Message SO-BCY-514

We are inviting you to become a Charter Member of our recently launched zagat.com subscription service for a special introductory price of only $9.95 (a 33% discount off the normal membership charge).

The benefits of membership include:

- **Ratings and Reviews:** Our trademark restaurant ratings and reviews for 45 cities worldwide. By year-end, our coverage will expand to 70 cities.

- **New Restaurants:** A look at restaurants as they open throughout the year.

- **ZagatWire:** Our monthly e-mail newsletter covering the latest restaurant openings, closings, chef changes, special offers, events, promotions and more.

- **Advanced Search:** With 50+ criteria, you'll find the perfect place for any occasion.

- **Discounts:** Up to 25% off at our online Shop.

- **Dining Diary:** An online record of your restaurant experiences, both positive and negative.

Given all these benefits, we believe that your zagat.com membership is sure to pay for itself many times over – each time you have a good meal or avoid a bad one.

To redeem this special offer, go to zagat.com and enter promotional code AmTop2003 when you subscribe.

Please join us.

Nina and Tim
Nina and Tim Zagat

P.S. Voting at zagat.com will continue to be free of charge.

ZAGATSURVEY®

2003

AMERICA'S TOP RESTAURANTS

Editors: Sinting Lai
and Daniel Simmons

Published and distributed by
ZAGAT SURVEY, LLC
4 Columbus Circle
New York, New York 10019
Tel: 212 977 6000
E-mail: americastop@zagat.com
Web site: www.zagat.com

Acknowledgments

Our special thanks to the thousands of surveyors who have shared their views with us and made this nationwide *Survey* possible. We would also like to thank our editors and coordinators in each city: Michele Axley, Karen Berk, Olga Boikess, Nikki Buchanan, Teresa Byrne-Dodge, Lauren Chapin, Suzi Forbes Chase, Andrea Clurfeld, Chris Cook, Pat Denechaud, Jeanne Dufour, Victoria Elliott, Jeanette Foster, Lisa Gray, Meesha Halm, Pam Harbaugh, Lynn Hazlewood, Carolyn Heller, Jill Hensley, Judy Houston, Philip Innes, Marty Katz, Michael Klein, Marilyn Kleinberg, Kathryn Kurtz, Gretchen Kurz, Ruth Lando, Sharon Litwin, Carolyn McGuire, Lori Midson, Colleen Moore, Maryanne Muller, David Nelson, Cynthia Nims, Jan Norris, Jennifer Pavlasek, Ann Lemons Pollack, Joe Pollack, Virginia Rainey, Susan Safronoff, Shelley Skiles Sawyer, Barbara Schmiett, Helen Schwab, Maura Sell, Deirdre Sykes Shapiro, Merrill Shindler, Mary Stagaman, Muriel Stevens, Bill St. John, Steve Stover, Jill Van Cleave, Alice Van Housen, Carla Waldemar, Julie Wilson and Kay Winzenried.

This guide would not have been possible without the hard work of our staff, especially Betsy Andrews, Constance Chang, Reni Chin, Anna Chlumsky, Larry Cohn, Anne Cole, Carol Diuguid, Griff Foxley, Jeff Freier, Shelley Gallagher, Curt Gathje, Randi Gollin, Jessica Gonzalez, Katherine Harris, Natalie Lebert, Mike Liao, Dave Makulec, Donna Marino, Laura Mitchell, Rob Poole, Benjamin Schmerler, Troy Segal, Robert Seixas, Yoji Yamaguchi and Sharon Yates.

The reviews published in this guide are based on public opinion surveys, with numerical ratings reflecting the average scores given by all survey participants who voted on each establishment and text based on direct quotes from, or fair paraphrasings of, participants' comments. Phone numbers, addresses and other factual information were correct to the best of our knowledge when published in this guide; any subsequent changes may not be reflected.

© 2002 Zagat Survey, LLC
ISBN 1-57006-417-2
Printed in the United States of America

Contents

What's New

After 9/11, the President counseled us to live our lives, hug our children and continue participating in our economy. Americans accepted that challenge – persevering in the face of recession, the ongoing war on terrorism and the lingering threat of further action. Since few businesses are more essential to our economy than the food industry, it's no surprise that America's restaurants have been a vital force in the nation's healing.

No Place Like Home: Obviously, world events have put a dent in both business travel and tourism. High-traffic visitor destinations have particularly suffered, with places such as Las Vegas, Orlando and San Francisco especially hard hit. Surprisingly, though, some major cities that were expected to fare the worst (New York, Chicago, Los Angeles) have managed relatively well. And fewer establishments than expected closed, while more than anticipated opened.

America Takes a BATH: The trend toward Better Alternative To Home ("BATH") restaurants – casual places where the food is hearty and the prices are modest – accelerated as Americans tightened their purse strings and sought comfort in familiar flavors. The result: Neighborhood haunts are thriving, regional American cuisines are enjoying renewed popularity and tabs have been reduced at many spots.

Fine Dining: Despite the surge in midrange eateries, upscale destination dining remains a powerful draw. After last fall's slump, most of the nation's finest restaurants are seeing their businesses rebound and, in some instances, outpace their performances of a year ago. However, the pattern here is mixed depending on location.

Strength in Numbers: Increased patriotism did not, however, mean isolationism. Showing its solidarity with the world, America embraced an even greater diversity of ethnic cuisines, 50 of which are represented in this book. And our culinary schools have never been more numerous or successful, pumping out thousands of chefs, new blood that guarantees the restaurant industry's rosy future.

Rock Solid: As the President said, the terrorists attacked a symbol of America's prosperity, but they did not touch its source. Similarly, the foundation of the restaurant industry remains solid. Coming on the heels of a boom that had become somewhat unrealistic, the slowed progress of the past year is more of a market correction than a downturn. The factors that have driven the restaurant revolution of the last three decades still support a pattern of growth in the quality and quantity of new restaurants nationwide.

New York, NY
November 15, 2002

Nina and Tim Zagat

About This Survey

Here are the results of our *2003 Zagat Survey of America's Top Restaurants,* covering 1,222 restaurants in 41 U.S. locales, including – for the first time – Charlotte, NC. The guide is designed to ensure that anyone can sample the best dining in virtually every major American city. For each area, we have included a list of the top restaurants (based on the results of our most recent *Surveys* in that area) as well as a list of "Additional Noteworthy Places."

Anyone who reads this book and knows these restaurants realizes that the U.S. is the leading place to eat in the world thanks to its extraordinary diversity. Twenty-five years ago, one couldn't have found a quarter the number of world-class restaurants in America, yet today the top spots in some of our smaller cities rival the best that New York has to offer.

By regularly surveying avid local restaurant-goers, we hope to have achieved a uniquely current and reliable guide. Given the huge number of people who participated in this *Survey* (some 77,000), virtually every restaurant was *visited at least several times a day, all year long*. Our editors have tried their best to synopsize our surveyors' opinions accurately, with their comments shown in quotation marks.

Since this guide is based on the ratings and reviews of our surveyors, we must first thank them. This guide is really "theirs". Of course, we are also grateful to our local editors, many of whom are professional food writers in their home cities. It was they who helped us choose the restaurants to be listed and edited the *Survey* results.

To help guide our readers to America's top restaurants, we have prepared two separate lists. See Top Food Rankings by Area (pages 7–9) and Most Popular by Area (pages 10–12). To assist readers in finding the cuisine they want in any region, without wasting time, we have also provided handy indexes.

As companions to this guide, we also publish *Top U.S. Hotels, Resorts & Spas*, as well as *Zagat Surveys* and maps to more than 70 other markets around the world. Most of these guides are also available on mobile devices and at zagat.com, where you can vote and shop as well. To join any of our upcoming *Surveys,* just register at zagat.com. Each participant will receive a free copy of the resulting guide when it is published.

Your comments, suggestions and even criticisms of this guide are also solicited. There is always room for improvement with your help. You can contact us at americastop@zagat.com or by mail at Zagat Survey, 4 Columbus Circle, New York, NY 10019. We look forward to hearing from you.

New York, NY
November 15, 2002

Nina and Tim

Nina and Tim Zagat

Key to Ratings/Symbols

Name, Address & Phone Number

Zagat Ratings

Hours & Credit Cards

F	D	S	C
▽ 23	9	13	$15

Tim & Nina's Pizza Kebab ◐ⓈⰔ⃠

4 Columbus Circle (8th Ave.), 212-977-6000

◪ Open 24/7, this "literal dive" is located in the subway station under Columbus Circle; as NY's first "kebab and soul pizza" stand, it offers "preposterous" pies with toppings of BBQ sauce and shish kebab to harried strap-hangers "for little dough"; but for the "cost of your fare" and the "need to shout your order" when the A train comes in, this would be "some trip."

Review, with surveyors' comments in quotes

Restaurants with the highest Food ratings and greatest popularity are printed in CAPITAL LETTERS.

Before each review a symbol indicates whether responses were uniform ■ or mixed ◪.

Hours: ◐ serves after 11 PM
Ⓢ open on Sunday

Credit Cards: Ⱄ⃠ no credit cards accepted

Ratings: Food, Decor and Service are rated on a scale of **0** to **30**. The Cost (C) column reflects our surveyors' estimate of the price of dinner including one drink and tip.

F Food	D Decor	S Service	C Cost
23	9	13	$15

0–9 poor to fair	**20–25** very good to excellent
10–15 fair to good	**26–30** extraordinary to perfection
16–19 good to very good	▽ low response/less reliable

For places listed without ratings, such as an important **newcomer** or a popular **write-in**, the cost is indicated by the following symbols.

I	$15 and below	E	$31 to $50
M	$16 to $30	VE	$51 or more

Top Food Rankings by Area

Atlanta
28 Bacchanalia
Ritz-Carlton Buck. Din. Rm.
Pano's & Paul's
27 Aria
Seeger's

Atlantic City
26 Medici
White House
25 Chef Vola's
Capriccio
24 Brighton

Baltimore/Annapolis
28 Prime Rib
27 Samos
Charleston
Stone Manor
Hampton's

Boston
28 L'Espalier
Aujourd'hui
Caffe Bella
27 Hamersley's Bistro
Olives

Charlotte
27 Barrington's
Toscana
McNinch House
McIntosh's
26 Sullivan's

Chicago
28 Seasons
Les Nomades
Ritz-Carlton Din. Rm.
Charlie Trotter's
Le Titi de Paris

Cincinnati
28 Maisonette
27 Palace
26 Dewey's Pizza
25 Daveed's at 934
Precinct

Cleveland
28 Johnny's Bar
27 Baricelli Inn
Phnom Penh
Giovanni's
26 Lola Bistro

Columbus, OH
28 Handke's Cuisine
27 Refectory
L'Antibes
Rigsby's
26 Yard Club

Connecticut
28 Jean-Louis
Thomas Henkelmann
27 Da Pietro's
Ondine
Restaurant du Village

Dallas
28 French Room
Riviera
27 Mansion on Turtle Creek
Café Pacific
Bob's

Denver/Mtn. Resorts
28 Keystone Ranch
Highlands Garden Cafe
Mizuna
Grouse Mountain Grill
Tante Louise

Detroit
28 Lark
Emily's
27 Zingerman's
26 Tribute
Common Grill

Ft. Lauderdale
27 Darrel & Oliver's Cafe
Mark's Las Olas
Casa D'Angelo
Cafe Martorano
26 Cafe Seville

Ft. Worth
28 Saint-Emilion
27 Del Frisco's
La Piazza
26 Cacharel
Randall's Gourmet

Honolulu
28 Alan Wong's
27 La Mer
Hoku's
3660 on the Rise
26 Roy's

Top Food

Houston
28 Mark's
 La Réserve
27 Ruth's Chris
26 Cafe Annie
 Rotisserie/Beef & Bird

Kansas City
26 Stroud's
 American
 Plaza III
25 Starker's Reserve
 Ruth's Chris

Las Vegas
28 Renoir
 Aqua
27 Picasso
 Andre's
 Le Cirque

Long Island
28 Mill River Inn
27 Mirabelle
 Kotobuki
 Mirepoix
 Peter Luger

Los Angeles
28 Matsuhisa
 Sushi Sasabune
 Sushi Nozawa
27 Patina
 Water Grill

Miami
27 Chef Allen's
 Romeo's Cafe
 Palm
 Norman's
26 Osteria del Teatro

Minneapolis/St. Paul
27 Goodfellow's
 La Belle Vie
26 Bayport Cookery
 D'Amico Cucina
 Lucia's

New Jersey
28 Ryland Inn
 Daniel's on Broadway
27 Cafe Panache
 Sagami
 Saddle River Inn

New Orleans
28 Peristyle
27 Bayona
 Brigtsen's
 Lafitte's Landing
 Galatoire's

New York City
28 Daniel
 Sushi Yasuda
 Jean Georges
 Le Bernardin
 Chanterelle

Orange County, CA
27 Napa Rose
 Aubergine
26 Pinot Provence
 Ritz-Carlton Lag. Niguel
 Gustaf Anders

Orlando
29 La Coquina
28 Victoria & Albert's
 Le Coq au Vin
 Del Frisco's
 Flying Fish Cafe

Palm Beach
29 Chez Jean-Pierre
27 Cafe L'Europe
 La Vieille Maison
 New York Prime
 Four Seasons

Philadelphia
29 Fountain
 Le Bar Lyonnais
 Le Bec-Fin
28 Vetri
27 Django

Phoenix/Scottsdale
28 Restaurant Hapa
27 T. Cook's
 Michael's at the Citadel
 Pizzeria Bianco
 Mastro's

Portland, OR
28 Genoa
 Paley's Place
 Tina's
27 Joel Palmer House
 Café des Amis

Top Food

Salt Lake City/Mtn. Resorts
27 Seafood Buffet
  Fresco Italian Café
  Metropolitan
  Mariposa
  Tree Room

San Diego
27 Sushi Ota
  El Bizcocho
  WineSeller & Brasserie
  Pamplemousse Grille
26 George's at the Cove

San Francisco Bay Area
29 Gary Danko
  French Laundry
28 Sierra Mar
  Masa's
  Ritz-Carlton Dining Rm.

Seattle
29 Rover's
28 Herbfarm
27 Georgian
  Mistral
  Campagne

Southern NY State
29 Xavier's at Piermont
  Xavier's at Garrison
28 Freelance Café
  La Panetière
27 Escoffier

St. Louis
26 Sidney Street Cafe
  Trattoria Marcella
25 Crossing
  Tony's
  Zinnia

Tampa/Sarasota
29 Ritz-Carlton Dining Rm.
28 Caffe Paradiso
  Lafite
  Blue Heron
27 Beach Bistro

Tucson
28 Dish
27 Grill at Hacienda del Sol
26 Vivace
  Ventana Room
  Janos

Washington, DC
29 Inn at Little Washington
28 L'Auberge Chez François
27 Makoto
  Kinkead's
  Maestro

Most Popular by Area

Atlanta
1. Bacchanalia
2. Bone's
3. BluePointe
4. Brasserie Le Coze
5. Canoe

Atlantic City
1. White House
2. Capriccio
3. Chef Vola's
4. Girasole
5. Brighton

Baltimore/Annapolis
1. Charleston
2. Prime Rib
3. Tio Pepe
4. Helmand
5. Ruth's Chris

Boston
1. Aujourd'hui
2. Blue Ginger
3. Olives
4. Hamersley's Bistro
5. L'Espalier

Charlotte
1. Upstream
2. Sullivan's
3. LaVecchia's
4. Guytano's
5. Mickey & Mooch

Chicago
1. Tru
2. Charlie Trotter's
3. Ambria
4. Everest
5. mk

Cincinnati
1. Maisonette
2. Precinct
3. Montgomery Inn
4. Palomino
5. Jeff Ruby's

Cleveland
1. Sans Souci
2. Lola Bistro
3. Johnny's Bar
4. Blue Point Grille
5. Baricelli Inn

Columbus, OH
1. Refectory
2. Rigsby's
3. Columbus Fish Market
4. Lindey's
5. Handke's Cuisine

Connecticut
1. Jean-Louis
2. Mayflower
3. Thomas Henkelmann
4. Rebeccas
5. Baang Café

Dallas
1. Mansion on Turtle Creek
2. Café Pacific
3. French Room
4. Riviera
5. Abacus

Denver/Mtn. Resorts
1. Highlands Garden Cafe
2. Barolo Grill
3. Strings
4. Briarwood Inn
5. Tante Louise

Detroit
1. Lark
2. Tribute
3. Whitney
4. Capital Grille
5. Zingerman's

Ft. Lauderdale
1. Ruth's Chris
2. Mark's Las Olas
3. Darrel & Oliver's Cafe
4. Charley's Crab
5. Outback

Ft. Worth
1. Bistro Louise
2. Del Frisco's
3. Reata
4. Saint-Emilion
5. La Piazza

Honolulu
1. Alan Wong's
2. Roy's
3. Hoku's
4. La Mer
5. 3660 on the Rise

 subscribe to zagat.com

Houston
1. Cafe Annie
2. Brennan's Houston
3. Mark's
4. Anthony's
5. Rotisserie/Beef & Bird

Kansas City
1. Fiorella's Jack Stack
2. Stroud's
3. Lidia's
4. Plaza III
5. McCormick & Schmick's

Las Vegas
1. Picasso
2. Rosemary's
3. Andre's
4. Palm
5. Steak House

Long Island
1. Peter Luger
2. Mill River Inn
3. Mirabelle
4. Panama Hatties
5. Bryant & Cooper

Los Angeles
1. Café Bizou
2. Cheesecake Factory
3. Campanile
4. Spago
5. Water Grill

Miami
1. Joe's Stone Crab
2. Norman's
3. Cheesecake Factory
4. Pacific Time
5. Chef Allen's

Minneapolis/St. Paul
1. Oceanaire
2. Kincaid's
3. Goodfellow's
4. D'Amico Cucina
5. Lucia's

New Jersey
1. Ryland Inn
2. Scalini Fedeli
3. Saddle River Inn
4. Manor
5. Highlawn Pavilion

New Orleans
1. Commander's Palace
2. Galatoire's
3. Bayona
4. Clancy's
5. Brigtsen's

New York City
1. Gramercy Tavern
2. Union Square Cafe
3. Gotham Bar & Grill
4. Daniel
5. Nobu

Orange County, CA
1. Cheesecake Factory
2. P.F. Chang's
3. California Pizza Kitchen
4. Il Fornaio
5. Ruth's Chris

Orlando
1. California Grill
2. Outback
3. Le Coq au Vin
4. Del Frisco's
5. Ruth's Chris

Palm Beach
1. Cafe L'Europe
2. Chez Jean-Pierre
3. Cheesecake Factory
4. La Vieille Maison
5. Cafe Chardonnay

Philadelphia
1. Fountain
2. Le Bec-Fin
3. Buddakan
4. Striped Bass
5. Brasserie Perrier

Phoenix/Scottsdale
1. P.F. Chang's
2. T. Cooks
3. Roy's
4. Mary Elaine's
5. Houston's

Portland, OR
1. Genoa
2. Wildwood
3. Higgins
4. Paley's Place
5. Castagna

By Popularity Rank

Salt Lake City/Mtn. Resorts
1. New Yorker Club
2. Fresco Italian Café
3. Metropolitan
4. Tuscany
5. Log Haven

San Diego
1. George's at the Cove
2. Laurel
3. Pamplemousse Grille
4. Mille Fleurs
5. Tapenade

San Francisco Bay Area
1. Boulevard
2. French Laundry
3. Gary Danko
4. Aqua
5. Chez Panisse

Seattle
1. Wild Ginger
2. Dahlia Lounge
3. Rover's
4. Metropolitan Grill
5. Canlis

Southern NY State
1. La Panetière
2. Crabtree's Kittle House
3. Xaviar's at Piermont
4. La Crémaillère
5. American Bistro

St. Louis
1. Trattoria Marcella
2. Sidney Street Cafe
3. Harvest
4. Tony's
5. Bar Italia

Tampa/Sarasota
1. Michael's on East
2. Bijou Café
3. Ophelia's
4. Bern's
5. Beach Bistro

Tucson
1. Café Terra Cotta
2. Grill at Hacienda del Sol
3. Ventana Room
4. Vivace
5. Janos

Washington, DC
1. Kinkead's
2. L'Auberge Chez François
3. Inn at Little Washington
4. Citronelle
5. Galileo

Restaurant Directory

Atlanta

Restaurant	Cuisine Type
28 Bacchanalia	New American
Ritz-Carlton Buck. Din. Rm.	New French
Pano's & Paul's	Continental
27 Aria	New American
Seeger's	Continental
Bone's	Steakhouse
Alon's	Bakery
La Grotta	Northern Italian
Chops/Lobster Bar	Steakhouse/Seafood
26 Soto	Japanese
Tamarind	Thai
Sia's	Asian/Southwestern
Sushi Huku	Japanese
Park 75	New American
25 Brasserie Le Coze	New French
Ritz-Carlton Buck. Café	New French
Asher	New American
Floataway Cafe	French Bistro
Food Studio	New American
di Paolo	Northern Italian

ADDITIONAL NOTEWORTHY PLACES

Abruzzi	N&S Italian
Atlanta Fish Market	Seafood
Babette's Cafe	European
BluePointe	New American/Asian
Buckhead Diner	New American
Canoe	New American
Chopstix	Chinese
dick & harry's	New American
Fogo de Chão	Brazilian/Steakhouse
Joël	New French
Kyma	Greek/Seafood
Mumbo Jumbo	New American
Nava	Southwestern
Nikolai's Roof	French/Russian
Oscar's	New American
Roy's	Hawaiian Fusion
Sotto Sotto	Northern Italian
Tierra	Pan-Latin
Van Gogh's	New American
Watershed	Southern

Abruzzi 23 | 17 | 24 | $43

Peachtree Battle Shopping Ctr., 2355 Peachtree Rd., NE (bet. Lindbergh Dr., NE & Peachtree Hills Ave., NE), 404-261-8186

◪ "Upscale" customers from the "old Buckhead crowd" "feel like family" at this "dependable" Italian; from the primi to the dolci (the "dessert cart is heaven on wheels"), the dishes are "authentic", but those who can't embrace the "aged" decor report an "expensive" experience that "should be better than it is."

Alon's [S] 27 | 16 | 19 | $11

1394 N. Highland Ave. (Morningside Dr.), 404-872-6000
High Museum of Art, 1280 Peachtree St., NE (16th St.), 404-733-4545 ⊄

■ For a "sweet-tooth fix", addicts "make excuses to stop by" the "best bakery in the city" for "lots of great gourmet goodies", notably "sensual cakes", "luscious pastries" and "heavenly cookies", while the "upscale sandwiches" (the artisanal breads are "ecstasy") pull in plenty of savory-seekers; regulars of the "modest" Morningside flagship (takeout only) lament "wish we could dine in", but for patrons of the High Museum of Art, the Midtown branch is pure bliss.

ARIA 27 | 26 | 25 | $47

490 E. Paces Ferry Rd. (Maple Dr.), 404-233-7673

◪ Hitting all the right notes in Buckhead is this "superlative" New American that "sings" with "imaginative, nuanced combinations of flavors"; orchestrating the action in the kitchen is chef Gerry Klaskala, whose "emphasis is on slow cooking" and who relies on ingredients so "fresh" they seem to have been plucked right "from the backyard"; equally "dazzling" is the "sexy", "sophisticated" interior replete with a "groovy lounge with beaded curtains", while the "thoughtful" service is simultaneously "efficient, warm and unpretentious", "but, boy, is it ever loud!"

Asher 25 | 23 | 25 | $52

1085 Canton St. (bet. Pine Grove & Woodstock Rds.), Roswell, 770-650-9838

■ "Bravo!" applaud boosters of this "breath of fresh air" in "historic" Roswell, an "oasis of fine dining in the North Fulton County desert of chain-restaurant mediocrity"; in a trio of "quaint" rooms in a "beautiful" Victorian house with a "quiet" "elegance", a "superior" staff proffers "innovative" New American cooking that "bursts with flavor" and is "exquisitely matched with optional wine pairings"; fit for any "special occasion", this "romantic" rendezvous is an "absolute treat."

Atlanta Fish Market [S] 23 | 19 | 20 | $33

265 Pharr Rd. (bet. Peachtree St. & Piedmont Rd.), 404-262-3165

◪ "Customers rush in like the tide for the gamut" of "exceptionally fresh" seafood "delicacies" prepared "almost any way you can imagine" at this "bright", "high-ceilinged" Buckhead fish house; diehards "go at an off-time to beat the crowds", but a swelling sea of foes carps about the "outrageous" "wait" ("flying to Hawaii might be less time-consuming"), "stressful" "noise" level and an "overrated" experience that's "losing its luster."

Babette's Cafe [S] 23 | 20 | 21 | $31

573 N. Highland Ave. (Freedom Pkwy.), 404-523-9121

■ An "oasis of Provence" transplanted to Poncey-Highlands, this "cozy" "charmer" is beloved for its "comfortably adventurous"

European country menu (starring "hearty and plentiful" dishes
like mussels with strawberries) "imaginatively served without the
attitude of many great restaurants"; only enhancing the "warm"
ambiance is the "friendly, knowledgeable" service.

BACCHANALIA

28 | 25 | 27 | $63

Westside Mktpl., 1198 Howell Mill Rd. (bet. 14th St. & Huff Rd.), 404-365-0410

■ Again the Most Popular restaurant in Atlanta, as well as No. 1
for Food, this "superlative" New American "feast for the palate
and the eyes" in West Midtown "continues to be ahead of the
pack" because chef-owners Anne Quatrano and Clifford Harrison
"make excellence look effortless"; "from the amuse-bouche to the
after-dinner chocolates", their "amazing" repertory is "sophisticated"
and "memorable", as are the "flawless" service and "cutting-
edge" decor; consider too the "unpretentious" vibe and you'll agree
that this "special-occasion" gem "deserves all its accolades."

BLUEPOINTE ⬧

24 | 27 | 22 | $45

3455 Peachtree Rd. (Lenox Rd.), 404-237-9070

☑ "Vogue, baby!" – this "ultra-trendy" Buckhead New American–
Asian is "Atlanta's place to see and be seen", be it at the "high-
energy" bar where "beautiful people" and "well-heeled patrons"
mingle with "gold-diggers" or in the "stunning", "sweeping" dining
room; the "edgy elegance" extends to the plate, where "creative"
"fusion cuisine" is "perfectly presented" by a "professional" staff;
it's "definitely an expense-account destination", but bashers
who are blue about "inconsistent" dishes, "noisy" environs and
"arrogant" service don't like "paying for attitude."

BONE'S ⬧

27 | 23 | 26 | $48

3130 Piedmont Rd. (Peachtree Rd.), 404-237-2663

■ A "perennial favorite" among the "power brokers" of Buckhead,
this "model" of "excellence" "beats all the pretenders and wanna-
bes in the men's club steakhouse category" thanks to its "big slabs"
of "flavorful" beef that's "always perfectly cooked"; enhanced by
a "deep wine list" (10,000 bottles), a "warm, old-fashioned" setting
and "gracious" service from an "impeccably" "seasoned" staff,
it results in a "superb" "red-blooded" dining experience that's
"worth the money"; it's "just what an institution should be", and
"you're not a true Atlantan unless you've been to Bone's."

BRASSERIE LE COZE

25 | 23 | 23 | $39

Lenox Sq., 3393 Peachtree Rd. (Lenox Rd.), 404-266-1440

■ Providing a "nice break from a day at the mall", this "vibrant"
New French "gem" (an offshoot of the renowned Le Bernardin in
NYC) easily "overshadows" its Lenox Square setting with "real
brasserie" food that's simply "marvelous" (notably its "perfect
fish" and the "best mussels in town"), served by an "unobtrusive"
staff in a "gorgeous" "Provençal"-inspired room that's "elegant"
without being "ostentatious" ("eat at the bar" for a more "casual"
meal); "there are no other French restaurants like this" for the franc.

Buckhead Diner ⬧

22 | 22 | 21 | $30

3073 Piedmont Rd., NE (Pharr Rd.), 404-262-3336

☑ "Even royalty will wait in line" along with the "locals, out-of-
towners and celebrities" at this "high-end diner" in Buckhead,
where the "hearty" New American "comfort food gone gourmet"
(like the "addictive" "homemade" potato chips with warm blue
cheese) "rocks"; the decor is "slickly" "beautiful" and the staff

"informative", but detractors warn "don't believe the hype", claiming that the "overpriced" eats "don't match its reputation."

CANOE [S] 24 | 26 | 23 | $39

Vinings on the River, 4199 Paces Ferry Rd. (I-75), 770-432-2663

■ Graced with a "luscious" "fairy-tale setting" on the banks of the Chattahoochee River replete with "gorgeous gardens" and a "lovely" patio, this utterly "charming" New American "winner" in Vinings is a pure "visual delight"; "very romantic", it makes for a "date spot extraordinaire", a "relaxing" refuge in which to relish "delectable" dishes and "incredible wines" brought to table by an "impeccable" staff; any wonder that it's "a perennial favorite" for a "special-occasion" destination?

Chops/Lobster Bar [S] 27 | 25 | 25 | $47

Buckhead Plaza, 70 W. Paces Ferry Rd. (Peachtree Rd.), 404-262-2675

■ Carnivores carry on and on about this "superb" Buckhead chophouse where a "flawless" staff makes you "feel like you've arrived" while proffering dry martinis and the "ultimate steaks" in "stunning", "clubby" environs; the downstairs Lobster Bar (dinner only), on the other hand, is a "seafood lover's paradise" charged with an "elegant energy" and a "less stuffy" vibe, tended to by equally "fine" servers who are a "class act all the way"; upstairs or down, "everything is tops."

Chopstix [S] 24 | 20 | 23 | $34

Chastain Sq., 4279 Roswell Rd. (W. Wieuca Rd.), 404-255-4868

■ "Startlingly upscale", this "truly gourmet" Buckhead "treat" takes Chinese cooking "to another level" with an "ambitious", "superior" menu courtesy of chef-owner Philip Chan; his dishes are delivered by "professional waiters" in "elegant" surroundings replete with candlelight, "beautiful flowers" and "live piano" music, so though frugal sorts fret it may be the "most expensive [of its kind] in the South", most maintain this "romantic" spot is a winner.

dick & harry's 25 | 19 | 21 | $38

Holcomb Woods Vlg., 1570 Holcomb Bridge Rd. (½ mi. east of GA 400), Roswell, 770-641-8757

◪ "Adventurous gourmets" tout this "upper-crust" Roswell New American as the "best reason to dine in suburbia", given the "creative", "first-rate" dishes (especially the "superb seafood" choices, including "out-of-this-world crab cakes") served by a "professional" staff in a "contemporary", open setting that's both "sophisticated and casual"; though a few grouches don't get "why people are so impressed" with this place, the majority applauds it as a "solid performer" all around.

di Paolo [S] 25 | 20 | 23 | $33

Rivermont Sq., 8560 Holcomb Bridge Rd. (Nesbitt Ferry Rd.), Alpharetta, 770-587-1051

■ Tucked away in a "nondescript strip mall" in Alpharetta, this "neighborhood" Northern Italian cucina is embraced by many residents as their "favorite suburban restaurant"; "well worth the trip outside the Perimeter", it appeals with "terrific" dishes (just about the "best in Atlanta" in its category) "cooked to order" and brought to table by a "great" staff that "makes you feel at home"; it'll "remind you of Tuscany", but the downside of this winning recipe is that it's "always crowded."

Floataway Cafe
25 | 22 | 22 | $38

1123 Zonolite Rd. (bet. Briarcliff & Johnson Rds.), 404-892-1414

◪ "Bacchanalia's little sister", this "standout" French bistro with an Italian accent, set in a "quirky" "industrial park" locale near Emory, may be "off the beaten path", but it's a worthwhile "adventure" for followers of chef Anne Quatrano's "simple" yet "sublime" preparations, "unique creations" that are delivered in "stunning" surroundings mixing "high-tech" with an "ethereal" "breeziness" by a staff that pays "attention to the details"; nevertheless, foes are "not that impressed" by the "miniscule" portions, "pretentious" vibe and high "noise" level.

Fogo de Chão [S]
25 | 21 | 26 | $45

3101 Piedmont Rd. (bet. W. Paces Ferry & Peachtree Rds.), 404-995-9982

■ Conventioneers and "Overeaters Anonymous" members know to "go starving" to this "fun" Brazilian churrascaria-style steakhouse in Buckhead, a link in a chain famous for it's "all-you-can-eat" "orgy" that includes a "sumptuous salad bar" that "raises the bar on all" others; brace yourself for "meat, meat and more meat" (15 types and all "perfectly" roasted over an open flame) "carved from skewers at your table" by "friendly", "knife-wielding gauchos"; it's a "fantastic, if a bit overzealous", experience that "everybody should try" "at least once."

Food Studio [S]
25 | 26 | 24 | $41

King Plow Art Ctr., 887 W. Marietta St. (bet. Ashby St. & Howell Mill Rd.), 404-815-6677

■ "Lots of brick and candlelight" warm up the "warehouse-chic" quarters of this "sexy", "romantic" New American "tucked away" in West Midtown; "architecturally stunning", the "art-gallery setting" totally complements the "picture-perfect", "orgasmic" creations "prepared with great affection" and presented by a "customer-focused" staff delivering "flawless, personal" service; with so much going for it, it's no wonder the "smart-looking clientele" "loves everything about it."

Joël
25 | 25 | 24 | $36

3290 Northside Pkwy. (W. Paces Ferry Rd.), 404-233-3500

■ "Hot, hot", this "welcome addition" has Buckhead all abuzz, with the cognoscenti predicting that it'll fast ascend to the "top ranks" of Atlanta's fine-dining establishments; already highly "promising", it's an airy oasis appointed with bright glazed glass and a "must-see" kitchen outfitted with reputedly the longest stove in the U.S., providing a "beautiful" backdrop for chef Joël Antunes' (ex Ritz-Carlton Buckhead Dining Room) "wonderful" New French (with Asian and Mediterranean accents) repertoire; keep an eye on this one.

Kyma
– | – | – | E

3085 Piedmont Rd. (E. Paces Ferry Rd.), 404-262-0702

Fabulous white marble columns flank the doors of this latest entry from the Buckhead Life Restaurant Group, where Pano Karatassos pays homage to his Greek homeland; boasting a gorgeous interior complete with a glittering constellation on the ceiling, as well as a waterfall, it's a dramatic backdrop for his son's (the chef) contemporary seafood preparations that star whole grilled fish (flown in daily from the Mediterranean).

La Grotta 27 | 23 | 26 | $44

2637 Peachtree Rd. (bet. Lindbergh Dr. & Wesley Rd.), 404-231-1368
Crowne Plaza Ravinia Hotel, 4355 Ashford Dunwoody Rd. (Hammond Dr.), 770-395-9925

■ "How do I love thee? – let me count the ways" rhapsodize reviewers about this "romantic" Northern Italian duo in Buckhead and Dunwoody, where "old-world charm and sophisticated cuisine" come together to make for an "elegant" affair with "contemporary flair"; amid "gorgeous" appointments, your "special-event" meal is "impeccably" served by "witty, sophisticated" staffers who are "attentive without being intrusive", which explains why this "longtime favorite" just "keeps on ticking."

Mumbo Jumbo [S] 22 | 23 | 19 | $36

89 Park Pl. (Auburn Ave.), 404-523-0330

◩ One of the "best reasons to go Downtown" is to visit this "dark and mysterious" New American haunt whose "fascinating" architecture and art provide a "unique" stage for the "beautiful people" who frequent this "slick scene"; "one of Atlanta's quirkiest" restaurants, it showcases an "interesting menu with some out-of-the-ordinary choices" that can be "exceptional", but brace yourself for an "unwarranted level of attitude."

Nava [S] 25 | 26 | 23 | $38

1 Buckhead Plaza, 3060 Peachtree Rd., NW (W. Paces Ferry Rd.), 404-240-1984

■ There's "nothing else like it" assert aficionados of this "edgy", "trendy" Southwestern "winner" in Buckhead, where "inspired", theatrical decor and a "wonderful terrace" attract a "great crowd"; as "fantastic" as its "impressive" "fine art" is chef Kevin Rathbun's "brilliant", "creatively conceived" fare, distinguished by "bold" Latin and Native American influences and brought to the table by an "incredible" staff; though it's "too damn noisy" for some sensitive sorts, the majority insists you "can't go wrong" here.

Nikolai's Roof 24 | 25 | 26 | $62

Hilton Atlanta Hotel, 255 Courtland St., 30th fl. (bet. Baker & Harris Sts.), 404-221-6362

◩ "Be treated like royalty" at this "fabulous", "uplifting" destination "atop the Hilton" Downtown, which boasts an "awesome vista" of the city; "everyone is celebrating something" here while "gracious" "waiters dressed as Cossacks" "pamper" them with "top-notch" French-Continental dishes and Russian specialties; thrifty comrades may gasp that it's "hideously expensive" (the prices are as "sky-high" as its location), but connoisseurs who "can't wait for the opportunity to go back" insist it's "worth" every ruble.

Oscar's 24 | 22 | 21 | $33

3725 Main St. (bet. Harvard & Princeton Aves.), College Park, 404-766-9688

■ "Finally, a terrific restaurant near the airport" gush gourmands about this "sophisticated but not stuffy" New American set in an "unlikely location" in College Park; one look at the "surprising depth" of chef Todd Immel's "fantastic", "creative" menu and you know that "this young kitchen has it going on"; his "wonderfully aromatic" dishes are delivered in a "neat" room dominated by an original Coca-Cola sign and worked by a staff that provides the "personal" touch; clearly, this "welcome addition to the Southside" "really has its act together."

PANO'S & PAUL'S
28 | 25 | 26 | $50

West Paces Ferry Shopping Ctr., 1232 W. Paces Ferry Rd. (Northside Pkwy.), 404-261-3662

■ Following a "spectacular" millennial redo, this "grand old dame" (the flagship of the Buckhead Life Restaurant Group) is even "better than before"; "lush, decadent and fabulous", it's revered by legions for its "superb" contemporary Continental menu (the famous "fried lobster tail is worth a splurge", but "you can't go wrong" with anything on the menu), so just "rest comfortably in your seat" and let the "impeccable", "gracious" staff take care of all; the only quibble: fashionistas who like to gussy up for "special occasions" plead "reinstate the dress code."

Park 75 S
26 | 24 | 26 | $46

Four Seasons Atlanta, 75 14th St. (bet. Peachtree & W. Peachtree Sts.), 404-253-3840

■ "An opulent oasis in the heart of Midtown", this New American "jewel" in the Four Seasons is "just the type of restaurant Atlanta was lacking" praise fans of Kevin Hickey's "exquisitely balanced dishes" that achieve an "interesting mix of flavors" (don't miss "the most amazing brunch in the world"); complemented by an "attentive" "but not fawning" staff and "beautiful", "elegant" surroundings, it's "perfect" for a "business lunch" or special event; P.S. "try the chef's table" in the main kitchen, which offers an eight-course menu paired with wines.

Ritz-Carlton Buckhead Café S
25 | 26 | 26 | $38

Ritz-Carlton Buckhead, 3434 Peachtree Rd., NE (Lenox Rd.), 404-237-2700

☑ "What a gracious, upscale restaurant should be" enthuse devotees enchanted by this "beautiful" New French cafe set in the Ritz-Carlton Buckhead hotel that's acclaimed for putting on the "most opulent brunch" in town; at lunch and dinner, a "great" Provençal menu is featured, but note that some patrons find the service rather "haughty."

RITZ-CARLTON BUCKHEAD DINING ROOM
28 | 27 | 28 | $62

Ritz-Carlton Buckhead, 3434 Peachtree Rd., NE (Lenox Rd.), 404-237-2700

■ "Pampering" with just about "the best fine dining in town, year in and year out", this "outstanding" New French dining room at the Ritz in Buckhead "keeps Atlanta on the map", impressing with a "beautiful", "elegant setting" and a "magnificent", "sincere" staff; keeping pace is chef Bruno Ménard's "sublime", "sophisticated" menu, touched with a Japanese accent and accompanied by a "first-class wine list"; "a special place for a special evening", this hotel experience is "off the charts", "dress code and all."

Roy's S
23 | 25 | 23 | $46

3475 Piedmont Rd., NE (Lenox Rd.), 404-231-3232

☑ Hawaiian Fusion cuisine reigns at this "smashing" newcomer, a "cavernous", "upbeat" outpost of Roy Yamaguchi's expansive empire; groupies gush about the kitchen's "terrifically" "unusual combinations of ingredients" (special kudos go to the "superb seafood" specialties and "killer desserts") and the "wonderful" staff that "takes care of your every need", but those not eager to hang 10 here dismiss it as a "hokey" formula that's all "flash, cash and Buckhead trash."

SEEGER'S 27 25 25 $75

111 W. Paces Ferry Rd. (E. Andrews Dr.), 404-846-9779

◩ "A four-hour meal" savored at this Buckhead "stunner" is "time deliciously spent"; an "adventure in food" designed by chef-owner Guenter Seeger, it's an "exquisite dining experience", dazzling with "inspired" Continental dishes so "gorgeously presented" that they "deserve contemplation" and "flawlessly paired" with a 1,000-bottle wine list; it's all delivered by "one of the best staffs anywhere", which explains why habitués "would eat here every night if we could afford it", but dissenters detect "too much attitude" and "the least amount of food for the most amount of money."

Sia's 26 24 25 $43

The Shoppes of St. Ives, 10305 Medlock Bridge Rd. (Wilson Rd.), Duluth, 770-497-9727

■ "Dining out in Duluth" was "never" "this good" swoon smitten sorts about this "elegant" "gem" that brings "class and style outside the Perimeter"; in "beautiful", "airy" surroundings with a "terrific" atmosphere, chef Scott Serpas "skillfully" "fuses" Asian and Southwestern flavors to "create" "fabulously" "exciting", "original" dishes, while a "superb" staff (overseen by owner Sia Moshk, "a truly enthusiastic and gracious host") "treats guests like kings and queens"; yes, it's a "little expensive" for the area, but this "happy" "find" is "perfection in the North Fulton suburbs."

Soto ◐ 26 15 16 $36

Kroger Shopping Ctr., 3330 Piedmont Rd. (Peachtree Rd.), 404-233-2005

◩ According to acolytes who worship "incomparable" chef-owner Sotohiro Kosugi, this Buckhead sushi "samurai" "raises" the craft "to another level"; widely esteemed as the "best Japanese in the South", it turns the "freshest" fish into "meticulously arranged" works of "art", making for an "ethereal experience"; be warned, though, that the "wait can be excruciating", the "extremely" "unassuming" digs "could be improved" and the service is "so slow" (and "rude" to boot), but diehards gladly "put up with it" – "nothing matters here but the food."

Sotto Sotto 25 19 19 $34

313 N. Highland Ave. (Elizabeth St.), 404-523-6678

◩ "If you can't afford a trip to Milan", this "high-energy" Northern Italian in Inman Park is "the next best thing"; "not much has been overlooked as far as the food goes" – the "simple, authentic and delectable" dishes ("impeccable pastas", "killer risottos and oven-roasted fish") are "worth eating over and over" and are delivered "promptly" by a "well-informed" staff in an "attractive" space – but detractors complain about a "shoulder-to-shoulder experience" with way "too much attitude" and "terrible acoustics."

Sushi Huku [S] 26 21 24 $30

Powers Ferry Landing, 6300 Powers Ferry Rd. (Northside Dr.), 770-956-9559

■ "Have we been beamed to Japan?" wonder diners transported by the "authentic", "top-quality" sushi and sashimi showcased at this Northside spot, one of the "best Japanese establishments in town"; regulars are "satisfied in every way" by the "freshest" fish ("great tempura and teriyaki" too), delivered "with a big smile" by a "warm" staff in "fantastic" surroundings.

Tamarind 🅂   26 | 20 | 22 | $29
80 14th St., NW (bet. Spring & Williams Sts.), 404-873-4888
■ The "best of its breed" in Atlanta, this "upscale" Midtown Thai thrills with "spectacular", "exceptionally presented" offerings that are "fit for the King of Siam"; a "husband-and-wife team" have "created a near-perfect dining experience" with their "beautiful" interior, "gracious" service and "attention to every detail", thus for a "special dinner" in the Far East, "nothing even comes close."

Tierra   23 | 17 | 20 | $29
1425-B Piedmont Ave. (Westminster Dr.), 404-874-5951
■ "Exceeding all expectations", this "refreshing" "breath of fresh air" in Midtown is a "yummy" Pan-Latin "travelogue" on a plate, featuring an "interesting" menu that wends through Central and South America, the Caribbean and Mexico (the Nicaraguan "tres leche cake is a must-have"); factor in a regional wine list, tango dancing (on some Wednesdays) and "pleasant" service overseen by "extremely nice and hardworking chef-owners", and it makes for a "delightfully" "festive" getaway "from the ordinary."

Van Gogh's 🅂   24 | 23 | 23 | $36
70 W. Crossville Rd. (Crabapple Rd.), Roswell, 770-993-1156
■ Roswell residents in search of a "romantic" "treat" "can't say enough" about this "classy" "jewel" that "continues to shine" with an "inspired" New American menu of "unique" "gourmet" dishes that "never disappoint" (the "unbelievable desserts" sweeten any "special occasion"); a few find it "overdone" and too "fussy", but it's a "perennial favorite" among the enchanted, who embrace it as a "wonderful" "oasis in the North Fulton culinary desert."

Watershed 🅂   23 | 19 | 19 | $27
406 W. Ponce de Leon Ave. (Commerce Dr.), Decatur, 404-378-4900
■ "Wow!" – definitely "not what you'd expect from a renovated garage", this "refreshing" Southern boutique in Decatur thrills with "killer" dishes masterminded by "genius" chef Scott Peacock; his "imaginative" fare always makes followers "happy" but never more so than on Tuesdays, when those in-the-know "get there early" for "fried chicken night" (simply "exquisite"); teamed with an "incredible" wine list and a "light and airy" space with a "laid-back" atmosphere, it adds up to an "extremely enjoyable meal", despite the "uncomfortable metal chairs."

TOP 10 FOOD RANKING

Restaurant	Cuisine Type
26 Medici	N&S Italian
White House	Sandwich Shop
25 Chef Vola's	N&S Italian
Capriccio	N&S Italian
24 Brighton	Steakhouse
23 Girasole	N&S Italian
22 Angelo's Fairmount Tavern	N&S Italian
21 Dock's Oyster House	Seafood
Los Amigos	Mexican/Southwestern
Knife & Fork Inn	American

F	D	S	C

Angelo's Fairmount Tavern

22	15	19	$28

2300 Fairmount Ave. (Mississippi Ave.), 609-344-2439

■ "Wipe up the last of the gravy and meatballs with a loaf of bread" at this "historic" "Atlantic City staple" (opened in 1935 and operated by three generations of the Mancuso clan) where "one big happy family" raises glasses of "homemade red wine" to toast the "homestyle", "old-fashioned Italian" cooking, seasoned with "lots of garlic, as it should be."

BRIGHTON STEAKHOUSE 🛇

24	23	24	$47

Sands Hotel & Casino, Brighton Park & Indiana Ave., 609-441-4300

■ "Stop gambling losses" with a "getaway" to this "impressive steakhouse" "located in the Sands", where even the least lucky players win with "wonderful steaks", a "great staff" that provides "top-notch" service and "elegant ", subtly evocative earth-and-wine-toned decor that'll make you "forget you're in a casino"; high rollers warn, though, that if you can't "get comped", be sure to "bring a hefty wallet."

CAPRICCIO 🛇

25	25	24	$48

Resorts Atlantic City Casino & Hotel, 1133 Boardwalk (North Carolina Ave.), 609-340-6789

■ "Eat like royalty" (especially at a table "overlooking the ocean") at this "top-scale Italian" at Resorts Atlantic City Casino & Hotel, where the "ambiance is superb", the "amazing" kitchen "never fails to deliver" "luscious dining" and service is "classy" and "polite"; of course, the food tastes even "better if you're comped" or using a "two-fer."

CHEF VOLA'S 🛇⊄

25	12	22	$39

111 S. Albion Pl. (Pacific Ave.), 609-345-2022

■ It helps to "know someone" at this bustling BYO ("unless you're a regular", "good luck getting a reservation!"), but if you're fortunate enough to get into this "happening basement" you'll find "superb", "can't-be-beat" Italian cooking served by a staff so "personal" that "they make you feel like family" within a "noisy", convivial scene; N.B. cash only.

Dock's Oyster House 🄢 | 21 | 16 | 20 | $38 |
2405 Atlantic Ave. (Georgia Ave.), 609-345-0092
■ "A landmark that improves with age", this venerable seafood house has been "the place to eat in Atlantic City" since 1897; not only does it serve ocean-"fresh" fare, but the owners "genuinely appreciate your business", and often "during the evenings" a "nice" "piano player adds" to the ambiance, mellowing the "loud, crowded" scene.

GIRASOLE 🄢 | 23 | 20 | 20 | $40 |
Ocean Club Condos, 3108 Pacific Ave. (bet. Chelsea & Montpelier Aves.), 609-345-5554
■ "Escape the casino" crush and slip into a "European" state of mind at this "top-flight" "feel-good place" with a "trendy ambiance, trendy people" and appropriately "cheerful" decor (considering its "name means 'sunflower' in Italian"); anticipate some "delicious food" and an "attentive staff" "that makes you and your significant other feel like you're the only people there."

Knife & Fork Inn 🄢 | 21 | 20 | 20 | $48 |
29 S. Albany Ave. (Pacific Ave.), 609-344-1133
☑ A "legend" in Atlantic City, this "classy" American "landmark" (circa 1912), which closed in the mid-'90s then reopened in '99, garners mixed reviews: traditionalists who are "glad to have it back" testify that it's "still a classic", while modernists maintain that its "old-fashioned menu" is a bit "stodgy" and "unimaginative"; still, a strong "emphasis on service" pleases all.

Los Amigos ●🄢 | 21 | 17 | 19 | $23 |
1926 Atlantic Ave. (bet. Michigan & Ohio Aves.), 609-344-2293
■ "Make sure you're hungry" before dropping into this "old standby" where the Mexican-Southwestern food is "delicious" and the prices are "reasonable"; insiders suggest you "stick with the chef's specials", while insomniacs note that it cooks up tortillas till the wee hours.

MEDICI | 26 | 26 | 25 | $48 |
Sands Hotel & Casino, Brighton Park & Indiana Ave., 609-441-4200
■ "If you're in AC with an expense account", try this "fun, classy" and pricey Italian at the Sands, a "special place" (rated No. 1 for Food among Atlantic City restaurants) that boasts a "creative bread basket" and such a "good variety" of "excellent" dishes that some surveyors swear it's "simply the best restaurant in South Jersey"; the "romantic" environs and "great service" earn high marks too.

WHITE HOUSE SUB SHOP 🄢⊄ | 26 | 12 | 18 | $13 |
2301 Arctic Ave. (Mississippi Ave.), 609-345-1564
■ "Hoagies from heaven" have made this humble "culinary icon" the Most Popular of Atlantic City restaurants; "check out all the pictures of famous people who've stopped here" (including George Clooney during filming for the recent remake of *Ocean's 11*), then get in line for "hall-of-fame" grinders so "sub-lime" they "can become an addiction."

Baltimore/Annapolis

TOP 10 FOOD RANKING

	Restaurant	Cuisine Type
28	Prime Rib	Steakhouse
27	Samos	Greek
	Charleston	New American
	Stone Manor	New American
	Hampton's	New American
	Joss Cafe/A*	Japanese
	Trattoria Alberto	Northern Italian
26	Milton Inn	American
	Lewnes'/A	Steakhouse
	Helmand	Afghan

ADDITIONAL NOTEWORTHY PLACES

Bicycle	Eclectic
Black Olive	Med./Seafood
Boccaccio	Northern Italian
Cantler's/A	Seafood
Harry Browne's/A	Continental/Chesapeake Bay
Linwood's	New American
Petit Louis Bistro	French Bistro
Ruth's Chris	Steakhouse
Soigné	Pacific Rim
Tio Pepe	Spanish

F | D | S | C

Bicycle 25 | 20 | 22 | $35

1444 Light St. (Fort Ave.), Baltimore, 410-234-1900

◪ Addicts "would pedal 100 miles" to this "hip" South Baltimore "storefront" for the chance to savor chef-owner Barry Rumsey's "playful perfection", exemplified by his Thai-style rockfish baked in banana leaves and teamed with chutney, red curry sauce and black sticky rice; the other dishes on the Eclectic menu are equally "complex and interesting", making this "tiny" "husband-and-wife"-run bistro a true "foodie haven", but better "reserve weeks in advance" and perhaps "bring earplugs."

Black Olive [S] 25 | 18 | 22 | $44

814 S. Bond St. (Shakespeare St.), Baltimore, 410-276-7141

◪ Be "transported to the Mediterranean" at this "charming" renovated row house in Fells Point, which is "heaven for serious seafood lovers"; "meet your treat before you eat" by taking the "fish tour" given by the "friendly owners", then have the "amazingly fresh" fare (including "exotic types that'll wow even aficionados") "simply prepared"; some wallet-watchers carp "sooo good but sooo pricey", but those who are hooked "always leave happy."

* A=Annapolis

Boccaccio 🅂 26 | 23 | 25 | $46
925 Eastern Ave. (bet. Exeter & High Sts.), Baltimore, 410-234-1322
■ "Memories of the meal linger for days" rhapsodize admirers of this "extraordinary" Northern Italian "paradise", a "longtime favorite"; the "delicate", "delicious and different" dishes ("not the standard" suspects) are served amid "beautiful", "inviting" quarters by an "impeccable" team, so though "it'll cost you" big ("thank God for expense accounts"), it's "first-class in every way" and it fully "deserves its reputation as one of Little Italy's best."

Cantler's Riverside Inn 🅂 23 | 16 | 18 | $28
458 Forest Beach Rd. (Browns Woods Rd.), Annapolis, 410-757-1311
☑ Boasting "atmosphere to the max", this "ultimate crab house" outside Annapolis is "nothing fancy", but if you "sit out on the deck" overlooking the creek and order a pile of steamed hard crabs and a frosty pitcher of beer, you'll have the "perfect afternoon"; that's enough to make "lines form in the street just to get into the lot", so consider "playing some summertime hooky" to "go during the week"; note, though, that "getting here is an adventure", making it essential to "get good directions" or "better yet, arrive by boat."

CHARLESTON 27 | 26 | 26 | $53
1000 Lancaster St. (Exeter St.), Baltimore, 410-332-7373
■ Surveyors swoon over chef Cindy Wolf's "sublime" "see-and-be-seen" scene at Inner Harbor East, voted the Most Popular restaurant in Baltimore; it's an "impressive" "special-occasion" destination that's just about "perfect" – from her "inventive" New American menu influenced by the Low Country and the wine cellar overseen by husband Tony Foreman to the "elegant" environs and "impeccable" service, this is a "top-notch" experience "to be relished and lingered over."

HAMPTON'S 🅂 27 | 28 | 27 | $59
Harbor Court Hotel, 550 Light St. (bet. Conway & Lee Sts.), Baltimore, 410-347-9744
■ This "opulent" hotel dining room with an "unbeatable view" "overlooking the Inner Harbor" virtually guarantees a "stellar" experience, "spoiling" guests with "refined, delectable" New American dishes served by a staff that "treats you like royalty"; when you demand "first-class everything" for a "big-time special occasion", this "classy place" is a sure thing; needless to say, it's "very expensive."

Harry Browne's 🅂 23 | 22 | 22 | $38
66 State Circle (bet. East St. & Maryland Ave.), Annapolis, 410-269-5124
■ "Hang out with politicians" and other "movers and shakers" at this "clubby" Annapolis "institution" with a "smashing view of the grand old State House" across the street; supporters say it "keeps doing it right" with "dependably excellent" Chesapeake Bay and Continental dishes turned out in "classy" surroundings by a "smooth" service team; some like the "people-watching" when the "legislature is in session", but others say it's more "wonderful without the lobbyists."

HELMAND 🅂 26 | 22 | 24 | $26
806 N. Charles St. (bet. Madison & Read Sts.), Baltimore, 410-752-0311
■ "Afghanistan's gift to B-more" has always maintained a "strong following for good reason", but now it's "enjoying" even more

"interest" due to world events; "no longer a hidden find in Mt. Vernon", it beckons with "exotic" dishes that "consistently" "hit the mark" (you "must try" the *kaddo* – "it'll forever change how you think about pumpkins" – and the *choppan*, "charcoaled rack of lamb at its absolute zenith"), "graciously" served by an "attentive" staff in an "elegant" room; to boot, it's an "incredible value."

Joss Cafe & Sushi Bar 🔲   27 | 18 | 21 | $28
195 Main St. (Church Circle), Annapolis, 410-263-4688
■ "Hearty greetings" welcome sushi connoisseurs of "all ages and types" at this "little nook" near the State House, "one of the top places" of its kind "in the U.S."; the "memorable" raw fish is so "fresh, fresh, fresh" "you'd think they caught it themselves", and the staff is "well-informed" and "entertaining", "impressing even native guests"; it may be "tight on space, but it's worth every bit of overcrowding."

Lewnes' Steakhouse 🔲   26 | 21 | 24 | $48
401 Fourth St. (Severn Ave.), Eastport, 410-263-1617
◪ "Local in every way", "Annapolis' own" steakhouse is a "manly kind of place" to celebrate a "special occasion"; it offers a "hard-to-beat" combination of "perfectly prepared prime beef" and a "fabulous wine list", along with "private booths" and "attentive" service; a few critical carnivores are left "disappointed" by the experience – and especially by the bill – but supporters are always ready to "prepare their appetites" for this splurge.

Linwood's 🔲   26 | 25 | 25 | $45
McDonogh Crossroads, 25 Crossroads Dr. (McDonogh & Reisterstown Rds.), Owings Mills, 410-356-3030
■ "Cool elegance and seductive fare" combined with "smooth" service make this "sleek" New American "the place to be seen" in Owings Mills; it's a "popular" gathering spot for "power lunches, business dinners" and "long meals with friends", appealing with dishes that "sparkle" and a "Manhattan nightclub-like" feel; if the "softly lit" dining room is too formal for your taste, "you can go more casual and sit at the counter around the open kitchen" or out on the new landscaped patio.

Milton Inn 🔲   26 | 27 | 25 | $50
14833 York Rd. (3 mi. north of Shawan Rd.), Sparks, 410-771-4366
■ "Far away from the city" above Hunt Valley is this "quaint", "romantic country inn" that has "survived" for more than half a century; quartered in a 260-year-old fieldstone house, it serves "excellent" "traditional" American "standards" in a series of formal stone-and-wood rooms replete with fireplaces; "expensive but worth it", "it's a perfect place to take your rich uncle when he visits."

Petit Louis Bistro 🔲   24 | 22 | 22 | $35
4800 Roland Ave. (Upland Rd.), Baltimore, 410-366-9393
◪ Like "a trip to Paris for $50, and they like Americans too" marvel devotees of this "perfect re-creation of a French bistro" "in the middle of Roland Park"; the "charming" brainchild of chef Cindy Wolf and wine director (and husband) Tony Foreman (the owners of Charleston), it's an "energetic" gathering place suitable for both "drop-in or special-occasion" dining, pleasing with "hearty" fare prepared with "panache" and paired with an "exciting" wine program; the "tables are close" together and "the din makes conversation difficult", but it "deserves its popularity."

PRIME RIB ●S 28 | 26 | 27 | $53 |
Horizon House, 1101 N. Calvert St. (Chase St.), Baltimore,
410-539-1804
■ "Old-time dress-up dining" distinguishes this "opulent" "'40s
Manhattan–style supper club" set in a Downtown apartment
house; voted No. 1 for Food in Baltimore, it promises a "special
evening out", proffering "sublime prime rib" and other cuts in
"luxurious" environs by "professional", tuxedoed waiters, with
live music playing softly in the background; of course the "dollars
add up", but this "venerable" "institution" elicits "wows on all
fronts"; N.B. jacket required.

RUTH'S CHRIS STEAK HOUSE S 24 | 23 | 23 | $49 |
600 Water St. (bet. Gay St. & Market Pl.), Baltimore, 410-783-0033
1777 Reisterstown Rd. (Hooks Ln.), Pikesville, 410-837-0033
☑ At this "classy" temple of meat, they sure know how to put the
"sizzle" in steak, so get set to "sink your teeth into" a "wonderfully"
"decadent" "hunk of beef"; "dressing up seems right" in such a
luxurious atmosphere (suitable for business entertaining and
"special occasions" alike), but critical carnivores feel that the
experience doesn't "rate the hype or the prices" (though they
don't seem to complain if "the company is paying").

SAMOS ⊅ 27 | 16 | 23 | $16 |
600 S. Oldham St. (Fleet St.), Baltimore, 410-675-5292
■ "Where Baltimore's Greeks eat", this "bustling" "neighborhood
community center" in Greektown is "nothing fancy", but it exudes
"true warmth", with a "welcoming staff that makes even sporadic
visitors feel like regulars"; from his open kitchen, hardworking
chef-owner Nick Georgalas satisfies his "big following" with
"down-to-earth" dishes that are both Hellenic and "heavenly",
and ridiculously "cheap" to boot.

Soigné – | – | – | E |
554 E. Fort Ave. (Jackson St.), Baltimore, 410-659-9898
"Everyone's talking about" this "hot spot" near Ft. McHenry, and
justifying the "great buzz" is Edward Kim's Pacific Rim "fusion"
menu, which showcases "unbelievable combinations" that result
in "delicious" "innovations"; "a real plus for Baltimore", it's already
"right at the top" of the town's restaurant pyramid according to fans
who "would eat here every night if we could afford it."

STONE MANOR S 27 | 27 | 25 | $57 |
5820 Carroll Boyer Rd. (Sumantown Rd.), Middletown, 301-473-5454
■ Promising a "great getaway", this "gorgeous stone manor
house" set on 114 acres of formal gardens and working farmland
in the Middletown countryside is an "intimate, relaxing" "destination"
for "memorable" New American cooking that amounts to "high
art"; it's "beautifully presented" in "romantic", "understated"
environs furnished with antiques and tended to by a "superb"
staff, making it a near-"perfect" "experience" that the enchanted
insist should "not be missed."

TIO PEPE S 26 | 22 | 23 | $44 |
10 E. Franklin St. (bet. Charles & St. Paul Sts.), Baltimore,
410-539-4675
☑ "We love it!" shout aficionados of this "wonderful" Downtown
"institution" that's renowned for preparing Spanish food "at its

best"; it's a "Baltimore favorite for all celebrations" given its "amazing" fare served by a "well-seasoned" team in a "feel-good" atmosphere; for a "special night out", it's an "enduring tradition", but dissenters who feel it's "overrated" cite dishes "adapted for the American palate", a "loud, cramped" setting and a "snobby" staff; P.S. "be prepared to wait, reservation" or not.

Trattoria Alberto   27   20   23 $49

1660 Crain Hwy. S. (Rte. 100 underpass), Glen Burnie, 410-761-0922

◪ Lurking in an "unlikely", out-of-the-way stretch of Glen Burnie, this "expensive" (for the neighborhood) "strip-center" Northern Italian is "not well frequented", but those who've discovered it rhapsodize about "extraordinary" cooking; it's definitely "not your typical suburban restaurant", so you better be "prepared to spend big bucks before you ask Alberto to take care of you."

Boston

Restaurant	Cuisine Type
28 L'Espalier	New French
Aujourd'hui	New American
Caffe Bella	Mediterranean
27 Hamersley's Bistro	French Bistro/New American
Olives	Mediterranean
Il Capriccio	Northern Italian
Prezza	N&S Italian
Saporito's	Northern Italian
26 Icarus	New American
Yanks	American/Californian
Julien	New French
Rialto	Mediterranean
Blue Ginger	Asian Fusion
La Campania	N&S Italian
Bistro 5	Northern Italian
Morton's of Chicago	Steakhouse
Radius	New French
No. 9 Park	European
Mistral	French/New French
Lumière	New French

ADDITIONAL NOTEWORTHY PLACES

Ambrosia on Huntington	New French/Asian
blu	New American
Blue Room	Eclectic/Med.
Caffe Umbra	French/N&S Italian
Clio	New French
East Coast Grill	Barbecue
Evoo	Eclectic
Federalist	New French
Ginza	Japanese
Grill 23 & Bar	American/Steakhouse
Harvest	American/New American
Le Soir	New French
Locke-Ober	Continental
Maison Robert	French
Mantra	French/Indian
Oleana	Med./Middle Eastern
Perdix	New American
Pigalle	French
Rowes Wharf	New England
Salts	New American/E. European

Ambrosia on Huntington [S] 24 | 24 | 23 | $50
116 Huntington Ave. (bet. Exeter & W. Newton Sts.), 617-247-2400
◪ Savor the "food of the gods" at this "hip" Back Bay "scene", which tantalizes curious palates with "inventive" New French–Asian "fusion" "combinations that push the envelope" ("like having a party in your mouth"); not only is the "dramatic" setting "drop-dead" "gorgeous" but the service is "silky smooth" and the "people-watching is a treat"; cynics, though, are turned off by the "pretentious" staff and warn that the prices are certainly "Olympian"; N.B. a post-*Survey* refurbishment may outdate the above Decor score.

AUJOURD'HUI [S] 28 | 28 | 28 | $64
Four Seasons Hotel, 200 Boylston St. (bet. Arlington & S. Charles Sts.), 617-351-2071
■ "Simply glorious", this "total treat for the body and heart" at the Four Seasons was voted the Most Popular restaurant in Boston; "when you have the urge to splurge", this "formal" room will "make any celebration spectacular" ("ask for a window table" overlooking the Public Garden); "such care, such flair" is clearly evident in the "exquisite" French-influenced New American dishes executed by chef Edward Gannon and brought to table by an "impeccable" staff, so though it's "pricey", this is the "pinnacle" of fine dining.

Bistro 5 26 | 17 | 23 | $31
5 Playstead Rd. (High St.), Medford, 781-395-7464
■ "An amazing restaurant in West Medford, of all places" gush boosters of chef-owner Vittorio Ettore's Tuscan-style "charmer" where his "gourmet" Northern Italian cooking "excites the palate" with "creative food pairings" and "big tastes"; no longer is it true that a "VW may have more room", as this once-"tiny storefront" has recently expanded, plus it now serves beer and wine.

blu – | – | – | E
Sports Club/LA, 4 Avery St. (bet. Tremont & Washington Sts.), 617-375-8550
A chichi health club in the Theater District may seem like an odd place for a sleek New American dining room, but don't tell that to all the trendies packing the raw bar at this latest venture from the Rialto team; there's plenty of seafood on the contemporary menu, though if you've done extra time on the treadmill, you can guiltlessly tuck into the rack of lamb with creamed spinach.

BLUE GINGER 26 | 23 | 23 | $43
583 Washington St. (Rte. 16), Wellesley, 781-283-5790
◪ "Rising above the fusion fray", chef-owner Ming Tsai "sets the standard for East-meets-West cuisine" with a "transcendent" menu that "more than lives up to" "the buzz"; no wonder it's immensely "challenging to get a reservation" – "even diners from Boston do the reverse commute" to this "sleek" suburban "phenomenon" where it's so perpetually packed "wall-to-wall" that you may "have to beg to be waited on"; though skeptics insist that "in LA, it'd be no big deal", plenty of groupies only hope that "the Ming dynasty continues to reign in Wellesley."

Blue Room [S] 25 | 21 | 22 | $36
1 Kendall Sq. (bet. Broadway & Portland St.), Cambridge, 617-494-9034
■ "Definitely a favorite", this "casually chic" Kendall Square "winner" is "full of energy", a "just right" showcase for chef

Steve Johnson's "adventurous" Eclectic menu; whether you settle in for the "awesome" Sunday brunch, "make a meal" of the "fabulous appetizers" or tuck into a "grillfest like no other", you'll be treated to "divine" Mediterranean-influenced dishes filled with an "intriguing mix of flavors"; "considering the high level" of quality and the "well-informed" service, it adds up to quite a good "value."

CAFFE BELLA   28 | 19 | 23 | $36

19 Warren St. (bet. Main St. & Rte. 139), Randolph, 781-961-7729
■ "What an amazing find!" fawn fans of this "exceptional" "suburban" "surprise" "hidden" "in a dingy little strip mall"; "once inside, you'll forget that you're in Randolph" because this is the "best spot between Boston and the Cape"; chef-owner Patrick Barnes, a "master of the culinary world", has designed a Med menu "so enticing that it's hard to choose", but "everything is of the freshest quality" and it's all served by a "knowledgeable" staff.

Caffe Umbra 🆂   – | – | – | E

1395 Washington St. (Union Park St.), 617-867-0707
At her cozy new South End trattoria in the shadow of the Cathedral of the Holy Cross, chef-owner Laura Brennan draws inspiration from Italy and France, turning out innovative dishes that might include a chilled velouté of zucchini and tomato, intriguing pastas like fresh-herbed pappardelle with pesto and mascarpone, and seared halibut with chanterelles and olive clafouti; paired with an interesting wine list, it's all served by a cordial staff in a narrow room with exposed brick and windows looking out onto the church.

Clio 🆂   25 | 26 | 24 | $58

Eliot Suite Hotel, 370A Commonwealth Ave. (Mass Ave.), 617-536-7200
☑ "Arguably the most creative chef in Boston", co-owner Ken Oringer "rules", conjuring up a "handsome", "high-style" Back Bay showplace for his "artfully prepared" New French dishes that "challenge the palate" and make any meal a "sublime" "special occasion"; backed by "terrific" service, it's an "extraordinary" "NYC-style experience", even though you should prepare for "micro portions at macro prices"; still, devotees are always "ready to spend the bucks" to join in this "orgy of dining bliss."

East Coast Grill & Raw Bar 🆂   25 | 18 | 20 | $32

1271 Cambridge St. (Prospect St.), Cambridge, 617-491-6568
■ "No wimps allowed" warn those addicted to the "dazzling, bold flavors" produced by owner Chris Schlesinger's crew at this "jumping" Inman Square joint that's always "packed to the gills" ("ask for the lava lounge", as it's a notch less "cacophonous" and you can "sit next to a volcano" – "beat that for kitsch"); not only does the kitchen prepare "sophisticated BBQ" that's the "best spicy food in town" but it's also renowned for "fantastically fresh seafood" dishes; "a favorite year after year", "this grill still thrills."

Evoo   24 | 21 | 22 | $38

118 Beacon St. (Washington St.), Somerville, 617-661-3866
■ Each "delicious", "luscious" taste savored at this "intimate" Eclectic bistro in Somerville "reveals chef Peter McCarthy's imagination"; only enhancing the "exciting" experience are "understated" surroundings with an "urban edge" and a staff that exemplifies a "passion for food and service"; so "though the name's a bit much" (it stands for extra virgin olive oil), "every neighborhood should be so lucky" to have such "a gifted chef."

Federalist ●☉S   24 | 25 | 23 | $62

XV Beacon Hotel, 15 Beacon St. (Bowdoin St.), 617-670-2515

☑ "Worth the splurge", a meal at this "opulent" Beacon Hill paean to power "isn't just dinner, it's an event" – from the "spectacular" decor to the "officious" service, each "extravagant" detail makes you "feel special"; equally "a beautiful treat" is the "exquisite" New French menu, matched with one of the "most extensive wine lists in Boston"; though "you may need to take out a mortgage", this is a "truly swanky" place to impress those snobby out-of-town guests"; N.B. the post-*Survey* arrival of chef David Daniels may outdate the above Food score.

Ginza ☉S   25 | 17 | 19 | $29

16 Hudson St. (bet. Beach & Kneeland Sts.), 617-338-2261 ●
1002 Beacon St. (St. Mary's St.), Brookline, 617-566-9688

■ Afishionados insist that it'd be "a sin to order anything but the unparalleled sushi" at this "traditional" Japanese duo in Chinatown and Brookline, renowned for "expertly preparing" raw fish that's "absolutely the best" in Boston – so "ultra-fresh" that "you can taste the sea"; though "getting a table is like a cattle call", the Hudson Street flagship is "a late-night" "lifesaver."

Grill 23 & Bar ☉S   26 | 24 | 24 | $50

161 Berkeley St. (Stuart St.), 617-542-2255

■ Just about "Boston's best" chophouse, this "boisterous" Back Bay "power scene" not only delights old-school carnivores with the "most tender steaks in town" but chef Jay Murray has made a number of "exciting" "updates" to the traditional American menu with "superb" results; the "courteous" staff "treats you like a king" amid "elegant" appointments that lend the room "a gentlemen's club feel", making it a "great place to bring clients."

HAMERSLEY'S BISTRO ☉S   27 | 24 | 25 | $53

553 Tremont St. (Clarendon St.), 617-423-2700

■ "Transcendent" French–New American "bistro cooking by someone who gets it" distinguishes this "class-act" "splurge" in the South End, where Gordon Hamersley "reigns supreme" with "perfectly prepared", "soul-warming" masterpieces; an "eclectic wine list" complements the "unfussy" yet "imaginative" cooking, while a "professional" staff works a room marked by "elegant simplicity"; "a favorite since it opened" in 1987, it's "still among the very best" in all of Boston.

Harvest ☉S   25 | 22 | 23 | $43

44 Brattle St. (Church St.), Cambridge, 617-868-2255

☑ "Aging well, like its own exceptional wines", this Harvard Square "institution" "has regained its former splendor", showcasing a "first-class" menu of "updated" American cooking in a "clubby", "understated" setting; "managers who know how to run the show" oversee an "efficient" staff, so even if a minority laments "it used to be unique and now it's just another expensive restaurant", most declare it just "keeps getting better"; N.B. the post-*Survey* arrival of chef Eric Brennan may outdate the above Food score.

Icarus ☉S   26 | 25 | 25 | $49

3 Appleton St. (bet. Arlington & Berkeley Sts.), 617-426-1790

■ "Wow!" exclaim elated epicures about this "well-appointed" South End luminary where the "modern renditions of classic cuisine" soar like its winged namesake; "Chris Douglass is a star chef without attitude", and his "artful" New American "creations" are "served with finesse" in a "serene", "rich-looking room" that resembles a "grand supper club"; though you may need to cash in "your 401(k) to pay" the bill, this is one of "the finest restaurants in Boston" in which to "celebrate a special evening."

Il Capriccio — 27 | 22 | 25 | $46

888 Main St. (Prospect St.), Waltham, 781-894-2234

■ "Worth the trip" to Waltham, this "refined" Northern Italian is "excellent by any standard, not just for the suburbs"; there may well be "too many praises to sing" here, but we'll try: chef/co-owner Richard Barron's "superlative" specialties are a "dreamy" "culinary treat", well complemented by a "wonderful wine selection" (the list must've been "compiled by a fanatic") and delivered by a "knowledgeable" staff with a "personal" touch; this is a "place you want to return to" time and again – "how could you not love it?"

Julien — 26 | 27 | 26 | $58

Le Meridien Hotel, 250 Franklin St. (bet. Oliver & Pearl Sts.), 617-451-1900

■ Bringing "a touch of France to the Financial District", this "opulent" "star" in Le Meridien Hotel is a "classy" "place for a celebration" or "romantic" dinner served by an "outstanding but not overbearing" staff in a "formal", "dramatic space"; chef Mark Sapienza's "imaginative" New French menu brims with "sumptuous" selections, so despite the "astronomical prices", this is a truly "memorable" experience – "what more could one wish?"

La Campania — 26 | 23 | 23 | $42

504 Main St. (bet. Cross & Heard Sts.), Waltham, 781-894-4280

■ Evocative of a "rustic cafe" "in Tuscany", this Waltham "jewel" is a "special" family-run "treat", tantalizing with "real" Italian food so "mouthwatering" you "could lick the plate"; an "amiable" staff "treats you as a beloved guest" in a teeny room with "charming country kitchen decor", which explains why despite "Downtown prices" it's always "hard to get in"; fans only wonder: "is there a way to make it bigger?"

Le Soir [S] — – | – | – | E

51 Lincoln St. (Walnut St.), Newton, 617-965-3100

Mark Allen toiled for years as the chef at a hotel dining room before opening his own place in Newton, an upscale neighborhood bistro featuring New French fare; dishes such as pan-roasted monkfish with lardons and rabbit pot pie, as well as all-time crowd-pleasers like steak frites, are smartly paired with a boutique wine list that focuses on French and California labels.

L'ESPALIER — 28 | 28 | 28 | $71

30 Gloucester St. (bet. Commonwealth Ave. & Newbury St.), 617-262-3023

■ "Absolute bliss" rhapsodize devotees of this "exquisite" Back Bay "stunner", a "lavish treat" ideal "for any special occasion"; "extraordinary" chef-owner Frank McClelland executes "seriously" "gourmet", "inventive" New French dishes (rated No. 1 for Food in Boston) that are "elegant in every way", turned out in a "romantic", "luxurious" townhouse setting that's equally "divine"; consider too the "unsurpassed" "personal attention" from the "unbelievable" staff and you'll concur that it justly "deserves all its acclaim."

Locke-Ober

– | – | – | VE

3 Winter Pl. (bet. Tremont & Washington Sts.), 617-542-1340

From the onion soup gratinée to the lobster Savannah, plenty of sentimental standbys remain on the menu at this Boston institution, reopened by Lydia Shire with Jacky Robert (ex Maison Robert) as executive chef; though Shire built her reputation on the wildly eclectic fare she prepares at Biba, here she's hewing to a mostly Continental line, while the restored dining room remains true to its Brahmin roots.

Lumière [S]

26 | 22 | 24 | $48

1293 Washington St. (bet. Waltham & Wilkes Sts.), West Newton, 617-244-9199

■ Arguably Newton's "best gastronomic contribution since the Fig Newton", this "sophisticated" "star" is a "suburban restaurant with city flavors"; chef Michael Leviton's "exciting", "exceptional" New French dishes are served by an "impeccable" staff in an "intimate" room with an ambiance of "easy elegance"; it's "a delectable experience in every way" – you just "have to plan weeks in advance", since it may be "harder to get into than Harvard."

Maison Robert

24 | 24 | 24 | $48

Old City Hall, 45 School St. (bet. Tremont & Washington Sts.), 617-227-3370

◪ "One of the first really gourmet restaurants" in the city, this "bastion of old Boston" dating back to 1971 remains an enduring "favorite that never disappoints"; "elegant and sophisticated", "with all the finishing touches" – from the "superior" classic French cuisine to the "grand" setting to the "formal", "thoughtful" service – it's "impressive" for any "special occasion"; trendoids may find it "conservative", but the chocolate soufflé surely "makes up for any sins."

Mantra

– | – | – | VE

52 Temple Pl. (bet. Tremont & Washington Sts.), 617-542-8111

Boasting a hookah den with fruit-scented tobaccos and comfy red couches, this chichi Downtown haunt tops the local hip meter; the elegant digs retain all the marble and granite trappings of the bank that used to occupy this space, while the polished service recalls the days of the Raj; it's a smart backdrop for Thomas John's French-Indian menu, which proves that this eclectic fusion can work.

Mistral [S]

26 | 25 | 24 | $54

223 Columbus Ave. (bet. Berkeley & Clarendon Sts.), 617-867-9300

◪ "Trendy to the last detail", this "hot spot" situated where the Back Bay meets the South End lures hipsters who swoon over chef Jamie Mammano's Provençal-inspired dishes that are "guaranteed fab"; "lots of pretty people" "in little black dresses" gather not only for the "memorable" fare but also for the "sexy", "très chic" "see-and-be-seen" "scene", made even more "seductive" by the "glamorous", "cosmopolitan" setting; "if you can get over the hype", consider it for a "decadent celebration" – just don't forget to "bring your attitude."

Morton's of Chicago [S]

26 | 20 | 23 | $50

1 Exeter Plaza (bet. Boylston & Exeter Sts.), 617-266-5858

◪ "A real steak in all its Midwestern glory", combined with an "opulent power-dining" setting with a "manly" ambiance, makes this "clubby" Chicago import in the Back Bay a "big hit with the business crowd"; though a minority moans that this "stodgy" "high-priced chain" "can't hold a charcoal" to the top homegrown temples of meat in town, contented carnivores can't wait to tuck into its "huge portions" of the "best-quality cow", scoffing "love it or leave it, baby."

No. 9 Park 26 | 23 | 24 | $54

9 Park St. (bet. Beacon & Tremont Sts.), 617-742-9991

◪ "Viva Barbara Lynch" cheer followers of the chef-owner whose "skill and imagination are evident in every dish" prepared at her "memorable" boîte in the shadow of the State House; the "low-key elegance" of the "swanky" yet "simple" interior "allows you to focus" on her "creative" European "culinary masterpieces" inspired by France and Italy; if some find it "too precious and pricey", most just get turned on by this "orgasm for the taste buds."

Oleana [S] 26 | 23 | 22 | $39

134 Hampshire St. (bet. Inman & Kendall Sqs.), Cambridge, 617-661-0505

■ The "excitement is palpable" at this "little gem", a "hip place to be" near Inman Square; credit chef Ana Sortun, who was "born to cook" and who brings her considerable Mediterranean expertise to this "darling" room, executing "intriguing" dishes enlivened by "surprising", "exotic" Middle Eastern flavors; whether indoors or out on the lovely patio, know that you'll be well taken care of by an "unpretentious, welcoming" staff.

OLIVES 27 | 22 | 23 | $48

10 City Sq. (bet. Main & Park Sts.), Charlestown, 617-242-1999

◪ "Please let this be where I eat my last meal on earth" pray fanatical worshipers of chef-owner Todd English's Mediterranean flagship in Charlestown, where his "big, bold, in-your-face" dishes are based upon "creative" – even "crazy" – "concoctions" that make the "taste buds dance"; note, however, that it can get "too frantic" and "noisy" and some are put off by the staff's "attitude", while the "no-reservations" policy (for parties smaller than six) "makes it a real hassle."

Perdix [S] – | – | – | E

597 Centre St. (bet. Pond & Spencer Sts.), Jamaica Plain, 617-524-5995

"Food is the star" at this "wonderful" bistro, a "tiny treasure" in Jamaica Plain that's easily "a cut above other local eateries"; chef-owner Tim Partridge's (ex East Coast Grill) "first-rate" New American cooking is full of "bold flavors", delivered to a handful of tables less than a stone's throw from the "open kitchen" (there's "no pretense" here); "intimate" and "welcoming", it brings "a touch of friendly elegance" to town.

Pigalle [S] 25 | 23 | 23 | $50

75 Charles St. S. (bet. Stuart St. & Warrenton Pl.), 617-423-4944

■ "Bravo" for this "brilliant" destination in the Theater District, one of Boston's "most exciting French restaurants"; chef-owner Marc Orfaly's classic dishes are "elegant and flavorful" and they're turned out in a "dark", "intimate" setting that seems to "suggest illicit activity"; not only is it "*très romantique* and *très cher*" but the servers are "extremely knowledgeable" and "everything they do has a personal touch"; P.S. "make reservations after 8 PM", when the "curtain crowd departs."

Prezza
27 24 25 $46

24 Fleet St. (Hanover St.), 617-227-1577

■ Just about the "best" Italian ristorante in Boston, this "polished" North End standout courtesy of chef-owner Anthony Caturano features "unique", "modern" interpretations (don't pass up the "awe-inspiring desserts", "artistic masterpieces" all), "fabulously presented" and matched with an "outstanding wine list"; kudos too to the "knowledgeable" staff that works the "sophisticated" room and "can't do enough to please"; this "winner" is for keeps.

Radius
26 25 25 $57

8 High St. (bet. Federal & Summer Sts.), 617-426-1234

■ "Eating in Boston is glamorous again" thanks to this "sleek", "chic" Financial District destination that's "among the best in the city"; chef Michael Schlow's "intriguing", "meticulously prepared" New French dishes are delivered by a "polished" staff whose "sheer professionalism" and "attention to detail are evident everywhere"; thus, despite "minimalist" decor that some find rather "stark", the "beautiful people" and "power brokers" "expect to spend here till it hurts" because more than a mere meal, this is an "artistic experience."

Rialto S
26 25 24 $53

Charles Hotel, 1 Bennett St. (Harvard Sq.), Cambridge, 617-661-5050

■ "Harvard Square's ritziest restaurant", this cherished "favorite for grand occasions" remains at "the top level" of Boston dining rooms; chef "Jody Adams is a goddess", crafting "exceptional" Med fare that's "always gratifying" and "sophisticated", "delivered with joie de vivre" by an "impeccable" staff in a "sumptuous", "modern" setting that's "a shrine to understated good taste"; the consensus: "love it."

Rowes Wharf S
24 27 24 $52

Boston Harbor Hotel, 70 Rowes Wharf (Atlantic Ave.), 617-439-3995

■ Boasting an "unbeatable harbor view", "elegant" room and "formal" service that proffers the "royal treatment", this "must do" at the Boston Harbor Hotel is a "place to be pampered"; it's a tough job to compete with such a "gorgeous" setting, but chef Daniel Bruce's daily changing menu of "classy", contemporary New England dishes shows "respect for simplicity and quality" and features lots of "local ingredients", particularly seafood; all in all, "superbly done" and "worth every $100 bill."

Salts
26 21 25 $45

798 Main St. (Windsor St.), Cambridge, 617-876-8444

■ At this "engaging" New American bistro in Cambridge, Steve Rosen's "unique" menu seeks inspiration from the East, though in this case it's Eastern Europe and the results are "inspired" – dishes that are "restrained yet flavorful and offered in interesting combinations"; despite the "understated elegance" of the petite room, diners may feel a little "jammed in", but the chef and his wife are a "charming couple who make this spot shine" and "they aim to please", making it "a real find for a romantic evening."

Saporito's S
27 18 24 $40

11 Rockland Circle (George Washington Blvd.), Hull, 781-925-3023

■ If your "passion for Northern Italian cuisine knows no obstacles", it's "worth the awful trip" to the South Shore to dine at this "homey" "treasure" where the "entire menu" of "innovative" dishes is "skillfully prepared and presented"; "don't let the exterior put you off" (it's set in "an old beach house") because this "expert" cooking is a "secret to be shared only with your best friends"; "even if it's way out in Hull", it's "one of the best in Boston."

Yanks [S] 26 | 23 | 23 | $49

717 Hale St./Rte. 127 (2nd Ave.), Beverly Farms, 978-232-9898

■ "Finally, refined food here on Cape Ann" swoon the cognoscenti about this "top-notch North Shore destination" distinguished by "NYC sophistication"; "though the name suggests a staid Brahmin dining room serving pot roast and cod cakes", the "superior" menu – classical American refreshingly updated with a "Californian influence" – and the "bright, contemporary" decor couldn't feel more "upscale" and "urban"; backed by "exemplary" service, it's "worth the drive" to Beverly Farms; N.B. a post-*Survey* chef change may outdate the above Food score.

Charlotte

TOP 10 FOOD RANKING

Restaurant	Cuisine Type
27 Barrington's	New American
Toscana	Northern Italian
McNinch House	Eclectic
McIntosh's	Steakhouse/Seafood
26 Sullivan's	Steakhouse
Volare	N&S Italian
25 Coffee Cup	Soul Food
Upstream	Seafood
Dearstyne's Bistro	Eclectic
Noble's	Med./New French

ADDITIONAL NOTEWORTHY PLACES

Bonterra	New American
Carpe Diem	New American
Guytano's	Tuscan/New American
LaVecchia's	Seafood
Mickey & Mooch	Steakhouse
Miró	Spanish
Pewter Rose	International
Sonoma	Californian
Woodlands	Indian/Vegetarian
Zebra	New French

F	D	S	C

BARRINGTON'S

27	21	24	$40

FoxCroft Shopping Ctr., 7822 Fairview Rd. (bet. Carmel & Colony Rds.), 704-364-5755

■ Rated No. 1 for Food in Charlotte, this "tiny gem tucked away on the side of a strip center" near SouthPark is the brainchild of "talented" chef-owner Bruce Moffett, whose "innovative" New American menu "will capture your loyalty after just one visit"; his "simply marvelous" dishes are served in a "charming", rustic-chic room with a "friendly" atmosphere by a "helpful, informative" staff; even if the "tight quarters may promote eavesdropping", it's "all worth it when the food packs such a powerful punch."

Bonterra ◗

23	25	22	$45

1829 Cleveland Ave. (Worthington Ave.), 704-333-9463

■ "We love the New South!" exclaim acolytes who worship at this "beautifully redone old church" in Dilworth, which draws the faithful with its "fabulous" wine list (400 selections by the bottle, "200 by the glass – oh my!") and a "creative" New American menu that's "exceptional from beginning to end" (the "dynamite fried lobster tail" is a must); enhanced by a "wonderfully" "unique" atmosphere and "knowledgeable, personable" service, it's "the place to be for all bon vivants in Charlotte."

Carpe Diem 25 | 23 | 22 | $34

401 E. Trade St. (Brevard St.), 704-377-7976

■ "Distinctive" New American food that's "interesting without being scary" awaits at this "starkly beautiful" Uptown "gem" where a "well-heeled hip" crowd gathers for a "thoughtfully" conceived menu from "scrumptious appetizers to decadent desserts"; "one of the truly original places in Charlotte", it's "always an adventure" to dine here, so "seize the meal!"; P.S. the cozy 'living room' bar is "perfect for after-work drinks."

Coffee Cup ⊭ 25 | 8 | 19 | $9

914 Clarkson St. (W. Morehead St.), 704-375-8855

■ "Button-down bankers meet the hard-hat crowd" at this "down-home" Uptown "institution" for fried chicken so "good" "we'd put it up against anyone's, even mom's", along with "superior" meat-and-three (vegetables, that is, "the way they're supposed to be – cooked to death"); it may be a "don't-look-in-the-kitchen" kind of place, but it prepares the "best Soul Food in Charlotte" and, besides, "where else can you order pig's feet?"; P.S. go early for lunch to avoid the "huge crowds."

Dearstyne's Bistro [S] 25 | 21 | 23 | $26

116 W. North Main St. (Hwy. 16), Waxhaw, 704-243-2090

■ Take a drive through "horse country" to the "sleepy little antique town" of Waxhaw to dine at this "hidden treasure" of a bistro; though the sweet of tooth make it a point to "order dessert first" ("you don't want to miss out on the incredible chocolate bread pudding"), others begin with the "excellent beef", "great fish of the day" or anything else on the "outstanding" Eclectic menu; add on "great, friendly" service and "reasonable prices" and the result is a "find" that's "worth the drive."

GUYTANO'S [S] 23 | 24 | 22 | $38

6000 Fairview Rd. (bet. Barkley Downs & Park South Drs.), 704-554-1114

◪ A "flashy" "Vegas-like" atmosphere (the "dining room ceiling alone is worth a visit") sets apart this "upscale" SouthPark destination, which presents "imaginative" Tuscan and New American dishes in "artful" ways; supporters praise it as a "much-needed injection of modernity" into the city's restaurant scene, but skeptics who find the decor as "overwrought" (if not "gaudy") as the "overblown" food ("oversauced, overgarlicked") ask "can you say 'overpriced'?"

LAVECCHIA'S SEAFOOD GRILLE 24 | 23 | 21 | $39

225 E. Sixth St. (College St.), 704-370-6776

◪ Accented with "huge sculptures of fish hanging from the ceiling", this "happening", "energetic" Uptown seafood grill is where the "beautiful people" "dress to impress" while "guzzling martinis" and dining on "amazing, melt-in-your-mouth" finny fare "prepared with verve"; fans urge "don't miss it" (you'll "feel like you're in NYC"), but foes frown "like eating in a barn, only not as quiet" ("bring your earplugs").

MCINTOSH'S 27 | 23 | 27 | $47

1812 South Blvd. (East Blvd.), 704-342-1088

■ Locally owned and offering the "best steaks in Charlotte" ("eat your heart out, Morton's"), this "warm, personal" South End surf 'n' turf house is a perennial "favorite" because proprietor Greg McIntosh "knows how to treat his guests"; though you "can't beat the meat", schools of surveyors urge "don't pass up the seafood either" (the "fried lobster tail is a must"); "they do things the right way" here (the "professional" "staff goes beyond" the call of duty), making for an "all-around wonderful" evening that's "worth" the "big dollars."

MCNINCH HOUSE
27 | 27 | 28 | $89 |

511 N. Church St. (bet. 8th & 9th Sts.), 704-332-6159

■ Utterly "romantic" and "intimate", this "exquisite" "Victorian" "jewel" quartered in a "private home" is where many prospective grooms in Charlotte "pop the question"; all patrons, though, can expect "total pampering", from the host who "tells stories of the local history" to the "attentive" staff that serves an "outstanding" six-course prix fixe Eclectic menu; "from soup to dessert", this is a "uniquely" "memorable" experience where "everything is taken care of for you", so just "sit back and enjoy."

MICKEY & MOOCH 🆂
23 | 23 | 21 | $31 |

Arboretum, 8128 Providence Rd. (Pineville-Matthews Rd.), 704-752-8080
9723 Sam Furr Rd. (I-77), Huntersville, 704-895-6654

■ "A chophouse that's like a ray of sunshine in the valley of chains" is how partisans describe this pair of '40s-style "finds" with "slick Rat Pack–era" decor ("you almost expect Frank Sinatra to come strolling around the bar"); it's a "great place for a great meal" – "everything we tried was excellent", plus the portions are "large" (expect to "bring a doggy bag" home) – and because it "feels like fine fining without the high prices", it's a "best value."

Miró 🆂
24 | 21 | 23 | $28 |

Stonecrest Shopping Ctr., 7804-A Rea Rd. (Ballantyne Commons Pkwy.), 704-540-7374

■ "Great fun with a group of friends and a pitcher of sangria", this "consistently excellent" Spanish grill wins friends with its "tasty" tapas, "perfect paella" and "tremendous" seafood specials, as well as a "wine list with many selections you won't see anywhere else"; it's all turned out in spare yet elegant environs accented with Miró prints by "genuinely nice" servers who "never hurry you"; P.S. "do not miss the tres leches cake" for dessert.

Noble's
25 | 26 | 24 | $45 |

3 Morrocroft Ctr. at SouthPark, 6801 Morrison Blvd. (Cameron Valley Pkwy.), 704-367-9463

■ "So many things are going on in the decor and on the plate" that you may be "exhausted by the time you leave" this "lavish" SouthPark "heavy hitter", but it's worth the effort because the European "country"-style setting is so "stunning" and the Med and New French fare "superb" and "innovative" (the "fried oyster salad is a must-try"); enhanced by an "excellent wine list" and "knowledgeable yet not overbearing" service, it adds up to an "all-around" "wonderful" experience.

Pewter Rose 🆂
23 | 24 | 21 | $30 |

1820 South Blvd. (East Blvd.), 704-332-8149

■ "Delightfully funky", this South End bistro quartered in a turn-of-the-(last)-century textile warehouse is a "bohemian" haunt with massive wood beams, soaring 30-ft. ceilings, walls of paned glass and lots of colorful knickknacks; it's a "cool" backdrop for an "eclectic, contemporary" International menu and equally "astounding wine list" served by a "solid" staff; "very popular" and a "great meeting place to people-watch", it's a "Charlotte tradition at this point."

Sonoma

24 | 23 | 23 | $38

129 W. Trade St. (Church St.), 704-377-1333

■ Demonstrating a "great vision for food", this "super", "wine-centric" Uptown bistro features a "witty" menu so tempting that it "makes you want to eat here every day"; that wouldn't be difficult, as its roster of "exciting", "modern" Californian dishes changes every week, though it's always based on "outstanding" local ingredients; just as "stylish" as the cooking is the spare, "almost edgy" interior, worked by a "truly dedicated" staff.

SULLIVAN'S STEAKHOUSE S

26 | 25 | 26 | $45

1928 South Blvd. (Tremont Ave.), 704-335-8228

■ "The bar is attractive, as are the regulars", at this "blow-out red-meat extravaganza" in the South End that showcases "melt-in-your-mouth steaks" and a "fantastic wine list"; the portions are "huge", so you may want to "skip lunch (and breakfast too)", the better to tuck into an "exceptional" bone-in Kansas City strip hauled out by "attentive" servers who "treat you real nice"; "upbeat" and "atmospheric", this is a "great place for a hungry, happy table of carnivores."

TOSCANA

27 | 24 | 25 | $41

Specialty Shops on the Park, 6401 Morrison Blvd. (Roxborough Rd.), 704-367-1808

■ Worth a visit just "for the basket of crusty bread and white beans, garlic and herbs drenched in olive oil that start every meal", this "comfortable, welcoming" Northern Italian in SouthPark will "make you feel like you're back in the homeland" with its "sublime", "authentic" cooking served by "charming waiters who all have accents"; a "real treat" ("coming here is as much an escape as a mini-vacation"), it's also a "great date place", especially "out on the romantic patio."

UPSTREAM S

25 | 25 | 23 | $43

Phillips Pl., 6902 Phillips Place Ct. (bet. Colony & Sharon Rds.), 704-556-7730

■ Voted the Most Popular restaurant in Charlotte, this "beautiful" "aquatic wonderland" near SouthPark is "inventive without being weird", luring in afishionados with its "magnificent" selection of "artfully prepared" seafood (the "bass is so good you'll want to lick the plate" clean) and "ornate" presentations; backed by a "polished", "hospitable" crew, it garners "a lot of buzz", and "if there are any celebrities in town, this is where you'll find them"; it's not inexpensive, but it's "worth the money and you'll leave satisfied."

Volare

26 | 20 | 26 | $42

545-B Providence Rd. (Laurel Ave.), 704-370-0208

■ "Intimate and incredible", this "hidden treasure" tucked away in an "unassuming storefront" in Myers Park is "one of the most romantic rendezvous around"; it appeals with an "interesting menu" of "authentic", "accomplished" Italian food, accompanied by a "respectable wine list" and served by a "marvelous", "cordial" staff; "seriously, don't miss this one", but remember to "make reservations early, as it fills up quickly."

Woodlands [S] ▽ 28 | 12 | 21 | $16

7128-A Albemarle Rd. (Harris Blvd.), 704-569-9193

■ "The only place to eat Indian in Charlotte", this "vegetarian's nirvana" turns out dishes so "top-notch" (including the "best ever samosas") that even hard-core carnivores "won't miss the meat"; these "excellent cheap eats" are "a must" for "adventurous seekers" of ethnic cooking because they're "different from the standard fare that you get elsewhere"; a "true winner", it allows even seasoned palates to experience the "joy of discovering what Indian food has to offer"; N.B. no liquor.

Zebra 24 | 24 | 22 | $48

4521 Sharon Rd. (bet. Fairview Rd. & Morrison Blvd.), 704-442-9525

■ "New and worth watching", this "sophisticate" near SouthPark will "challenge your palate" with "inventive", "delectable" New French fare (the "tasting menu is inspired") executed by a "witty chef" who "loves to mingle with his diners"; the "beautifully presented" plates and an "awesome" wine list that may be the "best in Charlotte" are brought to table by a "personable", "at-the-ready" staff in "refined" environs that are "elegant without being stuffy"; fans only "hope they never change their stripes."

Chicago

TOP 20 FOOD RANKING

Restaurant	Cuisine Type
28 Seasons	New American
Les Nomades	New French
Ritz-Carlton Din. Rm.	New French
Charlie Trotter's	New American
Le Titi de Paris	French
Carlos'	New French
Le Français	New French
Trio	New French
27 Ambria	New French
Tru	New French
Everest	New French
Tallgrass	New French
Spiaggia	N&S Italian
Les Deux Gros	French
Topolobampo	Mexican
Gabriel's	New French/N&S Italian
Arun's	Thai
26 mk	New American
Spring	New American
Morton's of Chicago	Steakhouse

ADDITIONAL NOTEWORTHY PLACES

Atlantique	Seafood
Avenues	New French
Blackbird	New American
Caliterra B&G	Cal/N&S Italian
Frontera Grill	Mexican
Gibsons	Steakhouse
Joe's	Seafood/Steakhouse
Kevin	New French/New American
Le Bouchon	French Bistro
Mirai Sushi	Japanese
Naha	New American/Med.
NoMI	New French/Asian
North Pond	New American
Oceanique	French/New American
one sixtyblue	New American
Pasteur	Vietnamese/French
Retro Bistro	French Bistro
Salbute	Mexican
302 West	New American
Twelve 12	New American

AMBRIA
27 │ 26 │ 27 │ $68

Belden Stratford Hotel, 2300 N. Lincoln Park W. (Belden Ave.), 773-472-5959

■ "No superlative is enough" to communicate the "polished" "excellence" of Lettuce Entertain You's "pure luxe" Lincoln Park "grande dame", a "romantic" "special-occasion" favorite "suited for classicists" (the "dress code's enforced . . . yay!"); it's "always a divine experience" "worth every dollar" thanks to chef-owner Gabino Sotelino and chef de cuisine Anselmo Ruiz's "fabulous" New French fare, an "outstanding sommelier", "servers who appear as if by magic" and an atmosphere of "hushed elegance."

Arun's ▣
27 │ 24 │ 26 │ VE

4156 N. Kedzie Ave. (bet. Belle Plaine & Berteau Aves.), 773-539-1909

■ Showcasing Arun Sampanthavivat's "culinary genius", this "intimate", "beautiful" Albany Park "haute" Thai "temple" "satisfies all the senses" with "superior" service and "one aphrodisiac after another"; be sure to "set aside a full evening" for the "leisurely" (and obligatory) $85 prix fixe menu, as "each of the 12 courses is a treat" "to eat and behold", featuring "artistic presentations" and a "gradual escalation of spice levels."

Atlantique ▣
24 │ 20 │ 23 │ $40

5101 N. Clark St. (bet. Carmen & Foster Aves.), 773-275-9191

■ Most mariners consider this Andersonville seafood house a prize "catch" for chef de cuisine Jared Wentworth's "imaginative", "beautiful presentations" of "fine, fresh fish" and other "well-prepared" delights from the deep (top toque–owner "Jack Jones is a genius!"), complemented by a "thoughtfully assembled" wine list; the "civilized", "softly lit" room with an "ocean motif" affords "intimate", "leisurely" dining, abetted by "on-the-ball" service from a "friendly staff."

Avenues
25 │ 26 │ 25 │ $70

Peninsula Chicago, 108 E. Superior St. (bet. Michigan Ave. & Rush St.), 312-573-6754

■ It's "high-end all the way" at this "perfect! perfect! perfect!" Peninsula venue, a Near Norther with a New French "seafood-intensive" menu compliments of executive toque Gerhard Doll and chef de cuisine David Hayden; expect "mighty-fine fine dining" in a "posh, proper" and perhaps just a soupçon "snobby" setting (the "gold color scheme is apt" given the "top prices"), where an "outstanding" staff "gives it their all."

Blackbird
25 │ 19 │ 23 │ $48

619 W. Randolph St. (bet. Desplaines & Jefferson Sts.), 312-715-0708

■ "Wear black" within the "white surroundings" of this "see-and-be-scene" West Loop New American where "brilliant" chef Paul Kahan employs French influences to take you on "a wonderful journey of amazing flavors" and "knowledgeable" servers "match the food" with "great wine selections"; "go with people you like", though, "because you'll be squeezed in tight" in a "minimalist" room that strikes some as "elegantly stark", others as "antiseptic."

Caliterra Bar & Grille ◐▣
24 │ 21 │ 22 │ $43

Wyndham Hotel, 633 N. St. Clair St. (Erie St.), 312-274-4444

■ Expect "consistently inventive" Cal-Ital fare at this "undiscovered gem" in Streeterville whose "seasonally obsessed" "monthly menus offer great variety"; the "beautiful room" is so "quiet and

civilized" and the service so "down-to-earth" you'll "forget it's in
a hotel"; P.S. the Food score does not reflect the post-*Survey*
departure of "brilliant chef" John Coletta.

Carlos' S   28 | 25 | 27 | $68
429 Temple Ave. (Highwood Ave.), Highland Park, 847-432-0770
■ "Worth the drive at twice the distance", this North Suburban
veteran is "always a sure bet" for "a special night out" thanks to
"outstanding", "palate-pleasing" New French cuisine that's so
"dependably wonderful" devotees "dream about" it; "invisible
attention" from a "stellar staff" overseen by "superb hosts Carlos
and Debbie Nieto" is another hallmark of its "small, comfortable"
room; P.S. the "great wine list" boasts 1,500 bottles.

CHARLIE TROTTER'S   28 | 26 | 28 | VE
816 W. Armitage Ave. (Halsted St.), 773-248-6228
■ Possessed of a "perfectionist's zeal", chef-owner Charlie Trotter
"overlooks no detail" at this "world-class" Lincoln Park New
American "innovator", "an epicurean's idea of heaven" where
"creative cooking", "a well-chosen wine list", "flawless service"
and "lovely atmosphere" add up to an "exhilarating", "one-of-a-
kind culinary experience."

EVEREST   27 | 27 | 28 | $74
One Financial Pl., 440 S. La Salle St., 40th fl. (Congress Pkwy.), 312-663-8920
■ "Dress to the teeth and allow lots of time" for a "prime-dining"
"splurge" at this "heavenly" "high-end" haven 40 floors above the
Loop; chef Jean "Joho has the touch", turning out "breathtaking"
New "French haute cuisine" "emphasizing Alsatian" flavors
"backed" by an "amazing" "booklike wine list" and "superior
service"; the "opulent" "safari" interior has detractors, but all
are awed by its "stellar views."

Frontera Grill   26 | 22 | 22 | $34
445 N. Clark St. (bet. Hubbard & Illinois Sts.), 312-661-1434
■ "A Chicago legend and deservedly so", this River Norther
(the more casual older brother of Topolobampo) is "the one that
started it all", showing "what depth Mexican food can have" with
"charming" chef-owner Rick Bayless' "world-class" "died-and-
gone-to-heaven" creations; add in "an interesting variety" of
"fabulous margaritas" and "great service" from a "professional
staff" and it's no wonder "it can be nearly impossible to get in."

Gabriel's   27 | 24 | 26 | $51
310 Green Bay Rd. (Highwood Ave.), Highwood, 847-433-0031
■ "A most enjoyable evening" awaits at this "classic" New
French–Italian on the North Shore where "sincerity is evident" in
the "excellent presentation" of "top-notch", "terrific food"; the
"creative" kitchen is overseen by "scrupulously attentive" "hands-
on chef-owner" Gabriel Viti, and the "elegant but casual" dining
room is staffed by "real professionals"; P.S. grape groupies gloat
it has "one of the best wine lists" around.

Gibsons Steakhouse ●S   25 | 21 | 23 | $48
1028 N. Rush St. (Bellevue Pl.), 312-266-8999
Doubletree Hotel, 5464 N. River Rd. (bet. Balmoral & Bryn Mawr Aves.), Rosemont, 847-928-9900
☑ "To see and be seen", a "fortysomething crowd" of "power
brokers", "glitterati", "wanna-bes" and "pinky ring"-ers, along with

"major-league ballplayers", packs this "exciting", "testosterone-filled hot spot" and "watering hole", an "expense-account heaven" for "A-1 martinis" and "obscene portions" of "excellent" "fresh meat"; those who find it a "noisy" "Gold Coast cliché" report its offshoot in "Rosemont is a little quieter."

Joe's Seafood, Prime Steak & Stone Crab [S] 25 | 22 | 24 | $47

60 E. Grand Ave. (Rush St.), 312-379-5637

■ "Are we in Florida?" ask claw-crackers complimenting this "retro-stylish" sophomore Near North "extension of the great Miami flagship", Joe's Stone Crab, which has been serving it up since 1913; a "successful Lettuce Entertain You partnership", it brings "big flavors" to Chi-town in "big portions" ("at big prices") of "hands-on seafood grub", as well as steaks "so good" that some can find "no words" to express their feelings.

Kevin [S] ▽ 28 | 27 | 26 | $48

9 W. Hubbard St. (State St.), 312-595-0055

■ When Kevin Shikami, "one of Chicago's most creative chefs", launched his namesake last year in River North, he immediately generated interest in his "excellent and adventurous" New French–New American fare (such as wasabi-spiked tuna tartare), which employs "the highest-quality ingredients" and "delivers pure pleasure"; the "stunning" yet "comfortable" storefront echoes the cuisine's Japanese accents.

Le Bouchon 25 | 19 | 20 | $35

1958 N. Damen Ave. (Armitage Ave.), 773-862-6600

◪ It "feels like Paris" has been "teleported to Bucktown" within this diminutive "darling" that devotees declare is "exactly what a bistro should be"; Jean Claude Poilevey's "real home cooking" yields "unbelievably delicious French" fare such as "outstanding duck", but some swear it's served up with a side of "authentic snobbery", and "claustrophobics" complain of an "uncomfortably" "cramped" setting where "long waits" are de rigueur.

Le Français 28 | 26 | 27 | $75

269 S. Milwaukee Ave. (bet. Dundee Rd. & Willow Rd.), Wheeling, 847-541-7470

■ Satisfied surveyors say chef Don Yamauchi is "keeping up the great tradition" of founding toque Jean Banchet – so judge jurists a year after a deed juggle jostled Northwest Suburban Wheeling's (once Classic, now New) French standard bearer known for "exceptional cuisine, wine and service"; "holding its own", the "beautifully prepared", "lighter" food remains "picture perfect" and "extremely pricey."

Les Deux Gros [S] 27 | 20 | 23 | $50

462 N. Park Blvd. (bet. Hill & Pennsylvania Aves.), Glen Ellyn, 630-469-4002

◪ Brothers Thomas and Michael Lachowicz, the self-proclaimed "two fat guys", "are not afraid of butter", and it shows at their West Suburban French, which is "formal" but "with a sense of humor"; the "thoughtful menu" of "excellent food" is "well prepared" (some savvy sybarites say "the degustation is the way to go"), making up for the "uninspiring" decor and "strip-mall" setting – though a post-*Survey* remodeling may outdate the Decor score.

LES NOMADES　　28 | 26 | 27 | VE

222 E. Ontario St. (bet. Fairbanks Ct. & St. Clair St.), 312-649-9010

■ A showcase for "talented chef" Roland Liccioni's "exciting", "visually stimulating" and "sensational" New French prix fixe–only menus, this popular spot is revered by well-heeled wanderers as an "oasis of refinement"; though it's no longer a private "club", "you'll feel a little privileged to be seated" within its "formal" yet "lovely Streeterville townhouse" where a "professional staff" "anticipates needs"; P.S. the wine collection is "stupendous."

LE TITI DE PARIS　　28 | 25 | 27 | $55

1015 W. Dundee Rd. (Kennicott Ave.), Arlington Heights, 847-506-0222

■ "They get everything right" at "always-nice owner" Pierre Pollin's haute French – from "imaginative" chef Michael Maddox's "ever-evolving" menu of "excellent", "superbly presented" fare to the "outstanding service" "without snobbery" and the "lovely" surroundings; a bastion of "elegance and quality", it has smitten surveyors saying it's "worth the drive" to the Northwest Suburbs and "the place to go when you want to be spoiled."

Mirai Sushi §　　24 | 22 | 19 | $38

2020 W. Division St. (Damen Ave.), 773-862-8500

■ This Wicker Park Japanese "screams 'repeat visit'", earning earnest encomiums for the "perfect presentations" of "inventive chef Jun" Ichikawa's "bold" "couture sushi" ("not cheap in either price or quality", it "compares favorably to Tokyo" spots'); P.S. the "beautiful people" head upstairs to the "sleek, hip lounge" to partake of the "awesome adult beverages" and "great sake list."

MK §　　26 | 24 | 25 | $51

868 N. Franklin St. (bet. Chicago Ave. & Oak St.), 312-482-9179

■ "Terrific food", a "stylish setting" and "expert service" are a "powerful combination" at this River North New American, where "genius chef[-owner] Michael Kornick" (the 'M.K.' of mk) is "at the top of his game"; his "innovative but approachable" food is paired with a "well-crafted and complementary wine list" and followed by "divine desserts", making this "a place to go back to as often as possible."

Morton's of Chicago §　　26 | 21 | 24 | $53

Newberry Plaza, 1050 N. State St., lower level (Maple St.), 312-266-4820
9525 W. Bryn Mawr Ave. (River Rd.), Rosemont, 847-678-5155
1470 McConnor Pkwy. (Meacham Rd.), Schaumburg, 847-413-8771
1 Westbrook Corporate Ctr. (bet. 22nd St. & Wolf Rd.), Westchester, 708-562-7000

■ "In the face of tremendous competition", these "clubby" cum lauders continue to claim the coveted steakhouse crown; the city original and its suburban spin-offs (part of a national chain) each get the meat-eaters seal of approval as a "primo" "red-meat heaven with attentive service" where "the bang lives up to the buck" – though many "thank goodness for expense accounts."

Naha　　25 | 24 | 23 | $54

500 N. Clark St. (Illinois St.), 312-321-6242

■ A "great addition to the fine-dining scene", this River North two-year-old "works" thanks to "chef Carrie Nahabedian's New American–Mediterranean fusion" featuring "seemingly simple dishes that uncover complex and fresh flavors"; the "polished", "passionate staff" "makes each diner feel special", and the "crisp, clean setting" "feels like a spa"; P.S. since you'll "eat like a king", loyalists laugh you'd better "bring the royal treasury."

NoMI 🖥   23 | 26 | 23 | $61

Park Hyatt Chicago, 800 N. Michigan Ave. (Chicago Ave.), 312-239-4030
☑ "You can't beat" the "stunning", "romantic view" at this "elegant", "sleek" New French–Asian fusion fantasy set in a "dazzling" room above the city lights that has the smitten sighing "can I live here? please?"; while foodies fawn over chef Sandro Gamba's "adventurous" and "artful" fare, a few frowners fuss over the "diminutive portions" and "high prices", adding it's time for the "arrogant staff" to "lose the attitude."

North Pond 🖥   24 | 25 | 22 | $43

(fka North Pond Café)
2610 N. Cannon Dr. (bet. Diversey & Fullerton Pkwys.), 773-477-5845
■ You'll feel like you're "dining at Frank Lloyd Wright's home" at this "wonderfully restored" "gem" of an "Arts and Crafts building" "hidden" in Lincoln Park, but the real architect here is "inventive" chef Bruce Sherman, who builds "delicious" New American dishes "using fresh ingredients" from "local organic farms"; P.S. though the "spectacular" "lagoon-and-skyline view" remains, a recent remodeling is not reflected in the Decor score.

Oceanique   24 | 20 | 22 | $45

505 Main St. (bet. Chicago & Hinman Aves.), Evanston, 847-864-3435
■ An "outstanding" variety of "exquisite" French–New American "seafood creations" made with "fresh, high-quality ingredients" is paired with the fruits of a "top-notch wine cellar" at this "romantic, comfortable" and "civilized" Evanston eatery; the kitchen's "precise preparation and presentation", as well as the staff's "polished service", make wallet-watchers wistfully "wish they could afford to eat here more often."

one sixtyblue   24 | 24 | 22 | $55

1400 W. Randolph St. (Ogden St.), 312-850-0303
■ "This could be the Michael Jordan of restaurants" fawn fans of this "airy" Market District New American, "a class act from start to finish" where "daring" chef Martial Noguier's "stellar", "stylish" French-influenced fare is complemented by "delicate wines and unobtrusive service" and set against Adam Tihany's "sleek", "chic" backdrop; it's "expensive", but most are happy to "pay for the hipness" and "the hope of seeing [silent partner] MJ."

Pasteur 🖥   23 | 23 | 20 | $34

5525 N. Broadway (bet. Bryn Mawr & Catalpa Aves.), 773-878-1061
☑ A "pleasant" meal is in store at this "elegant and seductive" "Edgewater oasis" where the "exciting taste treats" – "refined Vietnamese with French influences" – showcase "extremely fresh ingredients"; some surveyors say the staff is "unobtrusive" and the environment "relaxing", while others "would go more often if the service were as good as the food" and it weren't so "noisy."

Retro Bistro   26 | 19 | 23 | $35

Mt. Prospect Commons, 1746 W. Golf Rd. (Busse Rd.), Mt. Prospect, 847-439-2424
■ Mt. Prospect-ors panning for "excellent" French bistro fare that's a "good value" strike it rich at this "small", "intimate" spot,

an "oasis" in a Northwest Suburban strip-mall "wasteland", where "happy, friendly service" and the transporting "feeling of being in Europe" round out the "memorable" lunches and dinners.

RITZ-CARLTON DINING ROOM S | 28 | 27 | 28 | $68 |
Ritz-Carlton Hotel, 160 E. Pearson St. (Michigan Ave.), 312-573-5223
■ A "top dining experience" awaits at this "refined" New French in the Ritz-Carlton, a Four Seasons hotel; chef "Sarah Stegner is a treasure", and her "fantastic" food matches the "posh" yet "understated" surroundings; add in an "epic wine list", "fabulous cheese cart" and a "food-orgy-with-piano" Sunday brunch and this is "the place to splurge" "when elegance, not money, is the object."

Salbute | 25 | 17 | 20 | $30 |
20 E. First St. (bet. Garfield & Washington Sts.), Hinsdale, 630-920-8077
■ "Worth the wait at twice the drive", this West Suburban Hinsdale haven "deserves its raves" for "inventive" chef-owner Edgar Rodriguez's "thrilling, complex, delicious" "gourmet Mexican cuisine" and its "knowledgeable" staff; remember, "reservations are a must", especially since the "wait" for "the long-promised liquor license" has ended – now "all it needs is more space."

SEASONS S | 28 | 27 | 27 | $65 |
Four Seasons Hotel, 120 E. Delaware Pl., 7th fl. (bet. Michigan Ave. & Rush St.), 312-649-2349
■ Clients coo over this "crème-de-la-crème" New American whose "classic yet contemporary" "creations" are top-rated for Food among Chicago restaurants (the "lunch buffet is wonderful" and the "Sunday brunch is spectacular") and covet being "coddled by the loving staff" for whom "the customer is king" within the cosseting confines of its "classy" accommodations; N.B. the Food score does not reflect the post-*Survey* transfer of the toque from Mark Baker to Robert Sulatycky (ex Four Seasons Hotel Toronto).

Spiaggia S | 27 | 27 | 26 | $62 |
One Magnificent Mile Bldg., 980 N. Michigan Ave., 2nd fl. (Oak St.), 312-280-2750
■ "You know you've arrived when you enter the gorgeous dining room" of this "wildly expensive" "romantic splurge spot" in the Gold Coast; surveyors laud "talented chef" Tony Mantuano's "refined", "innovative" Italian cuisine as the "best [of its kind] in the city", adding that "attentive" service and "awesome views" from its "grand" setting contribute to a "special" experience; P.S. its next-door "cafe is wonderful and less" costly too.

Spring S | 26 | 25 | 25 | $53 |
2039 W. North Ave. (Damen Ave.), 773-395-7100
■ An "excellent addition" that's already a "favorite" of the "chic" set, this "hot", "hip" New American in Wicker Park "lives up to its hype" on the strength of "magnificent" chef-owner Shawn McClain (formerly of Trio) and his "gorgeous", "sublime" "Asian-influenced" cuisine (including "swimmingly fresh seafood") "professionally" served in a "stark", "stylish", "tranquil" space graced with a Zen garden; it's "pricey" but "worth springing for."

Tallgrass S | 27 | 25 | 27 | $63 |
1006 S. State St. (10th St.), Lockport, 815-838-5566
■ Diners deem it "worth the trip" to this "small", "romantic" Southwest Suburban New French in the "lovely canal town" of

Lockport, where chef Robert Burcenski "continues to amaze" with his prix fixe menus of "creative", "serious" fare highlighted by "innovative pairings" and "gorgeous presentations"; the "reserved, understated space" and "excellent" service contribute to the "world-class" experience; N.B. jacket and reservations required.

302 West 25 | 25 | 24 | $49

302 W. State St. (3rd St.), Geneva, 630-232-9302

■ "If this place were on the Near North Side, you wouldn't be able to get in" boast boosters of Joel and Catherine Findlay's "first-class" New American in the Western Suburbs, a "longtime favorite" for its "wonderful, inventive, always-changing menu" and "great selection of small-provider wines" "served with care" in a "beautiful, gracious dining room" set in a former bank; P.S. "they understand that desserts are supposed to be fun."

Topolobampo 27 | 24 | 25 | $50

445 N. Clark St. (bet. Hubbard & Illinois Sts.), 312-661-1434

■ A "star in a big food town", this River North Mexican (Frontera Grill's "upscale cousin") "continues to shine" thanks to "serious", "daring" cuisine admirers insist is "better than any in Mexico"; chef Rick Bayless dazzles fans with his "exciting treatment" of "the best ingredients", while "professional service", "beautifully artistic decor" and a "good tequila selection and wine list" contribute to an "all-around outstanding" experience.

Trio [S] 28 | 25 | 28 | $74

Homestead Hotel, 1625 Hinman Ave. (Davis St.), Evanston, 847-733-8746

■ "The French Laundry comes to Evanston" in the person of toque Grant Achatz (ex Thomas Keller's California legend), whose "finesse, bravado and quality" make him "as original a [chef] as you'll ever find"; his "exceptional cuisine" is "as serious as the setting" of this "true foodies' restaurant", while "inspired wine pairings" and "knowledgeable service" add to the "near-perfect experience", after which "all you can think about is doing it again."

TRU 27 | 27 | 27 | $85

676 N. St. Clair St. (bet. Erie & Huron Sts.), 312-202-0001

■ Chef-owners Rick Tramonto and Gale Gand "add humor and surprise to elegant cuisine" in their Streeterville Lettuce Entertain You partnership, a haven "for serious foodies" voted Most Popular in Chicago, where "splendid [New French] food and synchronized service" are showcased in a "spartan setting" and at a "leisurely pace" ("dinners last two to four hours", depending on your choice of prix fixe or "collection" menus); even "demanding diners" concede its "excellence" is "worth the astronomical price."

Twelve 12 24 | 22 | 21 | $51

1212 N. State Pkwy. (Division St.), 312-951-1212

■ At this "dazzling" Gold Coast New American, executive chef David Shea's "terrific balanced menu" of "imaginative dishes" (with an "excellent-bargain prix fixe"), enhanced by "beautiful presentations", "an impressive wine list", "chic", "well-appointed" decor and a "friendly, knowledgeable" staff, has fans hoping it enjoys a "long, happy run."

Cincinnati

TOP 10 FOOD RANKING

	Restaurant	Cuisine Type
28	Maisonette	French
27	Palace	New American
26	Dewey's Pizza	Pizza
25	Daveed's at 934	Eclectic/American
	Precinct	Steakhouse/Seafood
	Ambar	Indian
	Phoenix	Continental/American
24	China Gourmet	Chinese
	Pacific Moon Cafe	Pan-Asian
	JUMP Café	New American

ADDITIONAL NOTEWORTHY PLACES

Aioli	Eclectic
Beluga	Eurasian
Boca	N&S Italian/Eclectic
Brown Dog Cafe	New American
Jeff Ruby's	Steakhouse
Montgomery Inn	Barbecue
Nicola's	N&S Italian
Palomino	New American/Mediterranean
Primavista	Northern Italian
Vineyard Café	Eclectic

F | D | S | C

Aioli
23 | 17 | 16 | $31

700 Elm St. (7th St.), 513-929-0525

■ Julie Francis, a chef-owner "destined for culinary greatness", presides at this "nice addition to the Downtown scene" that offers "tempting", "well-prepared" "imaginative presentations" of Eclectic fare; though some cite a need for "improved service", the "casual, comfortable" ambiance and a "great selection" of *vins de pays* keep city-dwellers coming back for "affordable" meals that are "perfect before the opera or symphony."

Ambar India [S]
25 | 9 | 16 | $18

350 Ludlow Ave. (Clifton Ave.), 513-281-7000

■ "There's always a crowd" at this "bustling" "Clifton favorite" where the "scrumptious" cuisine (including "lots of wonderful vegetarian dishes" and "amazing naan") will "transport you right to India"; some wish management would "improve the decor" and say the "speedy service" can be "choppy", but if you want "great food and fair prices, this is the place to go."

Beluga ◐
21 | 25 | 18 | $39

3520 Edwards Rd. (Erie Ave.), 513-533-4444

■ "Contemporary with a minimalist mind-set" sums up this "sleek, inviting" East Side eatery where a "helpful", "good-looking" staff ministers to the cool crowd with martinis and "very good Eurasian food" that offers "a new twist on sushi"; if it's all a bit "pricey", well, a "hip location" in tony Hyde Park doesn't come cheap.

Boca — | — | — | E

4034 Hamilton Ave. (bet. Blue Rock St. & Spring Grove Ave.), 513-542-2022

Now under energetic new ownership, this reclaimed storefront in the funky Northside neighborhood has clearly been rejuvenated and is drawing an arty clientele with its Italian fare (as well as Eclectic options such as French and Korean dishes) made from impeccably fresh ingredients (try the inventive tasting menu); backed by more upscale quarters and more polished service, it's already become a solid crowd-pleaser.

Brown Dog Cafe 23 | 14 | 19 | $35

Pfeiffer Commons, 5893 Pfeiffer Rd. (bet. I-71 & Kenwood Rd.), Blue Ash, 513-794-1610

■ "Who woulda thunk" you'd find a "really neat funky gourmet" New American with "artfully prepared" "inventive cuisine" in a plain-Jane strip mall in suburban Blue Ash; the "attentive" staff manages to create "a friendly atmosphere" in the "tastefully decorated" space hung with chef-owner Mary Swortwood's paintings; perhaps it's "a bit overpriced", but "as neighborhood restaurants go, this one's a keeper."

China Gourmet 24 | 16 | 21 | $32

3340 Erie Ave. (Marburg Ave.), 513-871-6612

■ Connoisseurs confirm that the Moy family dynasty continues to operate "the best Chinese in Cincinnati", with a "refined and restrained menu" that may be "pricey" but "rises above" those of "other Asian establishments"; "charming service by a loyal staff" "makes you feel like an honored guest", even if the rooms replete with rosewood "could use some help"; P.S. regulars of this Hyde Park veteran know to "go with the waiter's recommendations."

DAVEED'S AT 934 [S] 25 | 21 | 19 | $49

934 Hatch St. (Louden St.), 513-721-2665

◪ A "trendy but casual" ambiance permeates the "cozy" rooms in this renovated Mt. Adams townhouse (regulars suggest you "get a banquette for good people-watching"); a majority crowns David Cook "Cincinnati's most creative chef" for satisfying "sophisticated palates" with his "daring" and "exceptional" Eclectic-American cooking, but critics complain of "small portions at big prices" and a "pretentious attitude", asserting that the "food isn't enough to overcome the belittling feeling."

DEWEY'S PIZZA [S] 26 | 15 | 16 | $16

Oakley Sq., 3014 Madison Rd. (Markbreit Ave.), 513-731-7755
Shops at Harper's Point, 11338 Montgomery Rd. (Kemper Rd.), Symmes, 513-247-9955
Newport on the Levy Mall, 1 Levy Way (E. 4th St.), Newport, 859-431-9700
265 Hosea Rd. (Clifton Ave.), 513-221-0400

■ The "best pizza in town" awaits at this quartet of "crowded" 'za meccas where pie-zans praise the "endless combinations" of "tasty, innovative" "gourmet" toppings and red sauce with a "nice little kick to it"; be sure to save room, though, for the "fantastic" house salad and the "good wines by the glass"; P.S. the "new location in Newport" and the "just-opened" Hosea Road branch are not rated.

JEFF RUBY'S 23 | 26 | 24 | $54

700 Walnut St. (7th St.), 513-784-1200

■ "Over the top" sums up this Downtown steakhouse where the "beautiful art deco decor" is "spectacular", the "top-notch" staff "treats you as the star attraction", the "great wine list" is 21 pages long and the "fantastic", "step-above-the-rest dry-aged beef" is displayed in a meat locker then served in "huge portions"; "unless you're rich", though, "be careful", as the prices at this "expensive" "place to be seen" are just as "flamboyant" as everything else.

JUMP Café 24 | 24 | 22 | $48

1203 Main St. (12th St.), 513-665-4677

■ "Jump to it" Over-the-Rhine locals say – this "hip spot" offers "terrific and imaginative" New American food accented with "nice little touches" like homemade bread with savory spreads amid "to-die-for decor" that's part New York chic, part California casual ("the best seats in the house" are at the food bar "with a view of the kitchen" or at "the private table in the old elevator shaft"); it's "very pricey", but the main gripe is that the restaurant gets "overwhelmed" by the noise "from the bar below."

MAISONETTE 28 | 27 | 27 | $64

114 E. Sixth St. (bet. Main & Walnut Sts.), 513-721-2260

■ After 53 years, this French Downtowner remains the "traditional choice for wow occasions", as well as Cincinnati's Most Popular and No. 1 for Food; a "lighter, modern" approach is evident in "the crème-de-la-crème" cuisine, the "warm, elegant decor" is full of "fine artwork and soothing lighting", the "unobtrusive" staff puts you "totally at ease" and the tab makes it a "fine-food bargain"; P.S. the Food score does not reflect the 2001 transfer of the toque from "longtime chef Jean-Robert de Cavel" to Bertrand Bouquin.

MONTGOMERY INN 🖪 20 | 17 | 17 | $30

9440 Montgomery Rd. (bet. Cooper & Remington Rds.), Montgomery, 513-791-3482

MONTGOMERY INN AT THE BOATHOUSE 🖪

925 Eastern Ave. (I-471), 513-721-7427

■ "Gazillions of customers" say "you just can't beat" these "blue-collar gourmet" barbecue shrines known for "massively meaty bones" and homemade chips; while waits for a table "can be over two hours" (offering time to study the "sports memorabilia" at both the Montgomery and the Downtown riverfront-with-a-view locations) and service can be "rushed", tourists and locals agree this "Cincinnati tradition" is "mm-mmm" good.

Nicola's 23 | 19 | 16 | $39

1420 Sycamore St. (Liberty St.), 513-721-6200

■ This sophisticate serves up a "varied menu" of "creative Italian" delicacies that are "worth the time" it takes to prepare them; owner Nicola Pietoso and his "informed and friendly" servers operate in a "lovely, airy room" in a historic building full of "eclectic touches" like old clockworks and local artwork; given the "wonderful food and ambiance", regulars can't figure out why it "doesn't get the crowds it deserves" (perhaps the edgy location in Over-the-Rhine's Pendleton Art district "keeps timid people away").

Pacific Moon Cafe 🗗   24 | 14 | 19 | $25

Market Pl., 8300 Market Place Ln. (Montgomery Rd.), Montgomery, 513-891-0091

■ For those sick of the "same old, same old offerings", this popular Pan-Asian cafe in suburban Montgomery offers one of the "most diversified" and "creative" menus in town, including "outstanding dim sum on weekends" that many partisans feel is "the only one to try in the tri-state area"; sure, "it's a little expensive", but this is "where the Chinese community eats" – preferably on the "cozy little patio."

PALACE 🗗   27 | 27 | 26 | $52

Cincinnatian Hotel, 601 Vine St. (6th St.), 513-381-6006

■ "Luxurious" and "refined", this "perennial favorite" Downtown shatters lingering stereotypes about hotel dining with its "inventive and delicious" New American menu; its other "key elements" are more traditional: "serene" surroundings and "impeccable service" ("they go out of the way to make an evening special for you"); P.S. while the main room remains the place for "celebrating or trying to impress someone", the adjacent Cricket Lounge hits just the right note for a "reasonably priced" late-night bite.

PALOMINO 🗗   21 | 24 | 18 | $34

Fountain Pl., 505 Vine St. (5th St.), 513-381-1300

■ "Above-average creativity", a "vibrant and exciting" atmosphere and a "knowledgeable" staff may be why this Downtown outpost of a national family of New American–Mediterranean restaurants "doesn't seem like a chain"; its "intriguing" space, decorated with vivid Northwestern art and blown glass, is always crowded with "Cincinnati's elite", who clamor for the rotisserie-cooked meats and the "best mushroom soup ever" while competing for the window tables that provide a "perfect perch" "to watch the happenings on the square."

Phoenix   25 | 27 | 24 | $39

812 Race St. (9th St.), 513-721-8901

■ "Elegant", "old-fashioned" surroundings with lovely Georgian appointments and a "gracious, club-like atmosphere" make this Downtown Continental-American a "good place to carry on a conversation" or to have a memorable "night out"; "exceptional pricing" (especially on the wine list), "beautifully served, rich" dishes and "hardly any turnover" among the experienced staff all ensure "you'll always feel special" here.

PRECINCT 🗗   25 | 20 | 22 | $48

311 Delta Ave. (Columbia Pkwy.), 513-321-5454

■ While it's no crime to call this "remodeled 19th-century police station" a "temple to steak", the raw bar and other "wonderful seafood" options are "just as impressive", and whatever you order, you get "a lot for your money"; yes, the "seating is cramped" in the warren of candlelit, mirrored rooms, but after 22 years on the East Side, this "clubby" "favorite" is still the best place "for a power dinner" or "to see celebrities and sports stars."

Primavista 🗗   23 | 24 | 22 | $42

Queen's Tower, 810 Matson Pl. (bet. 8th St. & Price Ave.), 513-251-6467

■ "The name says it all" – "the absolutely best view" of the Ohio River Valley and Downtown Cincinnati can be seen from this Price

Hillsider that "draws an older, local crowd" ("with a few heirs thrown in for good measure") that dines on an "extensive menu" of "delicious" Northern "Italian classics"; while you may pay a little extra for that prima vista, the cognoscenti claim it's still an "excellent value."

Vineyard Café & Wine Room S   – – – M
2653 Erie Ave. (Edwards Rd.), 513-871-6167
Vibrant Hyde Park is an ideal locale for this easygoing Eclectic cafe with a sunny disposition and a wall of windows, where well-dressed locals gather on the lovely patio for prime people-watching while dining on the signature crab cakes and sipping from an extensive, food-friendly wine selection; not only are the tabs marvelously modest, but live entertainment is featured in the cozy wine bar on Fridays and Saturdays.

Cleveland

TOP 10 FOOD RANKING

Restaurant	Cuisine Type
28 Johnny's Bar	N. Italian/Continental
27 Baricelli Inn	Continental
Phnom Penh	Pan-Asian
Giovanni's	Northern Italian
26 Lola Bistro	New American
Sans Souci	Mediterranean
25 Johnny's Downtown	N. Italian/Continental
Parker's	New American
Mise	Eclectic
Moxie	New American

ADDITIONAL NOTEWORTHY PLACES

Blue Point Grille	Seafood
Century	Seafood
Chez François	French
Circo Zibibbo	N&S Italian
fire	American
Johnny's Bistro	French Bistro
One Walnut	New American
Sergio's	Brazilian
Viva Barcelona	Spanish
Weia Teia	Asian Fusion

F	D	S	C

BARICELLI INN
27 | 24 | 24 | $59

Baricelli Inn, 2203 Cornell Rd. (Murray Hill Rd.), 216-791-6500

■ "Atmosphere abounds" at Paul Minnillo's "upscale" eatery housed in a "historic" brownstone mansion near "picturesque Little Italy"; the "flawlessly" served selections – "creative" contemporary Continental dishes and a "wonderful selection of cheeses" – are among the reasons devotees deem this a "favorite" "place for a celebration of any sort"; P.S. "stay overnight for a truly wonderful experience" (it's also a "quaint" B&B).

BLUE POINT GRILLE 🖬
24 | 23 | 22 | $43

700 W. Saint Clair Ave. (6th St.), 216-875-7827

■ Chef Jim Gillison scores points for the "finest fish in Cleveland" at this "refurbished" landmark "in the heart of the Warehouse District", where thirtysomething-and-up professionals converge for a "terrific bar scene" amid the "nautical" decor; despite gripes about the "outrageous prices", most recommend this "elegant establishment" when they "want to impress."

Century 🖬
24 | 25 | 22 | $47

Ritz-Carlton Hotel, 1515 W. Third St. (Huron Rd.), 216-902-5255

■ "Exactly what you would expect from a Ritz-Carlton" say surveyors of this Downtown dining room whose "sleek" setting "with a train motif" is "carpeted and draped so well you can actually carry on a conversation"; the "seafood-oriented menu" is "creative", while the "comprehensive sushi bar" and "cool" martini bar offer speedier options; opinions diverge on the service ("suave" vs. "overbearing"), but all agree that the "huge swirl of cotton candy that arrives with the check is a great touch."

Chez François ▫S   ▽ 28 26 26 $68
555 Main St. (Liberty Ave.), Vermilion, 440-967-0630
■ Whether you arrive by land or by sea – the restaurant offers docking, along with a "terrific view", on the Vermilion River – you'll be treated to a "truly wonderful" French dining experience at this "out-of-the-way" Far West "treat"; while prices can hit the high-water mark (even "some of the wealthiest are complaining"), the "special wine-pairing dinners" constitute the "best gourmet dining buy in northern Ohio", and the service is "top-notch."

Circo Zibibbo ▫S   20 24 17 $44
1300 W. Ninth St. (Saint Clair Ave.), 216-575-0699
◪ A cheery "rainbow of colored glass hanging from the ceiling and undulating along the walls" draws a "fun crowd" to this "can-you-say-trendy" "scene" "at the base of the Warehouse District"; the "jumping bar", though, may be "more enjoyable than the dining room" because while the "contemporary" Italian menu features some "inspired" dishes, disappointed detractors feel that the food is "overpriced" and "takes a looong time to arrive at the table."

GIOVANNI'S RISTORANTE   27 24 27 $60
25550 Chagrin Blvd. (Richmond Rd.), Beachwood, 216-831-8625
■ "Attracting well-dressed diners" to ritzy Beachwood, this "longtime favorite" is an "oasis of quiet (or stuffiness)"; while it's inarguably "expensive", supporters feel that the tabs are justified by the "attentive" service and top-notch Northern Italian menu (you "can't go wrong" with any of the selections), but skeptics complain that the kitchen "tends to overdo" things.

fire ◖S   –   –   –   M
Shaker Sq., 13220 Shaker Sq. (S. Moreland Blvd.), 216-921-3473
Giving new meaning to the word contemporary, this red-hot, ultramodern addition to historic Shaker Square demonstrates that minimalism can work, both on the clever seasonal American menu and in the industrial-chic interior; the open kitchen with brick and tandoori ovens and a chef's counter lets diners feel less like customers and more like guests while they tuck into simple yet creative comfort foods served by a personable crew; be warned, though, that the too-close quarters could send even the slightly claustrophobic running.

JOHNNY'S BAR   28 19 25 $52
3164 Fulton Rd. (Trent Ave.), 216-281-0055
■ "Reminiscent of the '40s", this "charming" West Side institution is the oldest of the three Johnny's establishments, and as with many a trilogy, the "first is always the best" assert the *amici* who voted it No. 1 for Food in Cleveland; though "dark" and a bit "cramped" with the stream of local "notables" flowing through, it's a must-try due to the "gorilla-size portions" of "fantastic" Northern Italian and Continental dishes delivered by a "superb" staff, and it's "worth every cent."

Johnny's Bistro 24 | 27 | 23 | $56

1400 W. Sixth St. (bet. Saint Clair & Superior Aves.), 216-774-0055

◪ Co-owner Paul Anthony's latest Johnny's venture, this "elegant" French beckons "special-occasion" revelers to the Warehouse District; advocates adore the "authentic dishes" ("if you don't try the truffled mashed potatoes, you've committed a culinary sin"), "plush" surroundings and "fabulous" service, but naysayers snap that "bistro food shouldn't be served in such a snooty environment."

Johnny's Downtown [S] 25 | 23 | 22 | $51

1406 W. Sixth St. (bet. Saint Clair & Superior Aves.), 216-623-0055

◪ When they need a "reliable spot for an important business dinner", the Downtown "suits" march to this "nice little brother" of Johnny's Bar, followed by a flock of "slicks and trendies" seeking a "swank" setting and "mouthwatering" Northern Italian and Continental dishes to match; the bottom line is "expensive", though most say it's "worth it for the occasional splurge."

LOLA BISTRO ◐[S] 26 | 21 | 23 | $46

900 Literary Rd. (Professor Ave.), 216-771-5652

■ He has posed naked with a Vita-Mix, he appears on the Food Network show *The Melting Pot* and still chef-owner Michael Symon has time to keep Tremont diners "oohing and aahing" with his "not-for-the-timid" New American menu that "makes food you don't think you like taste good"; "success hasn't spoiled" this "cutting-edge place", but it has made "reservations extremely necessary."

Mise 25 | 22 | 26 | $37

10427 Clifton Blvd. (bet. 104th & 105th Sts.), 216-651-6473

■ Chef-owner "Jeff Uniatowski has done a phenomenal job" cheer fans of his unexpectedly hip spot spanning two West Side storefronts; on the "creative", ever-evolving Eclectic menu, surveyors single out "imaginative" mainstays like coffee-crusted sea scallops and a "don't-miss" "coffee and doughnuts dessert", brought to table by "extremely knowledgeable" servers; just be warned that this mise-en-scène can get way "noisy."

Moxie [S] 25 | 19 | 21 | $44

3355 Richmond Rd. (Chagrin Blvd.), Beachwood, 216-831-5599

■ A "table-hopping crowd" crams into this "trendy" "deli on steroids" on the East Side to tuck into "consistently excellent" New American dishes like long-bone rib steak and the "out-of-this-world baked hot chocolate" dessert; even if some of the waiters seem straight out of the "Sprockets skit from *Saturday Night Live*" and the cavernous space can turn "oppressively loud", this "fun place" has plenty of moxie.

One Walnut 22 | 21 | 21 | $46

Ohio Savings Bldg., 1 Walnut Ave. (bet. 9th & 12th Sts.), 216-575-1111

◪ "Pricey and proud of it", this Downtown New American is the latest venture from chef-owner Marlin Kaplan; while the faithful rave about the "creative but classically inspired dishes" and "glitzy Gotham styling", the less reverent roar "overrated" – especially considering "not everyone is on an expense account."

Parker's 25 | 18 | 21 | $49

2801 Bridge Ave. (28th St.), 216-771-7130

◪ "Chef-owner Parker Bosley brings semi-formal haute cuisine" to Ohio City at this "refined" New American where his "exquisite use of local ingredients" ("fresh, fresh") results in "small portions but huge taste"; "for pure food, it's top-shelf" praise true believers, but critics counter "boring", citing the too-"simple" cooking and "no-glitz" atmosphere.

PHNOM PENH S⧽ 27 4 12 $18
13124 Lorain Ave. (131st St.), 216-251-0210

■ The "best cheap eats in town" (certainly not the "what-a-dump" digs) pull in plenty of takers at this West Side "hole-in-the-wall" where they gladly "line up outside" while waiting for a coveted table; the reward: a "wonderfully spicy", "extensive" Asian menu that highlights Cambodian and Vietnamese specialties but wanders all over the region; the cooking is the real deal, which means don't ask for "hot" unless "you can handle it"; P.S. "no liquor, but you're encouraged to BYO."

SANS SOUCI S 26 27 25 $47
Cleveland Renaissance Hotel, 24 Public Sq. (bet. Superior Ave. & 3rd St.), 216-696-5600

■ "Hands down the best Mediterranean" cooking in town, an "ever-changing menu, quiet rooms and relaxed service – what could be better?" ask the reviewers who have once again voted this Renaissance hotel dining room the Most Popular restaurant in Cleveland; "overlooking Public Square" and "oozing with charm", it's an "enticing" place to take "that special someone."

Sergio's in University Circle S 24 17 21 $38
1903 Ford Dr. (Bellflower Rd.), 216-231-1234

■ Brazilian influences shake up a menu that "never lets you down" at this "fascinating and flavorful" South American, "one of the better choices" in the arty University Circle area; live Latin-inspired jazz (Wednesday–Sunday) "makes the experience even more festive", though note that on concert nights the pre-symphony crowd takes over the already-"cramped quarters", so be sure to "book in advance."

Viva Barcelona S ▽ 23 20 26 $30
24600 Detroit Rd. (bet Clague & Columbia Rds.), Westlake, 440-892-8700

■ "Fine Spanish dining comes to the West Shore suburbs" crow converts to this neophyte, whose "incredible" dishes are well paired with "excellent sangria"; "exceptional" service from "tuxedo-clad waiters" and a "perfect" atmosphere (just the "right mix of soft lighting and music") are more reasons it's such a "real treat."

Weia Teia S 23 17 17 $25
Great Northern Mall, 140 Great Northern Mall (Brookpark Rd.), North Olmsted, 440-716-8381

■ "All mall restaurants should be this good" insist gourmands surprised to find an "artful", "funky" eatery so close to a Gap; its South suburbs locale makes it a convenient choice for shoppers, but it's worth visiting by anyone looking for an "inventive" "Asian-inspired" "fusion experience", even if more than a few respondents think that the "inattentive" service could use some work.

Columbus, OH

TOP 10 FOOD RANKING

Restaurant	Cuisine Type
28 Handke's Cuisine	International
27 Refectory	French/New French
L'Antibes	French
Rigsby's	Provençal/N. Italian
26 Yard Club	Irish/American
25 Lindey's	American
Restaurant Japan	Japanese
Cameron's American Bistro	New American
Morton's of Chicago	Steakhouse
La Tavola	N&S Italian

ADDITIONAL NOTEWORTHY PLACES

Alana's Food & Wine	Eclectic
Braddock's Grandview	Low Country
Columbus Fish Market	Seafood
M	Eclectic/New American
Mitchell's	Steakhouse
Shoku	Japanese
Starliner Diner	Cuban/Mexican
SuLan Eurasian Bistro	Eurasian
Trattoria Roma	Northern Italian
Vaqueros	Mexican

F	D	S	C

Alana's Food & Wine

| 24 | 13 | 21 | $31 |

2333 N. High St. (bet. Oakland & Patterson Aves.), 614-294-6783

☑ "Funky and strange yet comfortable", Alana Shock's (the "queen of flavor") "different" kind of eatery north of Ohio State's campus attracts "adventurous" appetites with her "innovative" Eclectic cooking (the "always-changing menu" "does well by vegetarians" too), matched by an "extensive" wine list with truly "great prices"; though a few find her "well meaning but cranky", supporters relish her "personalized" concept as a "refreshing" "diversion" and appreciate her "real commitment to quality ingredients."

Braddock's Grandview

| 22 | 17 | 20 | $32 |

1470 Grandview Ave. (Ida Ave.), 614-487-0077

☑ The kitchen's "magic with pork dishes" (don't say no to the "flavorful" hickory-smoked tenderloin) and other "imaginative" Low Country interpretations keeps loyalists returning to this "unpretentious" Southern treat on the main drag of the hip (yes, really) suburb of Grandview; it definitely "fills a niche" in the local dining scene, even if detractors gripe "lots of hype but not enough follow-through"; N.B. the post-*Survey* departure of namesake chef Michael Braddock may outdate the above Food score.

Cameron's American Bistro [S] 25 | 19 | 22 | $32

2185 W. Dublin-Granville Rd. (Linworth Rd.), Worthington, 614-885-3663

■ Columbus restaurateur Cameron Mitchell clearly "knows the business" well, which explains why this "friendly neighborhood" bistro in quaint Worthington, his first local venture, is "still going strong"; while it may be "less flashy" than his later enterprises, it remains an "all-time favorite" thanks to a New American menu that's "consistently" "awesome" (and includes some "very unique items") and a "super" staff; granted, it can get "crazy loud", but plenty of enthusiasts just "love" this place.

COLUMBUS FISH MARKET [S] 24 | 20 | 20 | $31

40 Hutchinson Ave. (Rte. 270), 614-410-3474

1245 Olentangy River Rd. (bet. 3rd & 5th Aves.), 614-291-3474

◪ Schools of fin fanatics seek out this "hit" pair of seafood houses (courtesy of Cameron Mitchell) with an "active, urbane" ambiance in North Columbus and in the Crosswoods area for "excellent fish" ("flown in fresh daily" and prepared with a "lively flair") that landlocked diners "can rely on"; the "unimpressed", however, say "good but never spectacular, and way too noisy."

HANDKE'S CUISINE 28 | 25 | 24 | $47

520 S. Front St. (bet. Beck & Blenkner Sts.), 614-621-2500

■ Certified Master Chef Hartmut Handke is the "genius" behind this "charming" "special-occasion" destination in the Brewery District, which has again been ranked No. 1 for Food in Columbus; featuring "unique subterranean dining" in a restored 19th-century rathskeller, it provides a "superb" International "feast for the eyes as well as the palate" (including "incredible" buffalo tenderloin steak and crème brûlée that "might be the best in the world"), along with "attentive" service; of course it's "expensive", but this "class act" is "still the best in town."

L'ANTIBES 27 | 22 | 24 | $45

772 N. High St. (Warren St.), 614-291-1666

■ "Very small and intimate", this Short North "gem" is "a definite asset" to Columbus because chef/co-owner Dale Gussett "knows what we want in fine dining" – "phenomenal" classic French fare ("go for the veal sweetbreads", "the best in town") proffered in an "elegant" environment with a "romantic" ambiance by a "professional" staff that satisfies "your every whim"; "expect a leisurely dinner" – there's "no rushing" here.

La Tavola 25 | 10 | 19 | $22

33 Beech Ridge Dr. (Powell Rd.), Powell, 614-848-4231

■ "From the outside, you'd never guess that this building is home to the best Italian food in town (the inside isn't much to look at either)", but this "family-run" trattoria in the Northwest delivers "truly outstanding", "authentic" Italian cooking (plus, the menu offers "half-size" helpings for smaller appetites, "a wonderful idea"), paired with a "great" all-Italian wine list that's "priced around retail"; to boot, the atmosphere is "laid-back" and the staff "super-friendly."

LINDEY'S [S] 25 | 24 | 22 | $37

169 E. Beck St. (Mohawk St.), 614-228-4343

◪ Even after two decades, "the beautiful people" still flock to this "lively" American bistro situated in a 19th-century building in

German Village because it's a "favorite" "institution that doesn't fail"; a "great gathering place" with "lots of action" at the bars and "interesting people-watching", it features a "wonderful variety" of "can't-go-wrong" dishes, but dissenters find it "overhyped" and "pretty snotty."

M – | – | – | M

2 Miranova Pl. (W. Mound St.), 614-629-0000

Chic, sleek and teeming with the beautiful people dressed to the nines, this venture from the Cameron Mitchell restaurant empire boasts a prime location in Downtown's hottest office/residential complex, as well as a terrace with the best view of the Columbus skyline; the sophisticated surroundings – state-of-the-art lighting, luxurious upholstery, light woods – provide an upscale background for an Eclectic–New American menu presented by a prompt, knowledgeable service team.

Mitchell's Steakhouse [S] 24 | 26 | 22 | $45

45 N. Third St. (bet. Gay & Lynn Sts.), 614-621-2333

Crosswoods, 7619 Huntington Park Dr. (Campus View Blvd.), 614-888-2467

◪ "Movers and shakers" patronize this "classy" steakhouse set in a "wonderful old bank building" in the heart of Downtown; it's a prime power place to "take clients" thanks to its "beautiful", spacious surroundings and an "excellent" staff that "treats you right", not to mention "well-prepared" aged cuts like its signature Kansas City strip; critics, however, who think that restaurant mogul Cameron Mitchell "may be spreading himself too thin", charge "overrated"; N.B. there's another branch at Crosswoods.

Morton's of Chicago [S] 25 | 20 | 21 | $50

2 Nationwide Plaza (High St.), 614-464-4442

◪ "More-than-generous portions" of "melt-in-your-mouth" aged porterhouses and "good" sides ("you could feed three kids with one potato") satisfy cadres of carnivores at this "traditional" Downtown chophouse; though fans praise the experience as "gluttony at its best", detractors shrug "more of the same", surmising that this "expense-account" chain link is "not as big a standout as in other cities because there are plenty of good steakhouses" in Columbus.

REFECTORY 27 | 26 | 26 | $48

1092 Bethel Rd. (Kenny Rd.), 614-451-9774

■ "The ecclesiastical atmosphere matches the heavenly food" at this "sumptuous", "flawless" French "benchmark" housed in a restored Northwest church with an air of "quiet elegance"; given "superb" chef Richard Blondin's "masterful" execution of both the classics and modern interpretations, beautifully accompanied by an "award-winning wine list" and brought to table by an "exquisite" staff that's "never intrusive", is it any revelation that it was yet again voted the Most Popular restaurant in Columbus by faithful worshipers?; P.S. check out the "bargain" bistro menu in the lounge.

Restaurant Japan [S] 25 | 15 | 19 | $25

1173 Old Henderson Rd. (Kenny Rd.), 614-451-5411

■ "One bite of the sublime spicy tuna roll will convince anyone that this is the best Japanese food in Columbus"; not only will the "expertly prepared, melt-in-your-mouth sushi make you an addict", but this "busy" "real deal" in the Northwest also features "top-notch" cooked dishes including "heavenly tempura and perfect noodles"; granted, the digs are strictly "no-frills" and it's "a little too bright", but the "great value" keeps fans coming back.

RIGSBY'S CUISINE VOLATILE 27 23 23 $38
698 N. High St. (Lincoln St.), 614-461-7888
■ "A happy place to eat", this "modern", "stylish" Provençal–Northern Italian in the trendy Short North district offers "lots of lively kitchen action on view and fun things on the menu"; the kitchen's "exciting" cooking yields "complex flavors" that are "sometimes unusual but always good", so though "it may be the place to be seen, unlike restaurants that focus on form over substance", this "adventure in food" "delivers excellent" fare "artfully presented" in a "metropolitan" ambiance by a "superb" staff; N.B. a post-*Survey* chef change may outdate the Food score.

Shoku S 23 20 20 $32
1312 Grandview Ave. (3rd Ave.), 614-485-9490
■ "Good, if not great", sushi in "chic", "dramatic" environs beckons scenesters to this "pleasant" Grandview Japanese "favorite" replete with a "spacious" patio that affords prime "people-watching"; though a few feel that the service can "vary", the majority recommends this "relaxing and enjoyable experience."

Starliner Diner S 24 13 18 $17
5240 Cemetery Rd. (east of Main St.), Hilliard, 614-529-1198
■ "Kitschy" "treasures" (think eccentric holiday ornaments, a collection of clocks from the '60s, etc.) earn this "down 'n' dirty" Hilliard diner acclaim as a "favorite funky place" to scarf down "huge portions" of "hearty", "out-of-this-world" Cuban-Mexican food, "wonderfully spiced" and "unusually good"; though there's often "a wait", when you "want to have some fun" and eat cheap ethnic, this "kooky" "oddball" satisfies.

SuLan Eurasian Bistro S 23 27 18 $35
2894 E. Main St. (east of Roosevelt Ave.), Bexley, 614-338-0788
■ "What a space!" exclaim enthusiasts of this "trendy" "rising star" in affluent Bexley, which distinguishes itself with a "fabulous interior design" and "soothing" ambiance; it's a "really cool" backdrop in which to sample a "smashing variety" of "creative", "exotic" even, Eurasian dishes; "a great addition to the Columbus scene", this "wonderful experience" just "keeps getting better."

Trattoria Roma S 24 17 18 $32
1447 Grandview Ave. (5th Ave.), 614-488-2104
■ Providing an "authentic" Northern Italian meal in Grandview, this "delightful" "treat" pleases with "inspired preparations" like "perfect al dente" "homemade pastas" with "incredible sauces" as well as "melt-in-your-mouth fish"; the "crowded" conditions and "noisy" room are the "only unfortunate distractions from the food", but at least "you can eat out front" on the sidewalk patio during nice weather.

Vaqueros S – – – I
Dublin Village Ctr., 6771 Dublin Center Dr. (Rte. 270), 614-659-0279
El Vaquero
3230 Olentangy River Rd. (Riverview Dr.), 614-261-0900
2195 Riverside Dr. (Lane Ave.), 614-486-4547
Aficionados of these lively Mexican fiestas can depend on them for classic south-of-the-border dishes offered at prices that won't

make them gulp *ay caramba*; the cooking is the real deal, and it's delivered by a speedy staff in kitschy surroundings decked out with sombreros, maracas and TVs that air Spanish-language shows.

YARD CLUB [S] 26 | 22 | 21 | $26

4065 Main St. (Norwich St.), Hilliard, 614-771-1400

■ Thanks to "a chef who thinks", the "surprisingly innovative" Irish-American selections offered at this "fun" hangout (set in an 1883 building registered with the National Historic Preservation Society) in old Hilliard are far "more gourmet" than the "pub grub you might expect from its name"; though the "service can be a little questionable at times", the "quality of the food" "makes up for it"; it's still an "underappreciated" "secret", which suits just fine the insiders who only "hope the word doesn't get out."

Connecticut

TOP 20 FOOD RANKING

Restaurant	Cuisine Type
28 Jean-Louis	New French
Thomas Henkelmann	French
27 Da Pietro's	Northern Italian/French
Ondine	New French
Restaurant du Village	French
Cavey's	Northern Italian/New French
Max's Oyster Bar	Seafood
Frank Pepe	Pizza
Rebeccas	New American
La Colline Verte	New French
26 Metro Bis	New American
Bernard's Inn	French
Valbella	Northern Italian
Jeffrey's	New American/Continental
Quattro's	N&S Italian
Sally's	Pizza
Meigas	Spanish
Max Downtown	New American/Steakhouse
Peppercorn's Grill	N&S Italian
Stonehenge	Continental

ADDITIONAL NOTEWORTHY PLACES

Baang Café	French/Asian
Cafe Routier	French Bistro
Carole Peck's	New American
Frank Pepe's The Spot	Pizza
Gennaro's Amalfi Grill	N&S Italian
Golden Lamb Buttery	American
Great Taste	Chinese
Harry's	Pizza
Max Amore	Northern Italian
Mayflower	American/Continental
Morton's of Chicago	Steakhouse
Piccolo Arancio	N&S Italian
Restaurant Bricco	N. Italian/Med.
Roger Sherman Inn	Continental
Roomba	Nuevo Latino
Ruth's Chris	Steakhouse
Steve's Centerbrook	New American
Terra Mar Grille	New American
Union League Cafe	French Bistro
West Street Grill	New American

BAANG CAFÉ [S] 24 | 21 | 19 | $41

1191 E. Putnam Ave. (I-95, exit 5), Greenwich, 203-637-2114

■ "Still hopping and happening" seven years after its opening, this "hot spot" is where "super-cool people" convene in Greenwich for "inventive", "expensive" French-Asian fusion cooking (like firecracker spring rolls) in a "modern minimalist" space; there are "long waits", the tables are "too close together" and the "noise level is painful", but that's exactly why "folks who want NY attitude and aura" head here.

Bernard's Inn [S] 26 | 24 | 24 | $53

20 West Ln. (Rte. 35), Ridgefield, 203-438-8282

■ Loyalists laud this Ridgefield landmark helmed by toque team Bernard and Sarah Bouissou (both ex NYC's Le Cirque) as "French elegance at its finest" in a "picture-perfect New England setting"; the "heavenly cuisine" "forces you to reset your standards" for a "wonderful array of appetizers", "great sauces" and even "sweetbreads for the shy", and with "superb service", there are "no weaknesses" here.

Cafe Routier [S] 25 | – | 22 | $35

1353 Boston Post Rd. (Rte. I-95, exit 65), Westbrook, 860-399-8700

■ The "incredibly consistent" kitchen at this Post Road French bistro (in larger digs following a post-*Survey* move to Westbrook) delights devotees daily with Franco favorites like the "steak frites of their dreams" (as well as some American dishes), not to mention a "great wine" list, "good prices" and a welcoming staff that has regulars reporting every visit is "like coming home"; N.B. now serving lunch.

Carole Peck's Good News Cafe [S] 25 | 19 | 21 | $38

694 Main St. S./Rte. 6 (Rte. 64), Woodbury, 203-266-4663

■ The "food is good news" at this Woodbury New American "gem" where "Connecticut's Alice Waters" has a "deft hand" with "fresh-from-the-farm" ingredients, resulting in "innovative but not coy" "takes on new and classic dishes"; a "gregarious crowd" finds it "well worth the drive" as well for the "professional service" and "chic", "casual setting"; P.S. "yes, that was Helen Hunt."

Cavey's 27 | 24 | 25 | $51

45 E. Center St. (Main St.), Manchester, 860-643-2751

■ "Black-tie service and blue-ribbon food in a blue-collar town" sums up the sentiment about this Manchester "close-to-perfection" "veteran" that's a "delightful" Northern Italian upstairs and a "formal but not pretentious" New French downstairs; both offer "excellent wine selections" and are "great for special occasions" – just be prepared for a "pricey" evening.

DA PIETRO'S 27 | 20 | 25 | $54

36 Riverside Ave. (Boston Post Rd.), Westport, 203-454-1213

■ The chef-owner's "pervasive influence makes you feel like a guest in his house" pronounce those passionate about Pietro Scotti's Northern Italian–French in Westport, where the "creative, "flawless" dishes are "worth a drive from anywhere in the tri-state area"; though some size-ists say the "teeny-tiny" storefront is "uncomfortably cramped", those who find it "romantic" advise "make reservations early."

Frank Pepe Pizzeria 🅂⊅　　27 | 12 | 16 | $17
157 Wooster St. (bet. Brown & Olive Sts.), New Haven, 203-865-5762
■ Devotees of Downtown New Haven's "king of pizza" debate
whether its "heavenly" white-clam pie is "the single best on earth"
or "in the galaxy", but either way they agree it's the greatest "of
all time"; still, those who say the "wait is unbelievable" ("bring
War and Peace") and the "service is brusque" advise opting for
takeout – "if you can get someone to answer the phone."

Frank Pepe's The Spot 🅂⊅　　25 | 12 | 15 | $16
163 Wooster St. (bet. Brown & Olive Sts.), New Haven, 203-865-7602
■ Though they "hate to spoil the secret", in-the-know New
Havenites confide that this smaller sibling of Frank Pepe Pizzeria
(which "catches the overflow" from its legendary big brother next
door) offers almost the same "tasty pizzas, chilly service and great
cheap Chianti"; plus, you're "usually seated in half the time",
making it just the spot for pie fanatics in a hurry.

Gennaro's Amalfi Grill　　25 | – | 23 | $35
196 Crown St. (Temple St.), New Haven, 203-777-5490
■ "Home is where the heart is, and the owners are all heart" at
this New Haven Italian rated "excellent" by regulars who return
for "an abundance of good choices" that includes "always-great
veal", "good red sauce" and "great desserts"; a 2001 move to
Crown Street resulted in more upscale digs that include a piano
bar that pulsates from Thursday–Saturday.

Golden Lamb Buttery ⊅　　25 | 27 | 25 | $54
499 Wolf Den Rd. (Bush Hill Rd.), Brooklyn, 860-774-4423
■ For 40 years, husband-and-wife owners Bob and Jimmie Booth
have overseen "once-in-a-lifetime experiences" that can include
a pre-prandial hayride ("you can see dinner frolicking in the fields")
on their 1,000-acre Brooklyn farm; the American menu is especially
"superb" in summer, when "fresh, fresh" vegetables turn up on
the table; just one caveat: it's "country cooking at city prices";
N.B. closed December 31–April.

Great Taste 🅂　　25 | 24 | 24 | $24
597 W. Main St. (Corbin Ave.), New Britain, 860-827-8988
■ Respondents rave about this "aptly named", "ultra-reliable" New
Britain Chinese where the "service is splendid", "the Peking duck is
always available" and the "owner's hand is evident in everything";
P.S. it's the "best use yet of an old IHOP" sing surveyors.

Harry's Pizza 🅂⊅　　25 | 17 | 20 | $17
West Hartford Ctr., 1003 Farmington Ave. (bet. LaSalle Rd. & Walden St.),
West Hartford, 860-231-7166
■ Regulars "get withdrawal symptoms" without "a weekly visit"
to this purveyor of the "best pizza in the Hartford area", which
is made with a "thin, almost cracker-like" crust and "toppings that
lean to what's fresh and in season"; it's "jammed most nights, but
they handle it", maybe because the staff "appears to be on skates."

JEAN-LOUIS　　28 | 25 | 26 | $62
61 Lewis St. (bet. Greenwich Ave. & Mason St.), Greenwich,
203-622-8450
■ Rated No. 1 for Food and Most Popular among Connecticut
restaurants, this Greenwich great is a gift from Jean-Louis Gerin,
the chef-owner, who "gets better every year", creating simply

"superb" New French food accompanied by a "wine list that would give any sommelier goose bumps"; the setting is "intimate" and "elegant" ("even the lighting is exquisite"), and the service is "perfection"; it's "pricey", but "from the warm welcome to the chef waving goodbye", "it doesn't get any better than this."

Jeffrey's 26 | 23 | 26 | $37

501 New Haven Ave. (Old Gate Ln.), Milford, 203-878-1910

■ "You'd never expect to find" "such incredible food" in an "unassuming" spot by "a busy [Milford] road" say fans of this New American–Continental "class act" overseen by owner "Jeffrey [Johnson], a perfect host"; "friendly service and piano music" (Thursday–Saturday) "enhance" the experience.

La Colline Verte [S] 27 | 25 | 26 | $52

Greenfield Hill Shopping Ctr., 75 Hillside Rd. (Bronson Rd.), Fairfield, 203-256-9242

■ Critics chorus "kudos" to the owner of this "surprising-for-a-shopping-mall" New French where "fine cuisine, elegant decor and superlative service equal an Olympic Gold"; "though prices aren't cheap", the equivalent experience is "higher at other spots", plus it provides "some of the best people-watching in Fairfield County" – "we've seen both Newman and Redford here."

Max Amore Ristorante [S] 25 | 22 | 22 | $31

Somerset Sq., 140 Glastonbury Blvd. (Main St.), Glastonbury, 860-659-2819

■ "Big fans of the Max chain" find this "trendy" Glastonbury Northern Italian that "feels like a California version of a Tuscan farmhouse" a "great" "scene to be seen" in; "your taste buds will do back flips" over "delicious food" ("pasta perfect"), while you "shout over the din and stuff yourself."

Max Downtown [S] 26 | 24 | 24 | $43

City Place, 185 Asylum St. (bet. Haynes & Trumbull Sts.), Hartford, 860-522-2530

■ "Don't save it for a special occasion" advise aficionados of Hartford's "power place", a Downtown New American steakhouse that's "very NY" and the "place to go" for "dinner with friends" or "the corporate bigwigs from out of town"; "steaks like buttah" share the table with "other man-size dishes", and "the bar is fully stocked with both liquor and patrons"; still, a "Maxed-out" minority calls it "overpriced."

Max's Oyster Bar [S] 27 | 26 | 25 | $44

964 Farmington Ave. (S. Main St.), West Hartford, 860-236-6299

■ Making a huge splash in happening West Hartford, this "snazzy", cathedral-ceilinged "addition to the Max empire" offers "excellent" shellfish 'hi-rise' platters, the "best" blackened swordfish and other superlative seafood; it's "packed", "pricey" and very "hot."

MAYFLOWER [S] 26 | 28 | 27 | $57

The Mayflower Inn, 118 Woodbury Rd./Rte. 47 (Rte. 109), Washington, 860-868-9466

■ If you're longing for "textbook country chic" consisting of "beautiful grounds", "pristine flower beds" and an "elegant" "*Masterpiece Theatre*" interior, then this Washington American-Continental is the place for you; its "excellent" seasonally changing menu (highlighting indigenous New England Atlantic ingredients and organic produce from local gardens) and "impeccable" service make for wonderful meals, "especially on the terrace in summer", so it's not surprising that some conclude "I could live here."

Meigas S   26 | 21 | 23 | $44
(fka Meson Galicia)
10 Wall St. (bet. High & Knight Sts.), Norwalk, 203-866-8800
■ A mainstay in Downtown Norwalk, this taste of "classic Madrid" is "maintaining its edge" with a new name, a freshening-up of its "pleasant" country inn–like interior and a more upscale menu of "pricey but delicious" Spanish specialties (including "perfectly prepared squid" with roasted beets and turnips in a shallot vinaigrette) served by an always-"solicitous" staff.

Metro Bis   26 | 21 | 24 | $41
Simsburytown Shops, 928 Hopmeadow St./Rte. 10-202 (Massaco St.), Simsbury, 860-651-1908
■ "Who would think a Simsbury strip-mall storefront could hide such great food and wine?" query surveyors who were "tempted to lie so this" New American "gem wouldn't be discovered"; conscience must have prevailed, because they report that chef-owner Christopher Prosperi oversees a "consistently enticing, innovative menu" that just "keeps getting better."

Morton's of Chicago S   25 | 22 | 22 | $54
30 State House Sq. (Asylum St.), Hartford, 860-724-0044
UBS Warburg, 377 N. State St. (bet. Atlantic & Washington Sts.), Stamford, 203-324-3939
■ "Beef is back and better than ever" at these Hartford and Stamford branches of a national steakhouse chain where "big meat", "big money" and "big shots" are the order of the day; still, wallet-watchers warn "take the clients, not the kids" to this "platinum-priced" ("come on, throw in the potato") "expense-account" spot, and sophisticates sigh "spare me the plastic-wrapped display" of meat rolled to the table on carts.

ONDINE S   27 | 26 | 26 | $50
69 Pembroke Rd./Rte. 37 (Wheeler Dr.), Danbury, 203-746-4900
■ "Worth the drive" to its "out-of-the-way" Danbury setting, this New Gallic destination is situated in a "romantic old house" with "paradigmatic Country French" ambiance ("look no further for Provence" atmosphere); moreover, the "first-class" prix fixe menu offers "many choices" and the service is "professional"; P.S. save room for the "must-try molten-chocolate dessert."

Peppercorn's Grill   26 | 22 | 22 | $40
357 Main St. (bet. Buckingham St. & Capital Ave.), Hartford, 860-547-1714
■ Lauders absolutely "love everything about" this "edgy, smart" and "happenin' place" they call "Hartford's best Italian"; its kitchen uses "hard-to-find ingredients" to create both "classic and trendy" meals that are considered "expensive but not overly" so, making for an "absolutely fabulous dining experience."

Piccolo Arancio   25 | 20 | 23 | $38
819 Farmington Ave./Rte. 4 (Rte. 10), Farmington, 860-674-1224
■ With Peppercorn's as its papa, no wonder this "romantic", "suburban" Italian serves "sleepy Farmington" "consistently excellent" "food that's too good to drive by"; "every bite" of

"awesome pasta", "innovative pizza" and "fabulous salad" is a "Tuscan-style" "delight", making this "cozy" and "comfortable" culinary keeper "easy to visit often."

Quattro's [S] 26 | 18 | 21 | $35

Strawberry Hill Plaza, 1300 Boston Post Rd. (Long Hill Rd.), Guilford, 203-453-6575

■ An "amazing selection" of "delectable specials" plus a "terrific wine list" has "junkies" of this "outstanding" Guilford Italian "addiction" vouching for its "quite excellent reputation" as "*the* restaurant on the shoreline" (albeit about two miles from the water), but be forewarned that the "delicious creations" are served in a "tight and noisy" space.

REBECCAS [S] 27 | 21 | 22 | $55

265 Glenville Rd. (Riversville Rd.), Greenwich, 203-532-9270

◪ A "NYC pulse beats" in Greenwich at this "sophisticated" New American "with strong European influences", "a showstopper on the rise" that serves some surveyors' "absolute favorite food" amid "austere decor"; though "the parking lot is full of Mercedes and BMWs", co-owner/manager "Rebecca [Kirhoffer] makes you feel like a VIP even if you pulled up in a Honda" (the same can't be said for some "snotty" servers on staff).

Restaurant Bricco [S] 25 | 21 | 21 | $37

78 LaSalle Rd. (Farmington Ave.), West Hartford, 860-233-0220

■ Duplicitous diners "want to give a poor review to keep people away" from this West Hartford Northern Italian–Mediterranean "hot spot", but most can't help "fawning" over chef/co-owner Billy Grant's "fabulous" "world-class" "creations"; he's won fans galore among the "social climbers in attendance" at this "loud, hectic" "yuppie nirvana."

RESTAURANT DU VILLAGE [S] 27 | 24 | 26 | $49

59 Main St. (Maple St.), Chester, 860-526-5301

■ It may be "the poor man's substitute for a trip to France", but boosters of this "cozy and quaint" Country French storefront in the "cute village" of Chester are hardly *les misérables*; "extraordinary" regional provender accompanied by "fabulous bread" "will knock your socks off", albeit in a "quiet and *tranquille*" way, at this "small, calm" "special-occasion" "oasis" that's "true to its" Gallic "origins."

Roger Sherman Inn [S] 25 | 26 | 24 | $50

195 Oenoke Ridge/Rte. 124 (Holmewood Ln.), New Canaan, 203-966-4541

■ Regulars report that "visiting is like being a guest in a private home" at this seventysomething New Canaan Continental in a "clubby country inn"; it's an "elegant" "gem" with a patio and "smoker's-heaven piano bar" that's "perfect" for a "scrumptious" Sunday brunch or "great-value prix fixe dinner" on Saturdays, though hipsters heckle it for being "fuddy-duddy" and warn "wear your plaid pants to fit in" with the "mainly blue-rinse crowd."

Roomba [S] 25 | 25 | 23 | $38

1044 Chapel St. (bet. College & High Sts.), New Haven, 203-562-7666

■ "The beat goes on" at this "hip and hot" New Haven Nuevo Latino with "fun Cubano" decor complete with "cool" "waterfalls"; whether seated in the "classy outdoor area" or "at the chef's table", the "noisy, lively" crowd cries "*me gusta mucho*" for the "killer drinks" and "inventive" dishes with "quirky combinations of tastes" and a riot of "tutti-frutti" colors that make "every plate look like a party."

Ruth's Chris Steakhouse S   25 | 20 | 22 | $46
2513 Berlin Tpke./Rte. 5/15 (Kitts Ln.), Newington, 860-666-2202
■ "For 'meatatarians', a real feast" can be found at what some Newington carnivores call the "best of the chain steak places"; if flesh is your fancy, you "can't miss" the "tender" beef "served with melted butter" and accompanied by "side dishes big enough for two"; but while most report this "old-style" chop shop is "worth the money", cost-conscious critics cry "too expensive."

Sally's Apizza S ⊅   26 | 11 | 15 | $17
237 Wooster St. (Olive St.), New Haven, 203-624-5271
■ "A testament to New Haven pizza", the "delicious" "brick-oven" offerings at this Wooster Street sexagenarian are "good enough to make Hillary want to run for senator from Connecticut" claim partisans; if she did campaign, she could pump hands in the "two-to three-hour" lines, since "waiting is part of the mystique" at this "superlative" pie purveyor.

Steve's Centerbrook Cafe S   25 | 24 | 24 | $43
78 Main St./Rte. 154 (Rte. 80), Centerbrook, 860-767-1277
■ A "wonderful menu and wine list" (250 selections) enhanced by the "lovely, intimate ambiance" of a "cozy old house" earn high marks for chef-owner Steve Wilkinson's "elegant" New American in Centerbrook; with its "attentive service", "fantastic food" and "reasonable prices", it's become a "favorite" for many who "dine here often" and "bring friends."

Stonehenge   26 | 26 | 25 | $54
Stonehenge Inn, 35 Stonehenge Rd. (Rte. 7), Ridgefield, 203-438-6511
■ A "civilized" "classic that's still at the top" and a "real treat for your entire being" are just a sampling of the superlatives surveyors lavish on this Ridgefield Continental "great old dame" in an "elegant country inn" with a "wonderful setting" and "lake views" that perfectly complement its "luxurious food" and "lovely service"; a "special-occasion" destination for "a romantic evening", it's even better if you "stay over."

Terra Mar Grille S   25 | 26 | 24 | $45
Saybrook Point Inn & Spa, 2 Bridge St. (Rte. 154), Old Saybrook, 860-388-1111
■ "Sail up and enjoy welcoming service" at this "classy" and "romantic" waterside spot in the Saybrook Point Inn & Spa that fans feel features nothing less than "wonderful everything" – "fantastic views" of Long Island Sound, "high-quality" "gourmet" New American fare with Italian and French accents, an "especially good Sunday brunch" and "great cocktails" to wash it all down.

THOMAS HENKELMANN S   28 | 28 | 27 | $64
Homestead Inn, 420 Field Point Rd. (bet. Bush Ave. & Horseneck Ln.), Greenwich, 203-869-7500
■ "*The* place for special occasions", this "truly elegant" "temple of tradition" (where "the elite meet to eat") in Greenwich's Homestead Inn gets "bravos!" for its "beautiful surroundings", "gentlemanly waiters" and "unparalleled" French food, including "the best roast duck of all time"; just "hold on to your hats and your wallets", as this "real dining experience" "comes at a high price."

Union League Cafe 25 25 24 $41

1032 Chapel St. (bet. College & High Sts.), New Haven, 203-562-4299

■ Take "a step back in time to when food tasted as good as it looked" at this "oasis of elegance", a "consistently excellent" "authentic French bistro" that many call "the best New Haven has to offer"; both the "classy", "top-notch" service and the "beautiful" "surroundings make you feel like someone special", so even if it is "a little pricey", it's "absolutely worth it."

Valbella 26 23 25 $53

1309 E. Putnam Ave./Rte. 1 (Sound Beach Ave.), Riverside, 203-637-1155

■ Deep-pocketed devotees find more than a "bit of Tuscany" in the "superb" cuisine at this "upscale", "pricey" Riverside favorite; the "specials are so good" some "never use" the "excellent menu", but those who do find an "incredible breadth" of Northern Italian dishes complemented by an "awesome wine list" and "seamless service"; savvy surveyors suggest you savor your "memorable dinner" "downstairs" in the "intimate setting" of the "must-see wine cellar."

West Street Grill [S] 25 20 21 $44

43 West St. (bet. Rtes. 118 & 202), Litchfield, 860-567-3885

■ You can "spot movie stars, authors or just your local friends" experiencing "first-class" "fine dining" at this "culinary mecca" on the green in the "Hallmark-card town" of Litchfield; loyalists "love the variety" of "delicious", "deftly prepared" dishes delivering "creative twists on" New American "standards", though many find the prices "a bit over the top" and suggest the sometimes "charming service" can suffer "if you're not part of the 'in' crowd."

Dalles

TOP 20 FOOD RANKING

Restaurant	Cuisine Type
28 French Room	New French/New American
Riviera	French/Mediterranean
27 Mansion on Turtle Creek	Southwestern
Café Pacific	Seafood
Bob's	Steakhouse
26 Hôtel St. Germain	New French/Continental
Pyramid Grill	New American
Nana	New American
Green Room	New American
Pappas Bros.	Steakhouse
Del Frisco's	Steakhouse
Old Warsaw	French/Continental
Star Canyon	Southwestern
Mi Piaci	Northern Italian
Abacus	International
25 Modo Mio	Northern Italian
Tei Tei Robata Bar	Japanese
City Cafe	New American
Chamberlain's	Steakhouse/Seafood
Capital Grille	Steakhouse

ADDITIONAL NOTEWORTHY PLACES

Al Biernat's	Steakhouse/Seafood
Arcodoro/Pomodoro	N&S Italian
Citizen	Pan-Asian
Ciudad	Mexican
Ferré	Northern Italian
Fogo de Chão	Brazilian/Steakhouse
Grape	New American/Eclectic
Il Sole	N&S Italian
Jeroboam	French Bistro
La Duni Latin Café	South American
Lola	New American
Mercury Grill	New American
Nick & Sam's	Steakhouse
Sea Grill	Seafood/Pan-Asian
Sevy's Grill	New American
Sonny Bryan's	Barbecue
Steel	Pan-Asian
Tramontana	New American
Voltaire	New French/New American
York Street	Eclectic

ABACUS
26 | 27 | 23 | $58

4511 McKinney Ave. (Armstrong St.), 214-559-3111

■ "If I could afford it, I'd eat here every night" gush acolytes of chef-owner Kent Rathbun's Uptown International where "novel appetizers" like "delicious lobster shooters", dazzling tasting menus and an "interesting wine list" are complemented by a "stunning", geometrically themed interior with "lovely orchids" on every table; in short: a smart choice for a "special occasion."

Al Biernat's [S]
23 | 23 | 23 | $49

(fka Al's Prime Steaks & Seafood)

4217 Oak Lawn Ave. (Herschel Ave.), 214-219-2201

◪ "Personal attention" from "consummate host-owner" Al Biernat wins over many at this Oak Lawn surf 'n' turf house where patrons dress up and "ask for a booth" to best take in the boisterous "see-and-be-seen" scene; "delicious salads" and "huge portions" of great beef go a long way as well, though a few tough-to-please types note that the service is "better when they know you."

Arcodoro/Pomodoro [S]
22 | – | 19 | $30

2708 Routh St. (McKinney Ave.), 214-871-1924

■ These two longtime Uptown Italian favorites join forces in a space renovated to resemble an Italian villa, where they share a kitchen and the same Sardinian menu, with the exception of the popular wood-oven pizzas, which are served only at Arcodoro, the more casual dining area.

BOB'S STEAK & CHOP HOUSE
27 | 22 | 25 | $47

4300 Lemmon Ave. (Wycliff Ave.), 214-528-9446

The Shops at Legacy, 5760 Legacy Dr. (Parkwood Blvd.), Plano, 972-608-2627

■ "As close as you can get to a private club without paying dues" is how close-knit regulars describe this "dark" Lemmon Avenue steakhouse, which serves the "best prime beef in Dallas", as well as a critically acclaimed rack of lamb and enormous glazed carrots that are "out of this world"; N.B. there's another branch in Plano.

CAFÉ PACIFIC
27 | 25 | 26 | $42

Highland Park Village, 24 Highland Park Village (Mockingbird Ln. & Preston Rd.), 214-526-1170

■ "Blue bloods and high-maintenance women" agree that this Highland Park seafood "institution" is "always at the top of its game" thanks to marvelous "maitre d' and local legend" Jean-Pierre Albertinetti and a "professional staff with personality and polish", not to mention an old-world setting that feels "like a private club", an "impressive wine list" and "the freshest fish in landlocked Dallas" (don't miss the "heavenly sole").

Capital Grille [S]
25 | 26 | 25 | $46

Crescent Shops & Galleries, 500 Crescent Ct. (bet. Cedar Springs Rd. & McKinney Ave.), 214-303-0500

■ "You know the drill" at this true masculine "power trip", the "quiet" Uptown outpost of a popular steakhouse chain – order a "great" cut of beef like the aged prime sirloin or the "best liver and onions" (at lunch only) and a bottle from the comprehensive wine list, then settle in and allow the unobtrusive, "well-taught" staff to tend to all your needs in "classy", "clubby" quarters appointed with animal heads, comfortable booths and a piano lounge; this is a slice of "high-roller heaven."

Chamberlain's [S] 25 | 22 | 23 | $46

5330 Belt Line Rd. (east of N. Dallas Tollway), Addison, 972-934-2467

Chamberlain's Fish Market Grill [S]

4525 Belt Line Rd. (Midway Rd.), Addison, 972-503-3474

■ "Always a class act", "charming" chef Richard Chamberlain's conveniently located Addison steakhouse wins over patrons with its superior cuts of beef; a "warm", "professional" staff, mahogany paneling and original lithographs from the '20s further explain why this is "where all the big-name people eat"; N.B. check out its seafood offshoot just down the street.

Citizen 24 | 25 | 21 | $39

Two Turtle Creek Vlg., 3858 Oak Lawn Ave. (Blackburn St.), 214-522-7253

■ "Chic and delicious" declare denizens of this "loud" Oak Lawn Pan-Asian that's a darling of the "go-to-be-seen" crowd thanks to its "dramatic", "contemporary" interior that gives off an "LA look and feel"; every bit as stylish as the decor is the "inventive" cooking influenced by every corner of Asia and "presented with flair."

City Cafe [S] 25 | 20 | 23 | $33

5757 W. Lovers Ln. (N. Dallas Tollway), 214-351-2233

■ "Consistently one of the finest in the city", this Lovers Lane New American offers the "comfortable" "feel of a neighborhood" eatery but with "first-class" food and service; its menu of "uniquely prepared" and "creatively presented" dishes "changes often enough to pique your curiosity", while the crowning touch is an "exquisite" wine list that oenophiles rank among "the best" in town.

Ciudad [S] 21 | 22 | 21 | $30

One Turtle Creek Vlg., 3888 Oak Lawn Ave. (Blackburn St.), 214-219-3141

■ "Wow" – it's "almost ahead of its time" marvel aficionados of this "trendy", "upscale" Oak Lawn Mexican, which focuses on the flavors of the Yucatán and Mexico City in turning out "authentic" yet "creative" dishes such as red mole–braised short ribs; it also cultivates friends with its "warm" service and "fun" atmosphere, though beware that it's often "very loud" – "unless you sit outside" on the "great patio."

Del Frisco's Double Eagle Steak House 26 | 24 | 24 | $53

5251 Spring Valley Rd. (N. Dallas Pkwy.), 972-490-9000

◪ Some of the "best steaks in the West" come off the grill at this "prime" North Dallas chophouse that's "tops", from its "perfectly cooked" beef and 850-bottle wine list to its clubby, high-"energy" environs and "superior" service; there's a price to be paid for being this "near to heaven", however: hefty tabs make it "strictly for the expense-account crowd", and its popularity means there's often a "long wait for a table", even "with a reservation."

Ferré Ristorante e Bar [S] – | – | – | E

West Vlg., 3699 McKinney Ave. (Lemmon Ave.), 214-522-3888

Courting trendy loft dwellers and the Highland Park establishment, this Uptown Northern Italian in the hot West Village complex scores a home run thanks to a seasoned team – owner Patrick Colombo and chef Kevin Ascolese – which delivers rousing Tuscan food in a casually elegant, honey-colored room with glass panels; N.B.

its adjacent wine bar, Crú, features an excellent selection of wines by the glass and small plates.

Fogo de Chão ⓢ | 25 | 21 | 24 | $41 |
4300 Belt Line Rd. (Midway Rd.), Addison, 972-503-7300

■ "Nirvana for carnivores", this Addison Brazilian churrascaria presents "food with a show", as "fantastic" gauchos carve off unlimited quantities of "excellent" skewered meats and poultry until you flip your coaster from green to red and beg them to stop; an "outstanding" salad bar only adds to the "gluttony", so "skip breakfast and lunch" before Chão-ing down here.

FRENCH ROOM | 28 | 29 | 28 | $69 |
Hotel Adolphus, 1321 Commerce St. (Akard St.), 214-742-8200

■ Elected No. 1 for Food in Dallas, this Downtown New French–New American "throwback to more elegant times" is appointed with a "magnificent" cherub-painted ceiling, soft candlelight and beautiful flowers; factor in "impeccable" service from a staff that makes you "feel like a king or queen" and "fabulous", exquisitely plated dishes and you have the city's "perfect" spot for "special-occasion dining"; N.B. gourmet diners on a budget should consider the prix fixe menus.

Grape ⓢ | 25 | 20 | 22 | $30 |
2808 Greenville Ave. (Vickery Blvd.), 214-828-1981

■ Three decades old, this "romantic" New American–Eclectic bistro on Greenville continues to be a "perennial winner"; credit its renowned mushroom soup (the "best ever"), award-winning wine list and "attentive" service, though close tables mean "unavoidable eavesdropping", which is just fine if you have a rather dull "first-date dinner" companion.

Green Room ⓢ | 26 | 19 | 23 | $40 |
2715 Elm St. (Crowdus St.), 214-748-7666

■ Put away those jackets and ties because this "noisy" Deep Ellum New American is a "brash", "refreshingly casual" spot where twentysomethings lap up chef Marc Cassel's "magnificent", "innovative" dishes, revel in a "delightfully funky" atmosphere and bond with the appropriately "trendy" staff; P.S. to best take advantage of this "bohemian" experience, consider the "superb" 'Feed Me, Wine Me' menu offered at "cherry-picking prices."

Hôtel St. Germain | 26 | 28 | 26 | VE |
2516 Maple Ave. (bet. Cedar Springs Rd. & McKinney Ave.), 214-871-2516

■ "Escape from reality" to this "quaintly European" Uptown New French–Continental whose mutely lit, widely spaced tables are staffed by attentive, white-gloved waiters; the "ultimate place for an intimate celebration", it offers exclusively a multicourse tasting menu (a "bargain" for the quality), so à la carte cats should think about rendezvousing at the Champagne Bar, which serves an array of appetizers and desserts.

Il Sole ⓢ | 23 | 23 | 21 | $38 |
Travis Walk, 4514 Travis St. (Knox St.), 214-559-3888

■ "Romantic" and subdued, this Italian in Knox/Henderson seduces with a second-story patio perfect for people-watching; it draws a "classy, not flashy", group of regulars who love the award-winning wine list (especially the smart offerings "by the glass or even half-glass") and the menu filled with "delicious" options like "to-die-for" calamari and maple crème brûlée.

Jeroboam   − − − E
Kirby Bldg., 1501 Main St. (Akard St.), 214-748-7226
Already as a Downtown destination, this sleek brasserie (the sibling of the Green Room) uncorks classic French fare including such favorites as pâté, cassoulet and selections from the cheese cart; habitués know that ordering one of the soups is the way to start a meal.

La Duni Latin Café 🖫   − − − M
4620 McKinney Ave. (Knox St.), 214-520-7300
Heads are turning at this bustling Knox-Henderson darling as patrons crane to see which film stars or concert headliners have found their way to this sleek South American oasis where husband-and-wife chef-owners Espartaco and Dunia (aka Duni) Borga bring upscale verve to their intriguing array of Latin dishes, served in a persimmon-hued interior on close-set tables that create a convivial atmosphere; N.B. the multi-tiered cakes are not to be missed.

Lola   − − − E
2917 Fairmont St. (Cedar Springs Rd.), 214-855-0700
This Uptown New American serves imaginative prix fixe meals in three or four courses by a suave staff in a house-turned-restaurant with a romantic ambiance; N.B. owner Van Roberts has assembled an award-winning collection of wines, which he's eager to discuss with oenophiles and novices alike.

MANSION ON TURTLE CREEK 🖫   27 28 27 $64
2821 Turtle Creek Blvd. (Gillespie Ave.), 214-559-2100
■ Once again voted the Most Popular restaurant in Dallas and the "gold standard" in its category, this Uptown Southwestern features acclaimed chef Dean Fearing's "consistently innovative" dishes, which may leave you "speechless"; the "outstanding" staff provides a "never-ending flow of attention" and the "beautiful rooms" convey an "exclusive feel" that's "like dining in someone's house", making for a "first-class night out", even if the "amazing wine list" is "overpriced."

Mercury Grill   25 22 22 $42
11909 Preston Rd. (Forest Ln.), 972-960-7774
Mercury
6121 W. Park Blvd. (Dallas Pkwy.), Plano, 469-366-0107
■ For "fine food in an improbable strip-mall location", head to this North Dallas New American where the "innovative" dishes "dazzle the senses" and a "trendy" clientele looks glamorous in the understated, modern setting; the only quibble: it's "one of the loudest restaurants" around; N.B. there's an offshoot in Plano.

Mi Piaci Ristorante   26 24 23 $38
14854 Montfort Rd. (Belt Line Rd.), Addison, 972-934-8424
■ "Luscious ingredients, creative combinations and most lovely presentations" add up to "absolutely spectacular" dining at this "upscale" Addison Northern Italian known for its "marvelous risotto" and osso buco; its "sleek", "open" room "overlooking the water" (a man-made duck pond) and "exemplary" service also win it kudos; P.S. a small room in the wine cellar can be rented out for private parties.

Modo Mio
Cucina Rustica Italiana S
25 | 21 | 22 | $35

Frankford Crossing, 18352 Dallas Pkwy. (Frankford Rd.), 972-671-6636
■ Despite a turnover in ownership, little has changed at this "great neighborhood" Northern Italian trattoria in North Dallas, where the "fantastic", "authentic" dishes are still always served "with a smile"; given such a "warm" atmosphere, no one minds much if it can get a bit "crowded" and "noisy."

Nana S
26 | 27 | 25 | $54

Wyndham Anatole Hotel, 2201 Stemmons Frwy., 27th fl.
(Market Center Blvd.), 214-761-7470
■ "What a view!" exclaim enthusiasts admiring the vista from the 27th-floor perch of this Downtown New American favorite; the "luxurious room", recently renovated and decorated with priceless Oriental art, is "where you go to impress someone", while the "excellent" fare (the eight-course chef's tasting menu, with optional wine pairings, is the smart way to go) and service complement the "wonderful" atmosphere enhanced by nightly live music.

Nick & Sam's S
24 | 24 | 23 | $50

3008 Maple Ave. (Carlisle St.), 214-871-7444
◪ This "see-and-be-seen" Uptown steakhouse herds in carnivores with amenities such as a rolling caviar cart, a grand piano in the open kitchen and "smart, sophisticated decor"; beef takes center stage, of course, but the lamb and fish dishes are also "excellent"; detractors, however, caution that it's "incredibly loud" and "priced for a roaring economy."

Old Warsaw ●S
26 | 24 | 23 | $56

2610 Maple Ave. (bet. Cedar Springs Rd. & McKinney Ave.), 214-528-0032
◪ An "elegant and romantic hideaway", this Uptown French-Continental grande dame has been exuding "old-world charm" for more than 50 years and it continues to formally serve "superb" fare (including the "best chocolate soufflé ever made"); wallet-watchers, though, warn "take your heaviest credit card."

Pappas Bros. Steakhouse
26 | 25 | 24 | $47

10477 Lombardy Ln. (I-35 & Northwest Hwy.), 214-366-2000
■ "Outstanding every time" declare devotees of this Northwest Dallas jewel in the crown of the Pappas family restaurant empire, which is "Texas to the core" and features "Lone Star State–size drinks, big steaks and great Southwestern decor"; a "huge wine selection" (priced "from $25 to $70,000") and commendable service only add to its reputation – just get "someone else to pay."

Pyramid Grill S
26 | 26 | 24 | $54

(fka Pyramid Room)
Fairmont Hotel, 1717 N. Akard St. (Ross Ave.), 214-720-2020
■ Formerly called the Pyramid Room, this elegant Uptown New American is still "one of our favorite" places to "celebrate an anniversary or promotion" due to its well-spaced tables, "terrific", courtly service, "excellent" grilled fare and many swell touches from its previous incarnation.

RIVIERA S
28 | 25 | 26 | $60

7709 Inwood Rd. (Lovers Ln.), 214-351-0094
■ Chef Michael Marshall (ex Hôtel St. Germain) is behind the stove at this "cosmopolitan" Oak Lawn French-Mediterranean

stalwart, which is where celebration-minded diners go "when they want to be pampered" by "graceful, welcoming" European-style service; the "superb" fare and a setting that's "like walking into a room in Provence" merely add to its "fancy-shmancy" allure.

Sea Grill S — | — | — | M

17617 Dallas Pkwy. (Trinity Mills Rd.), 972-733-4904
Chef Andy Tun performs his piscine magic with a Pan-Asian flair at this casual seafood house in North Dallas, executing a variety of simple fish dishes that can be ordered grilled, blackened, broiled, sautéed or steamed, all affordably priced; the only major complaint: it's very loud.

Sevy's Grill S 23 | 22 | 22 | $33

8201 Preston Rd. (Sherry Ln.), 214-265-7389
■ "All the essential elements" of a successful restaurant can be found at this Park Cities New American "favorite", which features a mission-style interior, a martini bar that's "quite the gathering place" and two hands-on owners, not to mention "impressive" cooking (especially "if you like roasted or wood-fired anything").

Sonny Bryan's Smokehouse 21 | 12 | 15 | $13

2202 Inwood Rd. (Harry Hines Blvd.), 214-357-1720 S
Macy's at Galleria Mall, 13375 Noel Rd. (bet. LBJ Frwy. & N. Dallas Tollway), 972-851-5131 S
Frankford Crossing, 4701 Frankford Rd. (Dallas Pkwy.), 972-447-0102 S
302 N. Market St. (Pacific Ave.), 214-744-1610 S
Republic Towers, 325 N. St. Paul St. (bet. Bryan St. & Pacific Ave.), 214-979-0102
1012 W. Hebron Pkwy. (Old Denton Rd.), 972-394-7076 S
5519 W. Lovers Ln. (Inwood Rd.), 214-351-2024 S
■ The "funky, original" Inwood locale "will always be the best" branch insist carnivorous connoisseurs of this famous BBQ chain, which has long been revered for its "tender", hickory-smoked brisket, pulled pork, ribs and "enormous onion rings."

Star Canyon S 26 | 26 | 24 | $48

Centrum Bldg., 3102 Oak Lawn Ave. (Cedar Springs Rd.), 214-520-7827
■ Superstar kitchen wizard Stephan Pyles has moved on, but executive chef Matthew Dunn keeps things "humming" at this Oak Lawn destination that "sets an example for great Southwestern food", ranging from "innovative" dishes like "fantastic *cuitlacoche* enchiladas" to classics like the "awesome bone-in rib-eye"; reviewers also rave about the "Texas-perfect decor, right down to the ceiling tiles branded with town names."

Steel S — | — | — | E

Centrum Bldg., 3102 Oak Lawn Ave. (Cedar Springs Rd.), 214-219-9908
Cloaked in metal, stone and cherrywood, this smart Pan-Asian addition to Oak Lawn presents an ambitious and interesting menu turned out with bold flair; emerging as a notable gathering place, it's quite the hot table thanks to its assortment of lacquered bento boxes and steaming clay pots, while its hyperactive sushi and sake bars pull in the urban-chic demographic.

Tei Tei Robata Bar S 25 | 23 | 23 | $42

2906 N. Henderson Ave. (Willis Ave.), 214-828-2400
■ "Hip patrons and trendy decor" are just the appetizers at this "pricey" Knox/Henderson Japanese where a "world-class chef"

prepares "fresh sushi and sashimi"; a "tremendous array" of *robata* (grilled) dishes also explains why some addicts will "travel 150 miles" to satisfy their yen here.

Tramontana
25 | 18 | 22 | $36

Preston Ctr., 8220B Westchester Dr. (bet. Cherry & Luther Lns.), 214-368-4188

■ "A tiny, romantic hideaway", this North Dallas New American bistro gets tons of accolades for its "superior", "inventive" cooking tweaked with French and Italian accents; surveyors add that "super-nice" chef-owner James Neel is a "treasure" whose skills are "moving this storefront to the forefront."

Voltaire
25 | 27 | 23 | $62

5150 Keller Springs Rd. (N. Dallas Tollway), 972-239-8988

◪ "Wow" swoon aesthetes over this "gorgeous" New French–New American in North Dallas, where trendsetters go to ogle the "fabulous" Dale Chihuly glass sculptures, as well as the "beautiful" patrons; while devotees delight in the "excellent", "creative" fare and "fantastic", "extensive" wine list, others find it "pretentious" and ask "what's the fuss?"

York Street
25 | 20 | 24 | $47

6047 Lewis St. (Skillman St.), 214-826-0968

■ Admirers say that "every intimate restaurant should aspire" to be this "enchanting" Eclectic "tucked inside an old house" in East Dallas; amid an unhurried pace, a "superb" staff provides angelic attention while delivering a "slice of culinary heaven" from chef-owner Sharon Hage's "interesting", market-fresh menu.

Denver Area & Mountain Resorts

TOP 20 FOOD RANKING

Restaurant	Cuisine Type
28 Keystone Ranch	Rocky Mountain
Highlands Garden Cafe	New American
Mizuna	New American
Grouse Mountain Grill	Rocky Mountain
Tante Louise	French
27 Del Frisco's	Steakhouse
Alpenglow Stube	Rocky Mountain
Charles Court	Continental/New American
Palace Arms	Continental/New American
Cafe Brazil	South American
Piñons	Rocky Mountain
Sweet Basil	New American
Wildflower	New American
Full Moon Grill	Northern Italian
Flagstaff House	New American/Eclectic
Penrose Room	Continental/New French
Renaissance	Med./New American
Left Bank	French
Sushi Den	Japanese
26 Hilltop Café	New American

ADDITIONAL NOTEWORTHY PLACES

Adega	New American
Aix	New American/French
Bang!	American
Barolo Grill	Northern Italian
Beano's Cabin	New American
Briarwood Inn	American/Continental
Clair de Lune	French
Conundrum	New American
Fourth Story	New American
India's	Indian
Kevin Taylor	New American
La Petite Maison	New American/French
Mel's	Med./New American
Panzano	Northern Italian
Q's	New American
Solera	Eclectic/New American
Splendido	New American
Strings	New American
Tamayo	Mexican
Vesta Dipping Grill	New American

subscribe to zagat.com

Adega Restaurant & Wine Bar ❶   — | — | — | E |
1700 Wynkoop St. (17th St.), 303-534-2222
Twentysomething trendsetters, fashion-conscious socialites and
other sophisticated urbanites are crowding this sleek, chic food
temple in the heart of Lower Downtown for chef Bryan Moscatello's
brassy, ambitious and exquisitely plated New American dishes
delivered with suave finesse by a top-tier staff and bolstered by
an astounding 800-bottle wine selection hand-picked by master
sommelier and owner Kenneth Frederickson; N.B. late-night diners
clamor for its excellent after-hours bar menu.

Aix   — | — | — | M |
719 E. 17th Ave. (bet. Clarkson & Washington Sts.), 303-831-1296
This small, exceedingly tasteful New American–French in Capitol
Hill takes its name and cooking style from Aix-en-Provence: the
kitchen simply buys the best ingredients possible and then leaves
them pretty much alone, allowing the distinct flavors to take center
stage; the attention to detail evident in the menu carries through to
the remainder of the restaurant, from the mustard-washed walls
to the tall, reed-like water glasses.

Alpenglow Stube Ⓢ   27 | 28 | 26 | $63 |
*Keystone Resort, 21996 Hwy. 6 (top of North Peak Mtn.), Keystone,
970-496-4386*
■ A blizzard of praise surrounds this Rocky Mountain "fine-dining
experience", the nation's highest restaurant at 11,444 feet, set on
North Peak in the Keystone Resort; take the "romantic gondola"
to the door where you're "greeted with warm, fuzzy slippers",
"fabulous old-world food and service" and "the best setting in the
state" – it's a "cool adventure" that feels almost "fairytale-ish";
N.B. open for dinner only Thursday–Sunday in the summer.

Bang!   26 | 18 | 20 | $19 |
3472 W. 32nd Ave. (bet. Julian St. & Lowell Blvd.), 303-455-1117
■ "Explosive down-home" American fare lures locals to this "kinda
funky", "crowded", "laid-back" "gem" in North Denver; surveyors
squeeze inside the "crowded" digs for "creative combinations" of
"soul-soothing" "comfy" food that "highlights seasonal ingredients"
(go ahead, "try the ever-popular meat loaf"), all served in a "lively
yet intimate", "upbeat, colorful and kooky" setting; a few are
"disappointed that prices have risen", but you still get lots of "bang
for the buck"; N.B. patio dining is now available.

BAROLO GRILL   25 | 25 | 24 | $39 |
3030 E. Sixth Ave. (bet. Milwaukee & St. Paul Sts.), 303-393-1040
■ "Comparable to Italy itself" is what fans call this "warm, inviting"
East Denver "place to be" that dishes out "the most authentic
ambiance" and Northern Boot cuisine "in the Rockies"; "it's in a
class by itself" thanks to the "fabulous food" and a "wine list that
will knock your socks off" (with plenty of offerings from the Barolo
region), served by an "intelligent", "knowledgeable" and, above
all, vino-"savvy" staff.

Beano's Cabin Ⓢ   24 | 28 | 24 | $62 |
Beaver Creek Resort, 1 Beaver Creek Pl. (Avon Rd.), Avon, 970-949-9090
■ "The trip up [Beaver Creek] Mountain is worth the price of the
meal" say those "enchanted" by this New American, but though the
"adventure" of getting there (by horseback or wagon in summer,

"wonderful sleigh ride" in winter or shuttle van year round) is a "memorable experience" in itself, it's the "intimate, woodsy", "gorgeous log cabin" setting, "elaborate and creative" fixed-price menu and extensive global wine list that make it "the ultimate romantic dinner date."

BRIARWOOD INN S | 25 | 27 | 26 | $41 |

1630 Eighth St. (bet. Hwy. 58 & US 6), Golden, 303-279-3121

■ Inn-mates insist they "can't say enough wonderful things about this" "old-fashioned" American-Continental "off the beaten track in Golden" that offers "huge portions" ("appetizers are a meal on their own") of "phenomenal food" served by a "friendly and efficient staff" within "elegant", "homelike surroundings"; though some say it's "too pricey", most maintain this "exquisite" spot is "worth it" as "the classic place to go to celebrate a special occasion", "impress guests" or enjoy "intimate conversation."

Cafe Brazil ⊅ | 27 | 18 | 23 | $28 |

3611 Navajo St. (W. 36th Ave.), 303-480-1877

■ It's like a trip "back to Rio" for revelers at this affordable, "hard to find, hard to forget" North Denver South American, a "cute" and "funky" facility featuring "fantastic", "flavorful" fare overflowing with a "riot of flavors"; the non-"claustrophobic" suggest you "reserve two weeks in advance" for a table in its "quaint" "little" "shoebox" of a space that feels "like someone's kitchen", and be sure to "bring cash", as they accept "no credit cards."

Charles Court S | 27 | 28 | 28 | $51 |

Broadmoor Hotel, 1 Lake Ave. (Mesa Ave.), Colorado Springs, 719-634-7711

■ Visitors to the "top-notch" Broadmoor Hotel resort deem this "classic fine-dining" "favorite in Colorado Springs" "a must" for "exceptional" Continental–New American fare complemented by an "excellent wine selection" and a "professional" but "relaxed" staff that offers "all the right pampering"; admirers adore both the "small, cozy" room and the "great lakeside patio", saying each is a "wonderful special-occasion" option; N.B. jacket suggested.

Clair de Lune ⊅ | – | – | – | E |

1313 E. Sixth Ave. (Marion St.), 303-831-1992

After closing his popular Aubergine Cafe, culinary star Sean Kelly is back in business as the owner-moonlighting-as-chef of this shoebox-size Capitol Hill classic French newcomer with all of 24 seats; using market-fresh foodstuffs, he fashions innovative yet simply prepared dinners ranging from fricassee of wild mushrooms to roasted organic chicken with eggplant Napoleon, complemented by an engaging wine list and savvy service; N.B. bring a wad of cash because credit cards are not accepted.

Conundrum S | 26 | 25 | 24 | $54 |

325 E. Main St. (bet. Mill & Monarch Sts.), Aspen, 970-925-9969

■ It's no brain-teaser – fans "dress up" for this "hip, high-energy" New American because of the "best people-watching around" plus "excellent" Med-influenced "cuisine prepared by a talented crew", coupled with a "great wine list" and "fantastic desserts and coffees", and served by a "professional, hospitable" staff amid "chic" "gold, sage and russet" decor that echoes the "colors of Aspen in the fall"; N.B. the Food rating does not reflect the post-*Survey* arrival of chef Perry Katsapis.

Del Frisco's
Double Eagle Steak House
27 | 25 | 26 | $50

Denver Tech Ctr., 8100 E. Orchard Rd. (I-25), Greenwood Village, 303-796-0100

☑ "As good as it gets" bellow "beef-eaters" aplenty about this "pricey" Greenwood Village branch of a mini-chain, where "top-shelf" staffers serve "football-size" cuts of "melt-in-your-mouth steak" with "mammoth portions" of "à la carte sides"; it's a "local favorite with sports figures" and "expense-account types" who also gather in the "dimly lit cigar bar", though detractors declare it's "for people with more money than sense" ("no one can eat that much"), adding "you pay to see the glitterati."

Flagstaff House S
27 | 28 | 27 | $50

1138 Flagstaff Rd. (on Flagstaff Mtn.), Boulder, 303-442-4640

☑ It's "the ultimate expensive-but-worth-it special-occasion place to go" in Boulder fawn fans of this mountainside "treat" set in a cabin (circa 1929) affording "gorgeous" views of the surrounding wildlife and city below; surveyors say the service is "exquisite" and call the "intricately prepared" Asian-inflected New American–Eclectic fare "imaginative" and "world-class"; P.S. "ask for a tour of the wine cellar", home to 20,000 bottles.

Fourth Story S
24 | 25 | 23 | $32

Tattered Cover Bookstore, 2955 E. First Ave. (Milwaukee St.), 303-322-1824

■ "Curl up in a booth" with a "literary classic" while dining on New American eats "among the stacks" at this "handsome" "local treasure" "perched atop" – and accessorized by – the famed Tattered Cover Bookstore, a "popular gathering place" in Cherry Creek; the "interesting seasonal menus" and "decadent desserts" are a "joy to the palate", and the bar offers "flights of fancy wines" delivered by a "meticulous" staff; P.S. it's also the spot to tune in to "Denver's best jazz."

Full Moon Grill S
27 | 21 | 24 | $33

Village Shopping Ctr., 2525 Arapahoe Ave. (bet. Folsom & 28th Sts.), Boulder, 303-938-8800

■ It's *amore* for admirers smitten by this "usually packed" Boulder Northern Italian, a "terrific discovery" "tucked in a strip mall"; lovers laud the "interesting variations" of its "inventive", "top-flight" fare, as well as the "friendly, accommodating" servers; while followers find the "unassuming" quarters "intimate", a handful consider it "cramped" and "crowded with too many tables."

GROUSE MOUNTAIN GRILL S
28 | 26 | 26 | $54

Beaver Creek Resort, 141 Scott Hill Rd. (Village Rd.), Avon, 970-949-0600

■ There's little to grouse about at this "superior" Beaver Creek Resort spot where "flawless food" from a Rocky Mountain menu, including "excellent meat" entrees and "great side dishes", is served in "hearty", "huge portions", bolstered by a "great wine list" with over 450 selections; a staff that's at "the top of its game" as well as "beautiful outdoor dining" and "stunning views" of the Valley only add to the luster of this "gem"; N.B. a jazz pianist plays six nights a week.

HIGHLANDS GARDEN CAFE
28 | 27 | 26 | $37

3927 W. 32nd Ave. (bet. Osceola & Perry Sts.), 303-458-5920

■ Gastronomes go gaga for this "garden of eatin'", a North Denver New American "beauty" where "amazing" flowers are matched by "inventive cuisine" and "impeccable service"; it's "stellar in all respects", and the two "quaint" old houses provide a "lovely refuge" any season, while patio dining by the greenery is a definite "summer must"; N.B. also available for private functions.

Hilltop Café
26 | 22 | 24 | $30 |

1518 Washington Ave. (16th St.), Golden, 303-279-8151

■ It's a "great addition to the suburbs" say locals who head west to this "quaint" "Golden nugget" within a "charming" Victorian-era residence for "delicious fine dining" upon "fabulous presentations" of "exciting", "expertly crafted New American" creations with "innovative" Asian embellishments courtesy of "artistic chef Ian Kleinman"; also "excellent" is the "impeccable" service from a "friendly" staff that provides "incredible customer attention."

India's 🖪
26 | 20 | 19 | $25 |

Tamarac Sq., 3333 S. Tamarac Dr. (Hampden Ave.), 303-755-4284

■ "Still the standard for Indian food in Denver", this "justly acclaimed" Southeast Denver mecca offers "consistently delicious" fare that devotees declare the "most authentic" in town and "worlds above and beyond" the competition's (including the "best chicken tikka [masala] this side of Delhi"); while most appreciate the "friendly" service and "warm decor", a few feel that "the look is tired" and the "strip-mall location is a turnoff."

Kevin Taylor
26 | 26 | 24 | $53 |

Hotel Teatro, 1106 14th St. (Arapahoe St.), 303-820-2600

■ "Paris, New York, San Francisco and London dining come to Denver" via this "expensive" Downtown New American, a "grown-up's restaurant" set in the "charming, classic" and "gorgeously decorated" art deco Hotel Teatro; "we love Kevin's food" say fans of chef-owner Taylor's "sublime" fare (a "superb" counterpoint to the "awesome wine list"), and most report that the "professional" staff provides "courteous and friendly service"; still, some find the milieu a bit "pretentious" and "stuffy for Denver."

KEYSTONE RANCH 🖪
28 | 28 | 28 | $61 |

Keystone Resort, 21996 Hwy. 6 (top of North Peak Mtn.), Keystone, 970-496-4386

■ "The elk melts" in your mouth "like butter" attest worshipers who regularly make the pilgrimage to this "grand" spot in the 1930s Keystone Resort homestead that's rated No. 1 for Food among Colorado restaurants for its "consistently excellent" seasonal Rocky Mountain fare (including "exotic wild-game dishes" and "delectable desserts") served in the "quiet, relaxed atmosphere" of a "superb", "rustic mountain setting"; "take a big sack of money", though, as it's an "expensive treat"; P.S. it's especially "great for birthdays and anniversaries."

La Petite Maison
26 | 23 | 25 | $37 |

1015 W. Colorado Ave. (bet. 10th & 11th Sts.), Colorado Springs, 719-632-4887

■ "Keep on keeping on" cheer habitués who hail this "wonderful" Colorado Springs veteran as their "all-time favorite"; "outstanding in every respect", it offers "innovative" New American fare with a "classic French influence" served by a "never-stuffy" staff within the "quiet and relaxed atmosphere" of a "charming Victorian" cottage (circa 1894) complete with two "small dining rooms that make it very intimate"; N.B. patio dining is also available in season.

Left Bank [S] ⊄ 27 24 24 $49

Sitzmark Lodge, 183 Gore Creek Dr. (Bridge St.), Vail, 970-476-3696

■ Vail's "quiet and elegant French" favorite "has become the standard by which to evaluate" all others gush Francophiles who consider it a "great" respite from the area's "nouveau places" thanks to "classic", "authentic" fare that's "delicious" (and "beautiful" to look at too); while some say "it's truly the best in service", a few snipers say it's "snooty", like "Paris with an attitude"; P.S. "bring cash" because "they still don't take credit cards – maybe next century."

Mel's [S] 25 22 23 $34

235 Fillmore St. (bet. 2nd & 3rd Aves.), 303-333-3979

◪ An "easygoing", "relaxed but upscale atmosphere" marks this Mediterranean–New American "steady standby" in Cherry Creek, a "winner" where "consistently" "creative dishes" (including "mussels to die for") are served by a "very friendly staff" that "has excellent knowledge" of the "great wine list"; "better-than-Broadway" people-watching at the bar and "great" "live jazz" also help "make the experience."

MIZUNA 28 23 27 $41

225 E. Seventh Ave. (bet. Grant & Sherman Sts.), 303-832-4778

■ Chef Frank Bonnano has a "ton of talent" declare devotees dazzled by this Capitol Hill New American, a "gustatory bonanza" considered one of the "finest restaurants in town"; the "service is elegant", the "menu is clever" ("mom didn't make macaroni and cheese – with lobster – like this") and the kitchen's "culinary artistry" renders "beautiful", "fabulous food"; while most call it "quaint" and "cozy", a handful gripe about "cramped dining" and "too-tight tables."

Palace Arms [S] 27 28 27 $50

Brown Palace Hotel, 321 17th St. (bet. Broadway & Tremont Pl.), 303-297-3111

■ If you want "hoity-toity", this "regal" Continental–New American, a Downtown "Denver landmark" in the 110-year-old Brown Palace Hotel, delivers with "classic cuisine" and "exquisite" service; "it's the epitome of old-world dining elegance, complemented by daring nouveau regional fare" as well as a selection of 1,500 wines (and "oh, those macaroons!"); while most adore the "one-of-a-kind French Empire decor" (some antiques date back to Napoleon's era), a few sniff that it's "stuffy"; N.B. jacket required for dinner only.

Panzano [S] 24 24 22 $33

Hotel Monaco, 909 17th St. (Champa St.), 303-296-3525

■ "Superstar" chef Jennifer Jasinski has taken this "wonderfully cozy" Downtown Northern Italian in a boutique hotel "to a new level" remark fanciers of her "yummy", "upscale" and "fabulous" food; add "prompt", "polished service" (especially "for patrons with theater tickets"), "warm atmosphere" and a "good vino selection" (including "hard-to-find wines") and you have "an elegant treat" that's "hard to beat."

Penrose Room 27 28 28 $50

Broadmoor Hotel, 1 Lake Ave. (Lake Circle), Colorado Springs, 719-634-7711

■ "Elegance, ambiance and excess" characterize this Continental–New French "resort tradition", a "romantic", "perfect-for-special-occasions" spot with "breathtaking views" of Colorado Springs and Cheyenne Mountain; the "spectacular", "imaginative cuisine", "featuring some dishes prepared tableside", rises to the "high Broadmoor Hotel standards", as does the "outstanding service" and live dinner music, including "great jazz for dancing."

Piñons S

27 | 25 | 26 | $56

105 S. Mill St. (E. Main St.), Aspen, 970-920-2021

■ It's "Aspen's best" exclaim enthusiasts who adore the "great" Rocky Mountain cuisine at this "never-changing" and "always reliable" spot "dressed up" to the nines in "cowboy-chic" style ("the most elegant of Western settings"); the "food is terrific", with "marvelous" elk and "incredibly delicious lobster strudel", set off by an "excellent wine list" and "service with a smile", all of which makes for "special nights"; N.B. be sure to call for information about seasonal closures.

Q's S

26 | 24 | 24 | $38

Boulderado Hotel, 2115 13th St. (Spruce St.), Boulder, 303-442-4880

■ Reviewers recommend the "sublime" selection of "dynamic modern" food and "nice wine list" served by a "well-trained staff" at this "way-good" Boulder New American, "a true class act" whose "elegant dining room" is set within the antique-filled "historic Boulderado Hotel"; trenchermen tout its tasting menu as an "indulgent splurge", while less ambitious epicureans insist that "an appetizer or two, a dessert and wine equals heaven!" – either way, you "can't go wrong" at this "special treat."

Renaissance S

27 | 25 | 26 | $63

304 E. Hopkins Ave. (bet. S. Mill & S. Monarch Sts.), Aspen, 970-925-2402

■ Instead of making it a "once-in-a-lifetime dinner", devotees of this "pricey" Med–New American in Aspen go often to sample the "daring" seasonal dishes that are "always pushing the envelope"; it's "outstanding on all fronts", with "beautiful" fare that reveals "avant-garde creativity", including a "tasting menu that's A+" and a wine list that features 450 selections; the "sumptuous, romantic decor" in the main dining room is offset by the newly remodeled private dining room upstairs.

Solera Restaurant & Wine Bar S

– | – | – | E

5410 E. Colfax Ave. (Grape St.), 303-388-8429

Though this Eclectic–New American bistro sits on a strip of road better known for tattoo parlors and fast-food joints, it's clear from the well-heeled crowds flocking here that chef-owner Christian "Goose" Sorensen has an East Denver hit on his hands; his menu puts a contemporary twist on classic comfort food, for instance gussying up mashed potatoes with creamy, dreamy mascarpone cheese; N.B. insiders report it's a favorite haunt of local chefs on their nights off.

Splendido S

26 | 26 | 25 | $59

The Chateau at Beaver Creek Resort, 17 Chateau Ln. (Scott Hill Rd.), Avon, 970-845-8808

■ Raves abound for this "stunningly superlative" New American in Beaver Creek offering "absolutely fabulous" food fashioned from "fresh ingredients" and served by an "impeccably professional", "intelligent and informed staff" within a "warmly romantic" setting; with "such attention to detail", it's among the "best dining and wining experiences in Colorado" and "even better than its glowing reviews", but bear in mind that it is "very expensive" – in fact, "the locals call it 'Spend-ido', and spend you will."

STRINGS [S] | 26 | 24 | 24 | $36 |

1700 Humboldt St. (17th Ave.), 303-831-7310

■ The "fabulous food presentations" are hard to beat at this "groovy" Uptown venue, a "lovely" "special-occasion" spot and a "dependable destination when entertaining or doing business"; reviewers rally for its "modern" menu of "delicious" Med- and Cal-influenced New American fare and savor its "chic" digs, saying it's an especially "premium experience" if "you want to see the beautiful people" (though a few squawk it's "too yuppie").

Sushi Den [S] | 27 | 23 | 20 | $33 |

1487 S. Pearl St. (E. Florida Ave.), 303-777-0827

■ If you're lucky enough to snag "a table, buy a lottery ticket later" advise fans of this "jam-packed", "no-reservations" Japanese near Washington Park where the "ecstasy" of "remarkably fresh fish" formed into "awesome sushi and sashimi", as well as other "scrumptious" "dishes for all palates", more than makes up for the "frustration of waiting" among "crowds" of "see-and-be-seen" "people with cell phones", so even if you "enter with a frown, you'll leave with a smile every time."

Sweet Basil [S] | 27 | 24 | 24 | $43 |

193 E. Gore Creek Dr. (Bridge St.), Vail, 970-476-0125

■ "No wonder reservations are hard to come by" say regulars who cherish this New American Vail Village "mountain favorite" for its "brilliant food", "kick-ass wine list", "chichi" yet "relaxed atmosphere" and "wonderful" "view of Gore Creek"; loyalists say "it's the quintessence of fabulous dining" thanks to "unique dishes" with a smidge of an "Asian influence" served by a "terrific staff", which is why after more than two decades this "supernova" is still burning brightly.

Tamayo [S] | – | – | – | M |

1400 Larimer St. (14th St.), 720-946-1433

Instead of burritos or tacos, expect complex, creative haute Mexican dishes that shed new light on south-of-the-border fare at this popular Larimer Square destination, the first local effort by chef-owner Richard Sandoval, who employs a cooking philosophy much like that of a French toque, building sauces step-by-step and stocking the refrigerator with only first-rate ingredients.

TANTE LOUISE | 28 | 27 | 27 | $45 |

4900 E. Colfax Ave. (Eudora St.), 303-355-4488

■ A French "treasure with history, style and sensational cuisine", this East Denver "gem has sparkled for years" and is "still one of Denver's best, in all areas"; "delectable", "impeccably prepared" "classic" Gallic fare and "superb" vintages from a "terrific wine cellar" are "lovingly served" by a "friendly and unpretentious" staff within the "perfectly intimate" and "romantic" environment of a "comfortable country"-style inn that's "simultaneously quaint and fabulous" – in short, it's a "memorable dining experience."

Vesta Dipping Grill [S] | 25 | 25 | 22 | $32 |

1822 Blake St. (bet. 18th & 19th Sts.), 303-296-1970

■ "Whether you're on a date or looking to find one", head to this "sexy" New American "LoDo tastefest", a "stylishly funky outpost" with a "really enjoyable bar" packed with "young, pretty people"; the "international flavors" of "mix-and-match entrees and sauces", "excellent soundtrack" and "helpful servers" conspire to make a "unique, divine" "dining experience"; still, nitpickers say the "dipping theme seems gimmicky" and grumble about "pompous" "service with an attitude."

Wildflower S   27 | 27 | 25 | $49 |

The Lodge at Vail, 174 E. Gore Creek Dr. (base of Vail Mountain), Vail, 970-476-5011

■ "Like a precious perennial", this New American in The Lodge at Vail is "always stunning" according to bloom boosters who hail its "sophisticated" and "superb food", "delightful atmosphere" and "impeccable service"; for a "special treat", indulge in "absolutely the most sybaritic brunch ever", or opt for a "terrific summer lunch outside" (served on the patio just steps away from the "beautiful flower" garden) or dinner within its "wonderful room" filled with silk floral arrangements.

Detroit

TOP 10 FOOD RANKING

	Restaurant	Cuisine Type
28	Lark	New French
	Emily's	Med./New French
27	Zingerman's	Deli
26	Tribute	New French/Asian
	Common Grill	Eclectic
25	Il Posto	N&S Italian
	Mon Jin Lau	Asian Fusion
	Cafe Bon Homme	New French
24	Daniel's on Liberty	New American
	Capital Grille	Steakhouse

ADDITIONAL NOTEWORTHY PLACES

Annam	Vietnamese
Earle	French/N&S Italian
Five Lakes Grill	New American
Golden Mushroom	Continental
Morels	American
Opus One	American/Continental
Ristorante Café Cortina	N&S Italian
Ritz-Carlton Grill	American/Continental
Steve's Backroom	Middle Eastern
Whitney	New American

F | D | S | C

Annam ▽ 26 | 20 | 23 | $23

22053 Michigan Ave. (bet. Mason & Monroe Sts.), Dearborn, 313-565-8744

■ The "first place we take out-of-town guests" is this Dearborn Vietnamese with a big-city, small-restaurant feel "reminiscent of a cramped auberge in Paris" (French-speaking owner Phuong Nguyen hails from Europe); in a "serene" room appointed with beautiful table settings and simple floral displays, a polished staff turns out "absolutely wonderful", "elegant" fare, resulting in a "sensational" meal, notwithstanding the "tiny" quarters.

Cafe Bon Homme 25 | 21 | 23 | $47

844 Penniman Ave. (bet. Harvey & Main Sts.), Plymouth, 734-453-6260

■ Marked by lots of "European touches and flavors", this "quaint" "little" "jewel" in "small town" Plymouth is a "classy" yet "relaxing" nook in which to "enjoy" "original", "outstanding" New French fare served by a "courteous" staff; "warm, intimate and romantic", it's "a great place for a casually formal rendezvous."

CAPITAL GRILLE [S] 24 | 23 | 23 | $54

Somerset Collection, 2800 W. Big Beaver Rd. (bet. Coolidge & Crooks Rds.), Troy, 248-649-5300

◪ The "ultimate businessman's expense-account restaurant", this "masculine" steakhouse with a "private club" feel pulls in movers and shakers as well as the "ladies who lunch" to Troy's tony Somerset Collection mall with its "tried-and-true" menu of dry-aged prime cuts, served in an "inviting", "swanky" setting by a staff that's "attentive without being obvious"; what's more, the bar is a "happening spot" for the "single senior" crowd, so though it's a chain, it's a "perennial favorite" because it's a "capital idea."

COMMON GRILL [S] 26 | 19 | 23 | $32

112 S. Main St. (bet. Middle & South Sts.), Chelsea, 734-475-0470

■ Occupying a pair of 1800s brick storefronts in the charming village of Chelsea, this "casual-chic" Eclectic grill shines with a "gourmet" menu of "scrumptious seafood" that's "always well prepared"; chef-owner Craig Common's "distinctly uncommon" dishes ("inventive though not so far out that the flavors don't mix") are "impressively presented" in a "boisterous" room by "friendly" folks; for such "excellent food without the attitude", admirers insist it's well "worth the scenic drive", but "plan on a wait at this popular" "getaway."

Daniel's on Liberty 24 | 23 | 23 | $40

(fka Moveable Feast)

326 W. Liberty St. (2nd St.), Ann Arbor, 734-663-3278

■ Set in an "old Victorian house" in Ann Arbor, this New American "treat" is still an "outstanding place to entertain" or "celebrate a special day" because owners Daniel and Carol Huntsbarger "carry on the tradition of excellence"; the fare is "always fabulous" and "lovingly prepared" and "sometimes surprisingly crosscultural", served by a "personable", "knowledgeable" staff in a series of "cozy, intimate" rooms with "understated" decor; N.B. it's now open only for parties of 10 or more.

Earle [S] 23 | 20 | 21 | $41

121 W. Washington St. (Ashley St.), Ann Arbor, 734-994-0211

■ A "true gem amid the collegiate chaos of Ann Arbor", this beloved "tradition" "warmly" appointed with exposed brick and dim lighting has long been acclaimed for its live jazz, but its menu hits the right notes too (fans vote it "the winner of the best-food-in-a-dark-basement category"); inspired by the provinces of France and Italy, the kitchen's country cooking is so "fabulous" that "it's all I could do not to lick my plate", and it's accompanied by a "grand" 1,400-bottle wine list.

EMILY'S 28 | 23 | 26 | $56

505 N. Center St. (8 Mile Rd.), Northville, 248-349-0505

■ Anticipate a "brilliant experience" in dining at this "cozy" "oasis" quartered in an old house in the "little hamlet of Northville", where chef-owner Rick Halberg's "imaginative" French-accented Med menu promises to "make a foodie's heart sing" (don't miss the "best duck in Detroit", glazed with balsamic vinegar and paired with sweet potato–vanilla bean puree); not only is "everything prepared to order" and delivered by servers who "take care of you as if you were a guest in their home", but the "monthly wine dinners are not to be missed."

Five Lakes Grill 24 | 17 | 20 | $41

424 N. Main St. (Commerce St.), Milford, 248-684-7455

■ "Bustling with friendly, noisy people who don't feel at all intimidated by the greatness" of "hardworking" chef-owner

Brian Polcyn's New American cooking, this "storefront" "treasure" is "worth the drive" to the "picturesque" village of Milford way north of Detroit; the "fantastic" menu changes seasonally, but it always offers "interesting choices from the traditional to the nouveau", all based on "local" ingredients and prepared with "a lot of flair"; "tell all your friends about this must" "destination."

Golden Mushroom 23 | 18 | 21 | $55

18100 W. 10 Mile Rd. (Southfield Rd.), Southfield, 248-559-4230

◪ Specializing in mushrooms, natch, and wild game ("love the pheasant"), this "perennial" Continental "favorite" in Southfield maintains a loyal following that relies on it as a "sure thing for a special occasion", praising its "classic old-school" menu and "quiet", "upscale" ambiance; "disappointed" dissenters, however, who lament that it's slipped "down a notch from its starry past" sigh this "old dame has lost her luster."

Il Posto Ristorante 25 | 23 | 25 | $57

29110 Franklin Rd. (Northwestern Hwy.), Southfield, 248-827-8070

◪ "Reminiscent of Italy without any Americanization", this "beautiful" "special-occasion" spot in Southfield boasts the "best" Italian food in the Detroit area, pleasing with a "marvelous" "gourmet" menu presented by "charming" waiters imported from the motherland (let them "steer you in the right direction" when ordering), who provide European-style kitchen-to-cart-to-table service; its "magnificent" appointments "set the mood for a romantic meal", though keep in mind that this is "definitely an expense-account type of place."

LARK 28 | 28 | 28 | $85

6430 Farmington Rd. (north of Maple Rd.), West Bloomfield, 248-661-4466

■ Voted both No. 1 for Food and the Most Popular restaurant in Detroit, this "memorable" country inn in West Bloomfield is "absolutely the best in the metro" region thanks to proprietors Jim and Mary Lark, who "do everything to make your visit a special occasion"; equal raves go to chef Marcus Haight's "seductive", "exquisite" New French fare (don't miss his "bountiful appetizer cart", "superb" rack of lamb Genghis Khan or Austrian soufflé) and the "impeccable" tuxedoed staff; though some detect a "pompous" air, devotees insist this is a "must."

Mon Jin Lau ◐ [S] 25 | 16 | 19 | $32

1515 E. Maple Rd. (Stephenson Hwy.), Troy, 248-689-2332

■ Daringly "imaginative", this "lively" "Nouvelle" Asian fusion "surprise" in Troy is a "big step up from your typical everyday Chinese"; chef-owner Marshal Chin's "unique approach" allows curious "taste buds to experiment" with "haute" dishes that are "always changing but always really delicious"; backed by an "unexpectedly good", eclectic wine list, a staff that's "usually right on" and "fine value for the quality", it's constantly "packed" with adventurous types who gather to "meet, greet" and eat.

Morels 22 | 22 | 21 | $43

Bingham Office Park, 30100 Telegraph Rd. (bet. 12 &13 Mile Rds.), Bingham Farms, 248-642-1094

◪ A "mushroom-lover's paradise", this "pretty" American bistro "built around an atrium" garden in a Bingham Farms office complex is a "dependable" bet for a "guaranteed good meal"; the menu offers "lots of nice choices" that "emphasize Michigan specialties" (order anything with the namesake morels in it) and it's enhanced by an "excellent wine list"; "you won't find any eyebrow-raising exotic items" emerging from the kitchen, but the service is "pleasant", if somewhat "spotty", resulting in an "enjoyable" experience for most.

Opus One 23 | 22 | 23 | $61

565 E. Larned St. (Beaubien St.), 313-961-7766

◪ "Downtown politicos" and "business leaders" "meet frequently" at this "elegant" American-Continental power-lunch haunt where the "high-caliber" fare, "fine" weekly changing wine list, "classy" surroundings and "unobtrusive" service help to "close the deal"; in the evening, it's a "great place to have dinner before the theater, as it offers package deals and a shuttle service", as well as live piano music, so even if doubters are "not sure what the appeal is here", fans appreciate it as "a dress-up-and-enjoy kind of place."

Ristorante Café Cortina 23 | 21 | 20 | $45

30715 W. 10 Mile Rd. (Orchard Lake Rd.), Farmington Hills, 248-474-3033

■ Ask for a "table near the fireplace" in the winter and a seat near the garden (once an apple orchard and now the site where the restaurant "grows its own vegetables" and herbs) in summer to best savor the dining experience at this "upscale" Italian in suburban Farmington Hills, long cherished for its "wonderful" menu of "cooked-just-right" pastas and "rich" entrees; combined with "tasteful" decor, "terrific" service and "owners who make patrons feel very welcome", it adds up to "a real treat."

Ritz-Carlton Grill [S] 23 | 26 | 26 | $56

Ritz-Carlton Hotel, Fairlane Plaza, 300 Town Center Dr. (Hubbard Dr.), Dearborn, 313-441-2100

◪ "Living up to the Ritz's high level of quality and service", this "sedate" American-Continental grill in Dearborn pays "attention to every detail", proffering an "excellent classic" menu in "luxurious" environs appointed with mahogany and warmed by a fireplace; the service is "impeccable", if "stiff", but the unimpressed say that though there's "nothing to really complain about, there's no special reason to go either."

Steve's Backroom 23 | 11 | 18 | $21

19872 Kelly Rd. (bet. 7 & 8 Mile Rds.), Harper Woods, 313-527-7240

■ "Hidden" away in the back of an ethnic market in Harper Woods, this "small" Middle Eastern "storefront" beckons with "absolutely first-rate" "treats" that attract even the tony crowd from the affluent suburbs across town; despite its humble digs (the "decor could use an upgrade") and "no ambiance", it's a real "find" for "fresh", "flavorful" cooking at "bargain" prices, and "on your way out the front door you can buy some of the great foods you sampled."

TRIBUTE 26 | 26 | 25 | $78

31425 W. 12 Mile Rd. (Orchard Lake Rd.), Farmington Hills, 248-848-9393

■ A "strong contender for the best in Michigan", this "grand" Farmington Hills "award winner" promises a "dining experience to remember", boasting "outstanding" Asian-accented New French "fusion" cuisine courtesy of Takashi Yagihashi that's a sheer "tribute to food" ("go for the chef's table in the kitchen for a really big show"); "unsurpassed in presentation", his "artistically prepared" "creations" are turned out in "stunning" surroundings by a "thoughtful and attentive" staff overseen by Mickey Bakst, the "best maitre d' in town"; "for a wow dinner, this is the place."

WHITNEY [S] 22 | 28 | 23 | $58

4421 Woodward Ave. (bet. Mack & Warren Aves.), 313-832-5700

◪ "Could any decor be better" than that of this "breathtakingly lovely" "step back in time" housed in a "restored" Victorian mansion? – not in Detroit attest admirers of this "special-occasion" Downtown "landmark" that ensures "truly elegant dining"; "in the main, it deserves its reputation as one of the fine restaurants in the area", though the New American menu and the service clearly "don't do justice" to the "enchanting" setting; still, it's "well worth a visit to take a look around and retire upstairs for dessert, coffee or after-dinner drinks."

ZINGERMAN'S [S] 27 | 14 | 19 | $16

422 Detroit St. (Kingsley St.), Ann Arbor, 734-663-3354

■ "Always a madhouse, always a treat" sums up "positively the greatest deli in the Midwest", located in a brick storefront a few blocks off the University of Michigan's Ann Arbor campus; it's a "must" for an "outstanding selection" ("if you can't find it here, it doesn't exist") of "world-class breads, pastrami" and other goodies, making it a "very special place for food lovers"; this is a "classic that does it right and doesn't mess with success"; the only caveat: "beware of the long lines."

Ft. Lauderdale

TOP 10 FOOD RANKING

	Restaurant	Cuisine Type
27	Darrel & Oliver's Cafe	New World
	Mark's Las Olas	Floridian
	Casa D'Angelo	N&S Italian
	Cafe Martorano	N&S Italian
26	Cafe Seville	Spanish
	Eduardo de San Angel	Mexican
	By Word of Mouth	New American
	Hobo's Fish Joint	Seafood
	Canyon	Southwestern
	Silver Pond	Chinese

ADDITIONAL NOTEWORTHY PLACES

Armadillo Cafe	Southwestern
Black Orchid Cafe	Continental
Blue Moon Fish Co.	Seafood/Caribbean
Cafe Vico	Northern Italian
Charley's Crab	Seafood
La Tavernetta	Northern Italian
Outback	Steakhouse
Primavera	N&S Italian
Ruth's Chris	Steakhouse
Sunfish Grill	Seafood

F | D | S | C

Armadillo Cafe [S] 26 | 19 | 23 | $42

3400 S. University Dr. (Frontage Rd.), Davie, 954-791-5104

■ For a "fun adventure" "involving all the taste buds", "go with a group of foodies" to this "radical Southwestern" cafe in Davie, which delivers a "wide variety" of "interesting", "delicious" dishes, from "outstanding fish" to "awesome chocolate fritters."

Black Orchid Cafe [S] 25 | 23 | 23 | $47

2985 N. Ocean Blvd. (south of E. Oakland Park Blvd.), 954-561-9398

◪ Safari-hunting surveyors with "tastes that lean toward game come home" to this Continental cafe in Central Broward, where the menu blooms with such "wonderful" "exotica"; the beach location, "candles and jazz guitar set the right mood" for "romantic" dining, though critics with contemporary tastes feel that the "outdated" menu and decor make it a "time warp back to 1978."

Blue Moon Fish Co. [S] 24 | 24 | 22 | $43

4405 W. Tradewinds Ave. (E. Commercial Blvd.), 954-267-9888

◪ The "lovely patio on the Intracoastal" is "big with boaters" at this "classy" Northeast Lauderdale seafood house with a Caribbean twist; gourmands cruise over for "superb" shellfish pan roasts and other "wonderful fish dishes" at dinner, as well as for an "amazing

Sunday brunch" and "bargain two-for-one lunch", though "small portions" and "uncaring" service mean that some drop anchor here only once in a blue moon when they're hungry for a "beautiful" view.

By Word of Mouth 26 | 16 | 24 | $39
3200 NE 12th Ave. (E. Oakland Park Blvd.), 954-564-3663

■ There's "no menu" at this "tiny" "culinary hot spot" in Northeast Lauderdale – they just "bring you to the showcase to let you see what they have for the day" – and though the New American "innovations" are "delicious", word of mouth has it that the "best part" of this "unique dining experience" is the "attentive servers" "entertaining you by describing each dish."

CAFE MARTORANO ◗ 27 | 17 | 21 | $53
3343 E. Oakland Park Blvd. (N. Ocean Blvd.), 954-561-2554

■ "*Sopranos*-cool before *The Sopranos* was cool", this "bada-bing!" cafe is "where Sinatra would eat" if he craved "awesome" "South Philly Italian" while in Northeast Lauderdale; there's "no menu", so when you land a table, "just ask what" "genius Steve Martorano" is "cooking today", and stick around till "late at night, when the disco ball comes down and the music starts pumping."

CAFE SEVILLE 26 | 20 | 24 | $33
2768 E. Oakland Park Blvd. (Bayview Dr.), 954-565-1148

■ "Ask for extra bread to devour every drop" on your plate at this "festive" Spanish "favorite" in Northeast Lauderdale; the "friendly owner" "isn't shy about telling you what to eat", like the signature paella or "some of the best fish specials in town", but he's such a "fantastic host" that even "kids" have "fun" here, though only adults have the pleasure of sipping the house's "hit sangria."

Cafe Vico S 25 | 19 | 25 | $35
IHOP Plaza, 1125 N. Federal Hwy. (north of Sunrise Blvd.), 954-565-9681

■ "When you enter, you're immediately greeted" by the "gracious" owner and "made to feel like family" at this "intimate", "outstanding neighborhood" Northern Italian in Central Lauderdale; regulars rave about the "best ravioli" and "real-treat" specials, though they "almost hate to say how good" this "reasonably priced" ristorante is, since they "still want to get in."

Canyon S 26 | 22 | 23 | $39
1818 E. Sunrise Blvd. (N. Federal Hwy.), 954-765-1950

■ "Oooh!" – the happy-hour posse just "loves those prickly pear margaritas", but the "Southwestern charms" of this "funky" Ft. Lauderdale "treasure" extend to its "inventive" meals as well; though the "bar noise" in the "crowded", "cozy" dining room can be a "bit loud", the "unusual dishes packed with character and spice" speak boldly enough to keep your palate's attention.

CASA D'ANGELO S 27 | 22 | 25 | $44
Sunrise Square Plaza, 1201 N. Federal Hwy. (bet. E. Sunrise Blvd. & NE 13th St.), 954-564-1234

■ The whole family pitches in at this "casual-dressy" Northeast Lauderdale "favorite": "wonderful" chef-owner Angelo Elias uses only "first-class ingredients" of "truly fine quality" to prepare his "killer" Italian dishes, wife Denise, "who greets you, is so nice she makes everyone feel" "like an old friend", and in season "mama comes from Italy" to cook; no wonder regulars visit throughout the year – it "always feels good to be here."

CHARLEY'S CRAB [S] 21 | 21 | 21 | $38

3000 NE 32nd Ave. (Oakland Park Blvd.), 954-561-4800

PAL'S CHARLEY'S CRAB [S]

1755 SE Third Ct. (bet. Federal Hwy. & Hillsboro Blvd.), Deerfield Beach, 954-427-4000

◪ Charley's chums choose these "classic" seafood houses along the Intracoastal and adjacent to Palm Beach "again and again for the view and the vittles"; "grandparents" bring the kids for "family comfort" and a "good early-bird value", while "out-of-towners" tout the "excellent Sunday brunch"; picky patrons pout, however, that these crab "traps" have been "fading into touristy blandness."

DARREL & OLIVER'S CAFE MAXX [S] 27 | 22 | 26 | $52

2601 E. Atlantic Blvd. (east of N. Federal Hwy.), Pompano Beach, 954-782-0606

■ Eighteen years marks one lengthy "orgasmic experience" for the clientele at this "California-style, open-kitchen" New World cafe, voted No. 1 for Food in the Ft. Lauderdale area; even if the "ordinary" decor fails to romance design divas, time and again Pompano Beach foodies "come to see what's new" on the "daily changing menu" of "creative", "delectable dishes."

Eduardo de San Angel 26 | 23 | 24 | $46

2822 E. Commercial Blvd. (bet. Bayview Dr. & 28th Ave.), 954-772-4731

■ "It's so nice to not have to scream over the music" when you want to discuss how "marvelous every dish" is at this "quiet" "nouveau" Mexican in Northeast Lauderdale, so "forget your preconceived notions", squeeze into a "postage stamp–size table" and thrill with the *fanaticos* to the "masterful" "fusion of all things from Baja to the Yucatan" at this "shining" "gem" amid the dross of the "Taco Bell world."

Hobo's Fish Joint [S] 26 | 18 | 22 | $40

Palm Spring Plaza, 10317 Royal Palm Blvd. (Coral Springs Dr.), Coral Springs, 954-346-5484

■ "One thing about Florida" lecture locals is that a "strip-mall location means nothing as far as quality" is concerned; "definitely not a 'joint'", this "creative" Coral Springs finster drops its line "where you least expect it", reeling in "serious fish-eaters" with its "wide variety" of "fresh" seafood served in a choice of "interesting ways"; hook a hungry friend and "tramp over" to "share the sampler", replete with "homemade tartar sauce."

La Tavernetta [S] 25 | 23 | 23 | $39

926 NE 20th Ave. (south of Sunrise Blvd.), 954-463-2566

■ If you're boating along the Intracoastal, this "intimate" Northern Italian "favorite" is "somewhat hard to find", but when you spy it you can dock and they'll "cook your catch"; "terrific" specialties like its Hawaiian sea bass in white wine sauce lure in schools of hungry sea dogs who board the water shuttle, as well as plenty of landlubbers who drive over to this "first-class" operation for a patio table with a "breathtaking" view.

MARK'S LAS OLAS [S] 27 | 24 | 24 | $52

1032 E. Las Olas Blvd. (bet. 10th & 11th Sts.), 954-463-1000

■ Fort Lauderdale's "people-watching headquarters" is this "trendy" Floridian where "chef Mark Militello's flair" for "fab" fare finds fans among the "hip and happening"; if so many "moguls on cell phones" makes the atmosphere too "NYC" and the "noise quotient a bit high" for your taste, "head for one of the booths in the back" to enjoy signature crab-crusted grouper and other "delicious" "culinary treats" in relative peace.

OUTBACK STEAKHOUSE [S] 19 | 16 | 18 | $25

650 Riverside Dr. (W. Atlantic Blvd.), Coral Springs, 954-345-5965
1801 SE 10th Ave. (17th St. Cswy.), 954-523-5600
6201 N. Federal Hwy. (bet. E. Cypress Creek & McNab Rds.), 954-771-4390
7841 Pines Blvd. (University Blvd.), Pembroke Pines, 954-981-5300
1823 Pine Island Rd. (Sunrise Blvd.), Plantation, 954-370-9956

◪ "Crikey!" cry reviewers – "are onions supposed to bloom?"; who knows, and who cares when they taste so "great, mate" at this "solid-value", "family-oriented" chophouse chain that pals say will "stun you with delights" from Down Under; a "party" atmosphere means it's "always packed", even if critics wonder why anyone would wait for these "slabs o' meat."

Primavera 26 | 22 | 22 | $45

Primavera Plaza, 830 E. Oakland Park Blvd. (west of N. Dixie Hwy.), Oakland Park, 954-564-6363

◪ Skip the local "rip-offs" and "step into a whole other scene past the portals" of this "small, warm" Italian "favorite" in Oakland Park, where "nearly perfect, artfully crafted" pasta, seafood and seasonal game dishes are complemented by an "extensive wine list"; the room is "elegant and romantic", but some say a "stuffy" staff that "fawns over regulars" and is "cold" to "newcomers" is only appealing "when you miss NYC snobbery."

RUTH'S CHRIS STEAKHOUSE [S] 25 | 23 | 24 | $49

2525 N. Federal Hwy. (bet. Oakland Park & Sunrise Blvds.), 954-565-2338

■ "Sizzle, sizzle!" – "despite being part of a chain", these "solid" "steak joints" possess the "right formula" to please "good old-fashioned meat lovers"; "huge portions" of "the best trimmings around", like "great creamed spinach" and "thin, crispy onions", are offered, but "nothing can match the arrival" of the "delicious", "buttery" beef; though "big taste" comes at a "big price", loyalists insist that these "superior selections" are worth it.

Silver Pond ◐ [S] 26 | 12 | 17 | $25

4285 N. State Rd. 7 (south of Commercial Blvd.), Lauderdale Lakes, 954-486-8885

■ "New Yorkers have no need to go back home" again say connoisseurs about this "authentic" establishment in Lauderdale Lakes, which woks up the "best Chinese for the price this side of Manhattan's Chinatown"; the "informed, friendly" staff helps diners select from an "awesome" menu that focuses on "incredible Hong Kong–style dishes"; note, though, that the digs are, ahem, "modest", so perhaps it'd be a good idea to "not look around" much.

Sunfish Grill 25 | 18 | 23 | $44

2771 E. Atlantic Blvd. (Intracoastal Waterway), Pompano Beach, 954-788-2434

■ "One nibble and you're hooked" as surely as the "fabulous" fish featured at this "colorful" "little jewel tucked away near the Intracoastal" in Pompano Beach; "true talent" Tony Sindaco "lovingly prepares seafood" so "world-class" that fin fanatics dare to "show up in the middle of a hurricane" just to be "blown away from start to finish" by his "outstanding" cooking.

Ft. Worth

TOP 10 FOOD RANKING

	Restaurant	Cuisine Type
28	Saint-Emilion	French
27	Del Frisco's	Steakhouse
	La Piazza	N&S Italian
26	Cacharel	French
	Randall's Gourmet	Eclectic
25	Bistro Louise	New American/Med.
	Kincaid's	Burgers
	Railhead Smokehouse	Barbecue
23	Angelo's	Barbecue
	Angeluna	Eclectic/International

ADDITIONAL NOTEWORTHY PLACES

Café Ashton	New American
Chisholm Club	Texan
Classic Cafe	New American
Cool River Cafe	Southwestern
Escargot	French
Grape Escape	Eclectic
Lonesome Dove	Western
Pegasus	International/Med.
Reata	Southwestern
Rough Creek Lodge	New American

	F	D	S	C
Angelo's Barbecue ⊄	23	14	17	$14

2533 White Settlement Rd. (University Dr.), 817-332-0357

■ "A tattered stuffed bear still greets you at the door" of this "no-frills", mesquite smoke–filled Northwest BBQ "institution", famous for serving "great chopped beef", brisket and the "coldest beers in town" to "lots of guys wearing cowboy hats"; P.S. "get plenty of napkins."

	F	D	S	C
Angeluna [S]	23	23	21	$35

215 E. Fourth St. (bet. Calhoun & Commerce Sts.), 817-334-0080

◪ "Convenient" before or after an event at Bass Performance Hall, this "cutting-edge" venue showcases an International menu of "artistically presented fusion dishes" ("Texas meets Asia and the angels sing") amid "cool" decor highlighted by a skylike ceiling covered with eclectic images (from Marilyn Monroe to Mr. Potato Head); still, spoilers shout that it's "so noisy I wanted to cry."

	F	D	S	C
BISTRO LOUISE [S]	25	24	23	$37

Stonegate Commons, 2900 S. Hulen St. (Oak Park Ln.), 817-922-9244

■ Sharing the No. 1 spot for Most Popular restaurant in Ft. Worth with Del Frisco's, chef Louise Lamensdorf's New American bistro is praised by admirers as one of the "best in the Metroplex" given its "wonderful brunch", a Mediterranean-accented menu that "challenges the local steak mentality" and an "improved wine list"; the "casually elegant" Provençal-themed space attracts a lot of well-heeled locals to the Southwest side, so don't be surprised if "you always see someone you know."

CACHAREL 26 | 25 | 25 | $44

Brookhollow Tower Two, 2221 E. Lamar Blvd. (bet. Ballpark Way & Hwy. 360), Arlington, 817-640-9981

■ An Arlington office tower surrounded by amusement parks and fast-food chain outlets is the unusual setting of this high-achieving classic French grande dame; in an "intimate, posh" dining room with an illuminated skyline view, choose a three-course prix fixe menu or order à la carte, but either way, the "great soufflés" should be a de rigueur sweet finale.

Café Ashton [S] – | – | – | E

Ashton Hotel, 610 Main St. (6th St.), 817-332-0100

While this New American bistro is set in a prestigious Downtown landmark building, now home to the luxurious new boutique Ashton Hotel, all historical overtones end at the glass front doors; inside is a streamlined space appointed with creamy yellow walls, bright blue opera chairs and modern artwork, making for a sleek backdrop for a menu that mixes European flavors with tropical nuances.

Chisholm Club [S] – | – | – | E

Renaissance Worthington Hotel, 200 Main St. (Second St.), 817-730-2222

Noted chef Grady Spears has resettled in Downtown's historic Renaissance Worthington Hotel as the headliner of this splashy Texan kitchen; the multilevel, leather-trimmed space with accents of black and dark green is appointed with private dining alcoves suited for deal making, while an open kitchen adds to the action at one end of the room, as does the on-site cooking school where the chef demonstrates recipes.

Classic Cafe ▽ 25 | 18 | 22 | $39

504 N. Oak St. (Denton St.), Roanoke, 817-430-8185

621 E. Southlake Blvd. (Byron Nelson Pkwy.), Southlake, 817-410-9001

■ While contrasting greatly in size, both the intimate Roanoke flagship (seating about 75) and the modern Southlake outlet (with room for 300) turn out "salmon at its best", in addition to other "exceptional" New American specialties; hands-on service and "friendly" managers who "always remember returning guests" further explain their popularity.

Cool River Cafe ◐[S] 21 | 23 | 19 | $33

1045 Hidden Ridge Rd. (MacArthur Blvd.), Irving, 972-871-8881

■ This Rocky Mountain–themed lodge set amid the Los Colinas/Valley Ranch sprawl has a lively "bar scene" (including a cigar/cognac lounge) peopled by corporate climbers and "beautiful women"; with the distraction of large-screen TVs and billiard tables, the Southwestern food may not be the focus, but it scores well, especially the rib-eye, which alone is "worth the trip."

DEL FRISCO'S DOUBLE EAGLE STEAK HOUSE 27 | 26 | 26 | $57

812 Main St. (8th St.), 817-877-3999

■ Tied with Bistro Louise as the Most Popular restaurant in Ft. Worth, this Downtown steakhouse chain link wows carnivores with the "best red meat", paired with "wonderful sides" and a showstopping wine list and served by an "impeccable" staff in "clubby environs"; so don your sports jacket and cowboy boots, double-check that "expense-account" limit and prepare for an "elegant power dinner"; N.B. reservations are essential.

Escargot   ▽ 26 | 24 | 23 | $37
Chicotsky's Shopping Ctr., 3427 W. Seventh St. (Montgomery St.), 817-336-3090
■ Frédéric Angevin's "wonderful" Cultural District French entry is quickly becoming a "favorite" thanks to his "outstanding" cooking; "elegantly" decorated, the narrow slice of a dining room is tended to by wife Michele; yes, "prices are high" and it can get "crowded", but that's to be expected for such a classy operation.

Grape Escape Wine Bar 🖺   20 | 22 | 21 | $26
500 Commerce St. (4th St.), 817-336-9463
◪ Small plates of Eclectic nibbles are teamed with flights of global wines at this compact Downtown tasting bar that makes for a "nice place to converse" after a concert at nearby Bass Performance Hall; while sour grapes whine "overpriced" with "not much food" to choose from, most say "we need more places like this."

Kincaid's Hamburgers 🖺⊄   25 | 14 | 17 | $10
4901 Camp Bowie Blvd. (Eldridge St.), 817-732-2881
■ "Excellent", "lean, juicy burgers" "dripping with mustard" and delivered in white paper sacks generate long lines at this peerless patty joint on the West Side, which pulls patrons from far and wide; "while not much for decor" (picnic tables and stand-up counters), its "old-fashioned friendliness" more than compensates.

LA PIAZZA 🖺   27 | 26 | 24 | $49
University Park Vlg., 1600 S. University Dr. (I-30), 817-334-0000
◪ Though clearly the "best Italian in Ft. Worth", this "expensive", "dressy" University Park Village destination is not without some controversy; while a "who's who" of regulars are welcomed as warmly as arriving relatives and whisked to prime tables to enjoy "a fabulous meal" based on the "freshest ingredients" (try the veal tenders with porcini mushrooms), a minority of frustrated outsiders chafes over the owner's playing favorites.

Lonesome Dove Western Bistro ▽ 23 | 18 | 20 | $33
2406 N. Main St. (24th St.), 817-740-8810
■ Chef Tim Love has set up his camp stove in the Stockyards with this "good addition" featuring polished Western ranch-style vittles turned out in a small, saloon-like room with plank doors, burlap draperies and a quintessential Western sunset painting; granted, fine linens, pewter platters and stemware are not typical chuck wagon accessories, nor is the grilled quail quesadilla or BBQ duck spring rolls, but culinary cowboys will easily adapt.

Pegasus   ▽ 24 | 25 | 22 | $35
2443 Forest Park Blvd. (Park Hill Dr.), 817-922-0808
■ Having "shown promise out of the gate", this elegant Forest Park pleaser continues to impress with its "cool", minimalist decor and "interesting" Mediterranean-influenced International menu; first-time visitors should consider ordering an array of meze, followed by one of the many intriguing entrees such as sumac-crusted filet mignon, Persian-spiced osso buco or duck with fruit mole.

Railhead Smokehouse
25 | 18 | 19 | $13

2900 Montgomery St. (I-30), 817-738-9808
5220 Hwy. 121 S. (Hall Johnson Rd.), Colleyville, 817-571-2525
■ Hot as the coals that smoke its meat is the "best BBQ" rivalry between this twosome and Angelo's; loyalists insist Railhead's ribs are "the final word" on the subject but add that "the brisket is out of this world" too (especially with "a tall schooner of Shiner Bock"); while the tables and patio perpetually overflow with patrons, the "cafeteria-style lines move quickly" and the "fun" atmosphere (T-shirts for sale read: 'Life is Too Short to Live in Dallas') keeps the mood light.

RANDALL'S GOURMET CHEESECAKE CO.
26 | 24 | 23 | $35

907 S. Houston St. (bet. 8th & 9th Sts.), 817-336-2253
■ This Eclectic cafe "tucked away on the nontouristy side of Downtown" features exposed-brick decor and a daily changing menu of impressive preparations, as well as a romantic "Paris-meets-New-Orleans-meets-San-Francisco-meets-Greenwich-Village" ambiance; N.B. don't forget to end your meal with a creamy wedge of its famous cheesecake.

REATA 🖂
– | – | – | E

Sundance Sq., 310 Houston St. (Third St.), 817-336-1009
Forced from its 35th-floor perch at the Bank One Building, this revered Downtown Southwestern now has its feet firmly planted in Sundance Square, where it continues its tradition of serving up hearty cowboy cuisine packed with smoky flavors and made-from-scratch goodness; the new incarnation still evokes the elegant ranch-style decor of the original and, though no longer blessed with a spectacular view, captures a feeling of the great outdoors with floor-to-ceiling photographs of unforgettable sunset vistas.

Rough Creek Lodge 🖂
▽ 29 | 29 | 29 | $54

County Rd. 2013 (US 67 S., 9 mi. south of Glen Rose), Glen Rose, 254-918-2550
■ Anticipate an "incredible experience" out on the "wide open prairie" at this haute hunting resort on Chalk Mountain; once seated in the elegant Western-accented room, saddled between a soaring, three-story limestone fireplace and a bustling open kitchen, you'll wax poetic over chef Gerard Thompson's intelligently stylish New American menu (which specializes in game birds); P.S. some "stay overnight" to avoid the long drive back.

SAINT-EMILION
28 | 25 | 26 | $47

3617 W. Seventh St. (Montgomery Rd.), 817-737-2781
■ Voted No. 1 for Food in Ft. Worth and embraced as "a French oasis in a steak-and-BBQ desert", owner Bernard Tronche's "romantic" brick cottage near the Arts District showcases "first-rate", classically prepared dishes made from "quality" ingredients, as well as a top-notch wine list that favors its namesake region; while the menu advises diners to pace themselves for a leisurely meal, let the staff know that you're on an American schedule if you want them to speed it up.

Honolulu

TOP 10 FOOD RANKING

	Restaurant	Cuisine Type
28	Alan Wong's	Hawaiian Regional
27	La Mer	New French
	Hoku's	Asian/International
	3660 on the Rise	Pacific Rim
26	Roy's	Hawaiian Fusion
	Chef Mavro's	New French/Hawaiian Reg.
	Ruth's Chris	Steakhouse
25	Mekong	Thai
	Hy's	Steakhouse
	L'Uraku	Japanese

ADDITIONAL NOTEWORTHY PLACES

Bali by the Sea	Eurasian
Diamond Head Grill	Hawaiian Regional
Golden Dragon	Chinese
Indigo	Asian/International
OnJin's Café	Asian/French
Orchids	American/Seafood
Padovani's	French/Mediterranean
Pineapple Room	Hawaiian Regional
Sansei	Japanese/Hawaiian
Side Street Inn	Hawaiian

F | D | S | C

ALAN WONG'S [S] 28 | 21 | 25 | $57

McCully Ct., 1857 S. King St. (bet. Hauoli & Pumehana Sts.), 808-949-2526

■ Again voted Most Popular and No. 1 for Food among Honolulu restaurants, this "consistent favorite" "hidden" on the edge of Ala Moana "never disappoints and always impresses" thanks to "heaven-in-your-mouth" Hawaiian Regional cuisine featuring a "wonderful blend of ingredients" ("try Da Bag" or the "flavorful signature ginger-crusted onaga") prepared by "inventive Alan Wong", the "masterful" chef-owner; with such "sumptuous" fare and "seamless service", "who cares" about the "tight quarters and constant din"?

Bali by the Sea 24 | 27 | 24 | $61

Hilton Hawaiian Vlg., 2005 Kalia Rd. (Ala Moana Blvd.), 808-941-2254

■ A "romantic" "special-occasion place", this "Beauty by the Sea" in "the huge Hilton Hawaiian Village complex" boasts an "elegant" open-air dining room with "awesome", "alluring views" of Waikiki Beach, not to mention "excellent" Eurasian cuisine and "friendly" service from an "efficient" staff; a few naysayers quibble that it's "overpriced" and "touristy", but most sum up the experience as "outstanding"; N.B. the Food score does not reflect the recent arrival of chef Roberto Los Baños.

Chef Mavro's 🆂

24 | 23 | 26 | $64

1969 S. King St. (McCully St.), 808-944-4714

◪ The "fantastic flavors" of "island ingredients" are "perfectly blended" with "Provençal" "culinary style" into "impressive" and "delicious" New French–Hawaiian Regional cuisine by a "first-rate" chef, the "mavrolous" George Mavrothalassitis himself, at this "beautiful" and "relaxing" venue on the edge of Ala Moana, then "wonderfully paired" with "amazing wines" and proffered by "attentive", "informed" servers who "pamper you"; a vocal minority grumbles about "tiny", "overpriced portions", but most "wish they could afford it more often."

Diamond Head Grill 🆂

24 | 25 | 23 | $51

W Hotel, 2885 Kalakaua Ave. (Diamond Head), 808-922-3734

◪ The "hip", "upwardly mobile" "all-dressed-up crowd" flocks to this "stylishly Zen" Hawaiian Regional eatery "in the W hotel", on the edge of Waikiki, where "enthusiastic chef" Todd Constantino "tries new things all the time" with his "innovative" and "fantastic" dishes ("not for the average meat-and-potatoes guy") served by a "knowledgeable", "accommodating" staff; still, some complain it's "expensive for what you get" and "too noisy" (thanks to the "trendy bar"), while lamenting that there's "no ocean view."

Golden Dragon 🆂

24 | 25 | 22 | $43

Hilton Hawaiian Vlg., 2005 Kalia Rd. (Ala Moana Blvd.), 808-946-5336

■ "This dragon isn't laggin'" according to surveyors "satisfied in every respect" with this "upscale" "fine-dining" Chinese "favorite", a bastion of "tranquility amid the bustle of the Hilton Hawaiian Village"; chef Steve Chiang's "delicious", "authentic Cantonese and Szechuan cuisine", as well as "innovative dishes" like the signature "lobster curry with fried haupia coconut pudding (a must-have)", are coupled with "impeccable" service and an "elegant", "luxurious" setting with "great views", making for "a really nice evening" "from the first cup of tea to the last fortune cookie."

HOKU'S 🆂

27 | 26 | 26 | $54

Kahala Mandarin Oriental Hotel, 5000 Kahala Ave., 808-739-8779

■ Located in the Kahala Mandarin Oriental hotel, this "top-of-the-line" eatery (whose name means 'star' in Hawaiian) shines thanks to "creative" chef Wayne Hirabayashi's "exquisitely prepared and presented" Asian-International cuisine, "fantastic" service and a "prime location" "by the sea" ("request a window table" for the "breathtaking view" of a "secluded beach"); it's a "dream place" of "understated elegance" that's "worth the splurge" and "the drive", as the "parking lot strewn with Ferraris, Mercedes Benzes and Lexuses" attests.

Hy's Steak House 🆂

25 | 23 | 25 | $55

Waikiki Park Heights Hotel, 2440 Kuhio Ave. (Uluniu Ave.), 808-922-5555

■ "A Waikiki institution", this "old-fashioned steakhouse" is "a must for the beef lover" according to fans of its "fabulous steaks" and "delicious prime rib", not to mention its "pleasant, attentive staff" and their "showmanship" in the "tableside preparation of salads and desserts" such as "to-die-for cherries jubilee", or its "traditionally elegant" setting, which "reminds some of an English castle library"; though the "modern"-minded lament the "dated decor and menu", purists predict it will remain "a mainstay for years" to come.

Indigo
22 | 22 | 19 | $37

1121 Nuuanu Ave. (Hotel St.), 808-521-2900

■ A "wonderful blend of East and West" awaits at this "exotic" Asian-International "in the middle of Chinatown" ("convenient to the Hawaii Theatre" Center), where chef Glenn Chu's "fun", "interesting menu" "delights the taste buds", the "fantastic lunch buffet" offers "value for the money" and the "great bar" makes "the meanest martinis in town"; nature enthusiasts suggest you "ask for a table outside" in the "romantic", "tropical"-"jungle" setting of its "beautiful patio"; P.S. though "parking is a nightmare", "valet [service] is available."

LA MER [S]
27 | 28 | 27 | $74

Halekulani Hotel, 2199 Kalia Rd. (Lewers St.), 808-923-2311

■ "Feel like royalty" at this "romantic", "idyllic restaurant" in the Halekulani hotel just steps from the "waves lapping" at Waikiki beach, where "inventive" chef Yves Garnier's "flawless" New French cuisine "with an island twist" combined with "an extensive (if expensive) wine list", "exquisitely" "superb service" from an "attentive-but-not-intrusive" staff and "beautiful sunsets over the Pacific" creates a "feast for all the senses"; such "elegance does not come cheap" or without a "dress code", so "bring your platinum card" and a jacket to this "special-occasion place."

L'Uraku [S]
25 | 22 | 23 | $42

Uraku Tower, 1341 Kapiolani Blvd. (Piikoi St.), 808-955-0552

■ From the "imaginative and spectacular" food to the "friendly, quick service" and "chic", "creative decor" featuring "colorful umbrellas" "hanging from the ceiling", this "real find" "off the beaten path" near Ala Moana "pleasantly surprises"; "up-and-coming" "master chef Hiroshi" Fukui "fuses Eastern and Western flavors" "with a Hawaiian touch" for a "unique take on Japanese" cuisine, and "don't miss his Weekender Lunch, a four-course gourmet meal for $16."

Mekong Thai [S]
25 | 15 | 18 | $21

1295 S. Beretania St. (bet. Keeaumoku & Piikoi Sts.), 808-591-8842
1726 S. King St. (McCully St.), 808-941-6184

■ Though they may have "less flash" than some competitors, these twin Ala Moana eateries attract "in-the-know people" who "enjoy" their "authentic", "flavorful Thai cuisine", which is not only "high quality" but dished out at "non-tourist prices" that make it a "great bargain"; sure, the "seating is tight" and the "decor could be improved", but "you really come for the food", especially the "yummy tom yum" soup, "great satays" and the "not-to-be-missed" Evil Jungle Prince, a famous creation of founding chef Keo Samanikone.

OnJin's Cafe
22 | 16 | 17 | $28

401 Kamakee St. (Kapiolani Blvd.), 808-589-1666

■ The "secret" is starting to get out about this "lovely little" "boutique" bistro on the edge of Ala Moana that "deserves to be better known"; midday *mangeurs* "delight" in its "outstanding" "gourmet" take on traditional Hawaiian "plate lunches" ("the fanciest in town"), while evening eaters enjoy a "totally different dinner menu" of "creative", "delicious" Asian-French fare, all at "bargain" prices; P.S. "attentive chef-owner" OnJin Kim is also a trained opera diva who's been known to sing during supper.

Orchids 🖸   25 | 26 | 25 | $50

Halekulani Hotel, 2199 Kalia Rd. (Lewers St.), 808-923-2311

◼ "Bravo! bravo!" boom bloom boosters bowled over by this "magical" and "romantic" venue at the Halekulani Hotel, "right on the beach in Waikiki", who say its "to-die-for views" coupled with "creative" American fare (including "fabulous seafood and beef selections" and "killer homemade pastries") and "impeccable service" make it a "favorite" for "special occasions", a "must for Sunday brunch" and a top "choice when taking out mainland visitors"; it's a bit "pricey", but fans say it's "worth every penny."

Padovani's   24 | 21 | 22 | $58
Restaurant & Wine Bar 🖸

Doubletree Alana Hotel, 1956 Ala Moana Blvd. (Kalakaua Ave.), 808-946-3456

☑ "Bursting with flavor", the "outstanding" and "refined French"-Mediterranean cuisine of "imaginative" chef Philippe Padovani (ex La Mer) draws devotees to this "nice, romantic" spot in the Doubletree Alana Hotel, as does the "stand-out service" and "sensational wine list" "a mile long" (with 50 by-the-glass pours); despite these attributes, dissenters are "disappointed" that it's "a little off the beaten path from Waikiki's main strip" and aren't impressed with some "stuffy" staffers.

Pineapple Room 🖸   24 | 20 | 21 | $37

Macy's, Ala Moana Shopping Ctr., 1450 Ala Moana Blvd. (Atkinson Dr.), 808-945-8881

◼ "Hidden" in an "odd location for an upscale" eatery – an "airy and comfortable room" "inside Macy's", within the "busy" Ala Moana Shopping Center – "innovative" owner "Alan Wong's second triumph" is hailed as "almost as good as" "his namesake restaurant", offering his signature style of "cutting-edge Hawaiian [Regional] cuisine" (here prepared by chef de cuisine Steven Ariel) at more "casual prices" but with the same "warm, friendly and attentive" service, making this "aloha experience" a "must-stop for all visiting foodies."

ROY'S 🖸   26 | 21 | 24 | $48

6600 Kalanianaole Hwy. (Keahole St.), 808-396-7697

◼ "Overlooking Maunalua Bay" in "peaceful Hawaii Kai", this "original" "flagship" "is still the best" location of "legendary" chef-owner Roy Yamaguchi's "classy" international "empire" and just "keeps getting better" thanks to his "consistently excellent" Hawaiian Fusion cuisine – including "mouthwatering fresh fish" dishes and "excellent chocolate soufflé" – plus "outstanding service" and "lovely sunsets"; since the "din and clatter" from the "open kitchen" can make the "crowded" "upstairs dining room too noisy", regulars recommend the "quieter downstairs" area.

Ruth's Chris Steak House 🖸   26 | 21 | 23 | $53

Restaurant Row, 500 Ala Moana Blvd. (bet. Punchbowl & South Sts.), 808-599-3860

◼ Carnivores clamor for this Restaurant Row chain outpost, "a chip off the ole block" that's "absolutely" "as good as it gets in Hawaii for top-quality steaks", with "huge portions" ("no stinginess here") of "scrumptious" meat so "juicy" and "tender" "you can cut it with a fork and skip the knife", accompanied by their "signature creamed spinach", a "delightful wine list" and "first-rate service" from an "incredibly attentive staff"; though some are worried about the "cholesterol level" and "eye-popping prices", most agree its "*extra* extraordinarily wonderful."

Sansei Seafood Restaurant & Sushi Bar ◐ [S] 24 | 17 | 19 | $39

Restaurant Row, 500 Ala Moana Blvd. (South St.), 808-536-6286

■ Following the success of his Maui original, "inventive" chef-owner Dave 'D.K.' Kodama opened this Restaurant Row sibling similarly specializing in "contemporary Japanese"-Hawaiian fare; with a "mind-boggling" "menu that's so big it can take all night to read", "there's surely something to please every palate", and though his "creative flair" results in some "nontraditional sushi" selections that might "make a purist cringe", those who "love" an "interesting twist" appreciate the "unique" take of his "original combos"; P.S. "check out the early-bird specials."

Side Street Inn ◐ [S] 24 | 7 | 15 | $21

1225 Hopaka St. (Piikoi St.), 808-591-0253

■ Though some say it's "more a bar than a restaurant", this "unpretentious" Ala Moana "hole-in-the-wall" is "known for" "simple", "out-of-this-world" Hawaiian "comfort food" at "bargain prices" and is "especially" "popular for its" "delicious" "fried pork chops", "the house specialty", as well as "very good blackened ahi" and "surprising chicken katsu"; an "always-busy favorite" of "in-the-know" "local folks", it's also "frequented by" some of "Hawaii's greatest chefs", who "can be found" "hanging out" and "feasting" "when off duty."

3660 ON THE RISE [S] 27 | 20 | 23 | $46

3660 Waialae Ave. (Wilhelmina Rise), 808-737-1177

■ "The best of Hawaii's cutting-edge Pacific Rim cuisine" awaits at this "hidden" "find in Kaimuki", a "quiet neighborhood" "away from the hubbub of Waikiki", where a "wizard" of a "creative chef"-owner, Russell Siu, "rises to the occasion" with "fresh, inspiring" specialties ("try the ahi katsu", "the best around") accompanied by a "great wine list" and offered with "pampering service" from an "accommodating staff"; P.S. "save room for" the "wonderful", "decadent desserts", such as the "truly *ono* Mile-High Waialae Pie" or the "No. 1 bread pudding in the known universe."

TOP 20 FOOD RANKING

Restaurant	Cuisine Type
28 Mark's	New American
La Réserve	French
27 Ruth's Chris	Steakhouse
26 Cafe Annie	Southwestern
Rotisserie/Beef & Bird	American
Brennan's Houston	Southwestern/Creole
Chez Nous	French
Tony's	Continental
Pappas Bros.	Steakhouse
Damian's	Northern Italian
Anthony's	Continental/New American
25 Café/Pâtisserie Descours	French Bistro
Ruggles Grille 5115	New American/French
Ruggles Grill	Southwestern/New American
Morton's of Chicago	Steakhouse
Aldo's	Northern Italian
Churrascos	South American/Steakhouse
Mosquito Cafe	Eclectic
Cafe Red Onion	Latin American Fusion
La Mora	Northern Italian

ADDITIONAL NOTEWORTHY PLACES

Américas	Latin American
Amerigo's Grille	Northern Italian
Aries	New American
benjy's	New American/Asian
Capital Grille	Steakhouse
Daily Review Café	New American
Da Marco	N&S Italian
Goode Co. Barbeque	Barbecue
Goode Co. Texas Seafood	Seafood
Indika	Indian
Irma's	Mexican
La Griglia	N&S Italian
Mockingbird Bistro	New American
Ouisie's Table	Southern/Eclectic
Quattro	New American/N&S Italian
Rainbow Lodge	Gulf Coast/Seafood
Saba Blue Water Cafe	Asian/Caribbean
Scott's Cellar	Asian/Continental
Tony Mandola's	Cajun/N&S Italian
Zula	New American

Aldo's Dining con Amore 25 | 19 | 21 | $63

219 Westheimer Rd. (bet. Brazos & Taft Sts.), 713-523-2536

■ When you're "in the mood" for an "opulent experience", it's hard to beat this "intimate" Montrose Northern Italian where "the word 'no' does not exist" for chef-owner Aldo El-Sharif, who "caters to your every culinary whim" while his "attentive" staff will even "put the doggy bag in your car"; though your "jaw may hit the floor" when the bill arrives, true believers say it's worth every penny to feast on the "exotic dishes" (like kangaroo, zebra, lion) showcased on the five-course prix fixe "spoken menu."

Américas 24 | 26 | 21 | $35

The Pavilion, 1800 Post Oak Blvd. (bet. San Felipe St. & Westheimer Rd.), 713-961-1492

■ The "fantasy-world" decor of this multilevel Latin American near the Galleria is so "amazing" it even threatens to "overwhelm" chef Michael Cordúa's "innovative", "magically" presented and "drop-dead delicious" cooking; similarly diverting are the "beautiful patrons" who fill this "trendy" spot to the "brim", especially during the "fabulous tapas happy hours" in the "funky bar"; the only quibble: it gets "way too loud."

Amerigo's Grille [S] 25 | 22 | 24 | $34

Grogan's Park, 25250 Grogan's Park Dr. (Sawdust Rd.), The Woodlands, 281-362-0808

■ Those looking for a "reason to trek out to The Woodlands" should consider this "top-notch" Northern Italian, "one of the only" places in the area that's "quiet" (i.e. there are "few children" around) and offers "lots of elegance for the money"; best of all is its "fantastic" menu, which makes it "wonderful for a special occasion"; P.S. check out the second-floor piano lounge.

ANTHONY'S 26 | 24 | 24 | $46

Highland Vlg., 4007 Westheimer Rd. (Drexel Dr.), 713-961-0552

■ Such a "dream dinner" is an "experience worth the price" at this "elegant" Highland Village "classic", one of the "top choices" in town for a Continental–New American "business power lunch", a "special occasion" or prime "yuppie-watching" (it attracts a "hip, well-heeled crowd"); nearly as impressive as the "excellent" menu are the "beautiful bar and sunken dining room", though the "smooth" service strikes some as "snobbish."

Aries – | – | – | E

4315 Montrose Blvd. (Richmond Ave.), 713-526-4404

From the ashes of 43 Brasserie, Scott Tycer and his wife Annika (both born under the sign of Aries) have raised up this elegant Montrose New American in heartwarming homage to fresh Texas ingredients; the wine list sports eye-opening picks, while exotic coffees and teas provide an ideal finale.

benjy's IN THE VILLAGE [S] 24 | 20 | 21 | $28

Rice Village, 2424 Dunstan St. (Kelvin Dr.), 713-522-7602

■ "Skinny people dressed in black" adore the "state-of-the-art" decor and "trendy" atmosphere at this "popular" Rice Village New American whose "inventive" Asian-influenced dishes are only slightly upstaged by the stylish staff (the "waiters are even prettier than the food"); it's "crowded" and "noisy", but that's to be expected for an "LA-in-Houston" experience.

BRENNAN'S HOUSTON 🖪 | 26 | 27 | 26 | $44 |

3300 Smith St. (Stuart St.), 713-522-9711

■ About "as close to perfection as you can get", this Downtown cousin of New Orleans' Commander's Palace puts a Texas twist on Louisiana cuisine with Carl Walker's "over-the-top fabulous" Southwestern-Creole creations; ideal for a "special occasion" or to "wow out-of-towners", it exemplifies "Southern charm" and "tradition" with its "sophisticated yet friendly" service, "wonderful" atmosphere and "peaceful courtyard."

CAFE ANNIE | 26 | 26 | 25 | $53 |

1728 Post Oak Blvd. (San Felipe St.), 713-840-1111

☑ "Still elegant and chic" – and still the Most Popular restaurant in Houston – Robert Del Grande's "richly designed" ("who does those flower arrangements?") Tanglewood Southwestern sets the "standard that others must meet" thanks to chef Ben Berryhill's "fantastic", "avant-garde" creations presented like "works of art", along with an "ooh-la-la wine list" and "impeccable" service; given such a "world-class" experience, the "elite" crowd that flocks here doesn't seem to mind the "expensive" tabs.

Café Descours | 25 | 16 | 18 | $20 |

1330 Wirt Rd. (Westview Dr.), 713-681-8894

Pâtisserie Descours

1330 Wirt Rd. (Westview Dr.), 713-681-8894

■ "Desserts that'll make you change your lunch plans", as well as "fabulous breads and sandwiches", are the specialty of this "delightful" Spring Branch patisserie and next-door cafe (open evenings only), which for dinner serves "delicious" bistro favorites; in short, it's a welcome source of "affordable fine" French fare.

Cafe Red Onion | 25 | 15 | 18 | $18 |

3910 Kirby Dr. (Southwest Frwy./Hwy. 59 S.), 713-807-1122
12440 Northwest Frwy./Hwy. 290 (43rd St.), 713-957-0957
1111 Eldridge Pkwy. (Enclave Pkwy.), 281-293-7500

■ This "inspired" Latin American cafe's "upscale", spacious Kirby offshoot may look completely different from the Highway 290 "hole-in-the-wall" original ("buy some tablecloths already!"), but both offer the same, "knock-your-socks-off" fusion cooking; N.B. there's now a third branch on Eldridge.

Capital Grille 🖪 | 25 | 25 | 24 | $48 |

5365 Westheimer Rd. (Yorktown St.), 713-623-4600

■ "Catering to power brokers", this "dark", "clubby" Galleria steakhouse with "old-boy lawyer style" is an ideal "place to impress" clients due to its "first-class" dry-aged beef, winning wine list ("heavy and complete") and "stellar" service; P.S. the "see-and-be-seen" scene at the bar is "packed with singles" of the 30-plus persuasion.

Chez Nous | 26 | 22 | 25 | $48 |

217 S. Ave. G (Staitti St.), Humble, 281-446-6717

■ For that "special occasion", "when French classics are what you want", take the "drive from Houston" to this "beautiful" venue in Humble whose "unusual home" is a "converted church", a fitting locale for its divine rack of lamb and "foie gras that's a life-altering experience"; for this "absolute treasure", "urban dwellers" are quite "willing to venture" far into "suburbia."

Churrascos   25 | 21 | 22 | $31

Shepherd Sq., 2055 Westheimer Rd. (S. Shepherd Dr.), 713-527-8300
9705 Westheimer Rd. (Gessner Rd.), 713-952-1988

◪ Carnivores enter "meat-eaters' paradise" at this pair of South
American steakhouses that always satisfies "cravings" for its
namesake *churrasco* – "melt-in-your-mouth tender" beef anointed
with "garlicky" *chimichurri* sauce – as well as "bring-more-please"
plantain chips and "can't-be-beat" *tres leches* cake; surveyors
deem it a "winner", despite some gripes that it's too "crowded."

Daily Review Café 🖪   23 | 16 | 19 | $24

3412 W. Lamar St. (Dunlavy St.), 713-520-9217

■ "Filling a niche" in Montrose, this "sophisticated, metropolitan"
cafe "hidden" down a side street is a "neighborhood hit" thanks
to its "creative without being wacky" New American menu (top
pick? – "what else but the chicken pot pie", though it's nothing
like mom used to make), "happy" atmosphere and garden patio.

Da Marco   24 | 20 | 21 | $36

1520 Westheimer Rd. (bet. Mandell St. & Montrose Blvd.), 713-807-8857

■ Chef Marco Wiles is a "genius" rave fans of this Montrose Italian
"winner" where his "dazzlingly good" – make that "stellar" –
cooking is fashioned from a palette of "authentic" regional flavors;
most everyone approves of the staff that "aims to please", but
the eye-popping golden orange color scheme draws varying
responses: admirers call it "cute" and "charming", while skeptics
demand "explain the paint job."

Damian's Cucina Italiana   26 | 23 | 24 | $38

3011 Smith St. (Rosalie St.), 713-522-0439

■ "Dark and full of business suits", this Downtown "paragon" of
"old-world elegance" and "sophisticated" Tuscan interpretations
encourages loyalists to "linger" and "enjoy" a "take-your-time
dining" experience; the downside of such "pleasant" loitering:
customers on the clock report that the "office wasn't happy" about
the "three-hour lunch."

Goode Co. Barbeque 🖪   24 | 17 | 17 | $14

8911 Katy Frwy./I-10 W. (Campbell Rd.), 713-464-1901
5109 Kirby Dr. (bet. Bissonnet St. & Westpark Dr.), 713-522-2530

■ Despite "lots of competition", owner Jim Goode's "not-to-be-
missed" "cafeteria-style" smokehouse duo slow-cooks the "best
BBQ in Houston", maybe even "in Texas"; what wins hearts here
are the "incredible brisket" and "coup de grâce" pecan pie.

Goode Co. Texas Seafood 🖪   23 | 18 | 20 | $21

2621 Westpark Dr. (Kirby Dr.), 713-523-7154
10211 Katy Frwy./I-10 W. (Gessner Dr.), 713-464-7933

■ "Thick and zesty" gumbo is what insiders seek "when it's cold"
outside at this "bustling" pair of seafood diners; whether you opt
for the "funky" railroad-car "classic" off Kirby or the newer, "more
upscale" offshoot out on I-10, you'll wonder too if there could be
"anything better" than its "terrific" fried or oven-roasted oysters,
mesquite-grilled fish or "extra-fantastic" *campechana*?

Indika   – | – | – | E

12665 Memorial Dr. (Boheme Dr.), 713-984-1725

Amid Memorial's way-out-west wasteland of urban sprawl, this
recent Indian addition courtesy of chef-owner Anita Jaisinghani

showcases classic, distinctive Punjabi dishes refracted through the lens of modern American cooking (think crabmeat samosas with papaya-ginger chutney) and paired with a smart little wine list; as sophisticated as the menu is the chic interior, done up in warm colors and accented with cool cubist paintings.

Irma's
22 17 21 $16

22 N. Chenevert St. (Ruiz St.), 713-222-0767

☑ "Don't tell anyone else how good the food is here" plead amigos of this "funky" Warehouse District Mexican where "sweet" Irma Galvan's lemonade quenches the thirst of the customers in her always "crowded" dining room; it's "perfect for a pre-game dinner", never mind the "irritating" (and limited) spoken menu.

La Griglia 🖪
24 23 22 $32

River Oaks Ctr., 2002 W. Gray St. (bet. McDuffie & Shephard Sts.), 713-526-4700

■ When the "River Oaks crowd wants to be casual", it often heads to Tony Vallone's Italian "prize winner", where the "funky interior" houses a "great kitchen", a staff that operates with "tag-team precision" and the "highest density of young, beautiful people" in town; no surprise that some down-to-earth types find it just "too noisy", too "snobby" and "too 'in.'"

La Mora Cucina Toscana
25 23 23 $32

912 Lovett Blvd. (Montrose Blvd.), 713-522-7412

■ "That's *amore*" sigh surveyors smitten with this "top-notch" Northern Italian "gem" that's "as romantic as it gets" thanks to its "serene", "lovely setting" in a "well-hidden" Montrose "villa"; chef-owner Lynette Mandola's "exquisite" Tuscan fare (such as "light and airy gnocchi" and the "best" *ribollita*) sets hearts aflutter, while her "charming" staff treats diners "like valued friends", all of which "makes the uncomfortable chairs worth sitting on."

LA RÉSERVE
28 27 26 $53

Omni Hotel, 4 Riverway (Woodway Dr.), 713-871-8177

■ "Serious" from its "quiet", "elegant" atmosphere to the "outstanding", meticulously rendered classic French menu, this "beautiful" Galleria hotel dining room "can't be beat" as a "place to dress up and have a special night out"; it boasts a "fabulous, seasonal menu" backed by a "well-selected" list of wines and "professional" service, but better "bring your platinum" card; N.B. a post-*Survey* chef change may outdate the above Food score.

MARK'S AMERICAN CUISINE 🖪
28 25 25 $43

1658 Westheimer Rd. (bet. Dunlavy & Ralph Sts.), 713-523-3800

■ "Feast at the altar of haute cuisine" at this "simply superlative" New American "cathedral of innovation" (voted No. 1 for Food in Houston) in Montrose, where acolytes report a near-"religious experience" thanks to "genius" chef-owner Mark Cox's "inspired" creations that find a fittingly "celestial" backdrop in this "chic" converted "brick church"; the only hint of impiety regards the "claustrophobically" "close quarters", though a recent renovation may be the answer to surveyors' prayers.

Mockingbird Bistro 🖪
– – – M

1985 Welch (McDuffie St.), 713-533-0200

Though the oddball cathedral decor at this Montrose newcomer owes something to Disney's *Hunchback of Notre Dame*, the food is straight-ahead New American bistro fare, executed to a fare-thee-well; chef John Sheely finds the soul of basics such as seared chicken, pork chops and grilled lamb steaks, comforting his customers with comfort foods of the most satisfying sort, not to mention a wine list priced at a below-average markup.

Morton's of Chicago [S] 25 | 23 | 24 | $48

Centre at Post Oak, 5000 Westheimer Rd. (Post Oak Blvd.), 713-629-1946

■ The "dark" lighting and "masculine" atmosphere at this Galleria link of the upscale chophouse chain (perhaps "the best thing Chicago ever exported") provide a "clubby" backdrop for its "superb", "fabulously presented" steaks; for many admirers, it adds up to the carnivorous "meal of the year" and *the* place to visit when you "want to impress", but for customers not on an "expense account", the "pretentious" experience may feel "overdone."

Mosquito Cafe [S] 25 | 20 | 21 | $18

628 14th St. (Winnie St.), Galveston, 409-763-1010

■ It's "worth seeking" this "out-of-the-way" "jewel" of an Eclectic cafe housed in a "hip, cute" renovated building in Galveston's historic district, because on an island fusty with fried fish, its "inventive", "healthy food prepared with inspiration" is a "breath of fresh air" for vegetarians and carnivores alike.

Ouisie's Table [S] 23 | 22 | 20 | $30

3939 San Felipe St. (bet. Drexel Dr. & Willowick Rd.), 713-528-2264

◪ There's "always something great on the chalkboard" at "nice lady" Elouise Cooper Jones' "welcoming" and "hip" Southern-Eclectic, which River Oaks denizens find a "pleasant lunch spot", as well as a top choice for "delicious" dinner dishes that spin "fresh takes on old favorites" (like shrimp-and-cheese grits); keep in mind, though, that it may "cost more than you'd expect."

Pappas Bros. Steakhouse 26 | 24 | 24 | $49

5839 Westheimer Rd. (Bering Dr.), 713-780-7352

■ Yes, "there are a lot of steakhouses in Houston", but this "handsome" Pappas family contender near the Galleria is "among the best" (though its cigar-friendliness prompts some to label it "more humidor than restaurant"); "oil tycoons" praise the "impeccable" service, "excellent wine list", "wonderful sides" and, of course, the "select" beef, but "just make sure someone else picks up the tab" because it can get "insanely expensive."

Quattro [S] – | – | – | E

Four Seasons Hotel, 1300 Lamar St. (Austin St.), 713-276-4700

Invigorated after a multimillion-dollar, up-to-the-second redo, the Four Seasons' once-staid dowager is now a sleek, less formal (and less intimidating) destination near Downtown's Convention Center; still a magnet for the high-stakes business crowd, it's attempting to attract a more diverse clientele as well with chef Tim Keating's approachable New American–Italian menu and a daily changing antipasti bar; the service, meanwhile, is as smooth and unobtrusive as ever.

Rainbow Lodge [S] 23 | 27 | 21 | $40

1 Birdsall St. (Memorial Dr.), 713-861-8666

■ Enraptured visitors to this charmer beside Buffalo Bayou "can't say enough good things" about its "beautiful setting", an upscale "hunting lodge" filled with hunting and fishing collectibles where diners can "watch for peacocks" and wildlife while roaming a menu of "excellent game" and Gulf Coast seafood dishes; it's quite a "wonderful choice for a romantic" meal (never mind if there are a few "too many prom dresses" here).

ROTISSERIE FOR BEEF & BIRD 26 | 23 | 25 | $43

2200 Wilcrest Dr. (Westheimer Rd.), 713-977-9524

■ In this mad, mad world, it's hard to find a restaurant that's been "very, very good" for a couple of dozen years, but this "superb" Far West American still garners raves from diners who indulge their "more exotic moods" with its "excellent wild game dishes"; an "inspired wine list" and "elegant" atmosphere round out the "delightful" experience at this "classic."

Ruggles Grill [S] 25 | 18 | 17 | $33

903 Westheimer Rd. (Montrose Blvd.), 713-524-3839

■ At Bruce and Susan Molzan's Montrose mothership, "enormous helpings" of "adventurous" Southwestern–New American fare eventually land on your table after an "always-long wait", "even with reservations"; for such an "awesome" meal, masochistic mavens are willing to "suffer" "claustrophobic" seating and "legendarily" "snobby" service, but not without griping that this is "not a tightly run ship."

Ruggles Grille 5115 25 | 25 | 21 | $36

Saks Fifth Avenue, The Galleria, 5115 Westheimer Rd. (bet. Post Oak Blvd. & Sage Rd.), 713-963-8067

■ Take a Galleria breather to "sink into a posh chair and dig into the richest desserts you've ever tasted", preceded by "creative" New American–French dishes served in "huge portions" at this "swanky sanctuary" tucked inside Saks; it's a "special place to dine within a special place to shop" say bag-laden shoppers who bless this "oasis of peace" for service that's "much better than at the original" Ruggles.

RUTH'S CHRIS STEAK HOUSE [S] 27 | 22 | 24 | $45

6213 Richmond Ave. (bet. Fountainview Dr. & Hillcroft Ave.), 713-789-2333
14135 Southwest Frwy./Hwy. 59 S. (bet. Dairy Ashford Rd. & Williams Trace Blvd.), Sugar Land, 281-491-9300

■ Houston's chophouse of choice, this "excellent" chain is simply the "best" swear carnivores partial to these beefy outposts west of the Galleria and in Sugar Land; "always perfect" and "sizzling" and accompanied by "fabulous" sides ("their asparagus – yum!"), the prime steaks are served in an "elegant" setting, offering a "quality" way to blow your oil millions.

Saba Blue Water Cafe – | – | – | M

416 Main St. (bet. Prairie & Preston Sts.), 713-228-7222

A jaw-dropping beauty of an aquarium with a beachy backdrop painting of cavorting nudes dominates this techno-sleek Downtown diner, complementing the menu of sexy salads and entrees inspired by islands spanning the seas from Asia to the Caribbean; at happy hour, bright young things crowd the bar for cocktails and tapas.

Scott's Cellar 24 | 25 | 24 | $50

6540 San Felipe Dr. (Voss Rd.), 713-785-8889

■ Supplicants "save up" for the "radical", "adventurous" Asian-Continental menu and a "wine list from the gods" at this chef-owned "fusion heaven" near the Galleria; the five-course "White Glove" tasting menu bestows an "evening's entertainment for the senses", stoking quiet foodie fervor amid the "beautiful" dining rooms and a "lounge with a fireplace"; bear in mind that the tabs "can really get expensive", but worshipers whisper it's "worth it" "at any price."

Tony Mandola's Gulf Coast Kitchen [S] 23 | 18 | 21 | $27

River Oaks Ctr., 1962 W. Gray St. (McDuffie St.), 713-528-3474

■ Its West Gray locale is "perfect for a long lunch away from the Downtown offices" say suits who "drop in" "at least once a week" at this "friendly, happy" Cajun-Italian "seafood heaven" and fight the "temptation to fill up" on the "outstanding appetizers" so that they'll have room for the "great variety" of "fresh" fish; with "excellent waiters" and "always-on-time reservations", no wonder its a "neighborhood favorite."

Tony's 26 | 25 | 26 | $60

1801 Post Oak Blvd. (bet San Felipe St. & Westheimer Rd.), 713-622-6778

■ "If God makes a reservation in Houston, it should be" at this Galleria Continental gush groupies of this "star of the Tony Vallone empire"; *the* place to "view Houston's society set in action", "Big T's" "continues to do a top-notch job" delivering "dreamy" dishes to the "diner who has everything", as well as to those who simply aspire to "feel like a baron or baroness" luxuriating in "sexy" surroundings "where any request is greeted warmly."

Zula – | – | – | E

705 Main St. (Capitol St.), 713-227-7052

Thanks to the concerted efforts of owners Dave Edwards and Steve Fronterhouse and showy chef Lance Fegen, this flashy, multimillion-dollar, split-level Downtown haunt is absolutely fabulous, right down to its glossy doggy boxes; spit-and-polish professionals flock here for glamorous dinners beginning with foie gras, while the budget-minded tend to congregate at lunch.

Kansas City

TOP 10 FOOD RANKING

Restaurant	Cuisine Type
26 Stroud's	American
American	New American
Plaza III	Steakhouse
25 Starker's Reserve	New American
Ruth's Chris	Steakhouse
Café Sebastienne	New American
Tatsu's	French
Grille on Broadway	New American
24 Fiorella's Jack Stack	Barbecue
zin	New American

ADDITIONAL NOTEWORTHY PLACES

Bristol Bar & Grill	Seafood
City Tavern	New American/Seafood
d'Bronx	Pizza/Sandwich Shop
40 Sardines	New American
Garozzo's	N&S Italian
Grand St. Cafe	Eclectic
Le Fou Frog	French Bistro
Lidia's	Northern Italian
McCormick & Schmick's	Seafood
MelBee's	New American

F	D	S	C

AMERICAN

26	25	26	$52

Crown Ctr., 200 E. 25th St. (Grand Ave.), 816-426-1133

■ As "romantic" as a "big Valentine", this "stunning" Downtown "icon" is the "perfect place if you're in the mood to be pampered"; a "favorite spot for a special occasion", it promises a "meal made in heaven" – a "fabulous" New American menu courtesy of chef Celina Tio, paired with an "exquisite wine list" and proffered by an "impeccable" staff in a "gorgeous room" with a "beautiful view."

Bristol Bar & Grill 🅂

24	22	22	$34

5400 W. 119th St. (Nall Ave.), Leawood, KS, 913-663-5777

■ "Fresh-from-the-oven" sugary biscuits that are "alone worth the trip", fish so pristine it "almost jumps off the plate" and a "glutton's-delight" Sunday brunch draw discerning diners to Leawood to this "suburban reincarnation of a classic Plaza restaurant"; "one of the busiest places in town", it's well manned by "enthusiastic" servers, but note that it can get quite "noisy" because "a lot's going on."

Café Sebastienne 🅂

25	24	21	$31

Kemper Museum of Contemporary Art, 4420 Warwick Blvd. (45th St.), 816-561-7740

■ Chef Jennifer Maloney's "quirky and delicious" New American cooking, distinguished by "intriguing combinations of flavor", "takes full advantage of what's fresh and seasonal"; as befits its setting in the Plaza's Kemper Museum, the cafe is adorned with a series of oil paintings by Frederick James Brown ("free art with every meal"), which makes it a "unique refuge from the ordinary"; just one "regret": dinner is served only on Fridays and Saturdays, but the "menu changes weekly" and it makes for a "great end to a day of viewing beautiful works."

City Tavern S   – | – | – | M
101 W. 22nd St. (Baltimore Ave.), 816-421-3696
Originally designed to be an outpost of NYC's venerable Oyster Bar, this New American seafood house in the Crossroads district now features Dennis Kaniger's inventive cooking; headlining a menu punctuated with straightforward steaks and seafood are specialties such as crab-and-corn-filled chile relleno and spicy grouper on a lentil pancake, all well paired with German or Scotch draught beers, small-batch bourbons or single-malt scotches and served in a room appointed with vintage architectural salvage pieces.

d'Bronx   24 | 12 | 15 | $11
3901 Bell St. (39th St.), 816-531-0550
Crown Ctr., 2450 Grand Ave. (25th St.), 816-842-2211 S
■ For "d'best" pizzas and deli sandwiches (notably a "Reuben to die for") "in town, period", head straight to one of these two "quintessential", "very busy" Italian joints ("run by a family loaded with personality") Downtown and in Westport to "take a break from the diet your cardiologist prescribed"; since you're already not counting calories, top off the meal with a slice of the "amazing" sour cream apple pie; any wonder that you'll always find a "good cross section of Kansas City" "hanging" out here?

FIORELLA'S JACK STACK S   24 | 21 | 20 | $20
13441 Holmes Rd. (135th St.), 816-942-9141
101 W. 22nd St. (Wyandotte St.), 816-472-7427
9520 Metcalf Ave. (95th St.), Overland Park, KS, 913-385-7427
■ "Don't wear your best shirt" if you're visiting this "killer" BBQ chainlet, voted the Most Popular restaurant in Kansas City, because the "amazing" vittles are finger-lickingly messy (especially the crown prime short ribs) and they're teamed with "out-of-this-world sides" (including "baked beans good enough to commit crimes for"); one caveat: no reservations accepted.

40 Sardines S   – | – | – | M
11942 Roe Ave. (119th St.), Overland Park, KS, 913-451-1040
James Beard award-winning chefs Debbie Gold and Michael Smith have left Downtown's American restaurant to open their own hip place in Overland Park; already packing them in are their satisfying New American dishes (think braised beef ribs over homemade pappardelle noodles, sautéed halibut in a summer vegetable stew and ethereal lemon meringue pie), approachable wine list and moderate prices.

Garozzo's   22 | 15 | 19 | $24
526 Harrison St. (Missouri Ave.), 816-221-2455
12801 E. Hwy. 40 (Norfleet Rd.), Independence, 816-737-2400 S
1547 NE Rice Rd. (Hwy. 291), Lee's Summit, 816-554-2800 S
9950 College Blvd. (Mastin St.), Overland Park, KS, 913-491-8300 S
☑ "Frank Sinatra is always playing" in the background and the "garlic just won't stop" at this "big, hearty, old-style" Italian

institution; it's "very noisy", constantly "busy" and the portions are so "large" they can "scare you", but you "won't find chicken spiedini as good anywhere else", nor servers as "entertaining."

Grand St. Cafe S   23 | 22 | 23 | $31
4740 Grand St. (47th St.), 816-561-8000

■ At this Plaza "jewel", the "wonderful variety" of "unique", "trend-conscious" Eclectic dishes "reflects the region's resources and tastes", making it a "good spot to take out-of-towners for a taste of KC" ("you must try the huge pork chop" and "decadent phyllo brownie dessert"); combined with pleasant patio dining, "affable" service and live jazz (on Mondays), it adds up to a "relaxing and enjoyable place" that's "well above average across the board"; P.S. check out the "wonderful Sunday brunch."

Grille on Broadway S   25 | 15 | 21 | $32
3605 Broadway (Valentine Rd.), 816-531-0700

■ "Tucked away in Midtown", this "cozy" "sleeper" is "one of the best spots for a romantic little getaway"; the New American menu emphasizes "excellent, creative seafood" dishes prepared "with flair" (the "Chilean sea bass is always a winner" and the "crab cakes alone are worth the trip"), and the "personable service reminds one of the days when unobtrusive friendliness was an art", but the quarters are "miniscule", so "claustrophobes" better "get used to very little elbow room."

Le Fou Frog S   24 | 15 | 20 | $40
400 E. Fifth St. (Oak St.), 816-474-6060

■ Don't be deterred by the "deceptively bland exterior" of this "cheeky" French bistro in the River Market area because the kitchen shows "a lot of dedication to food" and the "marvelous" cooking is well enhanced by a "smart wine list", which explains why "everyone from twentysomething hipsters to big-shot lawyers and judges eat here with gusto"; follow the lead of the "completely smitten" and just "enjoy the hustle and bustle" of this "splendid little place" while "friendly, prompt" servers tend to your needs.

LIDIA'S S   22 | 27 | 21 | $32
101 W. 22nd St. (Baltimore Ave.), 816-221-3722

☑ Boasting a "drop-dead gorgeous" interior designed by David Rockwell, this "lively" Northern Italian near Union Station is the co-creation of Lidia Bastianich; exuding a "sense of excitement and anticipation", it features "generously portioned" dishes at relatively "wallet-pleasing" prices, notably a daily changing "pasta sampler", along with a wine list filled with $20 bottles; detractors, however, find it "disappointingly mediocre" and lament "if only the food could be stepped up a few notches to match the atmosphere."

MCCORMICK & SCHMICK'S S   24 | 25 | 22 | $36
448 W. 47th St. (Pennsylvania Ave.), 816-531-6800

■ "For landlocked Midwesterners", this "upscale" seafood house is "the answer", thrilling fin fanatics with a "selection bar none" of "fish so fresh it may still be jumping on your plate" and an "impressive" oyster bar that "must be a wonderful dream"; perhaps even more "fabulous" is the "extraordinary" interior appointed with a "majestic stained-glass dome", mahogany woodwork and brass fixtures, and the "picturesque" deck "overlooking the Plaza"; even those who are "totally against chains have to admit that this one does a great job."

MelBee's ◐ – | – | – | E

6120 Johnson Dr. (Lamar Ave.), Mission, KS, 913-262-6121
Executive chef John Beasley's impressive resume – from Aqua in San Francisco to zin in Kansas City – speaks volumes on the New American menu at this dressy-casual Mission newcomer where his collection of beautifully composed small plates shows whimsy and intelligence; the only quibble: such thoughtfully conceived dishes deserve a more ambitious wine list.

PLAZA III THE STEAKHOUSE [S] 26 | 23 | 24 | $42

Country Club Plaza, 4749 Pennsylvania Ave. (Ward Pkwy.), 816-753-0000
■ Though the "world may change", thankfully this Plaza palace of beef "stays the same" say longtime loyalists; "red meat rules here, so just leave the guilt at home" and fork into the "best steak in Kansas City", so "perfectly cooked" and "deliciously tender" that "cows should line up for the chance to be served"; rounding out the picture is an award-winning wine list, "throwback" "classic" setting and "knowledgeable", "polite" staff.

RUTH'S CHRIS STEAK HOUSE [S] 25 | 21 | 22 | $46

700 W. 47th St. (Jefferson St.), 816-531-4800
◪ If you like your beef "sizzling, juicy" and "soaked in butter", amble over to this Plaza standby, which has earned begrudging respect from many locals ("a chain steakhouse in KC? – horrors!") and is "doing very well in a city that knows its meat"; "for the price, you may be able to buy your own cow", so "save this place for the expense account", though hometown supporters who are adamant that you certainly "can find better chops" in this town conclude an "admirable effort, but not quite the prime cut of other mainstays."

STARKER'S RESERVE 25 | 23 | 24 | $43

Country Club Plaza, 201 W. 47th St. (Wyandotte St.), 816-753-3565
■ Overlooking Country Club Plaza, this "charming hideaway" appointed with Country French decor is "renowned" for its "mind-boggling wine list", which beautifully accompanies a "quietly superb", regularly changing New American menu (the signature herb-roasted rack of lamb is "not to be missed") presented by a "classy" staff that "attends to every human need without hovering"; while a few find it all a "bit staid", admirers cherish it as a "special-occasion" "gem" that always promises a "magical evening."

STROUD'S [S] 26 | 13 | 20 | $19

1015 E. 85th St. (Troost Ave.), 816-333-2132
5410 NE Oak Ridge Rd. (I-35 & Vivion Rd.), 816-454-9600
■ "Forget your diet, forget your arteries" – "if it's pan-fried chicken you want, this is the place" exclaim enthusiasts of this "campy" pair of traditional American roadhouses on the South Side and Northland, whose "down-home" cooking is so "mouthwatering" (don't pass up the "absolutely sinful cinnamon rolls" either) that it was voted No. 1 for Food in Kansas City; sure, "there's always a line out the door", but "just bring a lawn chair, a novel and some snacks to tide you over" – it's definitely "worth the wait."

Tatsu's 25 | 19 | 22 | $36

4603 W. 90th St. (Roe Ave.), Prairie Village, KS, 913-383-9801
◪ "Consistently exquisite year after year after year", this "haute" French grande dame in "out-of-the-way" Prairie Village appeals to an "older crowd" with its "conservative" (or "overly traditional"?),

"rich" "classics" napped with "delectable sauces"; though it's a "solid performer", detractors lament that it's "rarely exciting or memorable" and suggest the "clichéd" "menu could use some new life" (bigger portions too).

zin

24　23　22　$43

1900 Main St. (19th St.), 816-527-0120

☑ "For a meat 'n' potatoes town", this "happy, hopping" New American addition to Downtown's Crossroads art district is "doing very well" thanks to a "clever", "constantly changing" menu that's always "a fresh surprise", teamed with a "brainy wine list" (natch, as it's named after the diminutive term for Zinfandel) and turned out in "swankily" "minimalist" environs; though dissenters find it a "bit contrived" and warn about "small" portions ("plan to leave hungry"), "nothing else in Kansas City feels as urban" as this "one-of-a-kind" "up-and-comer."

Las Vegas

TOP 20 FOOD RANKING

Restaurant	Cuisine Type
28 Renoir	New French
Aqua	Seafood
27 Picasso	New French
Andre's	French
Le Cirque	French
Nobu	Japanese/Peruvian
Prime	Steakhouse
Morton's of Chicago	Steakhouse
26 Rosemary's	New American
Delmonico	Steakhouse
Steak House	Steakhouse
Mayflower Cuisinier	Chinese
Trumpets	New American
Michael's	American/Continental
Wild Sage Café	New American
Palm	Seafood/Steakhouse
25 Emeril's New Orleans	Cajun-Creole/Seafood
Commander's Palace	Creole
Hugo's Cellar	Continental/Steakhouse
Charlie Palmer	Steakhouse/New American

ADDITIONAL NOTEWORTHY PLACES

Aureole	New American
Craftsteak	Steakhouse
Del Frisco's	Steakhouse
Eiffel Tower	French
808	Pacific Rim
Lutèce	New French
Mon Ami Gabi	French Bistro
NOBHILL	American
Osteria del Circo	Northern Italian
Pearl	Chinese
Piero's	Northern Italian
Piero Selvaggio Valentino	Northern Italian
Postrio	New American
Ruth's Chris	Steakhouse
Samba	Brazilian/Steakhouse
Spago	Californian
Spiedini	N&S Italian
Terrazza	Northern Italian
Top of the World	Continental
Verandah	Eclectic/American

subscribe to zagat.com

ANDRE'S
27 | 25 | 26 | $59

401 S. Sixth St. (bet. Bridger & Clark Aves.), 702-385-5016

ANDRE'S IN THE MONTE CARLO 🄢
Monte Carlo Resort & Casino, 3770 Las Vegas Blvd. S. (bet. Harmon & Tropicana Aves.), 702-798-7151

■ "Pure Andre" is local shorthand for "simply the best", which is how smitten fans view these two "romantic and special" Classic French "gems", one a "Downtown institution", the other a "Monte Carlo surprise"; chef Rochat is the man under the toque, and he knows how to produce "great cuisine", stock his cellars with "wonderful, rare wines" and then serve it all up in "comfortable, elegant" settings rich with "European charm."

AQUA 🄢
28 | 25 | 26 | $62

Bellagio, 3600 Las Vegas Blvd. S. (Flamingo Rd.), 702-693-7111

■ "Neptune would be proud" of this Bellagio branch of an acclaimed San Francisco seafood house, where admirers are hooked on "the best fish in the desert", including "to-die-for lobster pot pie" and other "flawless" fin fare, as well as "anything with foie gras"; its "beautiful, modern setting" in the Conservatory and "top-class service" tip the scales to make this a "fabulous" experience, and though some mutineers mutter it's "too pricey", others opine "it's worth every penny."

Aureole 🄢
24 | 27 | 23 | $66

Mandalay Bay Hotel, 3950 Las Vegas Blvd. S. (Tropicana Ave.), 702-632-7401

■ The four-story "glass-walled Tower of Wine" is a "vision", as are the cable-powered "glitzy 'angels'" who retrieve your bottle from over 3,000 choices at this Mandalay Bay New American, a flashier sibling of Charlie Palmer's NYC original; most hail the cuisine as "inventive" and of the "highest-caliber", and swoon for the separate Swan Court room, but the disgruntled deem it "overrated" with prices that "soar as high as the architecture."

Charlie Palmer Steak 🄢
25 | 26 | 25 | $62

Four Seasons Hotel, 3960 Las Vegas Blvd. S. (Hacienda Ave.), 702-632-5120

■ "Tucked away in the blissfully quiet Four Seasons", this New American steakhouse is a "popular" "oasis" with a "luxurious" atmosphere seemingly light years from all the razzle-dazzle, where Aureole's Charlie Palmer puts his special spin on "absolutely exquisite" beef and seafood selections offered up with "outstanding side dishes" and a "great" (though "pricey") wine list; also, as one would expect in this "classy setting", the "superior service" makes for an evening of "pure comfort."

Commander's Palace 🄢
25 | 25 | 26 | $52

Desert Passage at Aladdin, 3663 Las Vegas Blvd. S. (Harmon Ave.), 702-892-8272

■ "Y'all will find Southern hospitality" at this "elegant" Creole, a two-year-old offshoot of "the New Orleans original", in the Desert Passage; loyal subjects laud its "excellent stone-ground grits" with goat cheese, "must-try turtle soup" and "extremely fresh fish", though they're not easy on the wallet (it's "pricey"); Dixieland jazz on weekends, the "best" complimentary pralines and the presence of managing partner Brad Brennan (of the famed restaurant dynasty) add to the authenticity.

Craftsteak 🖬 — — — E

MGM Grand Hotel, 3799 Las Vegas Blvd. S. (Tropicana Ave.), 702-891-7318
In a city filled with fine steakhouses, this elegant and serene MGM
Grand Hotel newcomer from chef Tom Colicchio (of New York City's
Craft and Gramercy Tavern) already has carnivores crowing about
its aged grain- and grass-fed beef, as well as its plethora of seldom-
seen meats, fish and shellfish and housemade charcuterie; a
terrific lounge, good wine list and caring staff round out its appeal;
N.B. dinner only.

Del Frisco's — — — E
Double Eagle Steak House 🖬

3925 Paradise Rd. (Corporate Dr.), 702-796-0063
Just minutes from the Strip, this clubby two-year-old (the fifth
location of a small-but-growing family) brings a touch of Lone
Star–style hospitality to Sin City, with a friendly staff serving up
excellent steaks, such as the signature Double Eagle strip, and
schools of seafood (such as halibut with citrus vinaigrette) within
a handsome, wood-rich dining room; N.B. the spacious cigar
lounge is the place to savor a stogie before or after dinner.

Delmonico 🖬 26 24 25 $59

*Venetian Hotel, 3355 Las Vegas Blvd. S. (bet. Flamingo &
Spring Mountain Rds.), 702-414-3737*
■ It's "the very best of Emeril" at chef Lagasse's "gourmet"
New Orleans–style steakhouse in the Venetian Hotel, where you
can dine à la bam on "excellent garlic mashed potatoes" and other
favorites, washed down by wines from a list "longer than most
novels"; service is the "tops", "friendly but with a high degree of
professionalism", and though a few call the decor "too severe", it
doesn't stop the stampedes, so "book months in advance."

Eiffel Tower 🖬 22 26 22 $71

*Paris Las Vegas, 3655 Las Vegas Blvd. S. (bet. Flamingo Rd. &
Harmon Ave.), 702-948-6937*
■ The "incredible view of the Strip and Bellagio fountains" is an
eyeful at this literally "haute French" towering 11 floors above Las
Vegas Boulevard, in the Paris' scaled-down replica of Gustave's
glorious monument, where the "marvelous food", including "superb
foie gras" and "just-right lamb", is also to-sigh-for; even those who
find the "way expensive" *l'addition* absolutely in-Seine admit it's
an "unbelievable experience."

808 🖬 — — — VE

Caesars Palace, 3570 Las Vegas Blvd. S. (Flamingo Rd.), 702-731-7731
Chef Jean-Marie Josselin hula'd into town two years ago with this
seafood house in Caesars Palace named for Hawaii's area code,
and, appropriately, the phones have been ringing off the hook ever
since as diners dial for a table in the island-themed room; under
the toqueship of Wesley Coffel, the kitchen creates splendid Pacific
Rim fusion fare with a French accent, such as Deconstruction Ahi
Roll (tuna tartare, avocado and white truffle dressing).

Emeril's 25 22 25 $49
New Orleans Fish House 🖬

MGM Grand Hotel, 3799 Las Vegas Blvd. S. (Tropicana Ave.), 702-891-7374
☑ Starstruck surveyors say the "absolutely fabulous" Big Easy
eats "really kick it up a notch" at this MGM Grand Cajun-Creole

seafood house; though most say "everybody here has a great time", critics carp about "overhyped" fare and "sloppy service", wishing the telechef would "check up on his establishment" and offer more 'bam' "for the buck."

Hugo's Cellar [S] 25 | 23 | 25 | $44

Four Queens Hotel, 202 Fremont St. (Casino Center Dr.), 702-385-4011

■ "Elegant and timeless", this "Downtown institution" provides a "delightful dining experience" starting with "a rose for every lady"; the "classic" Continental steakhouse dinners include an "unbelievable salad cart" and "exceptional entrees" and end with "special chocolate-dipped fruit" after dessert, all served by a "charming" staff; though antagonists abase it as "past its prime", most maintain this stalwart is "still a winner."

LE CIRQUE [S] 27 | 26 | 26 | $74

Bellagio, 3600 Las Vegas Blvd. S. (Flamingo Rd.), 702-693-8100

■ "As good as the NYC original", this "fabulous" French at the Bellagio is "luxury defined" ("but not at all pretentious"), offering "impeccable service" in a "gorgeous" setting overlooking the lake; the "extraordinarily flavorful" fare is "elevated to art", "perfectly complemented by exquisite wines", with "delightful desserts" as an epilogue; epicureans agree "it's a joyous place to eat, drink and be merry" despite "eye-popping prices"; N.B. jacket required.

Lutèce [S] 25 | 23 | 24 | $71

Venetian Hotel, 3355 Las Vegas Blvd. S. (bet. Flamingo & Spring Mountain Rds.), 702-414-2220

■ The New French menu remains "elegant and fabulous" at this younger sibling of the NYC original in the Venetian, where "wonderful" food is set off nicely by what most call "beautiful" decor (though some find it "too stark") and "incredible" service; though it elicits a chorus of "overpriced", most adjudge it an "across-the-board winner."

Mayflower Cuisinier 26 | 20 | 23 | $34

Sahara Pavilion, 4750 W. Sahara Ave. (Decatur Blvd.), 702-870-8432

■ Pilgrims give thanks for this "unsurpassed" West Side Chinese "with French flair" where "incredible chef Ming See Woo" wows 'em with "the best noodles", "great fish" and "delicate sauces" that incorporate "unusual flavors"; the "delightful decor" includes "outstanding artwork", and the "personal service" helps make this a "must-visit."

Michael's [S] 26 | 22 | 26 | $64

Barbary Coast Hotel, 3595 Las Vegas Blvd. S. (Flamingo Rd.), 702-737-7111

■ "The staff fawns over you as you fawn over the food" at this Barbary Coast vet where VIPs have "every whim attended to" as they dine on "ultimate gourmet" American-Continental fare, preceded by a complimentary "relish tray full of delicacies"; the "classy", "quiet" setting features "lots of dark wood and red leather chairs" that produce an "old-world" feeling, but the "outrageous prices" are up-to-the-minute.

Mon Ami Gabi [S] 23 | 25 | 22 | $38

Paris Las Vegas, 3655 Las Vegas Blvd. S. (bet. Flamingo Rd. & Harmon Ave.), 702-944-4224

■ Francophiles profess it's "like eating on the Champs Elysées" at this "charming French bistro" at the Paris, where the "fantastic people-watching" and "beautiful view of the Bellagio fountains" are equaled by the *très* "yummy food" and "good wines"; some shun the "slow service", but most say it's a "great experience."

Morton's of Chicago [S] 27 | 25 | 24 | $52

400 E. Flamingo Rd. (Paradise Rd.), 702-893-0703

■ In a city where steakhouses abound, this East Side chain link of a "beef-eaters' bonanza" meets the "gold standard", serving "awesome steaks", "delicious seafood" and "decadent desserts" amid "elegant surroundings" that "enhance" the experience; though wallet-watchers warn "you'll pay a ton", weight-lifters retort it's "worth it every time."

NOBHILL [S] – | – | – | E

MGM Grand Hotel, 3799 Las Vegas Blvd. S. (Tropicana Ave.), 702-891-1111

Laid-back chic and dynamite cooking courtesy of chef Michael Mina and partner Charles Condy make this relaxing addition to the MGM Grand a happening spot; paying homage to San Francisco, the à la carte and tasting menus of American comfort fare include artisanal breads baked throughout the day and desserts warm from the showcase dining room oven.

Nobu ◐ [S] 27 | 25 | 22 | $58

Hard Rock Hotel, 4455 Paradise Rd. (bet. Flamingo Rd. & Harmon Ave.), 702-693-5090

■ "As good as its NYC namesake" rave the reverent about the Hard Rock's "outstanding neo-Japanese"; "sit at the sushi bar to marvel at the preparation" of "exquisite fresh fish" with a "spicy approach", or spring for the "heavenly" tasting menu consisting of a lineup of "exotic dishes with no anticlimax"; there's also "great celebrity spotting" in the "Zen-like setting", but a few dharma bums bash the minimalist portions and "way-out-there prices."

Osteria del Circo [S] 24 | 26 | 24 | $52

Bellagio, 3600 Las Vegas Blvd. S. (Flamingo Rd.), 702-693-8150

■ It's all in *la famiglia* at this Bellagio bistro managed by a son of Sirio (that's Maccioni, as in the more formal Le Cirque next door), who serves up "superb" Northern Italian fare inspired by mama Egidiana and prepared by chef de cuisine James Benson; the "whimsical" circus-themed, Adam Tihany–designed setting and "spectacular view of the fountain show" on 'Lake Como' provide a fitting overture for the "creative" yet "authentic" cooking.

PALM [S] 26 | 22 | 24 | $50

Forum Shops at Caesars, 3500 Las Vegas Blvd. S. (Flamingo Rd.), 702-732-7256

■ "Steak and lobster fit for Caesar" say those 'frond' of this spot at the Forum Shops, part of an "always-superb" "national chain without a missing link"; "big spenders" spring for "tremendous portions" of "excellent food" and little spenders vie for "Vegas' best $15 prix fixe lunch", all delivered in a "clubhouse setting" with "celebrity-adorned walls"; it may be "noisy as hell", but gents can retreat to the loo and dig the Elvis look-alike attendant.

Pearl [S] – | – | – | E

MGM Grand Hotel, 3799 Las Vegas Blvd. S. (Tropicana Ave.), 702-891-7380

Set in the MGM Grand's former Dragon Court space, this stylish Chinese newcomer features a tea trolley that offers individualized tableside service, and both à la carte and family-style menus with

Cantonese and Shanghai specialties, including many signature dishes of chef Kai-Wai Yau, a Hong Kong native, such as his succulent steamed Maine and Australian lobster tasting; in addition to the main dining room, the two private rooms also offer show-stopping contemporary decor.

PICASSO 🖫 | 27 | 29 | 28 | $79 |

Bellagio, 3600 Las Vegas Blvd. S. (Flamingo Rd.), 702-693-7223
■ The work of two "awe-inspiring" artists is featured at this "destination" in the Bellagio, the Most Popular restaurant in Las Vegas: in the kitchen, "genius" Julian Serrano creates "innovative" tasting and prix fixe menus comprising "spectacular" French dishes "flawlessly served", while the "opulent" interior includes "beautiful flowers", "lake views" and, oh yeah, Picasso paintings that make you "feel like you're dining in a museum"; in fact, the only thing that's not "*magnifico*" is a "hard-to-get" reservation, so book well in advance.

Piero Selvaggio Valentino 🖫 | 23 | 21 | 22 | $57 |
(aka Valentino)

Venetian Hotel, 3355 Las Vegas Blvd. S. (bet. Flamingo & Spring Mountain Rds.), 702-414-3000
◪ This "elegant" Venetian Hotel Northern Italian collects valentines from the cognoscenti, who call the cuisine "superb" (particularly the "wonderful pastas"), especially as it's accompanied by a "bang-up wine list" of more than 20,000 bottles and served by a staff that treats you "like royalty"; however, antagonists argue it's "oceans away from the LA" original, adding it's "overrated."

Piero's Italian Cuisine 🖫 | 24 | 22 | 23 | $52 |

355 Convention Center Dr. (bet. Las Vegas Blvd. & Paradise Rd.), 702-369-2305
■ If you're "looking for the old Vegas", you'll find it at this off-Strip bastion of "upscale Northern Italian" eats known as "the place to network with local shakers" and a "celebrity hangout"; a "good Caesar", "killer osso buco" and the "best Florida stone crabs" (in season) are served in a "romantic" setting with "dark lighting", but a few sniff at the "snooty waiters" and sneer it's "overpriced."

Postrio 🖫 | 24 | 24 | 23 | $48 |

Venetian Hotel, 3355 Las Vegas Blvd. S. (bet. Flamingo & Spring Mountain Rds.), 702-796-1110
■ "He's done it again" assert adherents of Wolfgang Puck's Venetian Hotel New American "delight" cloned from the San Francisco original; the "interesting menu" stars "great duck-sausage pizza" capped by the "planet's best crème brûlée", and though a few find it a bit "pretentious", its regulars recommend you "sit on the plaza and enjoy" the view of St. Mark's Square.

Prime 🖫 | 27 | 28 | 27 | $64 |

Bellagio, 3600 Las Vegas Blvd. S. (Flamingo Rd.), 702-693-7111
■ Jean-Georges Vongerichten is in his prime at this "transcendent" Bellagio Hotel steakhouse, about which even blasé beef lovers burble like the "breathtaking fountains" viewed windowside; beyond "perfect steaks", partisans proclaim the veggies "fabulous" and swoon for the "splendid", "airy" interior "draped in velvety blues and browns"; the staff is "concerned and prompt", and while you'll pay primo prices, it's "well worth it."

RENOIR
28 | 28 | 27 | $76

Mirage Hotel, 3400 Las Vegas Blvd. S. (Spring Mountain Rd.), 702-791-7353

■ The "sublime", "Paris-quality" meal is as much "a work of art" as the eponymous painter's originals adorning the walls of chef Alessandro Stratta's "superb" New French "heaven" at the Mirage, where the "imaginative" offerings were voted "the very Top" for Food among Las Vegas restaurants; the "expert" staff works together "like a ballet" in "plush, romantic surroundings" that make for "a calm and relaxing world away from the chaos."

ROSEMARY'S S
26 | 22 | 24 | $45

W. Sahara Promenade, 8125 W. Sahara Ave. (bet. Buffalo Dr. & Cimarron Rd.), 702-869-2251
Rio Suite Hotel, 3700 W. Flamingo Rd. (I-15), 702-777-2300

■ "The biggest hit in the desert" may be this New American three-year-old where husband-and-wife toque team Michael and Wendy Jordan "kick it up a notch" (Mike cooked under Emeril in New Orleans) with a "marvelous selection" of "innovative" fare; the "good service" and "attractive" art-filled decor also impress, though a few grouse the "tables are too close together"; N.B. the new location at the Rio opened post-*Survey.*

Ruth's Chris Steak House S
24 | 21 | 23 | $48

Citibank Park Plaza, 3900 Paradise Rd. (bet. Flamingo Rd. & Twain Ave.), 702-791-7011
Cameron Corner Shopping Ctr., 4561 W. Flamingo Rd. (bet. Arville St. & Decatur Blvd.), 702-248-7011 ◗

◢ "Always dependable", these steakhouse chain links on the East and West Sides are known for "unbeatable slabs o' beef" and a "range of wines" as well as a "knowledgeable staff"; opponents ruthlessly report that an overuse of "butter camouflages the meat" and claim that they're "overpriced."

Samba Brazilian Steakhouse S
23 | 23 | 23 | $36

Mirage Hotel, 3400 Las Vegas Blvd. S. (Spring Mountain Rd.), 702-791-7111

■ Gluttonous gourmands go to town at this "carnivore's paradise", courtesy of the Mirage and their "Brazilian-style feast" known as rodizio (which loosely translates as "more and more and still more keeps coming"); a hip-swaying "Latin beat" accompanies the rotisserie items, making the experience "dining and entertainment wrapped into one" – and all at a "reasonable price."

Spago S
25 | 22 | 23 | $42

Forum Shops at Caesars, 3500 Las Vegas Blvd. S. (Flamingo Rd.), 702-369-0360

■ "Always a favorite", this Wolfgang Puck pioneer in the Forum Shops at Caesars continues to "set the standard" with its "still cutting-edge menu" of Californian fare; the wolf pack devours the signature "succulent salmon pizza" and partakes of "great people-watching" on the patio or in the "more elegant dining room", and though service comments roam from "warm" to "disappointing", the gang agrees it "lives up to the hype."

Spiedini S
23 | 24 | 22 | $39

JW Marriott Las Vegas, 221 N. Rampart Blvd. (Summerlin Pkwy.), 702-869-8500

■ "It's fun to spend an evening" at this "it" Italian at the JW Marriott Las Vegas in Summerlin, where "hospitable owner"

Gustav Mauler and the "modern decor" create a "cozy" setting; the food's "excellent", the wine's "reasonable" and the "only drawback is the noise" from all the delighted diners.

STEAK HOUSE [S] 26 | 23 | 25 | $38

Circus Circus Hotel, 2880 Las Vegas Blvd. S. (Sahara Ave.), 702-794-3767

■ There's "no clowning around with the steaks" at this "icon" set in the Circus Circus Hotel, where promoters parade into a "romantic atmosphere" for "huge portions" of "fantastic meats", seafood and "excellent salads" at "best-bargain" prices; "be sure to reserve" in advance – it's a hot ticket – and check out the "out-of-this-world Sunday brunch."

Terrazza [S] 22 | 24 | 23 | $46

Caesars Palace, 3570 Las Vegas Blvd. S. (Flamingo Rd.), 702-731-7731

■ Facing the Garden of the Gods at Caesars Palace, this Northern Italian features "well-prepared dishes" that are "delicious to the last bite", while the dining room offers "wonderful" ambiance and "solid", "attentive" service; P.S. "go early", as it can get "crowded."

Top of the World [S] 23 | 27 | 22 | $48

Stratosphere Hotel & Tower, 2000 Las Vegas Blvd. S. (north of Sahara Ave.), 702-380-7711

■ Even the most worldly sigh for the "stunning views" at this "romantic" revolving room high atop the Stratosphere Hotel & Tower; the "gourmet" Continental menu includes many "excellent choices" to pair with the "special wine list", and the "experienced servers" are tops too, but wallet-watchers warn "bring lots of money" with which to tender the towering tariff.

Trumpets [S] 26 | 28 | 25 | $33

Sun City Anthem Ctr., 2450 Hampton Rd. (Anthem Pkwy.), Henderson, 702-614-5858

■ "Spectacular views of the city" hit the right note at this New American spot located in the recently built Anthem Center in Henderson; the menu is "wonderful", with service to match, and grown-ups go for the "quiet" ambiance (enhanced by a weekend jazz quartet) and get up early for the "great Sunday brunch."

Verandah [S] 24 | 24 | 24 | $36

Four Seasons Hotel, 3960 Las Vegas Blvd. S. (Tropicana Ave.), 702-632-5000

■ The "epitome of elegance", this Four Seasons Eclectic-American boasts a "charming" interior and gardenside patio dining that's "conducive to relaxing with friends" over breakfast, lunch, dinner and "very good high tea"; detractors dismiss it as "an overgrown coffee shop", but the majority maintains the "food's wonderful" and the "service is excellent."

Wild Sage Café [S] 26 | 21 | 23 | $31

600 E. Warm Springs Rd. (Amigo St.), 702-944-7243

■ "Puck prodigies" Laurie Kendrick and Stan Carroll run this "casual", "hip" New American, widely recognized as one of "the best off-Strip restaurants in town" thanks to an "imaginative menu and decor", "gorgeous preparations", "great breads" and "reasonable prices"; in short, it's just "what this city needed."

Long Island

TOP 20 FOOD RANKING

Restaurant	Cuisine Type
28 Mill River Inn	New American
27 Mirabelle	New French
Kotobuki	Japanese
Mirepoix	International
Peter Luger	Steakhouse
Panama Hatties	New American
La Plage	Eclectic
26 Tellers	Steakhouse
Stone Creek Inn	French/Mediterranean
Mirko's	Continental/Eclectic
Da Ugo	N&S Italian
Sempre Vivolo	N&S Italian
La Piccola Liguria	Northern Italian
Sen	Japanese
Polo	New American
Coolfish	New American
Trattoria Diane	Northern Italian
Piccolo	N&S Italian/New American
25 Louis XVI	New French
Stresa	N&S Italian

ADDITIONAL NOTEWORTHY PLACES

American Hotel	French
Barney's	New French/New American
Bryant & Cooper	Steakhouse
Casa Rustica	N&S Italian
Della Femina	New American
Focaccia Grill	New American/N&S Italian
Harvest on Fort Pond	N. Italian/Med.
La Marmite	French/N&S Italian
La Pace	Northern Italian
L'Endroit	French/N. Italian
Le Soir	French Bistro
Maidstone Arms	American
Mario	Northern Italian
Mazzi	Continental
Morton's of Chicago	Steakhouse
Palm	Steakhouse/Seafood
Palm Court at the Carltun	Continental/New American
Plaza Cafe	New American
Robert's	N&S Italian/Seafood
Tupelo Honey	New American/Eclectic

American Hotel S   25 | 24 | 22 | $55 |
The American Hotel, Main St. (Bay St.), Sag Harbor, 631-725-3535
■ The "elegant grande dame of the East End", this Sag Harbor "landmark" (circa 1846) is "the place to go for special wines" to accompany "awesome", "incomparable" classic French dishes served by a "professional" (if a tad "pretentious") staff; attracting an eclectic crowd of "celebrities", the "intelligentsia" and seasonal "tourists", its "romantic", "old-world" ambiance "takes diners back to a lost era."

Barney's S   25 | 22 | 23 | $51 |
315 Buckram Rd. (Bayville Rd.), Locust Valley, 516-671-6300
■ Like an "intimate" "country inn" with a "charming" setting, this "upscale" Locust Valley "gem" is beloved for its "superb, creative" New French–New American menu, "exquisitely presented" by a "terrific" staff in "warm and inviting" surroundings (try to get a "candlelit table by the fireplace"); add on a "good wine selection that complements the food" beautifully and the result is a near-"perfect" "getaway with your sweetie."

BRYANT & COOPER   25 | 20 | 21 | $50 |
STEAKHOUSE S
2 Middle Neck Rd. (Northern Blvd.), Roslyn, 516-627-7270
■ A "moneyed crowd" descends upon this "outstanding" "classic" chophouse in Roslyn for "wonderfully aged", "sizable slabs" of prime cuts "cooked to perfection" and paired with "delicious sides" like "great creamed spinach"; "newcomers", though, "better know someone", since "regulars get preferential" treatment ("reservations don't seem to mean a thing" and the "gruff" staff tends to "play favorites"), but if you don't mind "watching the steaks age" while you "wait" for a table, it's "worth it."

Casa Rustica S   25 | 21 | 23 | $45 |
175 W. Main St. (Edgewood Ave.), Smithtown, 631-265-9265
■ "Back at the top of its game", this "special-occasion" Smithtown Italian is an "elegant", "beautifully decorated" place to enjoy "interesting" updated dishes that are even more "fabulous" than before, served by a staff that's both "friendly and professional"; regulars are "always pleased" with this "fine-dining" experience, especially if they can "sit near the fireplace."

Coolfish S   26 | 23 | 21 | $46 |
North Shore Atrium, 6800 Jericho Tpke. (Michael Dr.), Syosset, 516-921-3250
■ Despite its "hard-to-find" location in the back of a Syosset office building, this "cosmopolitan" New American "scene" is "another winner" from chef-owner Tom Schaudel; it's "worth the drive from anywhere" for his "off-the-chart good" creations (especially what many vote as "the best fish on LI" and "awesome desserts" like his "magnificent" signature chocolate bag), "gorgeously" presented in "cool" but "comfortable" digs packed with the "beautiful people"; needless to say, it's very "tough to get reservations", but keep persevering – it's "worth it."

Da Ugo   26 | 20 | 24 | $42 |
509 Merrick Rd. (Long Beach Rd.), Rockville Centre, 516-764-1900
■ "Exceptionally high-quality" Italian cooking – zero in on the "best baked clams", "unforgettable seafood risotto" and a "wonderful veal chop" – makes this Rockville Centre standout a "class act

from top to bottom", not to mention the "on-the-ball" owner and "impeccable" "tuxedoed waiters"; the only drawbacks: the "lovely" room is extremely "intimate" (read: "claustrophobic"), and they "cater first to their weekly regulars", meaning it's "very hard to get a table."

Della Femina [S] 25 | 24 | 22 | $56

99 N. Main St. (bet. Cedar St. & Talmage Ln.), East Hampton, 631-329-6666

■ While the "see-and-be-seen show" at this "people-watching" "hot spot" in East Hampton could overshadow the "superb" New American cooking, gourmands are also "pleased" with the "wonderful", "creative" dishes, if not the "expensive" tabs; "attractive", "understated" decor and "professional" service create a "classy" experience (despite the "deafening" din), making it a "winner" in all respects.

Focaccia Grill [S] – | – | – | E

Gateway Plaza, 2010 Wantagh Ave. (Sunrise Hwy.), Wantagh, 516-785-7675

Brian Arbesfeld wields the whisk with "great" confidence at this Wantagh New American–Italian where his "original", "NYC-quality" cooking, accompanied by an "extraordinary", "unusual wine selection" and served by a "professional" staff, easily offsets an "unbearable noise level" and very subdued lighting ("could we turn up the lights?").

Harvest on Fort Pond [S] 25 | 23 | 22 | $42

11 S. Emery St. (S. Euclid Ave.), Montauk, 631-668-5574

■ "Well worth the drive to the end of the Island", this "superior", family-style Montauk destination takes the local dining standard "up a notch" with its "phenomenal" Northern Italian and Med dishes "made for sharing" and served by a "friendly" staff in a "beautiful" (if "noisy") setting; enthusiasts can't help but exhort: "do whatever you can to get" here.

KOTOBUKI [S] 27 | 16 | 19 | $32

86 Deer Park Ave. (Main St.), Babylon, 631-321-8387

377 Nesconset Hwy. (Rte. 111), Hauppauge, 631-360-3969

■ Widely regarded as the premier Japanese option on LI, these "fantastic" "winners" in Babylon and Hauppauge thrill with their "innovative choices" of "sumptuously fresh sushi" ("perfection on rice"); the "long" lines ("go early or you'll wait forever"), "bright lights and tight seating aren't exactly my cup of sake, but there's nothing like" their "dynamite" way with raw fish, and their "special for two has no equal anywhere" for the price.

La Marmite [S] 25 | 22 | 24 | $48

234 Hillside Ave. (bet. Campbell Ave. & Mineola Blvd.), Williston Park, 516-746-1243

■ "A Cadillac among Hondas" declare devotees of this "favorite" "old-timer" nestled for more than a quarter-century in a "charming Victorian house" in Williston Park; thanks to "superb" classic French and Italian dishes turned out by a "courteous" staff in a "luxurious yet relaxing" setting, it is for many the "epitome of fine dining" – "perfect, as it should be at these prices."

La Pace [S] 25 | 24 | 24 | $49

51 Cedar Swamp Rd. (2nd St.), Glen Cove, 516-671-2970

■ "Artful, edible towers" of "spectacular" savory creations and a "sumptuous", "romantic setting" ("especially near the fireplace") keep loyal customers coming back to this "first-class" Glen Cove Northern Italian; "be prepared to be pampered" with the "royal treatment" from the owner ("Angelo [Ventralla] always provides a warm welcome") and his "knowledgeable" staff at this "special-occasion" place ("one of LI's best") that's "worth every penny."

La Piccola Liguria 🖻　　26　20　25　$46

47 Shore Rd. (Main St.), Port Washington, 516-767-6490

■ Establishing the "standard" in Port Washington, this "heavenly" temple of "old-world charm" is the "best" Northern Italian on the Island thanks to its "superior" menu, "intimate" setting and "gracious", "immaculate" service; though it "deserves all the accolades", the "awe-inspiring" "list of nightly specials" "recited by waiters with very good memories" has even the most devoted worshipers praying "please write them down" lest "people fall asleep" during the "sermon."

La Plage 🖻　　27　21　24　$48

131 Creek Rd. (Sound Rd.), Wading River, 631-744-9200

■ "Bring a map and an empty stomach" to this "out-of-the-way" Eclectic "jewel" by the beach in Wading River, where the "superb", "creative" dishes, "intimate" ambiance and "professional" yet "friendly" service make it "worth the hunt"; though a few killjoys carp that the "quaint", "beach-bungalow" quarters are a "poor match" for such pricey "culinary artistry", laid-back types have no problem with "black-tie food in a jeans-and-sweater setting."

L'Endroit　　25　24　24　$51

290 Glen Cove Rd. (Park Dr.), East Hills, 516-621-6630

■ "Absolutely superb in every way" croon pampered patrons of this LI "classic", a bastion of "gracious dining" in East Hills that endures due to its "five-star" French cuisine (regulars say that chef-owner Avelino De Sousa "scores well" with Northern Italian specialties too), "elegant", "romantic" ambiance and, ahem, "interesting artwork"; consider also the "professional" staff overseen by a "concerned maitre d'" and it's easy to see why so many smitten habitués gush "*c'est magnifique!*"

Le Soir 🖻　　25　21　23　$41

825 Montauk Hwy. (Bayport Ave.), Bayport, 631-472-9090

■ "*Cuisine vraiment française*" distinguishes this "intimate, romantic" Bayport bistro that's renowned for "extraordinary" classic masterpieces "beautifully presented" in a "charming country inn" setting by a "caring", "dedicated" staff; as it's "too popular" on weekends, those in-the-know recommend coming for an "out-of-this-world" meal during the week.

Louis XVI 🖻　　25　28　25　$64

600 S. Ocean Ave. (Masket Dock), Patchogue, 631-654-8970

■ "Marie Antoinette herself would be jealous" of the patrons who are "treated like royalty" at this Patchogue New French "palace", which reigns as the most "beautiful" restaurant on LI courtesy of its "breathtaking" decor and "fabulous" views of Great South Bay; nearly as impressive are the "rich, savory" dishes, so "elegantly presented" that they're veritable "works of art", brought to table by a "first-class" staff; the "*très cher*" tariff may lead some peasants to revolt, but loyal subjects insist this is all that "fine dining should be."

Maidstone Arms 🅂   25   25   24 $51

Maidstone Arms, 207 Main St. (Mill Hill Ln.), East Hampton, 631-324-5006
■ Cherished as a "heavenly retreat in a hectic area", this "refined" American "superstar" in East Hampton may well be the "epitome of class" thanks to "perfectly prepared" dishes based on "impeccable flavor combinations", paired with "fabulous" wines and served in a country-inn setting with a "romantic" ambiance by an "excellent" staff practiced in "finesse"; N.B. the arrival of Paul del Favero behind the stove may not be reflected in the above Food rating.

Mario 🅂   25   21   23 $42

644 Vanderbilt Motor Pkwy. (bet. Marcus Blvd. & Washington Ave.), Hauppauge, 631-273-9407
■ "Amazingly good year in and year out", this "classy" Northern Italian standout in Hauppauge is renowned for its "fantastic" traditional fare ("you really get an authentic piece of Italy here") offered at "ridiculously reasonable prices"; backers boast that you "can't beat" the "simple elegance" of the room or the "attentive" service and come away confident that "it'll always be excellent."

Mazzi   25   22   23 $48

493 E. Jericho Tpke./Rte. 25 (bet. Depot & Melville Rds.), Huntington Station, 631-421-3390
■ The "all-time favorite" of many Huntington Station residents, this "top-quality" Continental delivers "delicious" dishes that "leave the taste buds dancing", complemented by an "exceptional", "offbeat" wine list and "superb" service; set in a "quaint" old house, its "warm, inviting" ambiance pleases most comers, though a few spoilsports fuss that the "romantic" lighting is "so dark you can't read the menu."

MILL RIVER INN 🅂   28   23   26 $57

160 Mill River Rd. (bet. Lexington Ave. & Oyster Bay-Glen Cove Rd.), Oyster Bay, 516-922-7768
■ Once again rated No. 1 for Food on LI, this perennial "favorite" housed in an unassuming little building in Oyster Bay didn't miss a beat after the departure of chef Henry Barone; current top toque Nick Molfetta maintains this "gem's" stellar standards by executing "elegant", "outrageously creative" New American dishes, served by a staff that "treats you like royalty"; though "tiny", it's quite "romantic", "especially by the fireplace in wintertime", and without doubt among the "best overall dining experiences" on the Island.

MIRABELLE 🅂   27   24   26 $60

404 N. Country Rd. (Edgewood Ave.), St. James, 631-584-5999
■ Esteemed as the "best French restaurant east of NYC", this St. James "destination" thrills adventurous palates with master chef-owner Guy Reuge's "ambitious" menu of "superlative", "flawlessly executed" contemporary creations, presented by an "absolutely" "professional" staff in a "charming" farmhouse setting; while a few grousers wish they'd "double the portions or halve the prices", most promise it's "worth every dollar" for an "amazing" experience that's not just "a meal but a trip" to Paris.

MIREPOIX   27   20   24 $55

70 Glen Head Rd. (Railroad Ave.), Glen Head, 516-671-2498
■ "You don't have to know how to pronounce the name" to indulge in the "superb", "innovative" International fare at this "romantic"

"little place" near the Glen Head train station that's so "intimate it's like eating in someone's dining room"; the kitchen turns "luxe ingredients" into "delicious" "creations" that are "heaven in your mouth" and it's all "presented beautifully" by "superb servers", so even though it's "expensive", it's "worth every penny"; N.B. the post-*Survey* arrival of chef Scott Bradley may outdate the above Food score.

Mirko's [S] 26 | 22 | 24 | $54

Water Mill Sq., 670 Montauk Hwy. (bet. Old Mill & Station Rds.), Water Mill, 631-726-4444

■ A "steady clientele keeps returning year after year" to this "hidden jewel" in Water Mill for "fabulous" Continental-Eclectic fare served in a "quiet", "charming" locale "away from the madding crowd" by a "professional" staff; though a few down-to-earth types protest that it "caters to the 'in' crowd", habitués chorus it's "wonderful in every way."

Morton's of Chicago [S] 25 | 24 | 23 | $57

777 Northern Blvd. (bet. Community Dr. & Lakeville Rd.), Great Neck, 516-498-2950

■ The most recent addition to Great Neck's famed "beef belt" and already one of the "best on LI", this palatial homage to meat showcases "huge" slabs of "phenomenal", "tender" steaks that "almost melt in your mouth", delivered by a "courteous" staff in a "men's club" arena; a few squeamish sorts prefer not to "see the meat before it's cooked" and cry ouch!, "my wallet", when the bill comes, but this "hot spot's" popularity seems secure.

Palm [S] 25 | 20 | 22 | $56

The Huntting Inn, 94 Main St. (Huntting Ln.), East Hampton, 631-324-0411

■ "Good luck getting a reservation during the summer on a Saturday night", but keep trying anyway because this "posh" "scene" set in the "beautiful" 300-year-old Huntting Inn in East Hampton is a "packed" "favorite", and it "can't be beat" for its "succulent" steaks, "famous" four-pound lobsters and "superb" blue cheese dressing, served by a "courteous, knowledgeable" staff; though a few grouches gripe that it's "full of the nouveau riche", fans are too busy "checking out who's at the next table" to much notice.

Palm Court at the Carltun [S] 24 | 27 | 23 | $51

Eisenhower Park (Merrick Ave.), East Meadow, 516-542-0700

■ "Elegant" surroundings, a "romantic" atmosphere and "superb" Continental–New American dishes make this "palace" in East Meadow's Eisenhower Park "the place to bring guests you want to impress" and "perfect" for any "special occasion", with "live jazz in the courtyard" in the summer as a bonus; though Miss Manners types "could do without the attitude" from the staff and frugal foes cry foul over "ridiculous" prices, the enchanted feel as if they've "walked into a dream."

PANAMA HATTIES [S] 27 | 25 | 24 | $61

Post Plaza, 872 E. Jericho Tpke./Rte. 25 (bet. Deer Park Ave. & Rte. 110), Huntington Station, 631-351-1727

■ Matthew Hisiger clearly proves that he's at the top of his game at this "exquisite" Huntington Station gem where he masterminds "stupendous" New American dishes that are "out of this world", "magnificently" presented in "picture-perfect" arrangements by a "knowledgeable" (if "snooty") staff; its strip-mall location belies the "suave" ambiance of its "elegant" room, though gourmands feel that dinner would be "worth it even if you sat in the parking lot"; yes, it's very "high-priced", but it's "also very high-class."

PETER LUGER [S]≠ 27 | 18 | 21 | $54

255 Northern Blvd. (bet. Lakeville Rd. & Little Neck Pkwy.), Great Neck, 516-487-8800

■ Yet again voted the Most Popular restaurant on LI, this legendary "institution" on Great Neck's beef belt is "in a class by itself", providing a "carnivorous experience" that "outshines all the competition" with "succulent", "exquisite" porterhouse teamed with "unbelievably fresh and tasty side dishes"; the decor may be "dull", it's "always" "loud, loud, loud" and the servers are "cranky" (though they "add character"), but in the end, legions will attest that "it's by far the best steakhouse this side of heaven."

Piccolo [S] 26 | 21 | 23 | $48

Southdown Shopping Ctr., 215 Wall St. (bet. Mill Ln. & Southdown Rd.), Huntington, 631-424-5592

■ "Still the one" for "truly divine" dining in the eyes of loyalists, this perennial pride of Huntington is a "classy establishment" legendary for "incredible" Italian–New American fare served in a "romantic" setting by a "top-notch" staff; reservations glitches and long "waits" for a somewhat "cramped" table notwithstanding, it gives virtually "all LI Italian restaurants something to aspire to"; N.B. a post-*Survey* chef change may outdate the above Food score.

Plaza Cafe [S] 25 | 22 | 25 | $51

61 Hill St. (Gin Ln.), Southampton, 631-283-9323

■ "It's about time that this community by the sea had a chef who really knows how to cook a fish" say appreciative admirers of this "tasteful" Southampton hideaway where Douglas Gulija orchestrates "absolutely delectable" New American dishes (his signature seafood shepherd's pie is simply "heavenly"); equally "phenomenal" is the service – "warm, friendly" and "caring" – so rest assured that you'll be "made to feel welcome and not rushed."

Polo [S] 26 | 26 | 25 | $53

Garden City Hotel, 45 Seventh St. (Franklin Ave.), Garden City, 516-877-9353

■ "The perfect place to impress a stuffy client" gush besotted boosters of this "luxurious" New American "haven" housed in the Garden City Hotel, which dazzles with "luscious" "creative combinations" that are "gorgeously presented" ("nonpareil") amid "elegant" surroundings (freshly refurbished); of course it's "expensive", but it offers "Manhattan poshness on LI", and you'll be "pampered" by "real professionals" from beginning to end – after all, this is "one of the best restaurants on the entire Island."

Robert's [S] 24 | 23 | 23 | $55

755 Montauk Hwy. (Water Mill traffic light), Water Mill, 631-726-7171

■ "If you want to impress someone, take them" to this refined, "sophisticated" Italian "charmer" set in an "attractive", historic house in Water Mill, where "hands-on owner" Robert Durkin and "talented" chef de cuisine Natalie Byrnes turn out "fabulous", "innovative" coastal dinners punctuated by "intense desserts"; by most counts, this is "one of the Hamptons' best bets" – "Robert's done it again!"

Sempre Vivolo 26 | 23 | 24 | $47

696 Motor Pkwy. (Old Willets Path), Hauppauge, 631-435-1737

■ "Consistently classy", this "elegant" Hauppauge Italian is a "real winner", a "grown-up place that's not stuffy" and "just the right size to be cozy"; it's a "good family operation and it shows" – the owners "know how to run a restaurant" and they're "always trying to please", as does the "impeccable but not overbearing" staff; "relax" and indulge in "outstanding" fare proffered in a "civilized" ambiance while being made to "feel special" – this is "romantic" "fine dining" that's "worth the high price tag"; N.B. jackets are required on Saturdays.

Sen [S] 26 | 20 | 21 | $44

23 Main St. (bet. Bay & Madison Sts.), Sag Harbor, 631-725-1774

◪ Splurge on just about the "best" sushi on LI at this "excellent" Japanese "favorite" in Sag Harbor, renowned for its "delicious, fresh and properly prepared" raw fish; it's "always crowded" and it doesn't take reservations, so it can seem "impossible to get into in the summer", but consider "going early"; critics, on the other hand, carp that it's now "overpriced" and frown that its once-"serene environment has been ruined by its popularity."

Stone Creek Inn [S] 26 | 25 | 24 | $49

405 Montauk Hwy. (bet. Carter Ln. & Wedgewood Harbor), East Quogue, 631-653-6770

■ "Kudos to the chef!" cheer the "hip" devotees of this "romantic hideaway" set in a "beautiful" Victorian-era former speakeasy in East Quogue that's appointed with "old-world" details; it's a "handsome", "inviting" backdrop for Christian Mir's "unbelievable" French-Med dishes prepared with "panache" and "elegantly presented" by an "outstanding" staff; a "perfect celebration" place, "everything is first-rate here – except the noise level"; N.B. closed January and February.

Stresa [S] 25 | 22 | 22 | $49

1524 Northern Blvd. (east of Shelter Rock Rd.), Manhasset, 516-365-6956

Stresa East [S]

Woodbury Best Western, 7940 Jericho Tpke. (Piquets Ln.), Woodbury, 516-364-1565

■ Like a "NYC spot in Nassau", this "elegant" Manhasset Italian draws in the "beautiful people" with "superb" "classics" paired with an "eclectic" wine list and complemented by a "beautiful" room (adorned with "amazing floral displays") and "divine" service; critics, though, croon "to know, know, know you is to love, love, love you", warning that unless you're a "favored regular" you may as well be "invisible" to the staff; N.B. the Woodbury sibling is new and unrated.

Tellers Chophouse [S] 26 | 27 | 24 | $52

605 Main St. (Veterans Memorial Park), Islip, 631-277-7070

■ "Deposit this one under delicious" rave gourmands about this "spectacular", "big-time" chophouse set in a "beautiful old bank building" (circa 1926) in Islip, where the "best steaks this side of Peter Luger" are accompanied by an "inspirational, award-winning wine list" (the vault now houses a wine cellar and humidor); equally "breathtaking" are the "dramatic" dining room and "gorgeously designed bar", so even if you have to "see the loan officer on the way in", it's "worth it" to live this "steak lover's dream."

Trattoria Diane 🅂   26 | 22 | 22 | $46

21 Bryant Ave. (Northern Blvd.), Roslyn, 516-621-2591

■ "Sophisticated" and "stylish", this Roslyn standout has "quietly emerged as one of the North Shore's best" thanks to chef (and co-owner) John Durkin's "superb", "sumptuous" Northern Italian dishes (make sure you "leave room for the fabulous desserts"); his culinary works of art are served in "bright, attractive" quarters with an "elegant" ambiance by a "capable", "professional" staff, making it a "real treat" – so of course "long waits" can often be expected.

Tupelo Honey 🅂   25 | 24 | 21 | $44

39 Roslyn Ave. (Sea Cliff Ave.), Sea Cliff, 516-671-8300

■ This "sophisticated" "slice of the city" brings a "breath of fresh air" onto the Sea Cliff scene with "bold, brassy" cooking and "iconoclastically good drinks" served by an "eager" staff in a "vibrant", "ultramodern" room with a "vacation-like" atmosphere; though it can occasionally take "weeks" to get a reservation, that just gives you time to "look forward to the innovative fare"; N.B. chef Henry Barone has debuted a New American–Eclectic menu that may outdate the above Food rating.

Los Angeles

TOP 20 FOOD RANKING

Restaurant	Cuisine Type
28 Matsuhisa	Japanese
Sushi Sasabune	Japanese
Sushi Nozawa	Japanese
27 Patina	Californian/New French
Water Grill	Seafood
Takao	Japanese
Joe's	Californian
Chinois on Main	Asian/French
Spago	New American
Mélisse	New American
Lucques	Californian/French
Belvedere	Californian/Eclectic
Diaghilev	French/Russian
Shiro	Californian/Asian
L'Orangerie	French
Frenchy's Bistro	French Bistro
Campanile	Californian/Med.
La Cachette	New French
26 Valentino	N&S Italian
Angelini Osteria	N&S Italian

ADDITIONAL NOTEWORTHY PLACES

Bel-Air Hotel	Californian/French
Bistro 45	Californian/French Bistro
Brent's Deli	Deli
Café Bizou	Californian
Capo	N&S Italian
Chaya Brasserie	Asian/Eclectic
Cheesecake Factory	American
Depot	Eclectic
Devon	Californian/New French
Grill	Steakhouse
JiRaffe	Californian
Josie's	New American
Lawry's	Steakhouse
Mimosa	French Bistro
Nobu Malibu	Japanese/Peruvian
Palm	Steakhouse/Seafood
R-23	Japanese
Ruth's Chris	Steakhouse
Saddle Peak Lodge	New American
Yujean Kang's	Chinese

Angelini Osteria [S] 26 | 16 | 22 | $38

7313 Beverly Blvd. (N. Poinsettia Pl.), LA, 323-297-0070

■ Finally, a place that's "as good as the reviews say it is" claim converts to this "instant classic", a "super-noisy" and "crowded" "real osteria in California" where "maestro" Gino Angelini is a "master at combining flavors" in "wonderfully presented" Italian dishes like the "sublime artichoke salad" and "scrumptious spinach lasagna"; the only quibble: there's really "no waiting area."

Bel-Air Hotel [S] 26 | 29 | 27 | $63

Bel-Air Hotel, 701 Stone Canyon Rd. (north of Sunset Blvd.), Bel Air, 310-472-1211

■ "Dining here is guaranteed to cure depression" ("and it costs the same as therapy too") note awed patrons of this "formal" Bel-Air Cal-French "place for special occasions", a "romantic", "Shangri-la" whose "breathtaking" environs include an outdoor dining room surrounded by a pond, swans and "exotic plants and fruit-bearing trees"; "gastronomic delights abound" and the "impeccable" staff "treats everyone like a star", so is it any wonder this is "the last word in elegance"?

Belvedere [S] 27 | 27 | 27 | $61

Peninsula Beverly Hills Hotel, 9882 Little Santa Monica Blvd. (Wilshire Blvd.), Beverly Hills, 310-788-2306

■ "You never know which star you'll run into" at this "refined" Beverly Hills hotel venue that's practically the "commissary" for the world-famous Creative Artists Agency next door, so be warned that you may "feel foolish if you're not gussied up a little"; admirers add that "a meal here is like taking a vacation", with "pampering" service, a "lavish" setting and "exceptional" Cal-Eclectic cuisine.

Bistro 45 [S] 26 | 22 | 24 | $46

45 S. Mentor Ave. (bet. Colorado Blvd. & Green St.), Pasadena, 626-795-2478

■ The consensus is that the "consummate host", "charming owner Robert Simon", "knows his business" at this Pasadena Cal-French bistro that's "holding its own after all these years"; set in a 1939 art deco building with lots of cozy, candlelit tables and soft jazz, it receives lavish praise for "fabulous food" folks "dream about", "exemplary service" and an "outstanding", "eclectic wine list" ("we love their winemaker dinners").

Brent's Deli [S] 26 | 11 | 20 | $17

19565 Parthenia St. (bet. Corbin & Tampa Aves.), Northridge, 818-886-5679

■ "Huge portions" mean "you'll need to be wheeled out if you finish your meal" at this Northridge "Jewish deli" that's "unquestionably the best" in town thanks to "unbelievable blintzes", "excellent pastrami", "cabbage soup like no other" and "cakes that are the tallest structures in the Valley"; "attentive service" and "wonderful catering" also make it "worth the schlep", though there is delivery.

CAFÉ BIZOU [S] 23 | 19 | 21 | $30

91 N. Raymond Ave. (Holly St.), Pasadena, 626-792-9923

Water Garden, 2450 Colorado Blvd. (bet. Cloverfield Blvd. & 26th St.), Santa Monica, 310-582-8203

14016 Ventura Blvd. (bet. Hazeltine & Woodman Aves.), Sherman Oaks, 818-788-3536

■ "Every restaurant should take lessons" from this "cute, comfy" and "consistently" "excellent" Cal trio (rated Most Popular among

LA restaurants); the "noise and jostling" might "not be relaxing", but "the food is so good", the prices "so reasonable" ("add soup or salad for a buck more") and the "attentive" staff so "friendly" that patrons "make reservations for [their] next meal while dining there"; P.S. "you can't beat that $2 corkage fee."

CAMPANILE 🇸   27 | 24 | 24 | $49

624 S. La Brea Ave. (bet. 6th St. & Wilshire Blvd.), LA, 323-938-1447

■ "Ask about the history of the building" when talking to the "extra-polite" staffers at Mark Peel and Nancy Silverton's Cal-Med, "deservedly a legend" with voters "consistently amazed" by its "creativity and quality"; the "fixed-price, family-style meal on Mondays is great", and Thursday's sandwich night is "something special" too, but this "serious but approachable" spot is "terrific" any day "for a business meal", "a romantic evening" or "a classy affair" with "out-of-town guests."

Capo   26 | 24 | 23 | $64

1810 Ocean Ave. (Pico Blvd.), Santa Monica, 310-394-5550

■ "A fanatic for the best ingredients", chef-owner Bruce Marder "knows how to use the local farmer's market" and "understands Italian food better than most" toques from The Boot declare devotees of his "romantic" Santa Monica "special-dinner" venue, but "bring your Brinks truck", as the "wonderful" "haute cuisine", "extensive wine list" and "incredible interior" aren't all that "wow" the crowds ("I almost fell off my chair when I saw the prices!").

Chaya Brasserie ❶🇸   25 | 24 | 22 | $45

8741 Alden Dr. (bet. Beverly Blvd. & 3rd St.), W. Hollywood, 310-859-8833

■ "Martinis are the drink of choice" with the "young", "hip", "beautiful" women – you know, the ones whose "shoes match their handbags" – at the "raucous" bar of this attractively lit, "beautifully decorated" West Hollywood Asian-Eclectic fusion entry; "after all these years" it's still "swinging with celebs, live jazz" and "fab" "creative food" (the "impressed" insist the rib-eye "steak is amazing" and the "Banana, Banana, Banana is the best dessert in the city").

CHEESECAKE FACTORY 🇸   20 | 17 | 17 | $23

364 N. Beverly Dr. (bet. Santa Monica & Wilshire Blvds.), Beverly Hills, 310-278-7270 ❶

11647 San Vicente Blvd. (bet. Barrington & Darlington Aves.), Brentwood, 310-826-7111 ❶

4142 Via Marina (Admiralty Way), Marina del Rey, 310-306-3344 ❶

2 W. Colorado Blvd. (Fair Oaks Ave.), Pasadena, 626-584-6000

605 N. Harbor Dr. (190th St.), Redondo Beach, 310-376-0466 ❶

Sherman Oaks Galleria, 15301 Ventura Blvd. (Sepulveda Blvd.), Sherman Oaks, 818-906-0700

Thousand Oaks Mall, 442 W. Hillcrest Dr. (Lynn Rd.), Thousand Oaks, 805-371-9705

6324 Canoga Ave. (Victory Blvd.), Woodland Hills, 818-883-9900

◪ "When you can't think of a place to eat", this chain's "something-for-everyone" American menu, "ridiculously huge portions", "consistently good" quality and "reasonable prices" make it an "all-around standby"; "long lines" are a drawback ("why don't they take reservations?"), but with 30-plus "out-of-this-world cheesecake" varieties, most "sweet" tooths swear it's "worth the wait" (and the "weight").

Chinois on Main S
27 | 20 | 22 | $52

2709 Main St. (bet. Ocean Park Blvd. & Rose Ave.), Santa Monica, 310-392-9025

■ Despite "tight quarters" and the "sonic ambiance of a jet-engine factory", "talented" "artist" Wolfgang Puck's "colorful" Santa Monica French-influenced Asian stalwart continues to be "one of the toughest tickets in town"; the reason: a "unique menu" with "wildly flavorful dishes" – including "a spectacular Shanghai lobster" and "mouthwatering" "sizzling catfish" – that can "shake even the most jaded palate."

Depot
23 | 21 | 22 | $39

1250 Cabrillo Ave. (Torrance Ave.), Torrance, 310-787-7501

■ "Bring someone you want to impress" to this Torrance Eclectic, because personable chef Michael Shafer is "a master at combining flavors" and is "more creative than ever", concocting dishes that his many fans extol as "worth the drive from anywhere in LA"; factor in a "very nice" space (in a former train station) and a "great bar" and it's easy to see why this has become a "power-lunch hang for the auto set" from the nearby Honda and Toyota headquarters.

Devon S
25 | 19 | 22 | $47

109 E. Lemon Ave. (Myrtle Ave.), Monrovia, 626-305-0013

■ Set in a "tiny", "intimate" "former carriage house" "on a side street" in the "most unlikely place" (Monrovia), this "minimalist" Cal-New French venue is "worth the trip" to experience "creative", "beautifully prepared" cuisine (including "exotic game"), an "unbelievable wine list" and "spectacular desserts"; by the way, "if it's not on the menu, ask – they love to please" their customers.

Diaghilev
27 | 28 | 28 | $60

Wyndham Bel Age Hotel, 1020 N. San Vicente Blvd. (Sunset Blvd.), W. Hollywood, 310-854-1111

■ "Dress up" for a "romantic dinner" at this West Hollywood Franco-Russian where you will "be pampered" "like a nobleman in an 18th-century palace" by legendary maitre d' Dmitri Dmitrov and his staff; featuring, among other czarist delights, "a mind-boggling selection of caviars and vodkas" ("I can't remember what I ate, but I loved it") and "long-stemmed roses", this "exquisite" evocation of St. Petersburg is "expensive but worth" every kopeck.

Frenchy's Bistro S
27 | 15 | 22 | $40

4137 E. Anaheim St. (bet. Termino & Ximeno Aves.), Long Beach, 562-494-8787

■ Chef-owner Andre Angles "loves his work and it shows" at this "excellent" French bistro "in an outlying Long Beach area" where it's "hard to choose between the filet mignon and Dover sole" or among the choices on the "sensible list" of "affordable wines"; just "don't be fooled" by its "improbable location" and "nondescript" exterior – this "wonderful needle-in-a-haystack" "charmer" more than "exceeds expectations."

Grill on the Alley S
23 | 19 | 22 | $45

9560 Dayton Way (Wilshire Blvd.), Beverly Hills, 310-276-0615

Grill on Hollywood S

Hollywood & Highland, 6801 Hollywood Blvd. (Highland Ave.), Hollywood, 323-856-5530

■ "Power-lunch central", this "industry players' heaven" exudes "money and importance" thanks to heavy "hitters" who huddle in its handsome room, brokering deals over "outstanding" steaks and "stepped-up comfort food" served by an "excellent", "professional staff"; P.S. the new Hollywood branch is already a "standard for a relaxing evening out", but some feel it's "too good for the location" (a "glorified mall") and lacks the "mover-and-shaker" clientele (i.e. there are "lots of tourists").

JiRaffe ⓢ   26 22 24 $47
502 Santa Monica Blvd. (5th St.), Santa Monica, 310-917-6671
◼ In the midst of creating "inspired", "original" Californian dishes, chef-owner and "mensch" Raphael Lunetta often "comes out of the kitchen to greet diners" at this "unassuming" high-achiever in Santa Monica; "a perpetual LA favorite", it features "awesome service", "an interesting and reasonable wine list" and "classy" digs ("the best seats are upstairs"); if that's not enough, there's also a "great $14.95 prix fixe lunch."

Joe's ⓢ   27 20 23 $44
1023 Abbot Kinney Blvd. (bet. Main St. & Westminster Ave.), Venice, 310-399-5811
◼ "Unpretentious" chef-owner "Joe Miller can cook better than almost anybody" swear the many devotees of his "absolutely wonderful food" at this "consistently excellent" Venice Californian that sports a "postmodern woodsy" look; if you can't make it for dinner (reservations are essential), try a prix fixe lunch (a "bargain") or "fabulous" brunch "on the patio."

Josie's   26 23 23 $52
2424 Pico Blvd. (25th St.), Santa Monica, 310-581-9888
◼ "Beautifully prepared" Texas wild boar, venison and other "game are specialties" on the "exotic", "creative" ("but not madcap") seasonal New American menu at "rising star" chef Josie Le Balch's taupe-toned "hidden" "gem" in Santa Monica; everyone knows "her cooking is wonderful", but the "quality wines" and "comfortable", "relaxing" setting with "well-spaced tables, booths" and banquettes are more reasons "you'll go back."

La Cachette ⓢ   27 24 24 $54
10506 Little Santa Monica Blvd. (bet. Beverly Glen Blvd. & Overland Ave.), Century City, 310-470-4992
◼ "Chef-owner Jean François Meteigner creates brilliant, light New French dishes (not an oxymoron)" employing fine Gallic ingredients (snails, frogs' legs, foie gras) at this "hard-to-find" "special-occasion" "gem" in Century City; no doubt "your date will be impressed" sitting at one of the "well-spaced tables" amid "nice artwork" while enjoying a "memorable meal" served by an "attentive but unobtrusive" staff; P.S. don't forget to "save room for the warm fruit tarts."

Lawry's the Prime Rib ⓢ   24 21 24 $42
100 N. La Cienega Blvd. (Wilshire Blvd.), Beverly Hills, 310-652-2827
◼ Reservations are recommended for this "legendary" Beverly Hills "celebration" steakhouse where "pleasant" waiters exhibit fine "showmanship" by "preparing your meal tableside from a silver-domed cart" stocked with "succulent slabs" of "the ultimate prime rib"; the "spinning salad will spin into your heart" and ditto for the "excellent Yorkshire pudding", but be advised, despite all the visitors from Tokyo, this is not "the Japanese embassy in LA."

L'Orangerie [S] 27 28 26 $75

903 N. La Cienega Blvd. (bet. Melrose Ave. & Santa Monica Blvd.), W. Hollywood, 310-652-9770

■ Put "on your suit, bring your big wallet" and prepare to be "wowed" by the "Versailles-like", "classically grand ambiance" of this dinner-only West Hollywood "French cuisine mecca" "hidden behind a wall of stone and foliage"; with "perfectly presented" dishes (try the prix fixe menus) that will "amaze your taste buds" and seriously "dedicated" staffers, it's no wonder surveyors "can't think of a better place for a special occasion"; N.B. Christophe Eme (ex NYC's Town) is the "great new chef."

Lucques [S] 27 23 24 $51

8474 Melrose Ave. (La Cienega Blvd.), W. Hollywood, 323-655-6277

■ "Phenomenal" chef Suzanne Goin cooks "exciting", "complex" Cal-French "soul food" (the "legendary" "short ribs deserve their reputation") at this "beautifully conceived and executed" West Hollywood "treat" where the "service is excellent", it's "fun to eat at the bar" or on the "heated patio" and "the Sunday night family-style prix fixe dinner is a steal"; N.B. a spin-off on Third Street in the former Antica Pizzeria space is in the works.

MATSUHISA [S] 28 17 23 $65

129 N. La Cienega Blvd. (Wilshire Blvd.), Beverly Hills, 310-659-9639

■ Move over, Lakers, Nobu Matsuhisa's Beverly Hills flagship has scored a four-peat as LA's No. 1 restaurant for Food; the "über-chef to the world" "amazes" with "magnificent", "innovative" Japanese cuisine ("don't miss the omakase") that "breaks traditions and makes new ones", served in a "marvelously unexciting" space by comparison; no surprise, it's all quite "expensive", so just be sure to "go with an empty stomach and a full wallet", and who knows, "you might rub shoulders with the famous."

Mélisse [S] 27 25 25 $66

1104 Wilshire Blvd. (11th St.), Santa Monica, 310-395-0881

■ "The cheese cart alone is reason enough to go" proclaim apostles of Josiah Citrin's "world-class" Santa Monica "event restaurant" where "magnificent", "ambitious" French-influenced New American cuisine ("the prix fixe is outstanding", the tasting menu "sublime") is complemented by a large but "focused" wine list, "beautiful" decor and "refined", "solicitous" service; it might be a good idea to "bring your banker" along for the meal, but what would you expect at one of "LA's finest restaurants"?

Mimosa 21 18 18 $37

8009 Beverly Blvd. (Crescent Heights Blvd.), LA, 323-655-8895

◩ "You'd have to go to Paris to match" the "excellent" French bistro cuisine at this "understated" "stalwart" that "delights" Francophiles with dishes such as the signature bouillabaisse, "authentic cassoulet" and, surprise, surprise, arguably the "best mac 'n' cheese in town"; the "cute" and "cozy" space, adorned with "charming" photographs, plays its role well too, completing the illusion of a corner of "France transplanted" to Fairfax.

Nobu Malibu [S] 25 20 21 $54

3835 Crosscreek Rd. (PCH), Malibu, 310-317-9140

■ The Malibu "elite" are "spoiled" having this "top" Japanese-Peruvian "favorite" "as their local sushi" spot, since "the freshness of the fish and the innovative talent of the chefs" result in "many delicious tidbits to sample (if your wallet's ample)", including some of "the best sashimi in the world", accompanied by a "huge selection of exotic sakes"; regulars recommend "rubbing elbows" "outdoors in the bamboo garden", where the term "stargazing" is a double entendre.

Palm S   25 | 19 | 21 | $54

9001 Santa Monica Blvd. (bet. Doheny Dr. & Robertson Blvd.), W. Hollywood, 310-550-8811

1100 S. Flower St. (11th St.), LA, 213-763-4600

☑ Sadly, "treasured maitre d'" Louis 'Gigi' Delmaestro recently passed away, but "testosterone dining" continues in his memory at this "manly palace of protein" in West Hollywood where "perfectly cooked" beef, "amazing lobster" and a "crab cocktail without which life is meaningless" garner universal cries of "fabulosa" from "expense-accounters"; N.B. a "new location" adjacent to the Staples Center brings "the Palm tradition" "Downtown."

PATINA   27 | 25 | 26 | $65

5955 Melrose Ave. (bet. Highland Ave. & Vine St.), LA, 323-467-1108

■ "Still the champ" to its many fans, this "granddaddy" of Joachim Splichal's culinary clan, featuring "drop-dead modern" Cal–New French fare as well as an "amazing wine list", makes for a "dream evening of eating" in an "elegantly" redone setting overseen by "constantly attentive" staffers; pondering a "spectacular" chef's sampler they'll "remember forever", surveyors sigh "I wish I was there at this very moment", even if they'd "need an investment banker to arrange financing for the food."

R-23   26 | 20 | 21 | $41

923 E. Second St. (bet. Alameda St. & Santa Fe Ave.), Downtown LA, 213-687-7178

■ With its "obscure location" ("a hidden back-alley spot in the Warehouse District Downtown"), this "top Japanese" can be "difficult to find", but "regulars" report "it's worth the hunt" for its "artful presentations" of "wonderful sushi" selections and cooked items (the "lobster tempura is a must here"), as well as "stylish" "minimalist decor" featuring "cool [Frank] Gehry–designed" "cardboard chairs"; P.S. a tip for those who "get lost every time": "R-23 means the railroad between Second and Third streets."

Ruth's Chris Steak House S   26 | 20 | 23 | $50

224 S. Beverly Dr. (bet. Olympic & Wilshire Blvds.), Beverly Hills, 310-859-8744

■ "When trying to show your father-in-law that you're doing well", "invent an occasion" to invite him to this "clubby", "costly" steakhouse chain link where it's smart to "share with friends" because "the side dishes are huge" and the "first-rate steaks" ("get the porterhouse for two" or the "sumptuous rib eye") are "awesome" in scope, "tender" in texture and come "sizzling in butter"; special kudos to the "excellent" staff that's "always friendly no matter how [customers] dress."

Saddle Peak Lodge S   26 | 26 | 24 | $53

419 Cold Canyon Rd. (Piuma Rd.), Calabasas, 818-222-3888

■ At once "a beautiful mountain refuge from the craziness of LA" and "a heaven for carnivores", this "romantic" hunting lodge high above Malibu "never disappoints" as "an incomparable adventure in New American dining" that "you'll talk about for years"; expect "fabulous game dishes" (enhanced by a 350-label indigenous wine list) and a setting that's part "over-the-top Ralph Lauren with stuffed animal heads" on the walls and part "Wild West bordello"; P.S. don't miss Sunday brunch ("who knew hare hash tasted so good?").

Shiro [S] 27 | 17 | 23 | $41

1505 Mission St. (Fair Oaks Ave.), South Pasadena, 626-799-4774

■ Year after year, this "low-key" South Pasadena Californian-Asian garners raves for its "to-die-for" deep-fried ginger catfish with ponzu sauce that'll make you "feel like a cartoon cat, leaving a perfect fish skeleton on your plate", but virtually every item on its "minimalist (but actually complex)" bill of fare is "superb"; those who've carped that its "limited menu" "needs to change" more often should be pleased by the new Tuesday–Thursday "prix fixe lunch – it's a bargain."

SPAGO [S] 27 | 25 | 24 | $62

176 N. Cañon Dr. (Wilshire Blvd.), Beverly Hills, 310-385-0880

■ Even "Jesus would have a hard time getting a table on a Saturday night" (especially in the garden) at Wolfgang Puck's Beverly Hills "showplace", which attracts "lots of beautiful people, movers and shakers" and "out-of-towner" "looky-loos" with eyes peeled for "stars on view"; "but you've got to notice the food" too – chef Lee Hefter's "cutting-edge", seasonal New American specialties "do not disappoint" even those with "sky-high expectations."

SUSHI NOZAWA 28 | 7 | 16 | $44

11288 Ventura Blvd. (Vineland Ave.), Studio City, 818-508-7017

■ "Dreams about crab rolls" are not uncommon after a visit to this "cramped", "rushed" Studio City Japanese where "acclaimed master" sushi chef Kazunori Nozawa "wonderfully prepares" "the best cuts" of "ultra-fresh" "ambrosial" fish on "lightly packed rice"; you'd better "play by his rules", though, as watching "customers get kicked out" for not "minding their Ps and Qs" ("no chitchatting" or requests – "just eat") is "practically a citywide pastime"; "just be prepared for a long line and a stiff bill."

SUSHI SASABUNE 28 | 6 | 17 | $49

11300 Nebraska Ave. (Sawtelle Blvd.), West LA, 310-268-8380

■ "Those who find Sushi Nozawa's Valley location inaccessible" should consider this "unassuming" outpost helmed by a protégé who "learned his lesson well"; like his mentor, Nobi Kusuhara sticks with traditional offerings (there are "no California rolls"), and you "eat what he gives you", which is fine with most fin-atics, since "everything melts in your mouth."

Takao [S] 27 | 14 | 22 | $45

11656 San Vicente Blvd. (bet. Barrington & Darlington Aves.), Brentwood, 310-207-8636

■ Ex Matsuhisa chef Takao Izumida's "superior", "creative sushi" garners rave reviews for this "cozy", "unassuming" Brentwood Japanese; you'll need to "make a reservation" before you can savor the likes of his halibut carpaccio, and it's "a bit expensive to go weekly", but the "staff treats you like family" and there's no denying that, while "tiny, it's mighty on the quality scale"; P.S. "you can't go wrong" if you "order the chef's special – he really does know best."

Valentino | 26 | 23 | 26 | $62 |

3115 Pico Blvd. (bet. 31st & 32nd Sts.), Santa Monica, 310-829-4313

◪ "Gracious host" and owner "Piero [Selvaggio] loves what he does", and it shows, at this "suave", "elegant" Santa Monica Italian that's "still the gold standard" in its category for "wonderful" service, "fantastic" cuisine and an "unequalled" 3,800-label cellar with "spectacular wines" (ranging in price from $40 to $25,000) that "match your food perfectly"; some cite "stuffy" staffers and a "somewhat pricey" menu as drawbacks, but most maintain "it's hard to find anything wrong here"; N.B. the enclosed patio was recently renovated to Boot.

WATER GRILL [S] | 27 | 24 | 25 | $51 |

544 S. Grand Ave. (bet. 5th & 6th Sts.), Downtown LA, 213-891-0900

■ "If you must impress a guest" with "perfectly done seafood of any description" and "can't risk an off night", "rely" on this Downtown "deep-sea treasure" convenient to the Music Center, a culinary "class act" that "never disappoints"; with prix fixe and custom-tasting menus, a "fantastic raw bar", "a fine" wine list, an "engaging space" that resembles an "art deco luxury liner" and a "knowledegable", "polished" staff, it's a "first-class" choice "for special-occasion" or "expense-account eating."

Yujean Kang's [S] | 25 | 18 | 21 | $35 |

67 N. Raymond Ave. (bet. Colorado Blvd. & Walnut St.), Old Pasadena, 626-585-0855

■ "Genius" "Yujean Kang could topple the Iron Chefs any day" swear acolytes of his "outstanding", red-walled "gourmet" "fusion Chinese" venue that's "worth the drive to Pasadena", especially for anyone "tired of egg foo yong"; the "beautifully" plated "creative dishes" offer "interesting combinations of flavors" ("the signature shrimp with polenta is the best", and the "tea-smoked duck is a must"), which are complemented by "excellent" wines thanks to an "attentive staff good at pairing" them with food.

Miami

TOP 20 FOOD RANKING

Restaurant	Cuisine Type
27 Chef Allen's	New World
Romeo's Cafe	Northern Italian
Palm	Steakhouse/Seafood
Norman's	New World
26 Osteria del Teatro	Northern Italian
Joe's Stone Crab	Seafood
La Palme d'Or	French/New French
Tropical	Chinese
Toni's Sushi Bar	Japanese
Ortanique on the Mile	Caribbean
Pacific Time	Pan-Asian/Seafood
Escopazzo	N&S Italian
Mark's South Beach	Floridian
Hy-Vong	Vietnamese
Crystal Cafe	Continental
Pascal's on Ponce	New French
Grazie Cafe	Northern Italian
25 Miss Saigon Bistro	Vietnamese
Morton's of Chicago	Steakhouse
Azul	New French/Asian

ADDITIONAL NOTEWORTHY PLACES

Baleen	New World/Seafood
Blue Door	New French
Cafe Prima Pasta	Northern Italian
Caffe Abbracci	Northern Italian
Carpaccio	Northern Italian
Casa Juancho	Spanish
Cheesecake Factory	American
Forge	Continental/Steakhouse
Garcia's	Seafood
Gaucho Room	Argentinean
Graziano's Parrilla	Argentinean
Joe Allen	American
Nemo	New American
Nobu Miami Beach	Japanese/Peruvian
Porcao	Brazilian
Rumi	New American
Shoji	Japanese
Tantra	Med./New French
Versailles	Cuban
Wish	New French/Brazilian

subscribe to zagat.com

Azul 25 27 25 $63

Mandarin Oriental Hotel, 500 Brickell Key Dr. (8th St.), Miami, 305-913-8358

■ One of Miami's "latest must-try" spots is this "terrific" two-year-old in the "super-beautiful" Mandarin Oriental Hotel on Biscayne Bay, where chef Michelle Bernstein, formerly of Tantra, "seldom falls" from the culinary "high wire" with her "stellar" "French-Caribbean fusion" fare with Asian accents; the "bare sophistication of the decor" and the "food mood" are so "Zen" that, despite what some call "outlandish prices", "it's a soothing experience."

Baleen [S] 25 27 22 $54

Grove Isle Hotel, 4 Grove Isle Dr. (S. Bayshore Dr.), Coconut Grove, 305-858-8300

■ For "the most beautiful view in all of Miami", "get a table outside and dine under the stars" on "breezy Biscayne Bay" at this "dazzling" New World seafood house in the Grove Isle Hotel; the "breathtaking setting" is as "magical" as chef Robbin Haas' "sumptuous" "touch", and the "whimsical" simian theme of its "sublime decor" makes it a "great place" to "hang" out with friends and "monkey around."

Blue Door ◐ [S] 24 27 21 $59

Delano Hotel, 1685 Collins Ave. (17th St.), Miami Beach, 305-674-6400

◪ Awash with "celebrities galore" and draped by Philippe Starck in "breezy, white, ceiling-to-floor curtains", "this chic spot in the Delano Hotel" feels like a "luxurious movie set", but the "dreamy" digs and "happening" "scene" don't "distract from the excellent" New French "seafood-heavy menu"; still, critics complain that "fantasy meets reality" when the big bill comes; N.B. the new prix fixe menu (under $50) is a boon for the budget conscious.

Cafe Prima Pasta ◐ [S] 24 18 21 $27

414 71st St. (Collins Ave.), Miami Beach, 305-867-0106

◪ "Take a break from that SoBe triple headache – parking, pricing and attitude" – at this "always-busy" "locals' favorite" ("a little off the beaten path for tourists") offering Northern "Italian food with a Latin beat", such as "delicious" Argentine steak and "fresh pastas" at "bargain" prices; a recent "expansion" means its "lively setting" isn't quite so "tight" as before, though some "old-timers" gripe that it "was better" when it was more "intimate."

Caffe Abbracci ◐ [S] 25 22 24 $41

318 Aragon Ave. (bet. Le Jeune Rd. & Ponce de Leon Blvd.), Coral Gables, 305-441-0700

■ You're bound to "see beautiful society people" and "flashy big shots" "schmoozing" and, true to the name of the place, embracing at this "warm", "wonderful" and very "alive" Coral Gables Northern Italian serving "strong standards and specials"; "hands-on owner Nino Pernetti" "manages to balance the highest levels of quality, service, decor and atmosphere", though some who come "for conversation" complain the "excellence" is matched by an equally extravagant amount of "noise."

Carpaccio [S] 24 20 22 $33

Shops of Bal Harbour, 9700 Collins Ave. (96th St.), Bal Harbour, 305-867-7777

■ "Even a bowl of soup is special here" claims the couture crowd about this "great break from shopping" at Bal Harbour, a "winning"

Northern Italian where you can sit on the patio and "gorge your eyes" on the "beautiful people" and "poodles in Gucci strolling by" as you feast on "excellent fresh pasta" and a dozen varieties of carpaccio at prices so reasonable "you'll have enough money left over to shop at Prada or Tiffany when you're done."

Casa Juancho ☾ [S] 22 | 22 | 21 | $35

2436 SW Eighth St. (bet. SW 24th & 25th Sts.), Miami, 305-642-2452

■ "Take out-of-town guests" for "a jumping evening" at this "authentic" "replica of a Spanish *meson*" (inn) in Little Havana, where "superior" tapas and paella, a vast Iberian wine list and a "lively bar scene with dancing" make "a great combination"; the "lovely", "traditional" setting not only features "hams strung up around the place" as decoration, but strolling ones as well in the form of guitarists, "accordionists and singers."

CHEESECAKE FACTORY [S] 21 | 19 | 19 | $24

Aventura Mall, 19501 Biscayne Blvd. (195th St.), Aventura, 305-792-9696 ☾

CocoWalk, 3015 Grand Ave. (Virginia St.), Coconut Grove, 305-447-9898 ☾

Dadeland Mall, 7497 Dadeland Blvd. (Kendall Dr.), Kendall, 305-665-5400

◪ They may be "factories", but these "reliable" outposts of an "upscale chain" have a "cookie-cutter recipe that works every time" – "industrial-size portions" of "tasty" Eclectic fare offered in "such variety" that some folks "never know what to eat"; though "the wait for a table is agony" and the "noise level" and "huge crowds" make it feel "like a visit to the zoo", the "hungry" packs here all agree that the 30-plus assortment of "divine" namesake cakes is "sinfully delicious."

CHEF ALLEN'S [S] 27 | 23 | 25 | $53

19088 NE 29th Ave. (NE 191st St.), Aventura, 305-935-2900

■ No. 1 for Food among Miami eateries, this New World "favorite" in Aventura "deserves the accolades" for its "adventuresome, tasty menu" of "tropical fusion flavors at their best"; "always evolving" yet "always superb", busy chef-owner Allen Susser is "the reigning king" of "Florida cuisine", and though he "travels a lot", he often "visits tables" when he's in-house, "making everyone feel special"; "if price is no object and you wish to impress or propose, this is the place."

Crystal Cafe [S] 26 | 20 | 25 | $38

726 41st St. (bet. Chase & Prairie Aves.), Miami Beach, 305-673-8266

■ "Sophisticates" find "fine dining" that "satisfies all the senses" at this "superb", almost-"secret" "spot" supervised by "super-talented" chef-owner Klime Kovaceski; "extraordinary European-style creativity from the kitchen" combines with "intimate", "formal ambiance" and "excellent service", adding up to a "wonderful" Continental experience that's got fans saying "hats off."

Escopazzo [S] 26 | 22 | 24 | $50

1311 Washington Ave. (bet. 13th & 14th Sts.), Miami Beach, 305-674-9450

■ "Romantic" and "refreshingly intimate", this "vest pocket"-size bistro "in the midst of the loud" "SoBe scene" is staffed by "courteous" "native Italians" who "know what they're doing" when it comes to "delivering" "delicate and delicious cooking" "with tender-loving care", providing "personable, knowledgeable service" and "accommodating whims" so well that customers "feel like celebrities."

Forge S
25 | 26 | 24 | $55

432 Arthur Godfrey Rd. (Royal Palm Ave.), Miami Beach, 305-538-8533

☑ Over the past three decades, this "costly", "classic" Continental chophouse "institution" with "stained glass" galore and a "'60s Miami Beach" vibe has forged its role as the "traditional place" for "old-fashioned, high-end dining"; "Caesar salad and prime rib are the stars" ("no calorie counting here"), and the "museum of a cellar" houses "the Mona Lisas of wines", so "go, splurge, enjoy!"

Garcia's S
23 | 15 | 18 | $20

398 NW North River Dr. (NW 4th St. Bridge), Miami, 305-375-0765

■ Locals "love to go by boat up the Miami River" to catch a "delish fish sandwich" at this "funky" waterfront seafood market near Downtown; "if you don't mind eating next to a bustling canal" amid a school of midday feeders, an "unpretentious", "great-value" meal here is "South Florida at its casual best"; N.B. it's soon to be open for dinner Thursday through Sunday.

Gaucho Room S
25 | 25 | 24 | $57

Loews Miami Beach Hotel, 1601 Collins Ave. (16th St.), Miami Beach, 305-604-5290

■ Set in SoBe's "beautiful Loews Hotel", this "solid performer" of a chophouse manned by an "attentive" and "courteous" staff "goes beyond the theme" of its "amazing decor" (a recreation of an Argentine horseman's estate), bringing "more than just super steak fare" from the pampas to the table in the form of adventurous offerings such as coriander-crusted Pacific sea bass; N.B. the arrival of chef Ted Peters may outdate the Food score.

Graziano's Parrilla Argentina S
– | – | – | E

9227 Bird Rd. (bet. 92nd & 93rd Aves.), 305-225-0008

Quantity coupled with quality bring in-the-know foodies and homesick Argentines to this popular South Dade *parrilla* (grill) with beef from the *asador* (spit), an award-winning selection of more than 450 bottles of vino and dozens of desserts, including its famed *panqueque*, a dulce-de-leche-filled crepe; don't be surprised to see Miami's celebrity chefs mingling with South American expats and luminaries in its low-key environment.

Grazie Cafe S
26 | 19 | 25 | $32

Suniland Plaza, 11523 S. Dixie Hwy. (bet. SW 14th & 15th Sts.), Pinecrest, 305-232-5533

■ Go figure – "nobody is Italian" at this "cozy" "storefront" in Pinecrest, but you'll "*mangia, mangia, mangia*" on "delicious" dishes from the North of The Boot nonetheless while the "zealous" "waiters sing"; the "chef will prepare anything you have a craving for", so "feel welcome" to "go back again and again" with "your requests", or "call ahead" for "favorites" like "mouthwatering filet-mignon ravioli", which must be ordered a day in advance.

Hy-Vong S
26 | 9 | 13 | $24

3458 SW Eighth St. (SW 34th Ave.), Miami, 305-446-3674

■ The "room's the size of the head of a pin", so "expect" a "long wait" for one of the few "elbow-to-elbow tables" at this "no-frills" "gem in Little Havana"; a fiercely loyal "cult following" swears its "superb Vietnamese is worth" "every minute" and isn't "bothered" at all by the "abysmal decor" or "slow", sometimes "rude, service", since at this "grubby hole-in-the-wall" it's "all about the food."

Joe Allen ●🄢 22 | 19 | 22 | $32
1787 Purdy Ave. (bet. 17th & 18th Sts.), Miami Beach, 305-531-7007
■ It's "counterintuitive" to expect a "transplanted piece of NYC" to become a "comfy" SoBe "neighborhood" "hang" with a vibe that feels "like a reunion"; nevertheless, this "most friendly place" fills up in the "early evening with fifty- and sixty- and later twenty- and thirtysomething" "locals" digging the tropical "deco motif", "scrumptious" "comfort food" and "bar with hard-boiled eggs as snacks"; "when you don't want fancy", this "glorified diner" is the ultimate in "understated" native "cool."

JOE'S STONE CRAB 🄢 26 | 21 | 23 | $51
11 Washington Ave. (1st St.), Miami Beach, 305-673-0365
☑ "Celebs, tourists and those spending other people's money" get their "fix" of "melt-in-your-mouth stone crabs" and "world-class sides" at this "legendary" South Beach "institution", Miami's Most Popular restaurant; it's "a must-go", though some "opt for the carry-out next door" and "make a mess at home", since (as the "crowds" "waiting in the bar" attest) "you have to know God to get in"; P.S. "it's a shame it's only open from" "the middle of May" "until mid-October."

La Palme d'Or 26 | 27 | 25 | $61
Biltmore Hotel, 1200 Anastasia Ave. (Granada Blvd.), Coral Gables, 305-445-1926
■ Perhaps "the most grown-up, romantic" dining in Coral Gables can be found at this "grande dame of French cuisine" at the Biltmore Hotel, where "gorgeous" frescoes and "flawless service" enhance the "drama" of "Philippe [Ruiz's] beautifully presented" "epicurean delights" (including a "quintessential Sunday brunch") and "sampler" menus by "visiting" toques "the first week of each month"; though it's "pricey", "celebrants" say this "ultra" experience is "worth every penny"; N.B. jacket required.

Mark's South Beach 26 | 23 | 24 | $57
Hotel Nash, 1120 Collins Ave. (11th St.), Miami Beach, 305-604-9050
■ For "trendy" fans of the 'Mango Gang' (the kitchen cadre that created New World cuisine in the '90s), the culinary "zenith" of South Beach just might be "wonderful chef" Mark Militello's "upscale original" in the "stylish" Hotel Nash, where "crisp, clean, pure" Floridian "flavors blended perfectly" "with a Caribbean touch" "satisfy" "chic" "palates" "alfresco" "around the pool" or in the "dining room that resembles a ship's" galley.

Miss Saigon Bistro 🄢 25 | 17 | 24 | $25
148 Giralda Ave. (Ponce de Leon Blvd.), Coral Gables, 305-446-8006
■ "Mama does it right" with her "fantastic creations" at this "all-in-the-family, homestyle" Vietnamese while, "if you're lucky", her "wonderful" "children"/"waiters sing some opera" for your supper; the "spicy" "treats" are "deservedly popular", so expect a "long wait", quickly "turned tables" and "noise" at this recently expanded, "inexpensive" "oasis on Coral Gables'" restaurant row.

Morton's of Chicago 🄢 25 | 24 | 24 | $53
1200 Brickell Ave. (Coral Way), Miami, 305-400-9990
17399 Biscayne Blvd. (NE 173rd St.), North Miami Beach, 305-945-3131
☑ At these "carnivore's heavens" in North Miami Beach and Downtown Miami, the "showing of the flesh" doesn't have the

usual sun-worshiper's connotation; here it means that "delicious red meat" is "presented raw" to each "entertained" table before orders are placed (the "very good seafood" is worth considering too); some critics find the cigar-friendly chainster's "pomp" and "à la carte" pricing to be "major turnoffs", cautioning "bring no teenage boys" because "they eat too much."

Nemo ●🅑🅢   24 23 21 $46

100 Collins Ave. (1st St.), Miami Beach, 305-532-4550

◼ Still an "all-around" "favorite" following the flight of former chef/co-proprietor Michael Schwartz, this "interesting" spot remains "a must-stop on the SoBe circuit" for Miami's "delicious people" determined to "gorge" themselves on "delicious" New American fare (with multicultural accents) followed by "heavenly desserts"; it's all about "location, location, location", so "sit outside in the courtyard" "under the trees" and you might get to "watch" "beautiful" folk like "Calvin Klein at the next table."

Nobu Miami Beach ●🅑🅢   – – – VE

The Shore Club, 1901 Collins Ave. (20th St.), Miami Beach, 305-695-3232

Since its pre-season debut in late 2001, the trendy Shore Club's Nouvelle Japanese has shaken and stirred the South Beach scene with a dash of Peru and lots of hype thanks to co-owner Nobu Matsuhisa, who has proven his culinary and marketing genius with outposts in several cities; the near-impossibility of getting a reservation leaves non-celebs clawing their way in for a taste of black cod with miso and other delectable, pricey tidbits.

NORMAN'S   27 25 26 $58

21 Almeria Ave. (Douglas Rd.), Coral Gables, 305-446-6767

☑ "Fans" feel this "incredible restaurant does indeed live up to its reputation", as "passionate" chef-owner Norman Van Aken is "still on top of his form", turning out "original" New World "dishes fit for a queen" served in "quietly sophisticated" digs by a "perfectly attentive" staff that makes diners "feel like royalty"; still, "hungry" sorts snipe that the "genius" does his "cutting-edge culinary masterpieces" in miniature, "literally leaving you asking for more."

Ortanique on the Mile 🅢   26 23 23 $45

278 Miracle Mile (Le Jeune Rd.), Coral Gables, 305-446-7710

◼ It's "Jamaica in the Gables" at this "wonderful" "addition" to the "Miami dining scene"; the "tropical atmosphere" "immediately puts you in the Caribbean", and the "inspired" "explosions of flavor" from "great island food" with "French fusion" "influences" "make that feeling linger"; the crowd is "festive", "young" and "noisy", but even oldsters who "don't like Florida" "would make a trip back just to eat" here – after all, "where else can you get a great glass of wine to go with your jerk foie gras?"

OSTERIA DEL TEATRO   26 18 24 $48

1443 Washington Ave. (Española Way), Miami Beach, 305-538-7850

◼ Foodies "can't be in SoBe without eating" at this "crowded", "tiny little place" where the "pastas are phenomenal" and the other "elegant" showstoppers are "seasoned to perfection"; it may be "in need of an interior decorator", but even "wealthy Italians" are "impressed" by the "sublime" Northern fare and its staff of "consistent pros" who "truly care."

PACIFIC TIME [S] 26 | 22 | 23 | $50

915 Lincoln Rd. (bet. Jefferson & Michigan Aves.), Miami Beach, 305-534-5979

■ "Talk about fusion!" – "everything and the kitchen sink" shows up at chef-owner Jonathan Eismann's "still-interesting" South Beach Pan-Asian where "very fresh fish" practically "jumps off the plate", "sauces are sublime" and desserts like the chocolate bomb are, you guessed it, "dynamite"; it's "tight" inside, so if you're not down with the din and "people bumping into your chair", a table "outside on Lincoln Road is a nice option."

PALM [S] 27 | 20 | 25 | $54

9650 E. Bay Harbor Dr. (Kane Concourse), Bay Harbor Island, 305-868-7256
4425 Ponce de Leon Blvd. (Ruiz Ave.), Coral Gables, 786-552-7256

◪ "The power" of the "ultimate steak" pulls "junkies" into this "NY landmark transported to Miami"; as befits a "place that's not for pecking at your food", everything here is outsized: "larger-than-life portions" come with "price tags to match" in a "barn-like space that's not conducive to conversation"; despite the "raves" of "regulars", some diners read too much "snobbery" in this Palm.

Pascal's on Ponce 26 | 19 | 22 | $44

2611 Ponce de Leon Blvd. (bet. Almeria & Valencia Aves.), Coral Gables, 305-444-2024

■ Francophiles call this "awesome" two-year-old in the Gables a "rising star" for its "sophisticated" New French fare offered at "reasonable prices" and with "excellent service" by a "friendly staff"; though "the tables are on top of each other" in the "small, spare" space, regulars report it's worth "squeezing into" this "intimate" spot and "hope it doesn't get spoiled by success."

Porcao [S] 23 | 18 | 21 | $39

801 Brickell Bay Dr. (SE 8th St.), Miami, 305-373-2777

■ Rodizio experts suggest you "fast for a week beforehand" and line up "someone to drive you home afterward", 'cause chances are this Downtown Brazilian beef "bacchanalia" will land you in a "meat coma"; the "amazing" "salad bar just won't quit", but "save room" to "try every cut you can think of" at this "noisy", "fill-'er-up" fleshfest full of "king" carnivores.

ROMEO'S CAFE 27 | 20 | 26 | $51

2257 Coral Way (bet. 22nd & 23rd Aves.), Coral Gables, 305-859-2228

■ With Romeo Majano as "your own private chef", you'll feel like a "pampered" Juliet at this "romantic" Coral Gables Northern Italian where the eponymous owner "individually tailors" an "excellent" "six-course meal" to the "liking" of each party in his "tiny", "pretty" place; with such "personal" attention, "you can go 50 times and never receive the same" dish twice."

Rumi ◐ – | – | – | VE

330 Lincoln Rd. (Washington Ave.), Miami Beach, 305-672-4353

Opened post-*Survey*, this super-hot SoBe supper club has already generated a huge buzz with its plush interior outfitted with cushy couches, multi-colored mirrors and even a queen-size Murphy bed; the model-gorgeous staff is couture-attired to match the decor, and the music is as mystical as a poem by the namesake Sufi master, while the stylish cocktails and surprisingly savory New American cuisine have night-crawlers whirling like dervishes.

Shoji ◐S | 23 | 22 | 20 | $40

100 Collins Ave. (1st St.), Miami Beach, 305-532-4445

■ Though former co-owner and top toque Michael Schwartz has moved on, master sushi chef Shingo Inoue remains at this stunning SoBe spot below Fifth Street, slicing up "inspiring", "authentic" raw-fish fare that voters vaunt as "not from the usual assembly line"; complementing his dishes is a "stellar sake selection", and an oh-so-"cool staff" adds to the stylish space's "nice vibe."

Tantra ◐S | 22 | 26 | 17 | $58

1445 Pennsylvania Ave. (Española Way), Miami Beach, 305-672-4765

◪ It's "more of a party scene than a restaurant" say supplicants about this "very expensive" SoBe "adult date place" with "dark and sultry" decor and "grass on the floor"; the "aphrodisiacal" Med–New French fare is "unbelievably good", but with everyone "smoking hookah pipes", dancing to "blaring trance music" and "lounging" beneath erotic wall reliefs and an endless loop of the movie *Kama Sutra*, the "action distracts from the eating"; N.B. the Food rating does not reflect a recent chef change.

Toni's Sushi Bar ◐S | 26 | 22 | 23 | $30

1208 Washington Ave. (12th St.), Miami Beach, 305-673-9368

■ "Seasoned" sea-savvy surveyors say you "can't beat this" "laid-back" fin den, SoBe's most senior sushi bar, for "big portions" of "the freshest and best-presented" *mer* fare offered at "great prices" by a "friendly", "highly professional" staff and accompanied by a "superior saki" selection; not only do they "love everything on" the "varied menu", but the "nice", "mixed crowd" makes this "comfortable", "pretty place" great "for people-watching" too.

Tropical Chinese S | 26 | 18 | 22 | $29

Tropical Park Plaza, 7991 SW 40th St. (79th Ave.), Miami, 305-262-7576

■ "Dim sum! dim sum! dim sum!" are the three top reasons it's "worth the drive" to this "top-notch" "Hong Kong–style" strip-mall hall in Southwest Dade; "large crowds" of Sinophiles "wait in line" "to watch the preparation" through the "huge glass window into the kitchen" and flag down "carts" loaded with a "massive array" of "alluring interpretations of traditional Chinese food."

Versailles ◐S | 19 | 15 | 18 | $19

3555 SW Eighth St. (SW 35th Ct.), Miami, 305-445-7614

■ Folks who hail from that nearby island-nation to the south say a "satisfying" meal at this "landmark" "Little Havana institution" "on Calle Ocho" is "like lunch at their family's home"; though the "mirrors" and "chandeliers" strike some as "a bit overdone", even "garish", this "quintessentially Cuban" diner peopled with "colorful locals" discussing "history and politics" is as "real" "as it gets."

Wish S | 24 | 24 | 22 | $53

801 Collins Ave. (8th St.), Miami Beach, 305-674-9474

■ Those who expressed a "we'll see" attitude when E. Michael Reidt took the toque from the much-touted Andrea Curto, the chef who helped this SoBe "jewel" skyrocket to stardom, have seen their "wishes come true": his "pricey" platters of New French–Brazilian cuisine (think chilled avocado vichyssoise) more than "live up to" his predecessor's legacy as well as Todd Oldham's "stylish" decor; P.S. both the lantern-festooned room and "lush" "tropical" patio garden are "perfect" for "romantic" tête-à-têtes.

Minneapolis/St. Paul

TOP 10 FOOD RANKING

	Restaurant	Cuisine Type
27	Goodfellow's	New American
	La Belle Vie	New French/Med.
26	Bayport Cookery	Eclectic
	D'Amico Cucina	N&S Italian
	Lucia's	New American
	Manny's	Steakhouse
25	Ristorante Luci	N&S Italian
	Punch Neapolitan	Pizza
	128 Cafe	New American
	Oceanaire	Seafood

ADDITIONAL NOTEWORTHY PLACES

Aquavit	Swedish
Dish	New American
Gardens of Salonica	Greek
Kincaid's	Seafood/Steakhouse
Origami	Japanese
Restaurant Alma	New American
St. Paul Grill	American
3 Muses	Eclectic
Vincent	New American/French Bistro
Zander Cafe	New American

F	D	S	C

Aquavit

24	25	23	$56

IDS Ctr., 80 S. Eighth St. (Nicollet Mall), Minneapolis, 612-343-3333
■ Nothing of the "mythically dour Scandinavian" about this place – "the first thing that comes to mind" when you enter is how the "sleek", "sophisticated" space is so "light and airy"; it makes for a "chic" background for Marcus Samuelsson's "minimalist but fabulous" "Nouvelle" Swedish menu, presented by an "excellent" staff; it's "fun to receive the little gifts from the chef between each course", which means that this Downtown "splurge" is "really an event" rather than a mere meal.

BAYPORT COOKERY S

26	17	23	$48

328 Fifth Ave. N. (Rte. 95), Bayport, 651-430-1066
■ "Definitely a quintessential foodie experience", this "charming", "romantic" "getaway" in the river town of Bayport near the state line has "yet to disappoint" gourmands with its five-course prix fixe Eclectic "culinary excursions", which change weekly but are always "imaginatively created and presented" (don't miss the "fabulous morel-fest" in the springtime); though a few impatient types find the very "leisurely" pace "quite a long ordeal", admirers are adamant that this is a "worth-the-drive restaurant if ever there was one"; N.B. one seating nightly at 7 PM.

D'AMICO CUCINA   26 | 24 | 25 | $55

Butler Sq., 100 N. Sixth St. (bet. 1st & 2nd Aves.), Minneapolis, 612-338-2401
■ "Impress out-of-town food snobs" or "make up with your wife over almost anything" by visiting this "upscale" "special-occasion" destination "somewhat hidden" in the Warehouse District, where the "heavenly" Italian dishes not only "never disappoint" but will also "push the boundaries of what you thought you liked to eat"; equally "refined" are the "palatial" surroundings and "incredibly knowledgeable" staff; the only drawback: "ouch, the price."

Dish S   − | − | − | M

1310 Hennepin Ave. (13th St.), Minneapolis, 612-339-1133
The folks from the former Table of Contents eatery have come out with a new edition – the same open space Downtown (finessed with nifty modern touches), the same classy martini list and wine finds and the same caring staff, but a brand-new name and New American menu concept, which sends up supper club classics as well as puts a fresh spin on fusion cuisine; N.B. don't miss the savory or sweet bento box samplers.

Gardens of Salonica   23 | 14 | 15 | $17

19 NE Fifth St. (Hennepin Ave.), Minneapolis, 612-378-0611
■ "In a city lacking for good Greek food", this Northeast "gem" is "definitely the pinnacle"; providing an experience that's "like a slice of the islands", it thrills the palate with "fantastic" cooking that yields "special flavors" ("must-have: the skordalia appetizer"); though the "wait is annoying" and it can get a "bit noisy" (and "service tends to be on the slow side"), "it's worth tolerating for the quality" of the dishes, not to mention the "'70s prices."

GOODFELLOW'S   27 | 25 | 25 | $59

City Ctr., 40 S. Seventh St. (bet. Hennepin & Nicollet Aves.), Minneapolis, 612-332-4800
■ "There's nothing like sipping a dry martini and gazing" at "stunning" "art deco" decor while dining on chef Kevin Cullen's ("the king of Minneapolis") "divine", contemporary "twists on American standards" at this Downtown standard-bearer, voted No. 1 for Food in the Twin Cities; his "flavor combinations are wonderful" and the "impeccable" staff provides "a pampering experience", making it a "good place to take high-maintenance clients"; even if a few sniff too "uppity", loyalists can't wait to return to "escape the mundane and pretend they're Zelda or F. Scott."

KINCAID'S S   22 | 22 | 22 | $41

8400 Normandale Lake Blvd. (84th St.), Bloomington, 952-921-2255
380 St. Peter St. (6th St.), St. Paul, 651-602-9000
▨ Immensely popular, this "bustling" pair of American surf 'n' turf "institutions" is a "solid performer" even if it's a "far cry from fine cuisine", which makes it "dependable, if a bit predictable"; legions of business suits feel it offers the "best power lunch around", so be warned that it's "often hard to get a reservation", both at the flagship in "suburban" Bloomington and the "newer hot spot in Downtown St. Paul."

LA BELLE VIE S   27 | 23 | 26 | $57

312 S. Main St. (Nelson St.), Stillwater, 651-430-3545
■ Take a "beautiful drive to Stillwater" and discover this "oh-so-romantic" "hidden gem along the St. Croix River", "a total joy from

the moment you walk in the door"; in a "lovely", "unpretentious environment", a "knowledgeable" staff delivers "superb" New French–Mediterranean dishes (executed by co-chefs Josh Thoma and Tim McKee) that are "grounded in classical techniques yet always include surprising twists", while a sommelier expertly advises on the "wonderful wine selection"; the "aromas, tastes, sights and sounds all contribute to the marvelous experience" – "*La Belle Vie* indeed!"

LUCIA'S 🅂   26 | 20 | 24 | $35
1432 W. 31st St. (Hennepin Ave.), Minneapolis, 612-825-1572

■ True, the "limited" New American lunch and dinner menus at this "chef-driven" Uptown "landmark" include "only four" entree items (only three or four appetizers too), but "genius" Lucia Watson's roster "changes weekly" and always stars "incredibly fresh, top-quality" "heartland ingredients" turned into "simple, pure preparations" with "amazing depths of flavor"; though the digs are "sardine-can" "cozy", the space is made comfortable by a "calm" atmosphere and "attentive yet relaxed" service, leading the "enchanted" to regard it as the "Chez Panisse of Minneapolis."

Manny's Steakhouse 🅂   26 | 19 | 25 | $56
Hyatt Regency, 1300 Nicollet Mall (Grant St.), Minneapolis, 612-339-9900

◪ "Everything is super-sized" at this Downtown "steakhouse of steakhouses", a "classic boys' club" that provides "big food and big drinks for big shots" in a "big room"; though the "loud, bright" quarters have "all the charm of a meat locker" and the staff is "as well aged as the beef" (but with "a great sense of humor"), meat lovers are convinced that they've reached "carnivore heaven."

OCEANAIRE 🅂   25 | 24 | 25 | $52
Hyatt Regency, 1300 Nicollet Mall (Grant St.), Minneapolis, 612-333-2277

■ Ranked the Most Popular restaurant in the Twin Cities, this "cosmopolitan" send-up of a vintage supper club that's styled after a '40s-era luxury ocean liner is appointed with cherrywood and red-leather booths and infused with a "clubby, old-money" atmosphere; the seafood "counterpart" of Manny's Steakhouse across the hall in Downtown's Hyatt Regency, its daily changing menu showcases "intelligently" prepared fish dishes that "recall an earlier time of elegant" dining; what's more, "nothing" is "snobbish here except the prices"; P.S. the "oyster bar is fantastic."

128 Cafe 🅂   25 | 12 | 20 | $32
128 Cleveland Ave. N. (Laurel Ave.), St. Paul, 651-645-4128

■ "Don't miss this gem" urge followers of this "cool" "diamond-in-the-rough" near the University of St. Thomas, even though it's "weirdly" set in the "basement of an apartment building"; you'll forget all about the humble digs once you tuck into Brock and Natalie Obee's "fabulous" New American "interpretations" (justly renowned are their "zippy" BBQ babyback ribs), delivered by a "caring" staff; romantic types laud it as a "great place to bring a date", even if a few wags quip they're "always expecting a washing machine to overflow."

Origami   23 | 17 | 18 | $35
30 N. First St. (1st Ave.), Minneapolis, 612-333-8430

■ "Even Japanese businessmen are impressed" by this "trendy" spot near the river in the Warehouse District, where "young locals" bask in the "urban" atmosphere; the sushi is so "fresh" it'll "knock your socks off" and the staff is "attentive and unobtrusive" (if "overworked"), but be forewarned that the "no-reservations policy" often leads to a "horrible wait" and the joint can get as packed as a Tokyo commuter train at rush hour.

Punch Neapolitan Pizza　　25 | 18 | 18 | $19

704 Cleveland Ave. S. (Highland Pkwy.), St. Paul, 651-696-1066

■ Discover the "deal of the century" at this "family-owned" "neighborhood spot" in Highland Park, where the "interesting flavors and great prices" make it "a religious experience" among the faithful; there are "very few items on the menu, but what they do have is perfect" – namely "wood-fired" "pizzas for adults", made with a "smoky" crust, the "sexiest tomato sauce in the city" and "delectable" toppings – which amply explains why a "diverse crowd" puts up with "long waits", "hard chairs, a cramped space" and a "deafening" "noise level."

Restaurant Alma S　　25 | 20 | 20 | $42

528 University Ave. SE (6th Ave.), Minneapolis, 612-379-4909

■ A "little" "jewel" in SE Minneapolis near the U of Minnesota, this "exciting" New American is a "dream come true" thanks to chef-owner Alex Roberts' "terrific homegrown menu" of "contemporary" dishes (based on local organic products) that leave fans "licking their plates clean"; accompanied by a "great", eclectic wine list, it's all turned out by a "helpful" staff in a "casual, urban" atmosphere; "these people know what they're doing."

Ristorante Luci S　　25 | 14 | 23 | $35

470 Cleveland Ave. S. (Randolph Ave.), St. Paul, 651-699-8258

■ "Don't be turned off by the low-key storefront" environs of this "definitive" "neighborhood" "hole-in-the-wall" in Highland Park because its "true" Italian cooking is "excellent – no other way to put it"; the "personable" family owners don't "try to pull your palate into submission" but instead feed you "normal-size portions" of "flavorful" food, including "homemade mozzarella", "delightful" pastas and "marvelous" seafood ("order the tasting menu and you won't be disappointed"); though it's "well worth the cost", note that there are only 36 seats, so "book way in advance."

St. Paul Grill S　　22 | 24 | 24 | $44

St. Paul Hotel, 350 Market St. (5th St.), St. Paul, 651-224-7455

■ Ever a "consistent standby for the scotch-and-cigar crowd", this "clubby", "classy" "tradition" in Downtown St. Paul has secured a place for itself as a premier "old boys' place" for "power dining"; quartered in a "historic" hotel, it boasts a "fabulous view of Rice Park" and an "elegant" backdrop for all-American fare ("it may not be inventive, but you know you're going to have a good meal") proffered by a "formal, knowledgeable" staff; furthermore, it gets plenty of votes for having the "best bar in town – period."

3 Muses S　　– | – | – | M

2817 Lyndale Ave. S. (28th St.), Minneapolis, 612-870-0339

Though this tiny Lyn-Lake charmer can be hard to find, word-of-mouth keeps its tables filled with diners eager to sample chef Nick Cronin's ever-changing menu of Eclectic small plates, such as blue-cheese wontons with pancetta, fennel, clementines and haricots verts (he'll even do a tasting menu upon request), smartly supported by an iconoclastic wine and beer list and served by a friendly staff in a relaxed, neighborhood setting.

Vincent ___ ___ ___ M

1100 Nicollet Mall (11th St.), Minneapolis, 612-630-1189
After just a few years in town, young chef and native Frenchman Vincent Françoual (a former sous chef at NYC's Le Bernardin) has established himself as a culinary star on the rise and now lends his name and hands-on enthusiasm to this hot new bistro on Nicollet Mall, which features a French-inspired, frequently changing New American bistro menu and an offbeat, affordable wine list delivered by a friendly, well-versed staff; N.B. its prime Downtown location behind Orchestra Hall makes it perfect for concertgoers.

Zander Cafe S 25 17 20 $35

525 Selby Ave. (Dale St.), St. Paul, 651-222-5224
■ Though "they clearly didn't spend a lot of money on the decor" at this "hip" storefront in Cathedral Hill, most patrons don't mind when they're rewarded with "brilliant" chef-owner Alexander Dixon's "inventive but always balanced" dishes; his New American menu is "limited", but it changes frequently and it's presented in a "buzzing" atmosphere that gets livelier still on nights when there's "great live jazz"; no wonder many first-timers "aspire to be habitués" – the "overall package is so welcoming and satisfying that I could eat here every week."

New Jersey

TOP 20 FOOD RANKING

Restaurant	Cuisine Type
28 Ryland Inn	New French
Daniel's on Broadway	New American
27 Cafe Panache	New French
Sagami	Japanese
Saddle River Inn	New American/French
Scalini Fedeli	Northern Italian
Cafe Matisse	Eclectic
Washington Inn	American
Moonstruck	American/Mediterranean
Serenäde	New French
410 Bank Street	French/New Orleans
Ebbitt Room*	New American
Le Rendez-Vous	French Bistro/Med.
Union Park	New American
26 Jocelyne's	New French
Dining Room	New American
Jeffrey's	New American
Fromagerie	French
Siri's	French/Thai
Bobby Chez	Seafood

ADDITIONAL NOTEWORTHY PLACES

Acacia	New American
Bernards Inn	New American
DeLorenzo's Tomato Pies	Pizza
Doris & Ed's	Seafood
Esty Street	New American
Frog & the Peach	New American
Harvest Moon Inn	New American
Highlawn Pavilion	New American/Continental
Karen & Rei's	New American
Little Cafe	International
Madeleine's Petit Paris	French
Manor	American/Continental
Mazi	Mediterranean
Park & Orchard	Eclectic/Vegetarian
Rat's	New French
River Palm Terrace	Steakhouse
Shumi	Japanese
Stage House	New French
Waters Edge	New American
Zarolé	New American

* Tied with restaurant directly above it

Acacia [S] 25 | 21 | 23 | $42

2637 Main St. (bet. Craven Ln. & Phillips Ave.), Lawrenceville, 609-895-9885

■ Shutterbugs just "want to take a picture of the plate" at this "smart" Lawrenceville New American that presents "pretty" dishes "flawlessly executed" in a "lovely", "lively" setting; nitpickers may grumble it's "a bit precious", but those seeking "civilized dining" deem it the "best in the Princeton area" "bar none" and note that its BYO policy makes this "sublime" spot "almost affordable."

Bernards Inn 25 | 26 | 24 | $53

27 Mine Brook Rd. (Quimby Ln.), Bernardsville, 908-766-0002

■ Chef Edward Stone's "marvelous" dishes, paired with "one of the best wine lists in NJ", set a "tony" tone at this "luxurious" New American in Bernardsville that's the epitome of "classic hunt-country sophistication"; indeed, it's such a "romantic getaway" that it's nearly "guaranteed to get a husband out of the doghouse"; P.S. "a stay at the inn after dinner is a must."

Bobby Chez 26 | 11 | 18 | $18

The Village Walk, 1990 Rte. 70 E. (Rte. 29), Cherry Hill, 856-751-7373
8007 Ventnor Ave. (Gladstone Ave.), Margate, 609-487-1922 [S]
Southgate Plaza, 1225 Haddonfield-Berlin Rd. (bet. Franklin Ave. & Laurel Rd.), Voorhees, 856-768-6660

■ "Heavenly", "chock-full-of-crab" cakes that just might be the "best in the universe" (the "spicy shrimp is to die for" too) are the house specialty at this trio of seafood joints that feature limited seating but a roaring take-out trade; the price of popularity: "long lines all day."

Cafe Matisse [S] 27 | 23 | 25 | $49

167 Park Ave. (bet. E. Park Pl. & Highland Cross), Rutherford, 201-935-2995

■ "Who needs NYC" when there's "flawless, original" Eclectic cooking in Rutherford that's "as artful as its name"?; what's more, chef-owner Peter Loria's dinner-only BYO, located in a former firehouse, is imbued with an ambiance so romantic it can even "turn a sparring couple into Romeo and Juliet."

CAFE PANACHE 27 | 21 | 25 | $49

130 E. Main St. (Rte. 17), Ramsey, 201-934-0030

■ Chef-owner Kevin Kohler just "keeps getting better" at this Ramsey BYO "favorite" where one frequently changing New French menu "always proves to be more spectacular than the last", thanks to his "innovative use of herbs and sauces"; the "tiny, country-cottage" surroundings are "unpretentious" yet "posh", and the "thoughtful staff" helps keep this one on everyone's special "celebration" list.

DANIEL'S ON BROADWAY [S] 28 | 27 | 25 | $46

416 S. Broadway (Sunset Ave.), West Cape May, 609-898-8770

■ Chef-owner Harry Gleason brings a "creative flair" to his New American BYO in West Cape May, where some of the "most imaginative" food in NJ includes "fantastic" dishes like his grouper Charleston; set in a "charming" "converted Victorian house", it features "first-class" service down to the "well-spaced timing of courses", making it "perfect for a special occasion" – "they care about everything" here.

DeLorenzo's Tomato Pies [S] 🚫 — 26 | 11 | 18 | $15
530 Hudson St. (bet. Mott & Swann Sts.), Trenton, 609-695-9534
■ "Tomato fans" insist that this "popular" "Trenton institution for thin-crust pies" serves the "best pizza in the tri-state area", even if there's "no salad, no pasta, no bathroom" and "nothing fancy" going on decor-wise; who cares, though, when the eats are so good that addicts "wake in the middle of the night with a craving"?

Dining Room — 26 | 28 | 27 | $64
Hilton at Short Hills, 41 JFK Pkwy. (Rte. 24), Short Hills, 973-379-0100
■ "The staff has sharp antennae" at this "flawless" New American in the Short Hills Hilton that reeks of "class", from the more than "capable kitchen" to the "exquisite", flower-laden dining room complete with "live harp music"; owing to its "consistent high standards", you should expect "top-of-the-line pricing", but "you get what you pay for" – "everything's perfect" here.

Doris & Ed's [S] — 26 | 20 | 23 | $46
348 Shore Dr. (Waterwitch Ave.), Highlands, 732-872-1565
■ "Mouthwatering seafood" whets plenty of appetites at this Highlands James Beard award–winner where you can expect a "whale of a meal, and that's no fish story"; besides the "art-on-a-plate" presentations, count on an "impressive wine list", "pleasant, knowledgeable" service and "lovely" "ocean views" – along with the inevitable "big summer crowds."

Ebbitt Room [S] — 27 | 26 | 25 | $49
Virginia Hotel, 25 Jackson St. (bet. Beach Dr. & Carpenter Ln.), Cape May, 609-884-5700
■ Foodies savor meals "beyond the beyond" at this New American "gem" in Cape May that provides a "yardstick for all others"; set in a boutique hotel and festooned with "breathtaking floral" arrays, this "romantic" spot is a "throwback to the elegance of the '50s", replete with "Swiss-level" service, so you're virtually guaranteed a "perfect evening."

Esty Street — 26 | 20 | 22 | $47
86 Spring Valley Rd. (Fremont Ave.), Park Ridge, 201-307-1515
■ "Pascack Valley's best", this "aristocratic" New American in Park Ridge showcases a "seasonal" menu of "innovative", "eclectic" dishes that admirers assert is the "equal of any in NYC"; it may be "noisy" and the "tables are too close together", but it's nevertheless "always a joy" thanks to its "sublime presentations" and "wonderful wine list", not to mention its "sophisticated" atmosphere and "knowledgeable" staff.

410 Bank Street [S] — 27 | 21 | 23 | $46
410 Bank St. (bet. Broad St. & Lafayette Ave.), Cape May, 609-884-2127
■ Putting Cape May "on the culinary map" is this "tropical retreat" set in Victorian digs where regulars continue to "explore the menu and find dishes to fall in love with"; whatever you select from the French–New Orleans menu (the fish is "heavenly"), be prepared for a "taste-bud explosion" – "after all these years, it still has what it takes"; N.B. good news for grape lovers: it now serves wine.

Frog & the Peach [S] — 26 | 23 | 24 | $51
29 Dennis St. (Hiram Sq.), New Brunswick, 732-846-3216
■ "A pioneer that doesn't age", this "landmark" New Brunswick "dream's" "magnificent presentations" of "inspired", "inventive"

New American cooking keep it on the "cutting edge"; from the "chic", "industrial" setting to the "impeccable service", devotees "can't say enough about the old girl" – just "be prepared to drop some mad loot."

Fromagerie S
26 | 25 | 25 | $55

26 Ridge Rd. (Avenue of Two Rivers), Rumson, 732-842-8088

☑ *Le* big cheese in Rumson for a *magnifique* meal, this "cozy" French is "perfect for a special occasion" given its "excellent" menu, "terrific" decor and professional service; though a minority frets that it's "not as inspiring as it used to be", the majority swoons that dining here is as "grand a night out" as ever.

Harvest Moon Inn S
26 | 24 | 23 | $49

1039 Old York Rd. (Rte. 202), Ringoes, 908-806-6020

■ The "Old World meets the 21st century" at this "historic inn" where chef-owner Stanley Novak presents cutting-edge New American cooking to a "crowd that's not quite NYC, though the food certainly is"; granted, it's a "bit of a ride" to Ringoes, but it's "more than worth it" to "eat from the time the moon rises till it sets" at this "perfect getaway."

HIGHLAWN PAVILION S
24 | 28 | 24 | $51

Eagle Rock Reservation, Eagle Rock Ave. (Prospect Ave.), West Orange, 973-731-3463

■ "Knockout", "magical" vistas of Manhattan "wow" diners at this bit of "heaven" in West Orange, where the New American and Continental dishes "hold their own" so well that some sigh the "view is merely gravy"; "be prepared to spend a bundle" for the chance to experience "how the better half lives", but for such "imaginative, lush dining", this "celebration" spot is hard to beat.

Jeffrey's
26 | 20 | 25 | $45

73 Main St. (Washington St.), Toms River, 732-914-9544

■ "Out-of-this-world delicious" cooking is the calling card of this New American BYO, a "wonderful surprise in Toms River", where chef Jeffrey Schneekloth's menu is based on the "finest, freshest ingredients"; though some say the decor "could use some sprucing up" and others feel "it has lost its touch since it got famous", true believers say this experience is exactly as it "should be."

Jocelyne's S
26 | 21 | 24 | $42

168 Maplewood Ave. (Baker St.), Maplewood, 973-763-4460

■ "Ooh-la-la!" – such "fabulous" food, "charming" ambiance and "darling" service trill the many devotees of this New French BYO in Maplewood, where chef Mitchell Altholz turns out exquisitely "delicate" dishes, "never serving an average meal"; wife Jocelyne works the front of the house, offering a "warm welcome" that makes "all guests feel special" at this "tiny suburban jewel."

Karen & Rei's S
▽ 27 | – | 24 | $39

1882 Rte. 9 N. (Brooks Ave.), Clermont, 609-624-8205

■ "How can one woman cook so well for so many?" marvel fans of this New American BYO in Clermont, where chef-owner Karen Nelson "must work around the clock to make everything taste so superb"; to enjoy her "innovative preparations" and "fantastic desserts", "you practically have to book the summer before – but it's totally worth it"; a post-*Survey* move to a spacious new setting with a fireplace and an open kitchen only ups the atmosphere ante.

Le Rendez-Vous [S] | 27 | 20 | 24 | $44 |

520 Boulevard (N. 21st St.), Kenilworth, 908-931-0888

■ "You won't believe you're in Kenilworth" after a taste of the "innovative", "slice-of-France" cooking at this "sweet" French-Mediterranean BYO bistro that's "one of NJ's undiscovered gems"; though the "really tight" quarters guarantee you'll "rub elbows" with fellow diners, the "food makes you forget that you're a sardine"; N.B. now open for lunch Monday–Friday.

Little Cafe | 26 | 19 | 23 | $35 |

Plaza Shoppes, 118 White Horse Rd. E. (Burnt Mill Rd.), Voorhees, 856-784-3344

■ "Big-city food" makes the scene in Voorhees at this "teeny-tiny" International BYO cafe that proves you "can't judge a place by its size"; the "storefront" setting may be "lacking in ambiance" and the "limited" "space is a problem" for claustrophobes, but it compensates with "unbeatable early-bird" deals and service that's "attentive without being pushy."

Madeleine's Petit Paris [S] | 26 | 21 | 24 | $46 |

416 Tappan Rd. (Paris Ave.), Northvale, 201-767-0063

■ Finally, "atmosphere to match the fabulous cooking" enthuse supporters of this classic French grande dame, which is now fully settled into its "spacious" site in Northvale after having relocated from Bergenfield; the owner's "warm hospitality" and the kitchen's "elegant" dishes keep this "winner" squarely in the "crème de la crème" league; P.S. don't miss the crêpe Madeline or the soufflés.

MANOR [S] | 24 | 26 | 24 | $52 |

111 Prospect Ave. (Eagle Rock Ave.), West Orange, 973-731-2360

■ They "treat you like a king" at this "glitz-to-the-hilt" West Orange American-Continental, aka the "Tavern on the Green of NJ", where "more people than at Grand Central Station" gather to dig into its "fresh seafood buffet"; though some dismiss it as "Jurassic dining", loyalists maintain that it's still a "must for a special occasion", as it "delivers the whole nine yards" – you can "present that engagement ring", then book the wedding here.

Mazi [S] | – | – | – | M |

401 Main St. (4th Ave.), Bradley Beach, 732-775-8828

Satisfying fans of authentic, regional Mediterranean cooking is this Bradley Beach BYO newcomer where music mogul-turned-chef Peter Mantas prepares specialties such as chicken piri-piri, scallops in gazpacho and vegetable cassoulet, while owner Leslie Feingold confects strictly seasonal desserts from the market's best; its all served up in a funky, flea market–chic setting with a vaguely Provençal vibe; N.B. open Wednesday–Saturday for dinner only.

Moonstruck [S] | 27 | 21 | 23 | $39 |

517 Lake Ave. (Grand Ave.), Asbury Park, 732-988-0123

■ Recently relocated to spacious new digs overlooking a lake in Asbury Park, this American pleaser still "never disappoints" its starstruck admirers thanks to the "consistently" "fabulous" Med-influenced creations "lovingly prepared" by its "talented chef"; the good news is that the move from its BYO site in Ocean Grove has brought it more than extra seats and legroom – it now also features a galaxy of spirits – but, alas, the "no-reservations" policy still makes entry a "real hassle."

Park & Orchard [S] | 24 | 15 | 20 | $34 |

240 Hackensack St. (Union Ave.), East Rutherford, 201-939-9292

■ "Come hungry" and "get here early", because this Eclectic "institution" in East Rutherford serves up "huge portions" but it accepts "no reservations"; though meat, chicken, fish and pasta dishes "abound" on the menu, it's most known for its vegetarian selections (the "most creative meatless choices we've ever seen") and "glorious wine list" (comprising 2,000 bottles, it's about the "size of a legal brief").

Rat's [S] | 24 | 28 | 23 | $60 |

16 Fairgrounds Rd. (Ward Ave. ext.), Hamilton, 609-584-7800

■ Fans say "beautiful doesn't begin to describe" this New French "fantasyland" perched on Hamilton's Grounds for Sculpture; it's "magnificent on all counts", from chef Eric Martin's "out-of-this-world" cooking to the "spectacularly decorated" rooms and "unbelievable" gardens; though its name refers to the creature in the kids' classic *The Wind in the Willows*, its existence comes courtesy of J. Seward Johnson Jr. and stands as testimony to "what you can create if you're a billionaire."

River Palm Terrace [S] | 25 | 19 | 21 | $49 |

1416 River Rd. (Palisade Terrace), Edgewater, 201-224-2013

41-11 Rte. 4 W. (bet. Paramus & Saddle River Rds.), Fair Lawn, 201-703-3500

209 Ramapo Valley Rd. (Rte. 17), Mahwah, 201-529-1111

■ "Here's the beef" – for "prime meat in a prime restaurant", these "upscale " North Jersey landmarks are "worth it no matter the price"; expect "tender", "tasty" cuts that set the "standard", delivered by a staff that's "amazingly patient", especially given the "high volume on Fridays and Saturdays."

RYLAND INN [S] | 28 | 28 | 27 | $69 |

Rte. 22 W. (Rte. 523), Whitehouse, 908-534-4011

■ "Mere mortals may not fully appreciate the complexity" of the New French fare created by "culinary god" Craig Shelton at this "magical" place in Hunterdon County, but suffice it to say that it was voted No. 1 for Food in NJ; not only is this "food heaven" simply "perfection" but the "deep wine list", "beautiful" setting and "classy, gracious" service have also helped make it the Most Popular restaurant in the Garden State.

SADDLE RIVER INN | 27 | 26 | 26 | $55 |

2 Barnstable Ct. (bet. E. Allendale Ave. & W. Saddle River Rd.), Saddle River, 201-825-4016

■ "Dream-making grand dining" awaits at this pond-side retreat set in an old barn in Saddle River, which has been executing "masterful meals in a country setting" for two decades; "inventive" chef-owner Hans Egg continues to "skillfully" turn out "excellent", New American–French dishes, served by an "immaculate" staff in a room infused with "European charm"; the cost-cutting BYO policy is just a "bonus", but make sure to "reserve ahead."

SAGAMI [S] | 27 | 17 | 22 | $34 |

37 W. Crescent Blvd. (Haddon Ave.), Collingswood, 856-854-9773

■ Just "ask the execs at Subaru of America" – they'll tell you about the "melt-in-your-mouth" "precision sushi" prepared by chef Shigeru Fukuyoshi and his crew at this Collingswood BYO that's "worth the price" for a taste of the "zenith in Japanese cuisine"; you may have to wait your turn for a seat in the "dark-wooded, low-ceilinged" room, but the "charming, efficient" staff will reward you with a pleasurable meal.

SCALINI FEDELI
27 | 26 | 26 | $60

63 Main St. (Parrot Mill Rd.), Chatham, 973-701-9200

■ Chatham has its own "masterpiece" in this "heavenly" Northern Italian BYO distinguished by its "superbly flavorful" dishes; though chef Michael Cetrulo may be spending time at its NYC sibling, that clearly hasn't interfered with the "off-the-scale" "pleasure" of the dining experience here, or the "marvelous", "romantic" ambiance; yes, it's "expensive" and the wait for a reservation can be long, but by all accounts, it's well "worth it."

Serenäde
27 | 25 | 25 | $59

6 Roosevelt Ave. (Main St.), Chatham, 973-701-0303

■ It's not only music lovers who "bliss out" over the "ingenious elegance" of the New French tasting menus at this "sensational" "CEO dining capital of NJ" in Chatham, where chef-owner James Laird employs the "highest-quality ingredients" and scores "straight A's"; credit too the "serene" surroundings and gracious service for always making diners "feel special."

Shumi S
24 | 12 | 18 | $34

30 S. Doughty Ave. (Veterans Memorial Dr.), Somerville, 908-526-8596

■ Some of the "best sushi in NJ" turns up at this Somerville spot where the "fish is so fresh you'd think it was caught out back"; ignore this BYO's "hospital-cafeteria" decor and just settle in for a "civilized" meal while chef-owner Kunihiko Aikasa "does his magic for you."

Siri's Thai French Cuisine S
26 | 23 | 24 | $36

2117 Rte. 70 W. (Haddonfield Rd.), Cherry Hill, 856-663-6781

■ "French elegance and sophistication" combine with "exotic" Thai flavors at this Cherry Hill venue that offers the "best of both worlds" and earns unanimous applause for its "gorgeous, creative" specialties ("each dish is better than the last"); this BYO's other elements are in perfect harmony too, from the "attractive" decor to the "well-trained, attentive" service to the "reasonable" tabs.

Stage House S
26 | 24 | 23 | $53

366 Park Ave. (Front St.), Scotch Plains, 908-322-4224

■ "From the *amuse* to the petit fours", anticipate "incredible culinary extravagance" via David Drake's "masterful" cooking at this New French in Scotch Plains; the "awesome" food's a cunning counterpoint to the "colonial setting" (it's quartered in a 1737 building), the "wine list is loaded with exceptional" bottles at "wonderful prices" and "they do all the little things that most places don't", so it promises to be a "longtime superstar on the scene."

Union Park S
27 | 27 | 27 | $47

Hotel Macomber, 727 Beach Ave. (Howard St.), Cape May, 609-884-8811

■ "Park yourself" in a "beautiful room" and get ready for a "thrilling experience" at this "superb" New American BYO in Cape May that "has it all" – "unique" dishes based on "delicious combinations", a "lovely" atmosphere and "meticulous attention to every detail"; it's a "must-stop for fine dining" in these parts.

Washington Inn 🅂   27 | 27 | 26 | $49

801 Washington St. (Jefferson St.), Cape May, 609-884-5697

■ "Everything's first-class" at this "perfect" American in Cape May that remains the epitome of "civilized, elegant dining", offering "traditional food prepared with finesse", an "unbelievable wine cellar" and "extremely professional" service; its 1840s plantation house setting is "gorgeous, especially at Christmas", prompting fans to gush "the whole package is fabulous."

Waters Edge 🅂   26 | 23 | 23 | $45

1317 Beach Dr. (Pittsburgh Ave.), Cape May, 609-884-1717

■ If you're dining at this Cape May New American on a "summer evening", try one of the "tempting", "highly imaginative seafood entrees with Asian and Caribbean touches" and you'll be assured of an "eclectic" repast; in addition, its "exceptionally beautiful" "waterfront setting" makes it one of the "trendiest places at the Shore"; the consensus: it "deserves its reputation in every way."

Zarolé 🅂   ▽ 26 | 27 | 19 | $45

20 E. Ridgewood Ave. (bet. S. Broad St. & S. Maple Ave.), Ridgewood, 201-670-5701

■ "Your companion will look great in the lighting" of this "upscale", "breathtaking" New American BYO, one of the "most innovative" eateries in Ridgewood; though the "different and delicious" fusion cuisine pairs easily with the "dramatic" decor, some say service is "a little off", but if it catches up, this spot will be truly "tops."

New Orleans

TOP 20 FOOD RANKING

Restaurant	Cuisine Type
28 Peristyle	French/New Orleans
27 Bayona	New American
Brigtsen's	Louisiana
Lafitte's Landing	Cajun-Creole
Galatoire's	Creole
Gabrielle	Creole
Grill Room	New American
La Provence	French
Commander's Palace	Creole
26 Clancy's	Creole
Ruth's Chris	Steakhouse
Artesia	New French
Jacques-Imo's Cafe	Creole/Soul Food
Irene's Cuisine	N&S Italian/French
Bistro at Maison de Ville	French Bistro
Dick & Jenny's	French/Creole
Mosca's	N&S Italian
Gautreau's	New French/Creole
Eleven 79	N&S Italian
Sal & Judy's	S. Italian/Creole

ADDITIONAL NOTEWORTHY PLACES

Antoine's	Creole/French
Arnaud's	Creole
August	New French
Brennan's	Creole/French
Cuvée	Louisiana
Dakota	Louisiana/New American
Emeril's	Creole/New American
Herbsaint	New French/New American
Kim Son	Asian
Martinique Bistro	French Bistro/Seafood
Mr. B's Bistro	Creole
Muriel's	Creole
Nine Roses	Vietnamese
NOLA	New Orleans
Pelican Club	New American
Rene Bistrot	French Bistro
Rib Room	Continental/Steakhouse
RioMar	Spanish/Latin American
Sake Cafe	Japanese
Upperline	Creole

Antoine's
22 | 25 | 24 | $49

713 St. Louis St. (bet. Bourbon & Royal Sts.), 504-581-4422
◪ Nostalgists hail this "old-fashioned" 1840 French Quarter Creole-classic French "landmark" where "half the fun is the history of it all"; those who live in the present, however, argue this "grande dame" is "getting a little tired" – "living on, not up to, her reputation" – and they wouldn't be "caught dead" in the touristy front room.

Arnaud's ◲
22 | 24 | 23 | $43

813 Bienville St. (bet. Bourbon & Dauphine Sts.), 504-523-5433
◪ Critics may carp this "fine old French Quarter lady" is "gliding on her reputation", but to most, she still "lives the legend", serving up "classic" Creole in an "elegant" setting where the "history of New Orleans is felt everywhere", even in the "nice" cigar bar and private dining rooms; "great trout meunière" and the "best" shrimp rémoulade garner as much applause as the live jazz, but it's the service that "sets it apart from the rest."

Artesia ◲
26 | 25 | 25 | $41

21516 Hwy. 36 (Hwy. 59), Abita Springs, 985-892-1662
■ This "elegant Country French inn" in Abita Springs, serving "fresh beautiful food", pulls urbanites across the lake for "unique dishes", a "very relaxed atmosphere" and "knowledgeable" service that combine to make it "worth the trip from the city"; N.B. a post-*Survey* chef change may outdate the above Food score.

August
– | – | – | VE

301 Tchoupitoulas St. (Gravier St.), 504-299-9777
No doubt about it: chef John Besh (ex Artesia) raises the culinary bar for the Big Easy, tempting diners with his New French dishes fashioned from local ingredients and beautifully presented within an 18th-century Warehouse District that's been restored to its original grandeur; the only concern is a world-class wine list that could use a few more reasonably priced bottles.

BAYONA
27 | 26 | 25 | $45

430 Dauphine St. (bet. Conti & St. Louis Sts.), 504-525-4455
■ "It's hard to miss with chef Susan Spicer", the "reigning queen" on the throne of this "perennial-favorite" French Quarter New American whose "spectacular" "innovative" creations please "both eye and tongue" ("the dishes are like works of art that make you want to weep"); add to the mix a "romantic patio" and an "on-the-ball" staff, and the result is an "absolutely exquisite" affair that fully deserves its "sterling reputation."

Bistro at Maison de Ville ◲
26 | 25 | 24 | $45

Maison de Ville, 727 Toulouse St. (bet. Bourbon & Royal Sts.), 504-528-9206
■ The most "Parisian of New Orleans' restaurants" rhapsodize Francophiles about this "cozy", "elegant" French Quarter bistro where chef Greg Picolo offers up "delicate, flavorful" fare; while a few find the small dining room a bit "claustrophobic", enthusiasts embrace the "beautiful courtyard" and "attentive" service, concluding this is "still one of the finest!"

Brennan's ◲
24 | 26 | 25 | $48

417 Royal St. (bet. Conti & St. Louis Sts.), 504-525-9711
◪ "Are there any great things left to say?" ask fans of this "true New Orleans" Creole-French "institution" in the Quarter where

"divine" eggs Benedict and "superb" bananas Foster, "elegant and charming" surroundings and "incomparable" (if "pretentious") service have regulars returning "not just for breakfast"; grumblers may groan it's an "overpriced tourist trap", but even so, "when you're in town you have to do it."

BRIGTSEN'S　　　　　27　22　25　$40
723 Dante St. (Maple St.), 504-861-7610

■ Only "master" chef Frank Brigtsen "could make andouille sausage taste better than foie gras" fawn flattering foodies fond of the "inventive" "top-flight" Modern Louisiana cuisine at this tucked away Riverbend veteran in a "turn-of-the-century New Orleans cottage"; "homey" service makes it "perfect for sharing", so get those hard-to-come-by reservations in advance.

CLANCY'S　　　　　26　21　24　$39
6100 Annunciation St. (Webster St.), 504-895-1111

■ "Don't let the secret out" plead perennial patrons – but it may be too late, since this "classic" Uptown Creole is "quickly being discovered"; "the fried-oyster-and-brie appetizer" "reappears in your dreams", accompanied by "the best ever" lemon ice box pie; it may be "too noisy" for some, especially in the front room, but the "congenial" staff gives a "warm welcome" and the "cool" setting makes you "want to dress up."

COMMANDER'S PALACE 🖥　　　　27　28　27　$47
1403 Washington Ave. (Coliseum St.), 504-899-8221

■ The "unrivaled" "queen of local cuisine" still rules with an "elegant" haute Creole hand, and subjects "feel the power", voting this Garden District "crown jewel" Most Popular among New Orleans restaurants for its "amazing" menu, "excellent" bread pudding soufflé and a Sunday jazz brunch that's "a must"; persnickety patrons pout that "there are too many tourists", but why wouldn't there be for "gracious Southern dining at its finest"?

Cuvée　　　　　26　26　24　$45
St. James Hotel, 322 Magazine St. (bet. Gravier & Poydras Sts.), 504-587-9001

■ Rising faster than a champagne bubble, this "bright star" in the CBD boasts "Richard 'Bingo' Starr, one of the best chefs in New Orleans today", whose "exciting" 'retro-Louisiana' menu is based on French, Spanish and Cajun-Creole accents; "professional, polished" servers provide "pampering" amid "plush, sophisticated decor" with "unique lighting" (the chandeliers are upside-down Nebuchadnezzars); just be sure to "bring your checkbook – and your spouse's" too.

Dakota　　　　　26　23　24　$40
629 N. Hwy. 190 (¼ mi. north of I-12), Covington, 985-892-3712

■ Cuvée's older sister, this North Shore Louisiana–New American offers "quality in every respect" – "terrific" specialties "beautifully presented" with "impeccable service" amid "refreshed new decor"; no question it's "worth a trip across the Causeway" for a "great eating experience" – especially if that includes the "amazing crabmeat-and-brie soup."

Dick & Jenny's　　　　　26　20　23　$35
4501 Tchoupitoulas St. (Jena St.), 504-894-9880

■ "Please take reservations" plead patrons tired of "waiting a long time" for a table at this "small", "charming bargeboard cottage" Uptown; it's just that everyone loves the dinner-only, Louisiana-inspired menu produced by chef Richard Benz and would "follow him to hell" for French-Creole "food that's out of this world"; fortunately, they can get it instead in this "friendly", "homey" and "casual" atmosphere overseen by wife and co-owner Jenny, who helps create a truly "class act."

Eleven 79
26 | 24 | 24 | $42

1179 Annunciation St. (Erato St.), 504-299-1179

■ Hidden under the expressway, this Warehouse District spot may be a little hard to find ("don't tell the tourists"), but that hasn't deterred devotees who love the "absolutely delicious" menu and the "quaint, charming atmosphere" of its renovated historic cottage; the "dimly lit surroundings" can get "much too noisy" and the usually "delightful service" sometimes "can't keep up with the crowd", but it's a "favorite" for folk who love "Italian food with a Creole heart."

Emeril's
25 | 23 | 24 | $51

800 Tchoupitoulas St. (Julia St.), 504-528-9393

◪ The "innovative" Creole-based New American fare "still excites" at you-know-who's "original" "happening place" situated in the Warehouse District, where a remodeling two years ago made it "much less noisy" and a visual "knockout"; while for many locals it's "too pricey", "too touristy" and a little "too big for its britches", and even advocates admit it "could use a little more Emeril", most maintain "you really do need to experience" it.

Gabrielle
27 | 19 | 24 | $42

3201 Esplanade Ave. (Mystery St.), 504-948-6233

■ "Fantastic surprises on and off the menu" await diners at this "tiny" Nouvelle Creole a few blocks from the New Orleans Museum of Art in the Faubourg St. John; "top Louisiana chef" Greg Sonnier gets "kudos for creativity" on "outlandishly good" rabbit, "luscious desserts" and other "consistently superior" fare, so who cares if it's "a little cramped"?

GALATOIRE'S [S]
27 | 26 | 27 | $44

209 Bourbon St. (Iberville St.), 504-525-2021

■ A "local favorite for generations", this haute Creole in the French Quarter may be the "most festive spot in the city", where the "atmosphere and tradition are as important as the food"; a "wonderfully renovated" upstairs "complements the old-school downstairs", and "waiters who will sit down with you and share great stories if you're there when the crowds aren't" make this a "uniquely New Orleans" "fine-dining" experience that "others aspire to" but can't quite replicate.

Gautreau's
26 | 23 | 24 | $44

1728 Soniat St. (Danneel St.), 504-899-7397

■ "Exquisite" New French–Creole fare has in-the-know noshers nipping to this "classy Uptown bistro" where devotees swear "everything is good" – from the "tantalizing" tastes and "top-notch" service to the "discreet" location and "unpretentious" vibe – and offered in a "beautifully" "converted old drugstore" complete with an antique apothecary cabinet; "go early or late", though, if you want to avoid "noisy" crowds; N.B. the Food rating does not reflect the post-*Survey* arrival of chef Mathias Wolf.

Grill Room [S] — 27 | 28 | 27 | $58

Windsor Court Hotel, 300 Gravier St. (bet. S. Peters & Tchoupitoulas Sts.), 504-522-1992

■ Aesthetes are awed by the "posh" "elegance" of this New American CBD veteran in the Windsor Court Hotel graced with an "unmatched" design that prompts romantics "to fall in love again"; with such "scrumptious" fare and "exceptional" wines, served by pampering waiters who move "like trained ballet dancers, this is "Southern hospitality" that's "worth the splurge."

Herbsaint — 24 | 20 | 22 | $36

701 St. Charles Ave. (Girod St.), 504-524-4114

◪ "Another thumbs-up for Susan Spicer" attest aficionados of her "hip home cooking" at this "informal but elegant" CBD New French–American; though comparers claim "it's not a Bayona experience" yet, as the service can be "indifferent" and the room "too confining" and "noisy" when things get "swinging", it's an up-and-coming "smash hit" with the "potential to be great."

Irene's Cuisine [S] — 26 | 22 | 22 | $36

539 St. Philip St. (Chartres St.), 504-529-8811

■ This "cozy", "romantic" Italian-Provençal serves "huge portions" of "wonderful food" to a largely local French Quarter crowd; while they adore the "best duck in the city" and fantastic "garlic chicken" (and accept the "cramped seating" and a wine list that "could use work"), fans "hate the wait" and ask "why not take reservations?"

Jacques-Imo's Cafe — 26 | 19 | 21 | $28

8324 Oak St. (S. Carrollton Ave.), 504-861-0886

■ For "five-star food on a one-star wallet", frugal foodies flock to this "informal delight" in Carrollton serving up "world-class" "Southern style at its best" – "amazing Creole" and Soul "home cooking" with Cajun flare, like "killer" cornbread and "unusual" alligator cheesecake; sure, the "happening" scene is "loud" and "funky", but the "element of chaos" in the "sometimes erratic" service just "adds to the fun" of the "authentic experience."

Kim Son — 24 | 12 | 17 | $20

349 Whitney Ave. (Westbank Expwy.), Gretna, 504-366-2489

■ An "unexpected surprise" awaits those who have not yet tried the "more-addictive-than-drugs" fare at this "inexpensive" West Bank Asian, a simply decorated spot where "excellent char-grilled" chicken and "super salt-baked shrimp and scallops" are among the "consistently good", "authentic" dishes on the "huge menu."

LAFITTE'S LANDING [S] — 27 | 27 | 26 | $44

Bittersweet Plantation, 404 Claiborne St. (Railroad Ave.), Donaldsonville, 225-473-1232

■ Chef-owner "John Folse is a legend", and smitten surveyors say that his "classic" Cajun-Creole in Donaldsonville's "lovely" Bittersweet Plantation is in "a league of its own" thanks to "terrific food and superlative service"; true, this "romantic getaway" is about an hour from town, but the "culinary delights" make a visit here "definitely worth the drive."

La Provence [S] — 27 | 26 | 24 | $44

25020 Hwy. 190 (bet. Lacombe & Mandeville), Lacombe, 985-626-7662

■ The trip across Lake Pontchartrain to reach this "wonderful Country French" "romantic hideaway" seems relatively short for an "authentic" piece of Provence itself, say drivers who delight in diving into "delicious" dishes prepared by "super chef" Chris Kerageorgiou; a "charming", "elegant" setting where you can "sit next to the fireplace, bask" with a glass of red wine and enjoy the "unbeatable service" has enthusiasts exclaiming *c'est magnifique*, "France should be so good."

Martinique Bistro [S] 25 | 21 | 21 | $35

5908 Magazine St. (bet. Eleonore & State Sts.), 504-891-8495

■ "It's always a delight to dine" on chef Hubert Sandot's "stellar" French seafood with a "Caribbean twist" at "Uptown's most charming bistro"; if you're on a "romantic" date or celebrating your "anniversary", "dine under the stars" on the patio by "a beautiful rose bush in front of the water fountain" and pray that things "don't ever change."

Mosca's ⊭ 26 | 13 | 19 | $35

4137 Hwy. 90 W. (bet. Butler Dr. & Live Oak Blvd.), Avondale, 504-436-9942

■ One stop at this cash-only "garlic lover's paradise" "will keep the vampires away forever" rave regulars of this Italian that's "worth every mile" of the "long ride" to Avondale; the "fattening" family-style fare is "not for the weak of heart", but that doesn't stop 'em from staking their forks into the "absolute best" grub "you'll ever eat outside your Sicilian grandmother's kitchen."

Mr. B's Bistro [S] 25 | 23 | 24 | $35

201 Royal St. (Iberville St.), 504-523-2078

■ "Another excellent Brennan" joint, this "casually elegant" French Quarter haute Creole is a "favorite spot to bring visitors"; start with "a cocktail at the bar, where you can watch the action" in a "stylish", "casual" room "humming with excitement", then move on to the "rich, luscious food"; while some prefer it for lunch or Sunday jazz brunch, finding it "touristy" for dinner, most maintain that whenever you go it's "consistently" "terrific."

Muriel's [S] 20 | 26 | 21 | $42

Jackson Sq., 801 Chartres St. (St. Ann St.), 504-568-1885

◪ Fans "can't say enough about" this "exciting" spot set in a "great location" "overlooking Jackson Square"; "one of the most beautiful restaurants in town", it boasts "incredible" ambiance, "wonderful" contemporary interpretations of traditional Creole dishes and "knowledgeable" service; the "not overly impressed" cite "growing pains", but most predict this "keeper" with "lots of potential" won't be "a well-kept secret" for long.

Nine Roses [S] 24 | 14 | 18 | $18

1100 Stephen St. (Westbank Expwy.), Gretna, 504-366-7665

■ In a town built on butter, "health"-conscious N'Awlins natives say it's "worth the schlep" "across the bridge" to try the "low-fat and delicious" "refreshing tastes" of Saigon at this Gretna spot; the fare on the "very lengthy menu" (which includes lots of vegetarian dishes) is "cheap and reliable", and locals argue "you know it's good when the entire place is filled with Vietnamese diners."

NOLA [S] 25 | 23 | 23 | $40

534 St. Louis St. (bet. Chartres & Decatur Sts.), 504-522-6652

◪ It's "Emeril's on a budget" at the superstar chef's "casual" "alternative" that gives "more bam for the buck" and, according to some folks, is "better than the original"; out-of-town "visitors love" the "delish" "contemporary New Orleans cuisine", but some locals think this "brassy, sassy" French Quarter cafe "seems more designed for tourists" who don't mind being "crammed in like sardines" to eat "gimmicky" grub.

Pelican Club [S] 25 | 24 | 23 | $42

312 Exchange Pl. (Bienville Ave.), 504-523-1504

■ The "fabulous fusion" of "old Louisiana Creole favorites with Asian flavors" is "worth a trip down the alley" to this French Quarter New American; it's a "unique and innovative dining experience", "yet very New Orleans" as well, even though an ambiance that "feels more like a club than a restaurant" means that this "special place" can get "crowded."

PERISTYLE 28 | 25 | 26 | $48

1041 Dumaine St. (N. Rampart St.), 504-593-9535

■ As per the No. 1 Food ranking among New Orleans restaurants, "Anne Kearney is the best chef" in town; sample the "focused flavors" of her "outstanding" French cuisine with a "perfectly matched" wine "beautifully presented" by a "spectacular staff" at her "refined and romantic" spot in the Quarter and you're bound to agree with locals who insist "trying to imagine a better dining experience would make my head explode."

Rene Bistrot [S] – | – | – | E

Renaissance Pere Marquette Hotel, 817 Common St. (Barrone St.), 504-412-2580

Master chef Rene Bajeaux is the guiding spirit at this charming, comfortable hotel dining room; his authentic French bistro menu focusing on flavorful *goût de terroir* (taste of the earth) cooking has the acclaim of picky local gourmands, and reasonable daily *table d'hôte* and special *plats du jour* bring in crowds at lunch and dinner.

Rib Room [S] 25 | 24 | 23 | $42

Omni Royal Orleans, 621 St. Louis St. (bet. Chartres & Royal Sts.), 504-529-7046

■ A "consistent treasure" in the heart of the French Quarter, this "oldie but goodie" Continental steakhouse is still a "favorite place to take business clients"; it's "hard to beat if you're in the mood for red meat" crow carnivores, who praise its prime rib "you can cut with a fork" between sips of the "best martinis in town"; ask for a window seat overlooking Royal Street for top-notch "people-watching" from the "comfortable, quiet dining room."

RioMar 23 | 20 | 20 | $31

800 S. Peters St. (Julia St.), 504-525-3474

■ For "innovative" Spanish and Latin American, fans favor this two-year-old Warehouse District eatery, "a breath of fresh air" amid the Creole congestion; the "limited but exceptional menu" offers "wonderful fish", a variety of seviches and other "zesty" dishes, while the "happy" setting has habitués hallucinating that they're harboring in "a seaside cafe in Spain."

Ruth's Chris Steak House [S] 26 | 22 | 25 | $46

711 N. Broad Ave. (Orleans Ave.), 504-486-0810

3633 Veterans Memorial Blvd. (Hessmer Ave.), Metairie, 504-888-3600

■ "You haven't had steak until you've eaten here" boast boosters who head to Metairie and Mid-City for "flavorful, tender" beef complemented by "superb" side dishes "generous" enough to "share with someone special"; sure, it's "very pricey", but the "staff makes you feel like family" and the original home on North Broad is still the "best site for politician-watching."

Sake Cafe [S] 25 | 26 | 22 | $25

2830 Magazine St. (Washington Ave.), 504-894-0033
Independence Mall, 4201 Veterans Memorial Blvd. (Houma Blvd.), Metairie, 504-779-7253
817 W. Esplanade (Chateau Ave.), Kenner, 504-468-8829

■ What fin fans want, what they really, really want, is a "very exciting Spice Girl roll" (with Ginger, of course) and more of the "unusual", "superb sushi" ferried by the "affable staff" at this "very elegant" (shall we say Posh?) Japanese trio; "the chic location on Magazine Street" feels like a "wonderful retreat", and followers also fawn over the "cool decor" at the original suburban site; N.B. the Kenner branch opened post-*Survey*.

Sal & Judy's [S] 26 | 15 | 21 | $31

27491 Hwy. 190 (24th St.), Lacombe, 985-882-7167

■ "Go hungry" for "prime rib cut as if from a brontosaurus" and other "large portions" of "outstanding", "old-world" Italian and "hearty" Creole at this Lacombe "tradition"; Sal himself is "still the man in the kitchen" here, and since his "consistently fabulous food" is "worth a trip across" Lake Pontchartrain, "reservations are a must."

Upperline [S] 26 | 23 | 24 | $39

1413 Upperline St. (bet. Prytania St. & St. Charles Ave.), 504-891-9822

■ "If cuisine were religion", the haute Creole fare at Uptown's "charming cottage" "would be salvation" say supplicants; the "unreal" "magic" of dishes like "superbly tender and flavorful lamb shanks" and a "duck with port wine sauce that makes your heart soar" is more than matched by the "sparkle" of "hostess with the mostest", owner Joanne Clevenger, and her decidedly "eclectic art collection."

TOP 20 FOOD RANKING

Restaurant	Cuisine Type
28 Daniel	French
Sushi Yasuda	Japanese
Jean Georges	New French
Le Bernardin	French/Seafood
Chanterelle	French
Nobu	Japanese/Peruvian
27 Gramercy Tavern	New American
Nobu, Next Door	Japanese/Peruvian
Peter Luger	Steakhouse
Gotham Bar & Grill	New American
Bouley	New French
Lespinasse	French
Alain Ducasse	French
Oceana	Seafood
Sushi of Gari	Japanese
Il Mulino	Northern Italian
Aureole	New American
Veritas	New American
Babbo	N&S Italian
Scalini Fedeli	Northern Italian

ADDITIONAL NOTEWORTHY PLACES

Aquavit	Scandinavian
Artisanal	French Bistro
Atelier	New French
Balthazar	French Bistro
Bayard's	French/American
Blue Hill	New American
Blue Ribbon	Eclectic
Café des Artistes	French
Carnegie Deli	Deli
Craft	New American
Danube	Austrian
db Bistro Moderne	French Bistro
Eleven Madison Park	New American
Fiamma Osteria	N&S Italian
Harrison	Med./New American
Ilo	New American
La Caravelle	French
La Côte Basque	French
Le Cirque 2000	New French
Milos, Estiatorio	Greek/Seafood
Montrachet	French
Park Avenue Cafe	New American
Picholine	Mediterranean
River Cafe	New American
Shun Lee Palace	Chinese
Smith & Wollensky	Steakhouse
Tavern on the Green	New American
Town	New American
'21' Club	American
Union Pacific	New American
Union Square Cafe	New American
Washington Park	New American

Alain Ducasse
27 | 26 | 27 | $193

Essex House, 155 W. 58th St. (bet. 6th & 7th Aves.), 212-265-7300

■ "Oh, what he can do with a truffle!" or even a trifle – chef-owner Alain Ducasse's "world-class" Midtown French gives NYers the "royal treatment" in its "ritualized" "parade" of "sublime" "culinary delights", "from foie gras to lollipops", delivered by a "super-attentive" staff in a "stunning" setting; despite "gimme-a-break" pricing (dinner prix fixe starts at $145), most maintain that the "meal of a lifetime" is well "worth the investment."

Aquavit [S]
26 | 26 | 25 | $64

13 W. 54th St. (bet. 5th & 6th Aves.), 212-307-7311

■ A "chic" "spa" for the "palate and eyes", Marcus Samuelsson's Midtown Scandinavian destination turns out "avant-garde" feats of "incredible herring-do", abetted by "flawless" service and a "sleek", "head-turning" atrium setting complete with a "dramatic waterfall" and birch trees; salmon "sticker-shock" survivors suggest a calming "infusion" of the eponymous "water of life" – or a spell in the more af-fjordable "upstairs cafe."

Artisanal [S]
23 | 21 | 20 | $51

2 Park Ave. (32nd St.), 212-725-8585

■ Those with a nose for curdish "delicacies" wheel by Terry Brennan's "pungent" Murray Hill French brasserie-cum-fromagerie for "delicious" dishes and "challenging cheeses" paired with a "super wine program"; despite "sometimes shaky" service, dining in this "brassy" Adam Tihany–designed room is the "most fun" a "cheese whiz" can have.

Atelier [S]
– | – | – | VE

Ritz-Carlton Central Park, 50 Central Park S. (bet. 5th & 6th Aves.), 212-521-6125

This Central Park South neophyte in the new Ritz-Carlton proffers chef Gabriel Kreuther's "perfectly balanced presentations" of Modern French cooking in comfortably swank quarters, backed by "impeccable" service; of course, these haute vittles come with haute prices, but NYC gourmands aren't complaining, since it's probably "best new restaurant of the year."

Aureole
27 | 25 | 26 | $76

34 E. 61st St. (bet. Madison & Park Aves.), 212-319-1660

■ Like a "blissful" "dream", Charlie Palmer's Midtown duplex flagship "runs rings around the trendies" thanks to the "complex", "delectable" New American fare prepared by new chef de cuisine Dante Boccuzzi, topped off with "vertical desserts" and "smooth", "finishing-school" service; brimming with "flowers and elegance", the "tranquil", "grown-up" space is the "epitome of class", where "paramours" with "something to celebrate" can "flex the credit card" and get "self-indulgent in a big way."

Babbo ☾ [S]
27 | 23 | 24 | $66

110 Waverly Pl. (bet. MacDougal St. & 6th Ave.), 212-777-0303

■ Ever "pushing the culinary envelope", this "*magnifico*" Village "showstopper" from (Molto Mario) Batali and (just plain Joe) Bastianich thrills with "robust", "adventurous" Italian cooking based on "bold" techniques that make for "heaven on a plate"; the "*bella*" bi-level townhouse setting and "warm, efficient" service ("despite the mobs") set the "simply luxe" tone, and though getting a table is akin to winning the "Powerball lottery", "all those limos outside can't be wrong" – it "doesn't get any better."

Balthazar ●🔾🇸　　　23 | 23 | 19 | $50
80 Spring St. (bet. B'way & Crosby St.), 212-965-1414

■ "Forget the flight to Paris" – Keith McNally's "buzzy" SoHo brasserie offers the same effect as a "spectacle" of French "style and substance", mixing "hustle-bustle" with "sex appeal" via a "pretty" crowd of "cool dudes" and "Sarah Jessica look-alikes"; "artful" food and "genial" service set the "high standards", and even if some shrug "*comme ci, comme ça*", it continues to be an "energizing" spot in which to "feel important."

Bayard's　　　　　23 | 24 | 23 | $63
1 Hanover Sq. (bet. Pearl & Stone Sts.), 212-514-9454

■ A step "back in time" to "Edith Wharton's" era, this "handsome" dinner-only Financial District French-American is a bastion of sophistication, featuring a "memorable" menu from chef Eberhard Mueller (ex Le Bernardin) and one of the city's best-value wine lists; the aptly "businesslike" tone is set by "attentive service from the minute you enter", and thanks to a number of private dining rooms, this is unquestionably the best place Downtown to give a party, big or small.

Blue Hill 🇸　　　　25 | 22 | 23 | $58
75 Washington Pl. (bet. 6th Ave. & Washington Sq. W.), 212-539-1776

■ They're clearly "on top of their game" at this "refined" "piece of heaven" set in a "stylish" Village brownstone where diners find their thrill with Daniel Barber and Michael Anthony's "superb", "spot-on" New American cuisine delivered with "panache" by a "gracious" staff; it's a "distinctive treat" for "grown-ups" that's "well worth" the price, though the "pretty" room may be "a little crowded" with "even prettier people."

Blue Ribbon ●🇸　　　25 | 17 | 21 | $47
97 Sullivan St. (bet. Prince & Spring Sts.), 212-274-0404

■ Prized for its "unadulterated high quality", this "super" SoHo Eclectic courtesy of the Bromberg brothers is a "joy any time" but a "lifesaver for the late eater", with "awesome", "no-nonsense" food to "suit every mood" served until the wee hours by a "courteous" staff; it's perpetually "packed" and "kicking", and though "no reservations" means a "mandatory wait", you can always cool your heels at the bar among "nice-to-look-at" patrons.

Bouley 🇸　　　　27 | 24 | 25 | $75
120 W. Broadway (Duane St.), 212-964-2525

■ He's back and it "seems like old times" – from the "original wooden door" and "fragrant bank of apples in the vestibule" to the "flawless" New French food – at David Bouley's reincarnation of his original TriBeCa "trendsetter", housed in the former Bouley Bakery space; this "solid rebound" comes complete with "darkly romantic" looks, "deft" service and, not surprisingly, prices to match – though the $35 prix fixe lunch is a bona fide "bargain."

Café des Artistes ●🇸　　22 | 26 | 22 | $63
1 W. 67th St. (bet. Columbus Ave. & CPW), 212-877-3500

■ George and Jenifer Lang's West Side "sybaritic" magnet can make anyone "feel like royalty" for the price of a meal; "fresh flowers" and gorgeous Howard Christy Chandler murals of nude young women set the "romantic" scene for "delectable" French food that's "imaginative without trying too hard" – and they also set the scene for not a few proposals; though a bit pricey, it's "worth the splurge" to "melt her heart."

Carnegie Deli ●🅢⌀　　　　20 | 8 | 12 | $24
854 Seventh Ave. (55th St.), 212-757-2245

■ "Skyscraper-size sandwiches" and "colossal cheesecakes" that "would make Dagwood proud" are the bait at this "quintessential" Midtown deli institution where "locals and tourists alike" squeeze into "communal tables" and endure "appropriately crusty" service for a taste of "overstuffed" bliss; it's "legendary for a reason" and "worth the occasional angioplasty."

CHANTERELLE　　　　28 | 26 | 27 | $87
2 Harrison St. (Hudson St.), 212-966-6960

■ David and Karen Waltuck's "ethereal" haute French treasure in TriBeCa "still shimmers" with "phenomenal" fare "magically presented" in a "calm", "sophisticated" setting enhanced by "well-choreographed" service that "leaves no detail unaddressed"; in short, it's the "gold standard of NYC restaurants" and priced accordingly (dinner is $84 prix fixe only), though the $38 lunch provides a "remarkable feast" for a remarkably low cost.

Craft 🅢　　　　26 | 25 | 24 | $65
43 E. 19th St. (bet. B'way & Park Ave. S.), 212-780-0880

■ "Fresh ingredients, simply prepared" are the hallmarks of Tom Colicchio's "casually classy" Flatiron New American offering a "culinary abacus menu" that allows you to "add or subtract items to build the perfect meal"; with "helpful" servers and "dramatic decor that's yin to the food's yang", it's "absolutely out-of-this-world", so though you'll "fork over some major change", it's worth it – there's "more art than craft" going on here.

DANIEL　　　　28 | 28 | 28 | $96
60 E. 65th St. (bet. Madison & Park Aves.), 212-288-0033

■ "As lavish and glamorous as it gets", Daniel Boulud's "life-altering" East Side French "temple" transports its "A-list" diners to "another world" with his "incredibly innovative" menu (once again it's ranked No. 1 for Food in NYC), an "exquisitely romantic" "palatial setting" and "sumptuous service from soup to soufflé"; granted, it all comes at "couture price tags", so "rob a bank" or "mortgage the kids" – it's "worth every expensive penny" for that "joyous feeling in the air."

Danube　　　　27 | 28 | 26 | $78
30 Hudson St. (bet. Duane & Reade Sts.), 212-791-3771

■ The "Hapsburgs rise again" at David Bouley's "artistic" TriBeCa "enchanter" where a "light hand with Austrian favorites" makes for "food to swoon over", especially when impeccably served in an "opulent", "Vienna Secessionist interior"; though you might want to double-check the "decimal place on the dinner bill", it's worth "saving the money you spend on analysis and applying it to this happy experience" that the enamored call "love at first bite."

db Bistro Moderne 🅢　　　　24 | 21 | 22 | $60
City Club Hotel, 55 W. 44th St. (bet. 5th & 6th Aves.), 212-391-2400

■ "Daniel Boulud goes modern" at this "stylish" Theater District French bistro offering the same "crafty" cooking as at the rest of his empire but at "more approachable prices"; famed for its "whimsical" foie gras–stuffed hamburger (an "instant classic", despite the $28 price tag), it's also known as a "power-lunch" locus for the publishing and rag trades, with the celebs favoring its "more formal" rear dining room.

Eleven Madison Park [S] 25 | 25 | 25 | $61

11 Madison Ave. (24th St.), 212-889-0905

■ There's "never a wrong note" struck at Danny Meyer's "airy" Madison Park New American where chef Kerry Heffernan's "high-concept" food is "as lofty as the ceilings", the "swank" "retro-metro" decor is equally "stunning" and the "unstuffy", "smooth-as-silk" service lives up to the "usual fine standards"; in short, this is "serious" "cosmopolitan dining at its best" – when prices don't matter, and where many "don't want to leave."

Fiamma Osteria ◐[S] 23 | 25 | 23 | $55

206 Spring St. (bet. 6th Ave. & Sullivan St.), 212-653-0100

■ Steve Hanson goes "upscale" at this "fine addition to the city's restaurant scene", an already "mature" SoHo Italian newcomer where "modest ingredients are combined into subtle, harmonious dishes" teamed with a "dictionary-size wine list" and "impeccable" service; the "high-class" triplex setup is simply "beautiful" and the prices only "moderately outrageous."

GOTHAM BAR & GRILL [S] 27 | 25 | 25 | $63

12 E. 12th St. (bet. 5th Ave. & University Pl.), 212-620-4020

■ This "elegant" Village New American is where "genius-at-work" Alfred Portale "still reigns", concocting "towering", "skyscraper"-like presentations that taste as good as they look; "faultless" service and "airy" environs shore up this annual winner's "staying power", as does the "deal-of-a-lifetime" $20.02 prix fixe lunch.

GRAMERCY TAVERN [S] 27 | 25 | 27 | $68

42 E. 20th St. (bet. B'way & Park Ave. S.), 212-477-0777

■ "As good as everyone says it is", Danny Meyer's Flatiron "triumph" has overtaken its sibling Union Square Cafe to become the Most Popular restaurant in NYC, thanks to chef Tom Colicchio's "pure and passionate" New American creations, the "exquisite" desserts, service that's "perfection personified" and handsome, neo-colonial decor; loyalties are divided between the "less pricey" "drop-in" tavern area and the "more formal back room", but wherever you sit, this is a "priceless experience"; P.S. try not to "hug the waiter."

Harrison [S] 23 | 21 | 22 | $51

355 Greenwich St. (Harrison St.), 212-274-9310

■ An "instant classic", this TriBeCa neophyte "deserves all the praise" showered on its "couldn't-be-better" Med–New American menu, "feel-right-at-home" ambiance and "sophisticated", "star"-studded crowd; even better, the "bill isn't a killer", leaving only one problem: "how to get a table."

Il Mulino ◐ 27 | 18 | 24 | $74

86 W. Third St. (bet. Sullivan & Thompson Sts.), 212-673-3783

■ "If you need a challenge", just "try getting reservations" at this mind-bogglingly popular Village Northern Italian; it could pack them in with its "aromas alone" – though the "perfectly prepared" food and "impeccable" service are certainly no handicaps; so "beg, lie, cheat or sell your soul to the devil" and "keep hitting redial" – "it's worth it" for the "best car payment" you'll ever eat.

Ilo [S] 24 | 22 | 22 | $74

Bryant Park Hotel, 40 W. 40th St. (bet. 5th & 6th Aves.), 212-642-2255

■ Ever since chef Rick Laakkonen (ex River Cafe) opened this "vibrant" New American across from Bryant Park, "serious foodies" have been flocking here; they report feeling "pure joy" as a result of the "clear, subtle flavors", "sparkling" service, "pristine surroundings" and "high-fashion", "glitterati" crowd; only the "relentless noise from the nearby bar" provokes any discord.

JEAN GEORGES 28 | 25 | 26 | $92

Trump Int'l Hotel, 1 Central Park W. (bet. 60th & 61st Sts.), 212-299-3900

■ "Everything works" like a charm at Jean-Georges Vongerichten's New French "nirvana", from the "gastronomic gold" mined in the kitchen to the "polished, unobtrusive" service to the "chic, understated" Adam Tihany decor; though you should be prepared to "drop a bundle", the $20.02 prix fixe lunch in the more "casual Nougatine Room" or out on the terrace overlooking Columbus Circle must be one of NYC's best "bargains."

La Caravelle 26 | 25 | 26 | $80

33 W. 55th St. (bet. 5th & 6th Aves.), 212-586-4252

■ Proving that "true civilization does exist in NYC", André and Rita Jammet's fortysomething Midtown French "favorite" maintains its "old-world perfection" via chef Troy Dupuy's "top-notch" creations, a warmly "posh" setting and a staff that "knows what you want before you do"; despite "jet set" dinner prices (prix fixe only, $72), lunch is a $38 bargain, leading devotees to insist "there is a heaven, and you don't have to die to get there."

La Côte Basque [S] 26 | 26 | 25 | $75

60 W. 55th St. (bet. 5th & 6th Aves.), 212-688-6525

■ "Like coming home – if you live in Versailles" – this "flawless" French Midtowner has supporters sighing "ooh-la-la" over Jean-Jacques Rachou's "sublime" food, the "lush" setting (decorated with paintings of the Basque seacoast) and the "formal" yet "comfortable" ambiance; sure, it's "pricey" (prix fixe $68 dinner) but "quicker than the Concord" for that "vacation to France"; indeed, many say this "grande dame" only "improves with age" – and the $36 prix fixe lunch costs less than taxi fare to the airport.

LE BERNARDIN 28 | 26 | 27 | $88

155 W. 51st St. (bet. 6th & 7th Aves.), 212-554-1515

■ "Hallowed ground" for seafood afishionados, Maguy LeCoze's "piscatorial paradise" in Midtown "spoils" you with "incredible" feats of French "culinary magic" from chef Eric Ripert, served with "balletic" "finesse" by a "seamless" staff in a "gorgeous", "formal" setting; "breathless" admirers don't mind the "whale of a bill" (prix fixe lunch $47, dinner $84) given the fact that this is "grand" dining "nonpareil."

Le Cirque 2000 [S] 25 | 26 | 24 | $83

NY Palace Hotel, 455 Madison Ave. (bet. 50th & 51st Sts.), 212-303-7788

■ "*C'est incroyable*" to "feel like royalty" "under the big top" at Sirio Maccioni's "unique" Midtown New French, a "visual delight" that "swirls" with "surreal" "opulence" as big spenders join "famous faces" ringside for "sumptuous" cooking and "top-notch", "preemptive" service; if the "ostentatious" "electricity" also makes it a "tourist destination", it's still the "gold standard" of "excess at its best" and a sure bet to "put a smile on your face" – especially if you dine in one of its handsome party rooms.

Lespinasse 27 | 27 | 26 | $95

St. Regis Hotel, 2 E. 55th St. (bet. 5th & Madison Aves.), 212-339-6719

■ Like a "taste of heaven", this "exquisite" Midtown French "masterpiece" exhausts "superlatives" with a "phenomenal" display of "creative" finesse from chef Christian Delouvrier, "flawless" service from a staff "with ESP" and a "regal" Louis XV–style dining room that's a "gorgeous" "place to celebrate" any type of deal; of course, all these luxuries may require "breaking the bank", but it's "definitely worth" it.

Milos, Estiatorio ◐ [S] 25 | 23 | 22 | $66

125 W. 55th St. (bet. 6th & 7th Aves.), 212-245-7400

■ There's "no comparison" to this "first-class" Midtown Greek where "impeccable seafood" is "grilled to perfection" and served in a "stunning", "airy" agora with "plenty of space"; finatics find "value" via the phenomenal first courses or lunch and pre-theater prix fixes, but those who elect to select from the alluring display "on ice" should "beware" of "per-pound pricing" that requires "pockets as deep as the ocean."

Montrachet 25 | 19 | 24 | $67

239 W. Broadway (bet. Walker & White Sts.), 212-219-2777

■ "Forever young", Drew Nieporent's "*magnifique*" TriBeCa French standby remains "one of the city's finest" for "rich", "sensational" food enhanced by an "amazing wine list" and "seamless" service; it's a "classic" made accessible by the prix fixe Friday lunch "steal", and if some suggest a "makeover" would get the "stuffy" room "out of the '80s", admirers who "barely notice" see only "solid excellence" "for years to come."

NOBU [S] 28 | 23 | 24 | $74

105 Hudson St. (Franklin St.), 212-219-0500

■ A meal at Nobu Matsuhisa's TriBeCa Japanese-Peruvian flagship can be a "religious experience", especially if you say "*omakase*" and let the chef pick your menu; not only does the "well-informed staff lead you through the experience" but you're "practically guaranteed celebrity sightings" in the "cool" birch-columned setting, all of which explains why acolytes are willing to pay a "bloody fortune" and endure "monthlong waits" for reservations – "provided you can get through on the phone."

Nobu, Next Door ◐ [S] 27 | 22 | 22 | $61

105 Hudson St. (bet. Franklin & N. Moore Sts.), 212-334-4445

■ A "great alternative" to its sibling next door, this "ultra-trendy" TriBeCan offers nearly the same "knock-your-socks-off" Japanese-Peruvian cuisine but for less money; plus, as "no reservations are accepted" (except for parties of six or more), "there's hope of actually getting a table" in the "simple", "Zen-like surroundings."

Oceana 27 | 25 | 26 | $72

55 E. 54th St. (bet. Madison & Park Aves.), 212-759-5941

■ For "fabulous fish" feasting, "cast your reel" at this prix fixe "piscean delight" that sails on smoothly even though chef Rick

Moonen has jumped ship; yes it's "pricey", but passengers pay happily for the "exquisitely considerate" service and "luxury yacht"–like decor that make you "feel as if you are on a cruise."

Park Avenue Cafe S   25 | 22 | 23 | $61

100 E. 63rd St. (bet. Lexington & Park Aves.), 212-644-1900

■ Rare is the restaurant "without a weak link", but devotees declare "everything's delicious" at this "really classy", "folk art"–filled New American Eastsider from executive chef David Burke; the "splendid" staff treats everyone "like you're their favorite customer", leading its "mover-shaker-dealmaker" crowd to urge "not to be missed – if your wallet can take it."

Peter Luger Steak House S   27 | 13 | 19 | $62

178 Broadway (Driggs Ave.), Brooklyn, 718-387-7400

■ It may be in Brooklyn, but this "cash-only" Williamsburg "landmark" is as "unbeatable" as the Yankees in their "prime"; acolytes of its "died-and-went-to-heaven" porterhouse and "can't-be-beat" sides, not to mention its "cantankerous" "old-world waiters" and German "beer-hall ambiance", say this "glorious" "NY ritual" is so "sublime", it makes a "regular" of nearly everyone.

Picholine S   26 | 24 | 25 | $75

35 W. 64th St. (bet. B'way & CPW), 212-724-8585

■ Though it may be "cheaper to fly" to the Riviera, you won't find Mediterranean cuisine any better than David Cox's "breathtakingly" "glorious" creations at this "sumptuous" Lincoln Center–area "class act"; everything from the "beautiful setting" to the "sublime" service encourages "lingering", and "don't forget" to leave room for the "glorious" cheese course orchestrated by *fromager* Max McCalman; N.B. the "smashing" $28 prix fixe lunch may be the best deal on the West Side.

River Cafe S   24 | 27 | 24 | $72

1 Water St. (bet. Furman & Old Fulton Sts.), Brooklyn, 718-522-5200

■ For a "romantic" meal in Brooklyn with "impeccable" New American fare and "solicitous" service, "it doesn't get any better" than this "former barge" on the waterfront turned into a "magical" "special occasion" "oasis" by renowned restaurateur Buzzy O'Keeffe; over the years it's produced some of NYC's best chefs, but it's always been most beloved for its "incredible view" of the Downtown Manhattan skyline, which makes "everything taste better" and helps justify the $70 prix fixe dinner tab.

Scalini Fedeli   27 | 25 | 24 | $73

165 Duane St. (bet. Greenwich & Hudson Sts.), 212-528-0400

■ "Wow" – "Jersey boy makes good in the big city" trumpet touters of Michael Cetrulo and his "fancy but not stuffy" Northern Italian TriBeCa "treasure", which has converts who "never even knew it was there" swearing it's "A+ all the way"; its "wonderfully crafted", "superb" dishes, "impressive wine list", "gracious, unobtrusive" service and "perfectly romantic", "regal setting" (the former Bouley space) make it a "memorable" "treat when you don't care about the bill" – who'd have guessed?

Shun Lee Palace ◑ S   24 | 21 | 22 | $49

155 E. 55th St. (bet. Lexington & 3rd Aves.), 212-371-8844

■ For the best experience, "toss away the menu and trust" the "excellent" staff at Michael Tong's "glamorous", "classy" East

Side "standard-bearer" where "superbly presented", "refined" "Chinese food with a few graduate degrees" is backed up by a "dignified" Adam Tihany–designed setting; as for the prices, "if Wall Street hasn't ruined you", you'll survive.

Smith & Wollensky Ⓢ　　22 | 16 | 19 | $57
797 Third Ave. (49th St.), 212-753-1530
◼ A "suit-wearing", "big-spending stockbroker crowd" calls this "noisy" East Midtown duplex "institution" "one honking great steakhouse"; it's a "manly-man", cigar-friendly place where "gruff", "colorful", "old-time" waiters tender "outrageous" slabs of beef and "fantastic" wines to revive the Wall Street Weary.

Sushi of Gari Ⓢ　　27 | 11 | 18 | $52
402 E. 78th St. (bet. 1st & York Aves.), 212-517-5340
◼ This "tiny" temple of "very creative sushi" on the Upper East Side counts among its clientele connoisseurs who "make reservations" to "sit at the bar" ("I saw Yoko Ono") and "pay big bucks" to "let Gari choose" what they'll eat; when they leave, they usually "do the happy food dance", though preferably outside, since there's "no room for elbows" inside.

SUSHI YASUDA　　28 | 25 | 25 | $61
204 E. 43rd St. (bet. 2nd & 3rd Aves.), 212-972-1001
◼ "Sublime sushi" to bring "tears to your eyes" is the specialty of this "spacious", "Zen-like" Japanese "oasis" near the UN, which boasts a "wide variety" of "unusual", "ultra-fresh" fish ("where does this guy find six kinds of mackerel?"); "for the ultimate dining experience", regulars suggest the omakase menu – "sit at the sushi bar" and let "master chef" Maomichi Yasuda work his magic; P.S. it's "expense-account necessary" for non-Rockefellers.

Tavern on the Green Ⓢ　　15 | 24 | 17 | $60
Central Park W. (bet. 66th & 67th Sts.), 212-873-3200
◪ While this over-the-top "glitzy", "circus-like Central Park classic" "tourist" "institution" is "fantastic in the winter" in the Crystal Room, with the "lights and the snow", "in the summer" in the garden or at any time for an elegant party, it does have its share of detractors who find it "tacky" and "under-serviced", with "mediocre", "overpriced" New American food.

Town Ⓢ　　24 | 25 | 22 | $67
Chambers Hotel, 15 W. 56th St. (bet. 5th & 6th Aves.), 212-582-4445
◼ A "hit" from day one, this Midtowner is where the "beautiful people", "power expense-accounters" and "serious diners" sip "trendy" cocktails at the "cool bar" then descend to an "ultra-modern" dining room to partake in Geoffrey Zakarian's "superb" New American cooking; no surprise – it's always "packed" and it's "expensive", but all smiles here.

'21' Club　　21 | 22 | 23 | $63
21 W. 52nd St. (bet. 5th & 6th Aves.), 212-582-7200
◼ "Still the ultimate" "NYC experience", this "institution" is seemingly "unchanged since Prohibition", yet it "never goes out of style" thanks to its "clubby" townhouse setting redolent with "exclusivity", "money and power", along with its "professional" service, "classic all-American" fare and "legendary" wine cellar; even though such good things come at a price, it offers lunch ($32) and pre-theater ($36) prix fixe menus, as well as 10 private party

rooms ("every one with its own tale") to give ordinary mortals the chance to live like a "bigwig"; naturally, jacket and tie are required.

Union Pacific 26 | 26 | 25 | $72

111 E. 22nd St. (bet. Lexington Ave. & Park Ave. S.), 212-995-8500

■ "Trailblazer" Rocco DiSpirito's reputation remains on track as "one of the most wonderfully inventive chefs in the city" at this "magical" Gramercy New American where all the elements – "spirited" creations "amazingly presented", a "spectacular" wine list, "tranquil" setting (complete with a "beautiful" waterfall) and "stellar" service – "come together in perfect harmony" to create a "totally Zen-suous experience."

UNION SQUARE CAFE [S] 27 | 23 | 26 | $60

21 E. 16th St. (bet. 5th Ave. & Union Sq. W.), 212-243-4020

■ Still a "winner after all these years", Danny Meyer's original "first-class restaurant" remains the place for an "all-around wonderful dining experience" that defines "perfection without pretension", from chef Michael Romano's "deceptively simple, exquisitely satisfying" New American cooking to the "always gracious" staff that "sets the benchmark for great service" to the "classy but not stuffy setting"; P.S. "even the most hardened NYers cry for joy upon getting an 8:30 weekend reservation" here.

Veritas [S] 27 | 22 | 26 | $80

43 E. 20th St. (bet. B'way & Park Ave. S.), 212-353-3700

■ A "wine list longer than the Old Testament" is the claim to fame of this "world-class" Flatiron New American, but diners who pony up for its prix fixe dinners ($68) also attest to chef Scott Bryan's "perfectly executed" cooking that "dazzles, from the eye to the stomach" and proves "commensurate" with the "fabulous" vintages; in short, "everything" is imbued with "intelligence" here.

Washington Park [S] 21 | 22 | 22 | $62

24 Fifth Ave. (9th St.), 212-529-4400

■ Jonathan Waxman, NYC's original celebrity chef, is "jamming again" at this "civilized" New American addition in the Village , something of an "Upper East Side hangout Downtown", where the "deceptively simple" "seasonal" fare, 1,200-label wine list and "professional" staff have won over a sophisticated crowd; those who knew Waxman in his heyday back in the '80s delight in reporting that he's "worked out the kinks" and is now performing "at the top of his game."

Orange County, CA

TOP 10 FOOD RANKING

	Restaurant	Cuisine Type
27	Napa Rose	Californian
	Aubergine	Californian/French
26	Pinot Provence	Provençal
	Ritz-Carlton Lag. Niguel	French/Med.
	Gustaf Anders	Swedish
	Troquet	New French
	Ruth's Chris	Steakhouse
	Hobbit	French/Continental
	Pavilion*	Californian/Med.
	Pascal	Provençal

ADDITIONAL NOTEWORTHY PLACES

Antonello	N&S Italian
California Pizza Kitchen	Pizza
Cellar	French
Cheesecake Factory	American
Il Fornaio	N&S Italian
Mr. Stox	New American
P.F. Chang's	Chinese
Ramos House Cafe	American/Southern
Ritz	Continental
Sage	New American

	F	D	S	C
Antonello	24	23	24	$50

South Coast Plaza Vlg., 3800 Plaza Dr. (Sunflower Ave.), Santa Ana, 714-751-7153

◪ "Every aspect is amazing" swear supporters of this South Coast Plaza Village venue where "excellent" "haute" Italian fare is served by a "friendly" yet "discreet" staff in the "warm, intimate glow" of a "romantic" (if ersatz) palazzo interior; naysayers jeer that it's "pretentious" and "overpriced", but longtime loyalists anoint it "the real thing."

	F	D	S	C
AUBERGINE [S]	27	24	24	$83

508 29th St. (Newport Blvd.), Newport Beach, 949-723-4150

◪ Disciples of chef-owner Tim Goodell, an "undisputed star of serious" Californian-French cooking, "make a pilgrimage" to his "enchanting" Newport Beach cottage to splurge on an "amazing wine list" and "wonderful", "innovative" prix fixe meals that are "reminiscent of the French Laundry"; quibblers may take issue with the "designer portions" and "excessive cost", but acolytes advise "go immediately if you truly care about food"; P.S. the "Sunday supper is a great deal", comparatively speaking, of course.

* Tied with restaurant directly above it

CALIFORNIA PIZZA KITCHEN   17 | 13 | 17 | $18

Park Place, 2957 Michelson Dr. (Jamboree Rd.), Irvine, 949-975-1585 🟥
*Laguna Hills Mall, 24155 Laguna Hills Mall (bet. El Toro Rd. & Regional Ct.),
Laguna Hills, 949-458-9600* 🟥
25513 Marguerite Pkwy. (La Paz Rd.), Mission Viejo, 949-951-5026 🟥
*Fashion Island, 1511 Newport Center Dr. (bet. Corporate Plaza &
Farallon Drs.), Newport Beach, 949-759-5543* 🟥
*Santa Ana Main Place, 2800 N. Main St. (Town & Country Rd.), Santa Ana,
714-479-0604* 🟥
*Brea Mall, 1065 Brea Mall, upper level (N. State College Blvd.), Brea,
714-672-0407* 🟥
*South Coast Plaza, 3333 Bear St. (W. Sunflower Ave.), Costa Mesa,
714-557-1279*
*The Market Place, 3001 El Camino Real (Jamboree Rd.), Tustin,
714-838-5083*

◪ While the "BBQ chicken version can't be beat", almost "any kind
of pizza you can imagine" is available at this wildly successful "Cal-
casual" chain that "pleases kids and adults" alike with "inventive
comfort food for the masses", including soups, salads and pastas;
its "simple", "tiled" setting won't win any awards, but that's offset
by its "predictably good product."

Cellar   25 | 23 | 24 | $49

Villa del Sol, 305 N. Harbor Blvd. (Wilshire Ave.), Fullerton, 714-525-5682
◼ If your "special night out" calls for "dark", "romantic" quarters,
this venerable "treasure of a place" underneath Fullerton's historic
Villa del Sol fills the bill with "wonderfully prepared" "old-school"
French cuisine and "one of the best wine lists in OC"; "top-notch"
service from a "knowledgeable" staff only enhances the "enjoyable
evening" at this subterranean landmark where everyone ends the
evening with a soufflé.

CHEESECAKE FACTORY 🟥   20 | 17 | 17 | $23

Irvine Spectrum Ctr., 71 Fortune Dr. (Pacifica), Irvine, 949-788-9998
*42 The Shops at Mission Viejo (I-5, Crown Valley Pkwy. exit), Mission Viejo,
949-364-6200*
*Fashion Island, 1141 Newport Center Dr. (Santa Barbara Dr.),
Newport Beach, 949-720-8333*

◪ "When you can't think of a place to eat", this national chain's
"something-for-everyone" American menu, "ridiculously huge
portions", "consistently good" quality and "reasonable prices"
make it an "all-around standby" – in fact, it ranks yet again as
the Most Popular restaurant in OC; the "unbearable wait" is a
drawback ("why don't they take reservations?"), but that just
gives you more time to choose from among its 40 cheesecakes,
all "worth the weight you'll put on."

GUSTAF ANDERS 🟥   26 | 23 | 24 | $51

*South Coast Plaza Vlg., 3851 S. Bear St. (Sunflower Ave.), Santa Ana,
714-668-1737*
◼ "A rare find anywhere", except Scandinavia, the "holiday
smorgasbord" at chef Ulf Anders' Santa Ana Swedish destination
is an "awesome eating adventure"; any time of year, though,
"superb" Arctic char, "outstanding herring" and "delicious"
gravlax are served in an "upscale", "contemporary" setting at a
"relaxed" pace by a staff that upholds a "standard of service few
others approach"; it's "not cheap", but it's "worth a drive from LA"
if you can afjord it.

Hobbit ⬛   26 | 23 | 26 | $65

2932 E. Chapman Ave. (Malena St.), Orange, 714-997-1972

■ "Mortgage the house for a once-in-a-lifetime experience" at this venerable Orange hacienda where "marvelous" "one-seating" evenings begin with "champagne and appetizers in the wine cellar" and proceed "up to the dining room for a sumptuous prix fixe meal" composed of seven "rich and saucy" courses of "high-tone" French-Continental dishes; it's "great for a special occasion" or an "outing with sophisticated out-of-town guests", but note that reservations are essential.

IL FORNAIO ⬛   20 | 19 | 18 | $29

Lakeshore Tower, 18051 Von Karman Ave. (bet. Main St. & Michelson Dr.), Irvine, 949-261-1444

■ "It's hard to believe this is a chain" remark impressed patrons of this "versatile" Italian outfit whose "super-yummy breads" are "sold at upscale grocers" and whose "solid" eats are perfect "for a late lunch on a lazy day" or when "the children are craving superb macaroni but parents want something more"; P.S. you've got to "love the rotating monthly regional menus."

Mr. Stox ◐⬛   24 | 23 | 25 | $44

1105 E. Katella Ave. (bet. Lewis St. & State College Blvd.), Anaheim, 714-634-2994

■ Long setting the "local standard" for "quiet", "enjoyable" dining in Anaheim, this "dependable" veteran continues to satisfy with New American dishes (and some "old Continental-style" touches such as soufflés) delivered by a "cosseting" staff; it's an ideal choice "before a game", especially since the decor has recently been "upgraded"; P.S. "get on the mailing list" to learn about "specials" like its winemaker dinners.

NAPA ROSE ⬛   27 | 26 | 25 | $52

Grand Californian Hotel, 1600 S. Disneyland Dr. (Katella Ave.), Anaheim, 714-300-7170

■ "Like the finest table in Napa" rave "adult Mouseketeers" who are dazzled by "creative" chef Andre Sutton's "very seasonal", "incredibly flavored" Californian cooking, rated No. 1 for Food in OC; factor in "articulate and helpful" GM/sommelier Michael Jordan's "cellar with all the big guns", an "attentive, personable" staff and Arts and Crafts–themed decor that lends a "fabulous country feeling" and you have "Disney's best effort in California."

Pascal   26 | 22 | 23 | $55

1000 N. Bristol St. (Jamboree Rd.), Newport Beach, 949-752-0107

◪ Pascal Olhats' flagship operation is an homage to Provence that overcomes its strip-mall location with a "country-style" room adorned with "marvelous" "fresh roses" as well as an "ethereal" menu (the "duck confit is out of this world"); a few gripe about "uptight" service, but most agree it's "hard to find fault" with this "great dining experience" that's "still excellent after all these years."

Pavilion ⬛   26 | 26 | 27 | $53

Four Seasons Hotel, 690 Newport Center Dr. (Santa Cruz Dr.), Newport Beach, 949-760-4920

■ "As good as it gets in OC" swoon fans of this "top-notch" hotel dining room in Newport Beach, where a "genuinely gracious" staff provides "service you dream about" and the kitchen turns out "brilliant", "creative" Cal-Med fare that clearly shows "meticulous attention to each ingredient"; not only does the "beautiful" space have an "understated elegance" that's "perfect" for a "special dinner" but the "nightly prix fixe menu" is a "great bargain" to boot.

P.F. CHANG'S CHINA BISTRO S   20 20 18 $24

Irvine Spectrum Ctr., 61 Fortune Dr. (Irvine Center Dr.), Irvine, 949-453-1211
800 The Shops at Mission Viejo (Crown Valley Pkwy.), Mission Viejo, 949-364-6661
1145 Newport Center Dr. (Santa Barbara St.), Newport Beach, 949-759-9007

■ "It may not be authentic, but it works for me" is the consensus on this "upmarket" American-style Chinese chain whose "well-executed" menu is a "hit" ("we come at least once a month for the lettuce wraps" alone); an Asian-themed setting that "feels like a ride at Disneyland" and a "lively bar" where "exotic martinis" are mixed round out the winning formula.

PINOT PROVENCE S   26 26 25 $50

Westin South Coast Plaza, 686 Anton Blvd. (Bristol St.), Costa Mesa, 714-444-5900

■ The "south of France comes to Costa Mesa" at this "unexpected surprise for a hotel restaurant" that boosters consider "by far the best of the Pinot" empire; the "exquisite" Provençal fare "reflects the chef's creativity" yet retains the "character of the French countryside", while the "refined but warm" room is worked by an "impressively" "knowledgeable" staff; a "perfect prelude to the opera or theater", the experience is so "wonderful you won't want to leave for the show."

Ramos House Cafe S   25 18 18 $23

31752 Los Rios St. (Del Obispo St.), San Juan Capistrano, 949-443-1342
■ "Small-town dining at its best" coo admirers of this adobe-style cafe that's "worth the hunt" through San Juan Capistrano's "historical district" to find because the reward is chef-owner John Humphries' "exciting" "tribute to American cuisine with a Southern accent"; all tables are out on the "charming" patio, so it "feels like brunch at somebody's home", and its proximity to the train station "only adds to its charm"; don't miss the "unique Bloody Marys."

Ritz   25 25 26 $55

Fashion Island, 880 Newport Center Dr. (Santa Barbara Ave.), Newport Beach, 949-720-1800
■ Fashion Island's longstanding site for a "special celebration", this destination earns kudos for its "old-world" service, "gloriously unchanged" Continental fare and "elegant" but "warm" interior with "nudes on the wall" that lend a mischievous note; the newish garden room beckons for "cigars after" dinner, while the "bar menu" works for "light", "post-event" noshing; P.S. a recent change in ownership may give loyalists pause, but regulars report it's "still so pleasing after all these years."

RITZ-CARLTON LAGUNA NIGUEL   26 27 28 $61

Ritz-Carlton Laguna Niguel, 1 Ritz-Carlton Dr. (PCH), Dana Point, 949-240-5008
■ If you're after a "lifetime memory", it "can't get much better" than this "romantic", "formal" hotel dining room in Dana Point; the "incredible" bluff-top site offers "one of the prettiest views in

California" ("walk along the cliffs" "overlooking the Pacific" "after dinner"), the "unhurried, attentive" staff seems right out of the "best places in Europe" and the "unsurpassed" French-Med dishes are "prepared with precision and flair."

RUTH'S CHRIS STEAK HOUSE S   26 | 20 | 23 | $50

2961 Michaelson Dr. (Carlson Ave.), Irvine, 949-252-8848

■ "When trying to show your father-in-law that you're doing well", "invent an occasion" to invite him to this "clubby" steakhouse chain link where it's smart to "share the sides" because the "awesome" "tender" steaks ("get the porterhouse for two") come "sizzling in butter"; kudos too to the "excellent" staff that's "always friendly no matter how we dress."

Sage S   25 | 19 | 23 | $36

Eastbluff Ctr., 2531 Eastbluff Dr. (Vista del Oro), Newport Beach, 949-718-9650

■ Those looking for a "bit of adventure in conservative OC" should seek out Rich Mead's "hidden" "storefront" in Newport, where there's "always something new and interesting" on his "innovative" New American menu; this is "food for the gods, available to mere mortals", and it's served by a "thoughtful", "relaxed" staff in both a "cozy", candlelit interior with lots of windows and out on the "pleasant garden patio", the place to be "when weather permits."

Troquet   26 | 22 | 20 | $52

South Coast Plaza, 3333 Bristol St. (Town Center Dr.), Costa Mesa, 714-708-6865

◪ "Pampered" patrons perusing the "gems at Tiffany" in South Coast Plaza know that the real "jewel" is this New French "class act" "on the third floor" of the mall; power couple "Tim and Liza [Goodell] know how to do it right" with "top-drawer" dishes like their signature truffle-crusted filet mignon and Valrhona chocolate soufflé; yes, it's "expensive", but insiders whisper that the "great-deal prix fixe menu at lunch is an excellent way to experience the fantastic fare."

Orlando

TOP 20 FOOD RANKING

Restaurant	Cuisine Type
29 La Coquina	International
28 Victoria & Albert's	American
Le Coq au Vin	French Bistro
Del Frisco's	Steakhouse
Flying Fish Cafe	New American/Seafood
Chatham's Place	Continental
27 Maison et Jardin	Continental
California Grill	Californian
Café de France	Continental
Christini's*	Northern Italian
26 Arthur's 27	Continental
Yachtsman	Steakhouse
Citricos	French
Ruth's Chris	Steakhouse
Emeril's	Creole
Thai House	Thai
Antonio's La Fiamma	N&S Italian
Manuel's on the 28th	International
25 Charley's	Steakhouse
Le Cellier	Steakhouse

ADDITIONAL NOTEWORTHY PLACES

Artist Point	Pacific Northwest
Boheme	Continental
Chef Henry's Cafe	German/Eastern European
Chefs de France	French Bistro
Cinderella's Royal Table	American
Delfino Riviera	Northern Italian
Dux	New American
Enzo's on the Lake	Northern Italian
Harvey's Bistro	New American
Houston's	American
Jiko	Eclectic
Narcoossee's	Seafood
Outback	Steakhouse
Peter Scott's	Continental
Rolando's	Cuban
Spoodles	Mediterranean
Stonewood Tavern & Grill	American
Thai Passion	Thai
Thai Place	Thai
Vito's Chop House	Steakhouse

* Tied with restaurant directly above it

Antonio's La Fiamma | 26 | 22 | 23 | $29 |

611 S. Orlando Ave. (Maitland Ave.), Maitland, 407-645-1035

■ "Superb" Italian food makes this "upscale" favorite overlooking Maitland's Lake Lily "as close to Italy as can be found in Central Florida"; the "fabulous" menu features dishes both "innovative" and "traditional", the wine list boasts more than 300 labels and the service is "friendly"; some say "horrible acoustics" mean that the "lovely", "contemporary" room is often "much too noisy", but others aver they only add to the "big-city" "party" atmosphere.

Arthur's 27 S | 26 | 27 | 27 | $56 |

Wyndham Palace Resort & Spa, 1900 Buena Vista Dr. , 27th fl. (Hotel Plaza Blvd.), Lake Buena Vista, 407-827-3450

■ "The best view at Disney" may be from this "posh" Continental perched on the Wyndham Palace's 27th floor, where "perfectly orchestrated" meals amount to "the ultimate in fine dining"; the "creative" dishes are "elegantly" presented by a "superb" staff, but by all accounts the crowning glory of this "very special place" is its "beautiful" panoramic park vista – especially if you can get a "late reservation by a window to enjoy the fireworks."

Artist Point S | 24 | 25 | 24 | $40 |

Disney's Wilderness Lodge, 901 Timberline Dr. (World Dr.), Lake Buena Vista, 407-824-1081

■ "Forget you're in Florida" at this retreat in Disney's Wilderness Lodge, where the Arts and Crafts interior is reminiscent of a "hunting" cabin deep in the "North woods" and the "fantastic" Pacific Northwestern menu is heavy on "wild game" and backed by "great wines" from California, Oregon and Washington State; N.B. the above Food rating does not reflect the recent arrival of chef Lenny DeGeorge.

Boheme S | – | – | – | E |

Westin Grand Bohemian, 325 S. Orange Ave. (South St.), 407-581-4700

With a plum address at the Westin Grand Bohemian hotel, this Continental is impressive thanks to its dining room filled with fine art and adjoining lounge boasting a rare Imperial Grand Bösendorfer concert piano; the menu also hits some high notes with dishes such as grilled ahi tuna and lemongrass shrimp, but its pièce de résistance may be the weekly changing Sunday jazz brunch.

Café de France S | 27 | 23 | 23 | $32 |

526 S. Park Ave. (Fairbanks Ave.), Winter Park, 407-647-1869

■ "Lots of locals" frequent the "best" Continental bistro in Winter Park to savor "consistently outstanding" fare ("try any fish dish" or "daily special"); the "small, cozy" space is "charming" and the staff as "personable" as can be, meaning it's "great for a special celebration" or just when you want to "feel like you're in France."

CALIFORNIA GRILL S | 27 | 26 | 25 | $41 |

Disney's Contemporary Resort, 4600 N. World Dr., Lake Buena Vista, 407-824-1576

☑ "The Mouse can cook, baby!" – so say surveyors about this Californian on "top of the world" (well, the 15th floor of Disney's Contemporary Resort, anyway), which has again been voted Orlando's Most Popular restaurant; "gifted" chef Clifford Pleau continually reinvents his "unique seasonal menus", creating "divine" dishes paired with an "equally eloquent wine list"; add "impeccable" service and "spectacular" views of the park and its fireworks, and the result is truly "great dining" – "tourists" in "shorts and Mickey Mouse ears" notwithstanding.

Charley's Steak House 🖫 | 25 | 22 | 22 | $36 |

6107 S. Orange Blossom Trail (1 mi. north of Sand Lake Rd.), Orlando, 407-851-7130
Goodings Plaza, 8255 International Dr. (Sand Lake Rd.), Orlando, 407-363-0228
Parkway Pavilion, 2901 Parkway Blvd. (Hwy. 192), Kissimmee, 407-396-6055
■ Steaks so tender you can "cut them with a fork" are the forte of this steakhouse mini chain where "thick", "incredible slabs of meat" are "cooked to perfection" over a "hardwood" fire, emerging "juicy" and "exceptionally flavorful" ("the best filet mignon I've ever had!"); add a "great martini" or a bottle from the "extensive wine list" and you're in "beef-lover's paradise."

Chatham's Place 🖫 | 28 | 24 | 26 | $39 |

7575 Dr. Phillips Blvd. (Sand Lake Rd.), 407-345-2992
■ Respondents continue to rhapsodize about this "top-grade" Continental in the Dr. Phillips area that's maintaining its tradition of gustatory "excellence" with "sublime" cuisine – such as its signature dishes, sautéed fillet of black grouper with pecans and scallions, and pan-roasted rack of lamb with rosemary au jus – "exquisitely prepared" and "elegantly served" in an atmosphere both "romantic" and "convivial", making for a "perfect evening."

Chef Henry's Cafe | 25 | 19 | 22 | $20 |

Howell Branch Shoppes, 3716 Howell Branch Rd. (Eastbrook Blvd.), Winter Park, 407-657-2230
■ "All's lovely on the eastern front" of Winter Park, where this "family-run" storefront with "a mom-and-pop" feel "adds variety" to the local dining scene with its "excellent" German–Eastern European menu of "high-quality" classics like creamy mushroom schnitzel and "authentic Hungarian goulash" prepared by chef Henry (aka Henrich Brestowski), whose wife, Estera, creates decadent desserts such as authentic Dobos torte and Gundel crêpes, all of which is served by sincerely "nice folks."

Chefs de France 🖫 | 25 | 25 | 22 | $37 |

Epcot Ctr., French Pavilion, Lake Buena Vista, 407-939-3463
■ "Like being in the heart of Paris" (except for the folks at the next table wearing "shorts, sneakers and baseball caps"), this upscale Epcot spot owned by famed chefs Paul Bocuse, Gaston Lenôtre and Roger Vergé is a "beautiful" recreation of a traditional French bistro; "excellent" duck à l'orange, boeuf bourguignon and other classics are delivered by "pampering" servers imported "from France", making for a "special dining experience" that's further enhanced by the "great" view of the park's fireworks.

Christini's 🖫 | 27 | 24 | 25 | $52 |

Bay Hill Mktpl., 7600 Dr. Phillips Blvd. (Sand Lake Rd.), 407-345-8770
■ "A treasure among restaurants", this "buttoned-up" Northern Italian "standby" in the Dr. Phillips area of South Orlando produces "feasts" of near-"perfect" execution, complemented by a 450-label wine list; among its many "charms" are "exquisite service", ornate, "beautiful" decor and "strolling musicians", who complete the "romantic" picture; just bear in mind that such "very special" dining doesn't come cheap – the prices are "high" even by "expense-account" standards.

Cinderella's Royal Table S   23 | 27 | 25 | $28
Walt Disney World, Cinderella Castle, Lake Buena Vista, 407-824-2222
■ Everyone "feels like a real nobleman" at this American housed in Disney's Magic Kingdom that's fabled for its elaborately "regal setting" ("you're dining in a castle – what else can I say?"), so it's certainly no fault of the "quality" dishes if "you barely notice them due to the pageantry" all around; "young children" especially "love" the "fairy-tale" "breakfasts with the princesses" (Cinderella and her entourage), even if they're sometimes "too excited to eat."

Citricos S   26 | 28 | 26 | $48
Disney's Grand Floridian Resort & Spa, 4401 Grand Floridian Way, Lake Buena Vista, 407-939-3463
■ The kitchen's "magnificent" creations are "rivaled only by the unique decor" at this "incredible" French "jewel" that boasts an impressive view of the Grand Floridian Resort – perfect for "enjoying the fireworks" – and an "elegant" modern interior with an exhibition kitchen; the "innovative", "always delicious" dishes are "nicely executed and finely served" and backed by a "superb wine list", making this "great celebration place" "one of Disney's best"; N.B. the Food rating does not reflect the post-*Survey* arrival of chef Gray Byrum.

Delfino Riviera   ▽ 24 | 27 | 22 | $51
Portofino Bay Hotel, 5601 Universal Blvd. (I-4, exit 29B), 407-503-1415
◪ "Elegant, beautiful" surroundings with a "superb ambiance" define this hotel Italian overlooking Portofino Bay at Universal Studios Escape; the "excellent" menu interprets "fabulous" specialties from Liguria, including handmade pastas, and the "romantic" mood is only enhanced by the "wandering musicians"; still, grouches grouse that it's "just not quite worth the price."

DEL FRISCO'S   28 | 22 | 27 | $45
DOUBLE EAGLE STEAK HOUSE
729 Lee Rd. (1½ blocks west of I-4), 407-645-4443
■ "Don't dare ask for a knife" – a fork is all you need when tackling "the best steaks in town" at this "dark, clubby" "cow heaven" where the "fabulous flavors" ("oh, those side dishes"), "excellent wine list" and "superb" service are a real "treat", despite decor that some say could stand a "redo"; yes, this is "expense-account" territory, but for such "huge portions" of "top-quality" fare, most find the prices "very fair"; N.B. check out the cigar-friendly piano lounge next door.

Dux S   25 | 25 | 25 | $53
Peabody Orlando Hotel, 9801 International Dr. (opp. Orange County Convention Ctr.), 407-345-4550
■ "For that special person you want to impress", this "epitome of class" at the Peabody Orlando is "very expensive but worth it" for its "first-rate" haute New American menu, opulent surroundings and attentive service; while a few find it "imposing" and "a bit stuffy", the majority lauds it as "fine dining at its best"; P.S. make sure you take time to "see the ducks in the lobby's" marble fountain.

Emeril's Restaurant Orlando S   26 | 23 | 24 | $50
Universal Studios Escape, Universal CityWalk, 407-224-2424
■ "Bam! – you can't take it a notch higher than the fabulous food and locale of this hot spot" rave the many fans of Emeril Lagasse's

"splendiferous" Creole centerpiece of Universal CityWalk, where the celebrity chef himself sometimes makes a surprise appearance in the show kitchen; rest assured the cuisine is "not just TV fluff" – it's "exhilarating", and though "expensive", most insist it's "all it's cracked up to be"; P.S. "plan way ahead" because it's very "hard to get in."

Enzo's On The Lake
| 25 | 23 | 23 | $40 |

1130 S. Hwy. 17-92 (State Rd. 434), Longwood, 407-834-9872

■ To fully enjoy the "enchanting" atmosphere of this "pretty" Longwood Northern Italian, "ask for a table with a view" of Lake Fairy and savor a "consistently excellent" "special dinner"; though insiders report being "treated like family", first-timers detect a "caste system" that favors some customers over others and warn about the "terrible acoustics"; still, the food is so "extraordinary" that it's "worth putting up with the pretensions and volume.

FLYING FISH CAFE S
| 28 | 28 | 26 | $43 |

Disney's BoardWalk Inn, 2101 N. Epcot Resorts Blvd. (Buena Vista Dr.), Lake Buena Vista, 407-939-3463

■ "Scrum-dittily-umptious!" exclaim enthusiasts of this New American seafood cafe at Disney's BoardWalk Inn that soars with "memorably" "well-prepared" catches "fresh off the boat"; its "fanciful" decor "beautifully" evokes Atlantic City's golden age of roller coasters, and it provides some of the "best service" around, all of which makes for very effective "date bait"; P.S. insiders say get a seat "near the open [show] kitchen."

Harvey's Bistro
| 24 | 23 | 22 | $28 |

Bank of America Bldg., 390 N. Orange Ave. (Livingston St.), 407-246-6560
Park Avenue Apartments, 6400 Times Square Ave. (Robert Trent Jones Blvd.), 407-313-2020 S

■ "Always dependable" for "upscale comfort food" (such as pan-crusted chicken and caramelized tenderloin medallions), this "fashionable" but "reasonably priced" European-influenced American bistro Downtown is appointed with lots of stained wood and brass; "especially convenient for a business meeting or pre- or post-theater" meal, it's an overall "solid" choice; N.B. though similar in decor and cuisine, the MetroWest branch offers more of a tavern menu.

Houston's S
| 24 | 24 | 21 | $25 |

215 S. Orlando Ave. (bet. Fairbanks Ave. & Lee Rd.), Winter Park, 407-740-4005

■ "Long waits" for a table seem "not so bad" when taking in the "best lake view" in all of Orlando at this "bustling" Winter Park branch of a national American chain where a "sophisticated crowd" enjoys "heaping portions" of "great food", an upscale lodge motif and "courteous", "attentive" service; singles add it's "a meat market galore."

Jiko – The Cooking Place S
| – | – | – | M |

Disney's Animal Kingdom Lodge, 2901 Osceola Pkwy., Lake Buena Vista, 407-939-3463

The more upscale of two restaurants within Disney's Animal Kingdom Lodge, this Eclectic offers a 'New African' menu that infuses traditional dishes from the cradle-of-humanity continent with European, Indian and Asian flavors; its extensive wine list is composed entirely of South African labels, and its dramatic decor evokes the vibe of the veldt, complete with lighting illusions that recreate a sultry savannah sunset every 20 minutes.

LA COQUINA [S] 29 | 28 | 27 | $51

Hyatt Regency Grand Cypress, 1 Grand Cypress Blvd. (State Rd. 535), 407-239-1234

■ Voted No. 1 for Food among Orlando restaurants, this "exquisite" "special-occasion" destination housed in the Hyatt Regency Grand Cypress is "a feast for the eyes and palate"; the contemporary International menu is "superb", showcasing a "great choice" of "expertly prepared" dishes that are served in a "stunning setting" by a very "fine" staff; of course it's "expensive", but you'll be "treated like royalty" and know that "you've had a real gourmet meal"; N.B. don't miss the "incredible" weekend brunch.

Le Cellier Steakhouse [S] 25 | 24 | 24 | $31

Epcot Ctr., Canada Pavilion, Lake Buena Vista, 407-939-3463

■ "You really feel like you're in a wine cellar" at this "atmospheric" Canadian steakhouse at Epcot, renowned for cooking up the "best steaks at Walt Disney World" (the house specialty, mushroom-stuffed filet mignon, is "heavenly"), as well as "excellent" burgers; add in "very good service" and it adds up to a "great stop."

LE COQ AU VIN [S] 28 | 21 | 25 | $34

4800 S. Orange Ave. (Holden Ave.), 407-851-6980

■ "Quaint, intimate and charming", this South Orlando French bistro is a "perennial favorite that's holding up well", continuing to prove that "fine things come in small packages"; so devoted is chef-owner Louis Perrotte's following that regulars claim to have the "phone number programmed on their cell phones", and why not? – the "simply excellent" menu "caters to the connoisseur" by "changing seasonally, so each visit is a delicious new experience."

Maison et Jardin 27 | 27 | 27 | $46

430 S. Wymore Rd. (½ mi. south of I-4 & State Rd. 436), Altamonte Springs, 407-862-4410

■ "When we win the lottery, we'll eat here once a week" vow vaunters of this "romantic" Altamonte Springs Continental, an "elegant" "class act" with a "gorgeous" interior overlooking "a beautiful grove of oaks"; the "exceptional" menu is done with "old-school finesse" and paired with a "fantastic" wine list; despite some grumbles about "pretentious" service, most feel that this "cream of fine restaurants" "sets the standard" in the Orlando area.

Manuel's on the 28th 26 | 28 | 27 | $54

Bank of America Bldg., 390 N. Orange Ave. (Livingston St.), 407-246-6580

■ Boasting a "breathtaking skyline view" from the 28th floor of a Downtown skyscraper, this "sophisticated" International is "a terrific place to take someone you want to impress", because the "eclectic, creative" dishes are simply "exquisite" and proffered by a "superb" staff that's "professional without being snooty"; this experience is "memorable", but prepare for expense-account tabs.

Narcoossee's [S] 25 | 26 | 25 | $37

Disney's Grand Floridian Resort & Spa, 4401 Grand Floridian Way, Lake Buena Vista, 407-939-3463

■ "What a view!" say visitors to this "memorable" seafood house in Disney's Grand Floridian that's "perfect for special evenings" thanks to a "fabulous" panoramic vista that encompasses the Seven Seas Lagoon and the Magic Kingdom beyond; add chef Celina Tio's "unusual" culinary touch, a "great wine list" and "friendly, attentive service" and voters conclude: "first-rate from drinks to desserts to fireworks."

OUTBACK STEAKHOUSE S   22 | 18 | 21 | $23

4845 S. Kirkman Rd. (Conroy Rd.), Orlando, 407-292-5111
Florida Mall, 1301 Florida Mall Ave. (Orange Blossom Trail & Sand Lake Rd.), Orlando, 407-240-6857
Shops at Lake Brantley, 990 N. State Rd. 434 (Jamestown Blvd.), Altamonte Springs, 407-862-1050
Formosa Gardens, 7804 W. Irlo Bronson Memorial Hwy. (Formosa Gardens Blvd.), Kissimmee, 407-396-0017
3109 W. Vine St. (Dyer Blvd.), Kissimmee, 407-931-0033
180 Hickman Dr. (State Rd. 46), Sanford, 407-321-5881
1927 Aloma Ave. (Lakemont Ave.), Winter Park, 407-679-1050
Albertson's Shopping Ctr., 5891 Red Bug Lake Rd. (Tuskawilla Rd.), Winter Springs, 407-699-0900

◪ Devotees declare they don't mind downing a "Wallaby Darned" (the steakhouse chain's popular frozen cocktail) while enduring "ridiculous waiting times" at these "fun", "friendly" franchises for the chance to chow down on "consistently" "tender, flavorful" beef and "who-could-resist bloomin' onions"; on the other end of the spectrum, grouches grumble that this "Australian fraud" is little more than a "dime-a-dozen" "theme" joint, and a "noisy" one at that.

Peter Scott's   24 | 24 | 25 | $47

Longwood Vlg., 1811 W. State Rd. 434 (I-4), Longwood, 407-834-4477

◪ "Dust off your dancing shoes" and traipse over to this "romantic" Longwood Continental, a "real supper club" "in the classic style"; showcasing a variety of eclectic lounge acts and offering a spacious dance floor, as well as a "great Dover sole" and a 500-bottle wine list, this "pricey" ("overpriced"?) haunt is ideal for a "very, very special night."

Rolando's S   24 | 13 | 20 | $15

870 E. State Rd. 436 (Red Bug Lake Rd.), Casselberry, 407-767-9677

■ A longtime "locals'" favorite , this Casselberry Cuban was bought in 1999 by experienced chef and Santo Domingo native Fausto Rodriguez who is working to "keep up" his predecessor's high standards so that it will remain "the place to go" for "authentic" food served by a "friendly" staff at prices that are a "fantastic value"; N.B. the Decor score does not reflect a recent redecoration.

RUTH'S CHRIS STEAK HOUSE S   26 | 24 | 25 | $49

Fountains Plaza, 7501 Sand Lake Rd. (Dr. Phillips Blvd.), 407-226-3900
Winter Park Vlg., 610 N. Orlando Ave. (Webster Ave.), Winter Park, 407-622-2444

■ "When it absolutely, positively has to be a great meal", seek out this "sooo good" chophouse chain that "lives up to its reputation" for "almost orgasmic" beef ("if tastier steaks exist, I've certainly never had one"); "everything here is first-class", from the "elegant dining room" to the "professional" service that's thankfully "not of the stuffed-shirt variety", but keep in mind such "wonderful experiences" don't come cheap.

Spoodles [S] 23 | 21 | 21 | $27

Disney's BoardWalk, 2101 N. Epcot Resorts Blvd. (Buena Vista Dr.), Lake Buena Vista, 407-939-2380

■ "Ignore the name" and check out the "eclectic mix of Med cuisines" at this "fabulous" fine-dining spot on Disney's Boardwalk known for its "creative", tapas-style menu (you'll want to "order all the appetizers" and share); as befits the Disney reputation for family entertainment, the hopping show kitchen ensures that everyone will have "a ball" – "eat here and you may never leave."

Stonewood Tavern & Grill [S] 23 | 24 | 23 | $25

Oakmont Shopping Ctr., 1210 International Pkwy. S. (Lake Mary Blvd.), Heathrow, 407-333-3292

5078 Dr. Phillips Blvd. (Conroy Rd.), Orlando, 407-297-8682

■ "Sumptuous" decor provides an "upscale" backdrop for casual gourmet American meals at these eateries (part of a growing two-state chain) that are "doing very well" in central Florida – in fact, they can be "hard to get in" to due to all of the locals who line up to enjoy seafood and oak-grilled steaks amid "dark-wood" environs; in sum, savvy supporters say it's "a great chain in the making"; N.B. the Dr. Phillips Boulevard location opened post-*Survey*.

Thai House [S] 26 | 17 | 23 | $15

2117 E. Colonial Dr. (Bumby Ave.), 407-898-0820

◪ Though it's now located a few doors down from its original site on East Colonial Drive (a move not reflected in the above Decor rating), this Thai "favorite" remains among "Orlando's best" thanks to its "varied menu" of "flavorful", "always-excellent" options (curries, satays and the like).

Thai Passion [S] – | – | – | E

Fountains Plaza, 7533 W. Sand Lake Rd. (Dr. Phillips Blvd.), 407-313-9999

Sumptuous surroundings replete with both Western and traditional seating (low tables with a well underneath for your legs) set the stage at this happening new Siamese near International Drive; the creative kitchen turns out specialties such as crispy angel wings (boned chicken stuffed with minced pork and clear noodles) and curried seafood soufflé, as well as familiar favorites like pad Thai and satays, all eye-catchingly presented to a mixed crowd of locals and tourists.

Thai Place 25 | 17 | 19 | $18

501 N. Orlando Ave. (bet. Hwy. 17-92 & Lee Rd.), Winter Park, 407-644-8449

■ "If grandma were Thai" she'd cook up "tasty" classics like the "excellent", "quick and inexpensive" renditions offered at this "good neighborhood stop" in Winter Park, where regulars "love the complimentary salad" and recommend the crispy fish or one of the "great red curries"; service is as "fast and courteous" as ever.

VICTORIA & ALBERT'S [S] 28 | 28 | 29 | $81

Disney's Grand Floridian Resort & Spa, 4401 Grand Floridian Way, Lake Buena Vista, 407-824-1089

■ "Proof that Disney can amaze adults as well as children", this "ultimate" Grand Floridian American achieves near-"perfection from start to finish": chef Scott Hunnel masterminds "glorious" prix fixe extravaganzas (especially at the "chef's table in the kitchen", where the meals are personalized), and "you couldn't possibly get better service", given that each table is pampered by a "maid-

and-butler" team that attends to "you and you only"; of course, as "the pinnacle of fine dining", it's "very expensive."

Vito's Chop House [S] ▽ 28 | 25 | 26 | $33

8633 International Dr. (Austrian Ct.), 407-354-2467

■ "Classy without being stuffy", this upscale International Drive destination is a favorite option for carnivores who rave its steaks and chops are "the best they've had in a long time"; the "high-quality" beef is "cooked exactly as requested" and presented by "attentive servers" who can also recommend "excellent" choices from the ambitious wine list boasting more than 800 bottles.

Yachtsman Steakhouse [S] 26 | 25 | 26 | $42

Disney's Yacht Club Resort, 1700 Epcot Resorts Blvd., Lake Buena Vista, 407-939-3463

■ "Morton's for the Disney set", this steakhouse in Disney's Yacht Club Resort truly "has all the elements" – "succulent" beef that some swear is simply the "best" on Mouse property, as well as other "mouthwatering" dishes, served amid "clubby decor" by a "top-notch" staff; in fact, fanatics proclaim that if they "had to pick a last meal" location, this "favorite" would be at the top of their list.

Palm Beach

TOP 10 FOOD RANKING

	Restaurant	Cuisine Type
29	Chez Jean-Pierre	French Bistro
27	Cafe L'Europe	Continental
	La Vieille Maison	Provincial French
	New York Prime	Steakhouse
	Four Seasons	Floridian
	Kathy's Gazebo	Continental
26	Renato's	N&S Italian
	Cafe Chardonnay	New American
25	John G's	American
	Marcello's La Sirena	N&S Italian

ADDITIONAL NOTEWORTHY PLACES

Captain Charlie's	Caribbean/Seafood
Cheesecake Factory	American
11 Maple Street	New American
Fathom	Seafood
La Belle Epoque	New French
Le Mistral	New French
Le Mont	Continental/Floridian
L'Escalier	New American/New French
32 East	New American
Zemi	Eclectic

F | D | S | C

CAFE CHARDONNAY [S] 26 | 23 | 24 | $45

Garden Square Shoppes, 4533 PGA Blvd. (Military Trail), Palm Beach Gardens, 561-627-2662

■ "Year after year", "you can count on" the "solidly" "superb" menu and "exciting wines" at this Palm Beach "favorite", a "gourmet gem" from "inventive appetizers" to "delicious", "fresh fish" to decadent desserts; given all its "panache" and "upscale" yet "casual" atmosphere, it's really rather "reasonably priced."

CAFE L'EUROPE [S] 27 | 28 | 26 | $60

331 S. County Rd. (Brazilian Ave.), 561-655-4020

■ For the "ultimate chic", you "must" try this "magnificently well-run" Continental standard-bearer, voted the Most Popular spot in Palm Beach; it "delights all the senses" with its "fabulous" fare, the "beautiful smell of fresh-cut roses" in the "lovely" dining room and prime people-watching perks; plus, it features an "unbeatable caviar bar" and "lively" jazz piano in the "bustling bistro."

Captain Charlie's Reef Grill [S] 25 | 14 | 22 | $27

12846 US Hwy. 1 (Juno Isles Blvd.), Juno Beach, 561-624-9924
251 US Hwy. 1 (Indiantown Rd.), Jupiter, 561-746-8857

■ "Don't bother with the makeup", just "put on your shorts and T-shirt" and head to this "loud", "shabby-chic" Caribbean seafood grill in Juno, "where locals go" in droves despite the "huge lines"; the reason: "generous portions" of some of the "best fresh fish around", all "reasonably priced" and matched with 50 "good wines by the glass"; N.B. an offshoot just opened in Jupiter.

CHEESECAKE FACTORY ●❺ | 21 | 19 | 19 | $24 |
5530 Glades Rd. (Butts Rd.), Boca Raton, 561-393-0344
CityPlace, 701 S. Rosemary Ave. (bet. Hibiscus & Irish Sts.),
West Palm Beach, 561-802-3838
✔ "Factories for sure", yes, but these popular American arenas are based on a "cookie-cutter recipe that works every time": feed customers "industrial-size portions" of "reliable, tasty" eats and offer them so much "variety" that they might "never know what to eat"; though the "wait for a table is agony" and the "noise level" and "huge crowds" make it feel "like a zoo", the "hungry" packs all agree that the 30-plus varieties of the namesake cheesecake are "sinfully delicious."

CHEZ JEAN-PIERRE BISTRO | 29 | 24 | 26 | $56 |
132 N. County Rd. (bet. Sunrise & Sunset Aves.), 561-833-1171
■ "Far and away the best" meals in town are found at this "quaint", "family-run" French "charmer" whose outstanding "quality" is "not to be believed", which explains why it was voted No. 1 for Food in Palm Beach; "sophisticated" "locals" "love" the "consistently excellent", "authentic" dishes (including "exquisite sea bass" and "really fresh Dover sole") brought to table by a "friendly, expert" staff in a comfortable room decorated with trompe l'oeil paintings, and they can't wait to return.

11 Maple Street ❺ | – | – | – | M |
3224 NE Maple Ave. (11th Ave.), Jensen Beach, 561-334-7714
Tucked away on a tiny, sandy alley "up in Jensen Beach" is this 1909 picket-fenced delight where "creative" chef-owners Mike and Margie Perrin "really know their way around the kitchen", dishing up New American fare with an emphasis on organic and natural ingredients; the "wonderful", tropical-themed room and the porch are open only five nights a week, so when you "dine in this beautiful house with the twinkly lights", you too may "wish it were an inn so you could spend the weekend."

Fathom ❺ | 23 | 25 | 21 | $47 |
11611 Ellison Wilson Rd. (PGA Blvd.), Palm Beach Gardens,
561-626-8788
✔ "Exquisite", "bold" seafood creations teamed with a "notable" wine list lure Palm Beach Gardens gastronomes to this "stylistic" fish house on the Intracoastal; though many say the art nouveau interior is "gorgeous", others "feel lost in the big room" where the "high ceilings" merely augment all the "noise", while money-wise critics can't fathom the steep prices or the "pretentiousness."

FOUR SEASONS ❺ | 27 | 28 | 27 | $59 |
Four Seasons, 2800 S. Ocean Blvd. (Lake Ave.), 561-582-2800
■ "If you need pampering", sink into a swanky seat at this "elegant showstopper" set in the "lovely" Four Seasons hotel, where the "gorgeous" ocean views and hand-painted Chinese murals set the stage for "heaven-on-a-plate" Floridian dishes executed by chef Hubert Des Marais, followed by "wondrous" desserts by Tom Worhach and served by "pure professionals"; it leaves supplicants swooning that the "Greek gods must have built this place."

John G's [S] ≠ 25 | 15 | 22 | $18

10 S. Ocean Blvd. (Lake Ave.), Lake Worth, 561-585-9860

■ "You'll need to loosen your belt" after tucking into one of the "best breakfasts and lunches in South Florida" warn regulars of this oceanside "local legend" in Lake Worth; don't mind the "long lines", because while you cool your jets waiting for a table you can enjoy the "beach view and salty air"; the traditional American vittles are a "great value", but note that it's cash only and it's open only till 3 PM.

Kathy's Gazebo Cafe [S] 27 | 24 | 25 | $53

4199 N. Federal Hwy. (Spanish River Rd.), Boca Raton, 561-395-6033

◪ "Dover sole to die for" and other "exquisitely prepared" "classic" Continental dishes "please even the most finicky diner" at this "traditional" Boca cafe where an "older, well-heeled crowd" "treats itself to an elegant evening"; the staff working the "beautiful little room" is "extremely attentive", though even customers "with reservations" are sometimes kept "waiting" for a table.

La Belle Epoque [S] ▽ 26 | 26 | 25 | $48

253 SE Fifth Ave. (Atlantic Ave.), Delray Beach, 561-272-5800

■ Few surveyors seem to have discovered this "wonderful" New French "find" "off the beaten track", but those who have praise it for ushering in a beautiful epoch of fine dining for Delray Beach denizens; overseen by "friendly" Swiss owners, a "charming" staff delivers dishes so "exquisite" that patrons may be prompted to pitch pennies in the fountain at the center of the "stylish" room to wish for a speedy return trip.

LA VIEILLE MAISON [S] 27 | 28 | 27 | $58

770 E. Palmetto Park Rd. (bet. NE Olive Way & Spanish Trail), Boca Raton, 561-737-5677

■ The "grande dame of Boca" garners plenty of "kudos" for its world-class service team, led by the "best captain in the U.S.A."; drawing nearly as much praise is the kitchen's "consistently divine" Provincial French fare, turned out in a "beautifully furnished old house" where its "small, private rooms" make it *the* "place to come and not be seen" when you're looking to get "*très romantique.*"

Le Mistral [S] 25 | 21 | 23 | $46

Northbeach Plaza, 12189 US Hwy. 1 (PGA Blvd.), North Palm Beach, 561-622-3009

■ "Appearances can be deceiving" because tucked inside this "ordinary" North Palm "strip mall" is a "cozy charmer" of a French restaurant; the bouillabaisse is "outstanding", though "everything" on the "authentic", "top-notch" menu is "extraordinary", making this "wonderful gourmet" treat a "favorite for a special evening."

Le Mont ▽ 23 | 26 | 23 | $51

Northbridge Ctr., 515 N. Flagler Dr., 20th fl. (bet. 4th & 5th Sts.), West Palm Beach, 561-820-2442

◪ High in the sky on the 20th floor of a West Palm bank tower, this "very glitzy" Pittsburgh import is perfect "if you need la-di-da" "bordello decor" and a "spectacular view" to seduce your date; supporters say the Floridian-style Continental fare is "delicious", but foodies who've 'been there, eaten that' crave "more selection" from the "overpriced" menu.

L'Escalier [S] – | – | – | VE

The Breakers Hotel, 1 S. County Rd. (Royal Palm Way), 561-659-8480
The venerable Breakers Hotel has renovated its Florentine Room and rechristened it after the stairway leading to this haven; in an intimate room appointed with silky banquettes and flower-adorned polished tables, a "pampering" staff serves "outstanding" French-accented New American dishes, an unusual cheese selection and a winning wine list; it's a thoroughly "elegant" experience, but be forewarned that a meal here can be a bank breaker.

Marcello's La Sirena [S] 25 | 19 | 23 | $46

6316 S. Dixie Hwy. (bet. Forest Hill & Southern Blvds.), West Palm Beach, 561-585-3128
◪ Inside this "small, charming" West Palm A-frame is an Italian ristorante that's definitely a "cut above" most others, pleasing with "simple, perfectly prepared" dishes with an emphasis on seafood; accompanied by "one of the best wine lists ever", the "wonderful" fare is presented "without pretense", making the "expensive" tariff worth it.

NEW YORK PRIME [S] 27 | 23 | 24 | $56

2350 Executive Center Dr. NW (Glades Rd.), Boca Raton, 561-998-3881
■ "Fuhgeddabout New York" – the "mack daddy of steakhouses" is in Boca; it's always "boys' night out" at this beef bacchanalia where the "huge", "delicious" cuts virtually guarantee "Great Dane-size doggy bags"; a "clubby" "attitude", though, means that if you're not one of the "boisterous" "regulars", you may find it "hard to get a reservation in season" at this "popular" "glutton"-fest.

Renato's [S] 26 | 25 | 24 | $55

87 Via Mizner (Worth Ave.), 561-655-9752
■ Palm Beach residents who "want to eat well" but also have "romance" on their minds patronize this "charming" retreat "off Worth Avenue" that simply "oozes atmosphere"; whether inside the "spectacular" dining room filled with "fresh flowers" or out in the "lovely courtyard", you'll enjoy "wonderful" meals plated on "beautiful Limoge china" and served in a "courteous manner."

32 East [S] 23 | 20 | 21 | $42

32 E. Atlantic Ave. (bet. SE 1st & S. Swinton Aves.), Delray Beach, 561-276-7868
■ A "creative, daily changing menu" based on "simple ingredients" prepared well "keeps the locals" and the far-flung alike "coming back" "again and again" to "Delray's fun place for grown-up" gastronomes; though the "noisy, busy" bar scene "feels like Manhattan", it's chef Nick Morfogen's "plentiful" New American "fusion" fare that takes this "upscale joint" "beyond South Florida."

Zemi [S] 25 | 24 | 23 | $49

Boca Ctr., 5050 Town Center Circle (S. Military Trail), Boca Raton, 561-391-7177
◪ This "sophisticated" see-and-"be seen" "hot spot" is where "trendy" Boca folks congregate; don't think, though, that the food plays second fiddle here, because chef John Belleme's Eclectic menu (with a "bit of an Asian influence") is "exquisite" and "exotic" and it's "beautifully presented" in a space so "chic" that "even the bathroom is pretty"; introverts, however, may want to "avoid the weekends", when "they sure do pack them in."

TOP 20 FOOD RANKING

Restaurant	Cuisine Type
29 Fountain	New French/New American
Le Bar Lyonnais	French Bistro
Le Bec-Fin	French
28 Vetri	N&S Italian
27 Django	European
Deux Cheminées	French
Buddakan	Asian Fusion
Swann Lounge	New French/New American
26 Striped Bass	Seafood
Susanna Foo	Chinese/New French
La Famiglia	N&S Italian
Mainland Inn	New American
Jake's	New American
Prime Rib	Steakhouse
Dilworthtown Inn	New American
Birchrunville Store Cafe	N&S Italian/French
Savona	Northern Italian
Inn at Phillips Mill	French Bistro
¡Pasión!	Nuevo Latino
Nan	New French/Thai

ADDITIONAL NOTEWORTHY PLACES

Alma de Cuba	Cuban
Bistro St. Tropez	French Bistro
Brasserie Perrier	New French
Capital Grille	Steakhouse
Dmitri's	Mediterranean/Seafood
Fork	New American
Founders	New American
Kristian's	N&S Italian
La Bonne Auberge	French
Morimoto	Japanese
Opus 251	New American
Overtures	French/Med.
Pif	French Bistro
Pigalle	French Bistro
Ristorante Panorama	N&S Italian
Saloon	N&S Italian/Steakhouse
Tangerine	Moroccan/Med.
Tre Scalini	N&S Italian
20 Manning	Asian/New American
Yangming	Chinese/Continental

Alma de Cuba [S] 21 | 23 | 22 | $46

1623 Walnut St. (bet. 16th & 17th Sts.), 215-988-1799

◪ Celebrity chef Douglas Rodriguez and über-restaurateur Stephen Starr help the "beautiful" people "forget where they are" at this "hip" Restaurant Row Cuban collaboration; where the "mojitos have mojo", the modern fare is "fabulous fusion" and the decor features "flashing scenes" of the island, it is indeed "hard to believe you're in Philly", though diners who find it "too dark", "too loud" and "too trendy" pout that a "trip to Havana should be more fun."

Birchrunville Store Cafe ⊭ 26 | 20 | 22 | $40

1407 Hollow Rd. (Flowing Springs Rd.), Birchrunville, 610-827-9002

■ "Half the joy is finding" Francis Treciak's Italian-French BYO "retreat" "in the woods" of "nowheresville", aka the Chester County "hills"; the other half, at least, is the chance to savor "exquisite", "mouthwatering" "country" cooking turned out in a "cute" "village store" setting; you need to "make reservations way in advance", it's "cash only" and the "110-decibel" noise level is "not conducive" to conversation.

Bistro St. Tropez 23 | 20 | 20 | $35

Marketplace Design Center, 2400 Market St., 4th fl. (23rd St.), 215-569-9269

◪ Patrice Rames has French bistro style "down pat" at his fourth-floor "hideaway" in the Marketplace Design Center; it's where "arty" urbanites "send suburbanites" for "imaginative" prix fixe meals served in a "kitschy" setting with a "spectacular" "view of the Schuylkill"; there's a "groovy bar" too, and after a repast aesthetes like to "browse through the displays" in the building, but sensitive sorts sniff that the "rude" staff has too much Gaul.

BRASSERIE PERRIER [S] 26 | 25 | 24 | $52

1619 Walnut St. (bet. 16th & 17th Sts.), 215-568-3000

■ "Bring your best client" to Georges Perrier's other Center City standout, because even if this New French belle is known as the "poor man's Le Bec-Fin", it promises an "almost perfect dining experience" that'll make you seem "rich and trendy"; expect an "Armani-clad clientele" slouching about the "power bar" jabbering on "cell phones" while a "professional" staff glides through the "sleek", "Manhattanesque" room delivering chef de cuisine Chris Scarduzio's "elegant", "scrumptious" fare to diners who only wish the portions weren't so "tiny."

BUDDAKAN [S] 27 | 27 | 24 | $47

325 Chestnut St. (bet. 3rd & 4th Sts.), 215-574-9440

■ Stephen Starr plays up the "wow factor" at his "edgy" Asian "fusion" "production" in the Historic District, where "the 'in' crowd" experiences "gastronomic nirvana" thanks to chef Scott Swiderski's "beautiful" dishes, turned out "in the shadow of a big, golden Buddha"; though there's nothing "Zen-like" about the "deafening" noise, you can "enjoy a more relaxing dinner" upstairs, where "you get no stares" – except from the "servers who are as stone-faced" as the statue of the Enlightened One himself.

Capital Grille [S] 24 | 24 | 23 | $49

1338 Chestnut St. (Broad St.), 215-545-9588

◪ Take "a welcome trip back to the '50s, when food was guiltless fun", at this "clubby", "old-school" Avenue of the Arts beef palace; the "expense-account" legions "feel like senators" chomping on "melt-in-your-mouth" meat and swilling "great martinis" amid a "dark wood" interior brightened by a "sunny staff"; jaded jurists jibe "seen one chophouse, you've seen them all", but how many have servers "who send out thank-you notes"?

Deux Cheminées | 27 | 27 | 26 | VE |
1221 Locust St. (bet. 12th & 13th Sts.), 215-790-0200
☑ Culinary "king" Fritz Blank's prix fixe "shrine to haute" French is "straight out of a Victorian novel"; within the "sumptuous old-world setting" of a "charming mansion" in Center City, disciples willingly "sacrifice dieting" to indulge in "superior" fare brought forth by an "impeccable" staff; it's a "real special-occasion place", even if some find it a "bit stuffy."

Dilworthtown Inn 🆂 | 26 | 26 | 25 | $50 |
1390 Old Wilmington Pike (Brenton Bridge Rd.), West Chester, 610-399-1390
■ "For an inn from Revolutionary times, it sure is hip" marvels the "horsey set" about this "stately" "colonial" survivor of the Battle of Brandywine that's "hard to beat" for an "evening of absolute class"; whether seated in one of the "small, beautiful, candlelit dining rooms" or out in the "lovely stables", you'll be treated to "sophisticated" New American dishes; it's so "very special" that you'll "feel like you're visiting the elite of Chester County" – only "without the stuffiness."

DJANGO 🆂 | 27 | 20 | 23 | $32 |
526 S. Fourth St. (South St.), 215-922-7151
■ Bryan Sikora and Aimee Olexy's "little gem of a BYO" off South Street "already rivals other favorites" "in the hearts" of Brotherly Lovers due to its "mind-bogglingly" "fresh, fresh, fresh" "monthly menu highlighting seasonal produce"; the European menu brims with "inventive combinations", though the complimentary "bread in a flowerpot" and the "exquisite cheese plate" alone are "worth the trip"; enhanced by "warm, inviting" surroundings, this is a "keeper for years to come."

Dmitri's 🆂 | 25 | 14 | 20 | $27 |
795 S. Third St. (Catharine St.), 215-625-0556 ⌻
2227 Pine St. (23rd St.), 215-985-3680
■ "It doesn't pay to cook at home" when the "stuff that dreams are made of" is available at Dmitri Chimes' "minimalist", moderately priced Mediterranean seafood houses in Queen Village and Fitler Square; highlighting the "mouthwateringly fabulous" fare is the "superb grilled octopus", so though these cash-only BYOs are as "crowded" and "noisy as airports", with equally "hurried" service, "you won't mind the wait", as you'll be taking a trip to "heaven and Santorini all at once."

Fork 🆂 | 24 | 22 | 22 | $39 |
306 Market St. (bet. 3rd & 4th Sts.), 215-625-9425
■ The "ultimate in casual cool" might be this "respectably mod" New American in Old City, which is a bit "New York", but not too much so; "sit at the bar and enjoy the lack of scene" or settle in the dining room and let the "cordial" servers bring you "seasonal" dishes that are "innovative without being weird"; despite "noisy", "cramped" quarters, fans who "savor every delicious bite" of the "pleasant" Sunday brunch, lunch or dinner just sigh "stick me with a fork, I'm in heaven."

Founders [S] | 26 | 27 | 25 | $57 |

Park Hyatt at the Bellevue, 200 S. Broad St. (Walnut St.), 215-790-2814

■ "They treat you like royalty" at the Park Hyatt's "elegant" New American "institution" where patrons "ride the elevator" up to a "special room" that "screams class all the way"; providing an almost "lost kind of dining experience", it delivers a "memorably" "exquisite" meal replete with weekend "ballroom dancing" and an "outstanding" view of the city through its floor-to-ceiling windows; N.B. jacket required on Fridays and Saturdays.

FOUNTAIN [S] | 29 | 29 | 29 | $66 |

Four Seasons Philadelphia, 1 Logan Sq. (Benjamin Franklin Pkwy. & 18th St.), 215-963-1500

■ This "smashing" Logan Square "landmark" at the Four Seasons is "hard to overpraise", though legions of supporters are happy to try; "guaranteed to impress" are top toque Martin Hamann's "triumphant" New French–New American culinary feats, decor that's even more "gorgeous" following a redo and "terrific" service, making the "super-high" tariffs "worth every gilded penny."

Inn at Phillips Mill [S] ⊄ | 26 | 26 | 24 | $46 |

2590 N. River Rd. (Phillips Mill Rd.), New Hope, 215-862-9919

■ "In New Hope but away from the hustle", this "romantic" BYO "country inn" set in a mid-18th-century house is a "joy to visit" for many reasons; the French bistro dishes are "delicious" and the service so "phenomenal" that "every request is fulfilled, and with good cheer" to boot, but the kicker may be its "absolutely charming" surroundings featuring a quartet of fireplaces and a "delightful courtyard garden."

Jake's [S] | 26 | 22 | 24 | $47 |

4365 Main St. (bet. Grape & Levering Sts.), 215-483-0444

■ Bruce Cooper's "stylish" New American "started it all in Manayunk" back in the '80s and "it hasn't lost anything" in the ensuing years – in fact, "lots of regulars" agree that "on all fronts" it "just gets better and better, like fine wine"; "choose anything on the menu – nothing will disappoint" – though the standouts must be the "sinful crab cakes" and "must-try cookie taco dessert"; it's a "neighborhood favorite", so "don't plan to just drop in" – "reservations are a must."

Kristian's Ristorante [S] | 25 | 21 | 22 | $43 |

1100 Federal St. (11th St.), 215-468-0104

■ "Bravos" abound for the Leuzzi family's "elegant" South Philly Italian ristorante, deemed a "delight" for chef Kristian's "great osso buco" and other "top-notch" dishes; the "charming" staff and "welcoming" surroundings make this "favorite" "worth every penny", as well as every minute spent "waiting for a table."

La Bonne Auberge [S] | 25 | 26 | 25 | $66 |

Village 2 Apartment Complex, 1 Rittenhouse Circle (Mechanic St.), New Hope, 215-862-2462

◪ "What a night out!" exclaim Francophiles about this "special-occasion" "classic" in New Hope that's "consistently superb"; the "excellent" cooking, "voluminous wine list", "wonderful" service and "romantic", "church-quiet" ambiance are *très bonne* indeed, but its "much-too-expensive" tariffs and a "difficult" location "tucked away in a condo complex" that's grown up around a 1750 farmhouse have critics crying *sacré bleu!*

La Famiglia Ⓢ   26 24 25 $57

8 S. Front St. (bet. Chestnut & Market Sts.), 215-922-2803

■ A "memorable" experience awaits at the Sena family's "grand" Italian "jewel" in Old City, but "be prepared to spend big bucks"; while wallet-watchers warn that it's "obnoxiously" "overpriced", the "remarkable" fare, a wine list that "reads like a telephone book", "*bella*" decor and a staff that "fawns" over you "like you're a king" make this "class act" a "favorite" "special-occasion" destination among many admirers.

LE BAR LYONNAIS ◕   29 24 26 $49

1523 Walnut St. (bet. 15th & 16th Sts.), 215-567-1000

■ "When you want" the "Le Bec-Fin touch" at a fraction of the cost, follow the lead of those in-the-know and "slum" it at this "plush yet unstuffy" "baby bistro" nestled below chef-owner Georges Perrier's Center City flagship; not only is it a "real find" for "exceptional" French fare served by a "knowledgeable" staff but you can always expect to have a "great conversation with whoever's eating at the bar"; N.B. no reservations accepted.

LE BEC-FIN   29 28 28 $85

1523 Walnut St. (bet. 15th & 16th Sts.), 215-567-1000

■ Georges Perrier's "once-in-a-lifetime" "star" on Restaurant Row continues to turn out "perfection on a plate", dazzling pampered patrons with "stupendously" "superior" French cuisine (and a "magical" triple-tiered "dessert cart") proffered in a "formal" Louis XVI–style dining room appointed with "elegant" period furnishings; equally "world-class" is the "absolutely impeccable" service team, which makes everyone "feel like royalty", adding up to a "memorable experience" that's "as close to heaven as you can get"; N.B. jacket required.

Mainland Inn Ⓢ   26 23 25 $45

17 Main St. (Sumneytown Pike), Mainland, 215-256-8500

■ When the city has you down, take a trip to this "charming" "country" retreat near Lansdale that's "far from the rat race"; it's a "top-drawer" choice for "beautiful" New American meals leisurely delivered by "respectful, knowledgeable" servers across "creaky floors" in a series of "old-fashioned" rooms that bespeak a "formal" yet "cozy" "quaintness."

Morimoto ◕Ⓢ   –   –   –   VE

723 Chestnut St. (bet. 7th & 8th Sts.), 215-413-9070

Iron Chef Masaharu Morimoto and golden boy Stephen Starr "rock" Philly with their "cool", "much-anticipated" Japanese joint on Jewelers Row; amid a "gorgeous interior" designed by wunderkind Karim Rashid, diners embark on an "extraordinary" culinary cruise to "sushi heaven" and other heights, while the captain "makes the rounds to all the tables"; the only catch: "it's so pricey you can't go often" enough.

Nan   26 18 22 $33

4000 Chestnut St. (40th St.), 215-382-0818

■ It might "look like a corner store from the outside", but inside is a "diamond in the rough", a "pleasant", if "spartan", space that allows University City restaurant-goers to focus on chef-owner

Kamol Phutlek's "fabulous", "artistically presented" "fusion" of New French and Thai flavors that positively "sparkle"; it's a "great" BYO "bargain" staffed by "lovely people" and "quiet enough to actually talk", leading scores of smitten sorts to urge "don't miss it."

Opus 251 S   24 | 24 | 22 | $48
Philadelphia Art Alliance, 251 S. 18th St. (bet. Locust & Spruce Sts.), 215-735-6787

☑ An "artful alliance" at the Art Alliance, this New American "tucked" into the "mansion" off Rittenhouse Square combines "scrumptious" fare, a "charming" "jewel box" of a room and a "gracious" garden into a "transporting European"-style dining experience; too bad too many say there's "too little" food and too much "attitude" "for the price."

Overtures S   25 | 22 | 23 | $44
609 E. Passyunk Ave. (bet. Bainbridge & South Sts.), 215-627-3455

■ "Bring your Château Margaux" to this "elegant gourmet BYO" off South Street where you and "that special person" will be "pampered and pleased" by French-Mediterranean "perfection" on a plate, presented by a "wonderfully friendly and capable" staff; just "don't go after you get a tattoo across the street" lest you clash with the "beautiful trompe l'oeil" decor.

¡Pasión! S   26 | 24 | 24 | $50
211 S. 15th St. (bet. Locust & Walnut Sts.), 215-875-9895

■ Passion runs high for Guillermo Pernot's "cutting-edge" cooking at this Center City Nuevo Latino where "everything is superlative", from the "tantalizing" seviches to the "orgasmic" grilled meats; factor in "sexy" decor that "tells the story without being a theme park", plus service from a staff with "loads of personality", and the experience results in a "splurge" "worth writing home about."

Pif S   25 | 14 | 20 | $33
Italian Mkt., 1009 S. Eighth St. (Washington Ave.), 215-625-2923

☑ A South Philly "destination for wine aficionados" toting their own prized vins, this BYO French bistro is "still finding its way", but it's certainly off to a "good beginning"; chef-owner David Ansill shops for "fresh ingredients from the Italian market" for his "limited" but "wonderfully" "creative", "daily changing menu", and if you don't agree that the "tiny" room's "charm is its lack of charm", "hopefully they'll be successful enough to redecorate the place."

Pigalle S   – | – | – | E
702 N. Second St. (Fairmount Ave.), 215-627-7772

Hoping to put the developing neighborhood of Northern Liberties on the culinary map, this handsome Parisian brasserie is where a diverse crowd of hipsters, artists and foodies goes for hearty classics prepared by Stacey DiPlacido; backed by an affordable little wine list, warm ambiance and low-key service, it leads devotees to cheer *tout est magnifique!*

Prime Rib S   26 | 26 | 24 | $55
Radisson Plaza Warwick Hotel, 1701 Locust St. (17th St.), 215-772-1701

■ "Melt-in-your-mouth" and "laughably large", its "name is its specialty" at this "glamorous" "carnivore's delight" in the "elegant" Warwick Hotel in Center City; a "class act" all the way, it's a "grand", "opulent" showstopper that makes you feel like "dressing for the occasion", which is most fitting, since jackets are required –

but don't fret "if you forget yours" – they're so "professional" that "they'll loan you one."

Ristorante Panorama 𝕊   23 | 22 | 21 | $42
Penn's View Hotel, 14 N. Front St. (Market St.), 215-922-7800
■ Oenophiles fancy the "fabulous flights" at Luca Sena's Old City Italian ristorante and wine bar; with "knowledgeable bartenders" pouring 120 selections by the glass, "everybody talks about the wine, but the food is excellent" too, and the setting, graced by a "beautiful wall mural", is "dark and romantic"; the only problem: the prices seem to be on their own upward flight.

Saloon   24 | 22 | 22 | $53
750 S. Seventh St. (bet. Catharine & Fitzwater Sts.), 215-627-1811
■ "Big, bold and amazingly consistent" since 1967, this "clubby" "pub" of an Italian steakhouse is a "home away from home" for anyone from the "heart of South Philadelphia" who "wants to go back to their roots"; the food is so "absolutely fabulous" that followers say the "chef should teach other chefs how to cook", but the service swings between "fawning" and "abusive", and some are convinced that you're "paying extra for the possibility of seeing or being seen."

Savona 𝕊   26 | 26 | 24 | $59
100 Old Gulph Rd. (Rte. 320), Gulph Mills, 610-520-1200
■ "Two more payments and the meal is mine!" quip those who save up for a "vacation" at this "big leaguer" on the Main Line, a Northern Italian "class act" that's "worth the train date" from the city; the atmosphere might be "ostentatious", but there's no quibbling about Dominique Filoni's "superb" Riviera-inspired menu, the "awesome" wine cellar, the appealing Mediterranean decor or the "pampering" service from a staff led by wife Sabine.

STRIPED BASS 𝕊   26 | 28 | 25 | $59
1500 Walnut St. (15th St.), 215-732-4444
■ Neil Stein's "absolutely posh" big-ticket "treat" on Restaurant Row remains one of Philadelphia's most popular power trips thanks to Terence Feury's "bite-by-bite succulent" seafood dishes, served by a staff that "knocks itself out to please you"; it's all turned out in digs so "hip" and "glamorous" (you'll "feel like a star") that the "atmosphere is worth the price" in itself.

Susanna Foo 𝕊   26 | 25 | 25 | $55
1512 Walnut St. (bet. 15th & 16th Sts.), 215-545-2666
☑ Chef-owner Foo's "justly famous" and "high-rent" Restaurant Row "landmark" "tingles the palate" with "light but complex" Chinese–New French "original" creations served with "perfect pacing" by an "impeccable but not snooty" staff in an atmosphere of "understated" "elegance"; it's an "exquisite" experience "fit for an emperor", but commoners who come to celebrate "those super-special life events" implore "can't we make the portions just a bit bigger?"

Swann Lounge ●𝕊   27 | 27 | 27 | $48
Four Seasons Philadelphia, 1 Logan Sq. (18th St. & B.F. Pkwy.), 215-963-1500
■ The "poor man's Fountain" is a "classy joint" in its own right; down the hall from that "other place" at the Four Seasons, this standout's "scrumptious" New French–New American dishes, "casually

elegant" quarters and "waiters who cater to your every need" place it squarely among the city's top establishments; not only is the "dessert buffet a chocolate heaven" but it's "perfect for tea" or brunch too.

Tangerine [S] 24 | 26 | 23 | $48

232 Market St. (bet. 2nd & 3rd Sts.), 215-627-5116

■ Stephen Starr rocks the "casbah" at his "sexy" "dream" in Old City, where the Moroccan-Mediterranean fusion cuisine amounts to a "fez-tival of fantastic flavors" served "family-style"; "draped in red and gold brocade", it's an "exotic" place that "transports you to another world", and you'll want to take a date along, because "see-and-be-seen" takes on a "wildly" "romantic" meaning in this "candlelight"; in a word: "wow!"

Tre Scalini [S] 25 | 14 | 22 | $33

1533 S. 11th St. (Tasker St.), 215-551-3870

■ "Mother hen" Franca DiRenzo "delivers more than you'd expect" at this "unpretentious" BYO Italian set in a "converted row house" in South Philadelphia; "in a city of expense-account eateries where half your bill goes toward paying for the decor", her "dumpy" joint is the "real deal", dishing up "scrumptious" food with "intense flavors", served "promptly" at refreshingly "affordable" prices.

20 Manning [S] 21 | 21 | 19 | $39

261 S. 20th St. (bet. Locust & Spruce Sts.), 215-731-0900

◪ "Where the beautiful people go", you'll find "another Audrey Claire hit"; at this "sleek" Asian–New American off Rittenhouse Square, chef Kiong Banh "proudly" prepares "creative", "tasty" treats; be warned, though, that the "noise storm" inside makes "conversation impossible", but if you're "curious" as to what's "trendy", this joint sure is 'in.'

VETRI 28 | 23 | 26 | $62

1312 Spruce St. (bet. Broad & 13th Sts.), 215-732-3478

■ "There aren't enough superlatives" to describe this "most excellent" of Philadelphia's Italian ristorantes, but we'll try; in a "charmingly designed townhouse", a near-"flawless" staff proffers Marc Vetri's (a "culinary genius") "lovingly prepared and beautifully presented treasures", including "spinach gnocchi unlike anything else in this world"; diners lucky enough to score an "almost impossible-to-get reservation" at this Center City "jewel" rejoice "may it always thrive."

Yangming [S] 24 | 21 | 22 | $35

1051 Conestoga Rd. (Haverford Rd.), Bryn Mawr, 610-527-3200

■ Main Liners "fall in love with the food" "again and again" at this "classy-to-the-core" Chinese-Continental "institution" in Bryn Mawr; the "innovative" specials "melt in your mouth" and the service is "stellar", so it's no wonder that it rates as the "suburbs' best" for a "beautiful" Sino supper, plus, as the "bartenders know what they're doing", it always "feels like a party" here.

Phoenix/Scottsdale

TOP 10 FOOD RANKING

Restaurant	Cuisine Type
28 Restaurant Hapa	New American/Asian
27 T. Cook's	Mediterranean
Michael's at the Citadel	New American
Pizzeria Bianco	Pizza
Mastro's	Steakhouse
26 Mary Elaine's	New French
Marquesa	Mediterranean
Medizona	SW/Mediterranean
Gregory's World Bistro	International
Vincent Guerithault	French/SW

ADDITIONAL NOTEWORTHY PLACES

Convivo	New American/SW
Eddie V's Edgewater Grille	Gulf Coast/Seafood
Houston's	American
Leccabaffi	N&S Italian
Lon's at the Hermosa	New American/SW
P.F. Chang's China Bistro	Chinese
Rancho Pinot	New American
Roaring Fork	Western
RoxSand	Eclectic
Roy's	Hawaiian Fusion

F	D	S	C

Convivo

25	15	23	$38

Walgreens Shopping Ctr., 7000 N. 16th St. (E. Glendale Ave.), Phoenix, 602-997-7676

■ "Glad it's in my neighborhood" cheer cultists who could happily eat Jeffrey Beeson's "fantastic" Southwestern-inspired New American cooking (think lobster tamales and sugar-and-chile-cured lamb tenderloin) "every day"; though the "nondescript strip-mall" setting "leaves a lot to be desired", regulars don't mind, since the "friendly" chef "uses the freshest local ingredients possible" in his weekly changing menu and presents his dishes in a most "imaginative way."

Eddie V's Edgewater Grille S

25	24	21	$43

20715 N. Pima Rd. (E. Thompson Peak Pkwy.), Scottsdale, 480-538-8468

☑ The "superb" Gulf Coast seafood, "expertly prepared" and "imaginatively" plated, hooks in fin fanatics at this "sleek" North Scottsdale newcomer; though service is so far "uneven", admirers deem this "welcome addition" "promising" given the "impeccable" cooking, "sophisticated", "inviting" surroundings and live nightly entertainment (jazz, blues); P.S. you'll "love the patio" overlooking the McDowell Mountains.

Gregory's World Bistro 26 | 19 | 24 | $48

8120 N. Hayden Rd. (Via De Ventura), Scottsdale, 480-946-8700

■ Despite its location in an "unassuming strip mall" in McCormick Ranch, this International bistro is an "exciting" "find" thanks to the "polished" cooking of Gregory Casale, "one of the most creative chefs in town"; his "inspired" menu, enhanced by a select, award-winning wine list, is presented in a "warm", "inviting" room accented with "interesting photographs" of faraway places, making it a "superb place to return to many times"; now if only he'd do something about those "teeny portions."

HOUSTON'S [S] 21 | 19 | 20 | $27

Camelback Esplanade, 2425 E. Camelback Rd. (N. 24th St.), Phoenix, 602-957-9700

6113 N. Scottsdale Rd. (bet. E. Lincoln & E. McDonald Drs.), Scottsdale, 480-922-7775

◪ "Utterly consistent", these "safe bets" are an "excellent value" for "solid" American food, including the "best spinach dip in the universe", "yum yum" soups and salads and "juicy hickory burgers"; to avoid the "long lines" and "after-work crush" of "young professionals" at the bar, insiders know to "go at off-hours", when the "team-server approach" makes for a "well-oiled machine"; detractors, however, dismiss the "unremarkable" "chain food" and "hurried" atmosphere.

Leccabaffi [S] 25 | 18 | 21 | $44

Mountain View Plaza, 9719 N. Hayden Rd. (E. Mountain View Rd.), Scottsdale, 480-609-0429

◪ "Like being in Italy" say devoted diners about this "authentic" North Scottsdale trattoria where chef-owner Giovanni Scorzo wanders all over The Boot, cooking up "great grilled antipasti", "wonderful pastas" and "incredible" regional specialties; his dishes are so "infused with rich flavors" that you'll be "licking your mustache" (per the translation of its whimsical moniker) clean, but "disappointed" dissenters who deem it "overrated and overpriced" want to know "what's the big deal?"

Lon's at the Hermosa [S] 25 | 27 | 23 | $49

Hermosa Inn, 5532 N. Palo Cristi Rd. (E. Stanford Dr.), Paradise Valley, 602-955-7878

■ Once the "classic adobe" ranch house of cowboy artist Lon Megargee, this "secret hideaway in Paradise Valley" overlooking Camelback Mountain is "picturesque" rhapsodize admirers who swoon over the "romantic" ambiance created by the beehive fireplaces, rustic wood beams and vintage photos; most patrons race right outdoors for "glorious" "patio dining" "under the stars", but regardless, you'll be treated to "incredible" Southwestern-inflected New American cuisine.

Marquesa [S] 26 | 27 | 26 | $61

Fairmont Scottsdale Princess, 7575 E. Princess Dr. (bet. Pima & N. Scottsdale Rds.), Scottsdale, 480-585-4848

■ "Absolutely beautiful", this "top-notch" North Scottsdale Mediterranean is a "foodie's delight", "from the imaginative appetizers" to the "exotic" entrees to the "fabulous desserts" (including a tiny chocolate replica of a Dali painting); the "flawless" service means that guests are "treated like royalty", resulting in a "truly marvelous experience that makes any meal a special occasion"; of course it comes with a "big price tag", but "what's not to love" here?; P.S. its "amazing" Spanish market-style Sunday brunch is "second to none."

MARY ELAINE'S
26 | 28 | 27 | $74

The Phoenician, 6000 E. Camelback Rd. (N. 60th St.), Scottsdale, 480-423-2530

■ "Bring your sweetheart" to this "gorgeous" room at The Phoenician for an "incredible dining experience" replete with a "breathtaking view" of Camelback Mountain and live jazz nightly; not only does chef James Boyce create "exquisite" New French dishes "fit for a sultan – at prices to match" (his "tasting menu is a must for foodies") but the "doting" servers tend to the "tiniest details", even giving ladies "special footstools for their handbags", because "heaven forbid your Prada should touch the floor."

MASTRO'S STEAKHOUSE 🖸
27 | 23 | 25 | $55

La Miranda, 8852 E. Pinnacle Peak Rd. (Pima Rd.), Scottsdale, 480-585-9500

■ Never mind that the "stylish lounge" at this "bold and brassy" chophouse in North Scottsdale is "populated by spaghetti-strapped young things" and "ancient swingers", because if you proceed to the "smartly decorated" dining room, you'll be treated to the "best steaks in town", accompanied by an impressive list of California wines and "martinis the size of fishbowls"; even if it's "noisy" and "pricey", the "people-watching is super" and you'll "love that doggy bag" tomorrow.

Medizona
26 | 18 | 25 | $42

7217 E. Fourth Ave. (Winfield Scott Plaza), Scottsdale, 480-947-9500

■ For "extraordinary" Med-inspired Southwestern cooking that "you can't get anywhere else" (think "awesome veal cheeks", rabbit baklava, prickly pear tiramisu), head straight to "innovative" chef-owner Lenny Rubin's "small", "cute" bistro in Downtown Scottsdale, where his "bold" food is "deliciously" "off the wall"; it's "not for the unadventurous", but that's fine by the gourmands who "return" often for an "exciting, rewarding dining experience."

MICHAEL'S AT THE CITADEL 🖸
27 | 24 | 25 | $51

The Citadel, 8700 E. Pinnacle Peak Rd. (Pima Rd.), Scottsdale, 480-515-2575

■ Chef Michael DeMaria's "eclectic" New American menu, which begins with "artful tasting-spoon appetizers" and concludes with "inventive desserts", is just one reason admirers say it's "worth the drive to Pinnacle Peak"; also earning kudos are the "relaxing, elegant setting" enhanced by an indoor waterfall, as well as the "superb" staff and "knowledgeable sommelier"; P.S. Sunday brunch out on the patio overlooking a leafy garden is "a real treat."

P.F. CHANG'S CHINA BISTRO 🖸
21 | 21 | 19 | $28

Chandler Fashion Ctr., 3255 W. Chandler Blvd. (Rte. 101), Chandler, 480-899-0472
Kierland Commons, 7132 E. Greenway Pkwy. (N. Scottsdale Rd.), Scottsdale, 480-367-2999
Scottsdale Fashion Sq., 7014 E. Camelback Rd. (bet. N. Goldwater Blvd. & N. Scottsdale Rd.), Scottsdale, 480-949-2610
740 S. Mill Ave. (E. University Dr.), Tempe, 480-731-4600

☑ Even diehards concede that the "no-reservations" policy is a "giant problem" at this perpetually packed chain, ranked the Most Popular restaurant in the Phoenix area, but they're willing to put up with the "long wait" and constant "noise" to tuck into "snazzy" "nouveau" Chinese fare, especially "the best lettuce wraps ever"; though purists pan the "Americanized" results, the majority believes that this is "traditional Chinese food made even better."

PIZZERIA BIANCO [S] 27 | 20 | 21 | $22

Heritage Sq., 623 E. Adams St. (N. 7th St.), Phoenix, 602-258-8300

■ Anointed "the patron saint of pizza" by legions of pie partisans, chef-owner Chris Bianco makes the "best wood-fired pizzas in town" – "hands down" – thanks to his relentless "focus" on "good, simple" ingredients and "attention to quality"; of course, this "historic" "little brick building Downtown is always busy", but the "freshness" of his handmade mozzarella alone makes it "well worth the wait"; besides, patrons can "chill in his wine bar" next door.

Rancho Pinot 25 | 20 | 23 | $43

Lincoln Vlg., 6208 N. Scottsdale Rd. (E. Lincoln Dr.), Scottsdale, 480-367-8030

■ "Let's see, where to start?" muse regulars as they explain why this "local favorite", a "comfortable" "little gem", always exudes such "a good buzz"; first, Chrysa Kaufman's New American dishes are "awesome" (her "homey" signature fare includes Nonni's Sunday chicken – so "good" "you may never order anything else" here – and mom's honey-pecan pie); then there's husband Tom's "top-flight" wine cellar, the "secluded setting" and the "most individualized" service; "bravo!"

RESTAURANT HAPA 28 | 20 | 25 | $45

Lincoln Vlg., 6204 N. Scottsdale Rd. (E. Lincoln Dr.), Scottsdale, 480-998-8220

■ Get ready for an "orgasmic" dining experience at this "exciting" "treasure", because James McDevitt's cooking is so "brilliant" his restaurant was voted No. 1 for Food in the Phoenix/Scottsdale area; the surroundings are "understated" and "calm", making it a "perfect backdrop for focusing on the subtlety" of his "exquisite" Asian-accented New American dishes and wife Stacey's "to-die-for desserts" (don't miss her "unique ice creams"); "by far, this is one of the most memorable meals" you'll have in the Southwest.

Roaring Fork 25 | 21 | 23 | $40

Finova Bldg., 4800 N. Scottsdale Rd. (Chaparral Rd.), Scottsdale, 480-947-0795

■ "Charming" chef-owner Robert McGrath, a former Texan with a flair for cooking "hearty campfire food", rules the range at his recently relocated bistro, which turns out Western cooking "with a true gourmet touch"; though many look forward to settling in at dinnertime over his pork porterhouse with a side of green-chile macaroni, others prefer to show up early for the "best happy hour in town", washing down their 'big-ass burger' with a huckleberry margarita; with "everyone having such a good time", expect it to be "crowded" and "noisy."

RoxSand [S] 24 | 21 | 22 | $43

Biltmore Fashion Park, 2594 E. Camelback Rd. (N. 24th St.), Phoenix, 602-381-0444

◪ "Still terrific after all these years", this "metropolitan" Phoenix "fixture" accented with challenging art continues to satisfy curious palates who are looking for something "unusual" on their plate, thanks to chef-owner RoxSand Scocos, whose Eclectic menu highlights such dishes as African piri piri and curried rice tamales ("the stuff dreams are made of"); even those who contend that this "overrated" stalwart is "getting a little tired" admit that it remains the last word for "dessert, dessert, dessert."

ROY'S | 25 | 22 | 22 | $43 |

Camelback Esplanade, 2501 E. Camelback Rd. (26th St.), Phoenix, 602-381-1155
Scottsdale Seville, 7001 N. Scottsdale Rd. (E. Indian Bend Rd.), Scottsdale, 480-905-1155 🖲

◪ "Hip" and "energetic", these "see-and-be-seen" Arizona outposts of Roy Yamaguchi's Hawaiian Fusion dynasty "don't have that chain feel" say loyalists who love the "must-have" lobster potstickers, "heavenly" chocolate soufflé and "everything in between"; while a disgruntled few are put off by their "shopping center" locations and "inconsistent" service, most are always ready to "sit outdoors in the misted coolness" of their patios and "imagine themselves on a tropical isle."

T. COOK'S 🖲 | 27 | 28 | 26 | $53 |

Royal Palms Hotel & Casitas, 5200 E. Camelback Rd. (bet. N. Arcadia Dr. & N. 56th St.), Phoenix, 602-808-0766

▪ Nestled at the base of Camelback Mountain in a "charming", "upscale resort" that still bears traces of the Spanish estate that it once was, this "gorgeous" "special-occasion" "destination" is "the epitome of fine dining" in Phoenix; enthusiasts make it a point to "bring out-of-town guests" here for the "whole package", which includes "outstanding" Mediterranean fare, "classy but not stuffy" service and a "cozy piano bar" that reeks of "romance."

Vincent Guerithault | 26 | 21 | 24 | $52 |
on Camelback 🖲

3930 E. Camelback Rd. (N. 40th St.), Phoenix, 602-224-0225

◪ A "pioneer" in French-Southwestern "fusion", "delightful" chef-owner Vincent Guerithault turns out "phantasmagorical" fare that screams "special occasion" in every bite; long setting the "standard" in Phoenix, his "romantic" refuge (just redone to make it reminiscent of a Provençal country inn) still provides a "great dining experience", but doubters who find it "disappointing after all the hype" feel it suffers from "missed details."

Portland, OR

TOP 10 FOOD RANKING

	Restaurant	Cuisine Type
28	Genoa	N&S Italian
	Paley's Place	Pacific NW/French Bistro
	Tina's	Pacific NW/French Bistro
27	Joel Palmer House	Pacific Northwest
	Café des Amis	French
	Couvron	New French
	Wildwood	Pacific Northwest
26	Saburo's	Japanese
	Castagna	N. Italian/New French
	Winterborne	Seafood

ADDITIONAL NOTEWORTHY PLACES

Restaurant	Cuisine Type
Bluehour	Mediterranean
Café Azul	Mexican
El Gaucho	Steakhouse
Heathman	Pacific NW/French
Higgins	Pacific Northwest
Mint	Latin American
Pazzo	Northern Italian
Pho Van	Vietnamese
Sungari	Chinese
Zinc Bistrot	French Bistro

F	D	S	C

Bluehour 🖂
24 | 27 | 22 | $42

250 NW 13th Ave. (Everett St.), 503-226-3394

■ "Master" restaurateur "Bruce Carey has done it again" with this "trendy" "hit" in the Pearl offering an ever-changing yet always "good" menu of "inventive" but "surprisingly unpretentious" Med dishes accompanied by "swanky drinks and scrumptious desserts"; the "lovely surroundings" feature high ceilings and "sexy curtains" that create "quiet, private" areas, and "superb service" ensures an experience that's "elegant from start to finish."

Café Azul
25 | 21 | 22 | $33

112 NW Ninth Ave. (bet. Couch & Davis Sts.), 503-525-4422

☑ "Haute Mexican" that would make "Diane Kennedy proud" transforms this Pearl spot into a "sophisticated" experience; "homemade chips and salsa" are hard to resist, and the "vibrantly flavored" "mole is darn close to what you'd find in Oaxaca"; though the "service is impeccable" and the "ambiance lovely", a few gringos gripe it's "too expensive" and "overly noisy."

CAFÉ DES AMIS
27 | 23 | 26 | $40

1987 NW Kearney St. (20th Ave.), 503-295-6487

■ A "long-standing favorite" of Francophiles, this Gallic "classic" in the Northwest District features a "charming setting" that's the backdrop for "intimate dining"; its many friends say *encore* to "satiny soups", the "duck with blackberry sauce" and an "excellent wine list" but save loud cheers for the "superior service"; N.B. there's also a franc-friendly bistro menu.

CASTAGNA   26 | 22 | 25 | $41
1752 SE Hawthorne Blvd. (18th Ave.), 503-231-7373
CAFE CASTAGNA S
1758 SE Hawthorne Blvd. (18th Ave.), 503-231-9959
■ This Hawthorne French-Italian is an embodiment of the "clear vision" of husband-and-wife owners Kevin Gibson ("former Genoa chef") and Monique Siu, where the kitchen "artistically" creates "spectacular scallops, quail and rack of lamb" using "clean, pure flavors that echo the minimalist decor"; with a "varied, affordable wine list" and "gracious service", it's a "chic place for clients" and out-of-towners; N.B. the more casual cafe also offers burgers and pizza.

Couvron   27 | 22 | 25 | $66
1126 SW 18th Ave. (bet. Madison & Salmon Sts.), 503-225-1844
■ "Every bite is truly delicious" at this "elegant" Downtown New French – the crème de la crème in local "haute cuisine" – famed for its "fanatical devotion" to "world-class" flavors, "architectural presentations" and "personalized service"; featuring "amazing" seven-course prix fixe meals only (the "vegetarian offering", which must be ordered a day in advance, "brings tears" to some eyes), it's an "expensive splurge", but go ahead – "sell the family jewels and enjoy."

El Gaucho ●S   23 | 24 | 24 | $52
319 SW Broadway (bet. Oak & Stark Sts.), 503-227-8794
■ Buckaroos bypass the pampas and go Downtown to this relatively "new kid on the Portland steakhouse block" (located next to the Benson Hotel, where visiting presidents bunk) for "big portions" of "fabulous steaks", including "excellent" classics such as Châteaubriand, followed by "bananas Foster to rival Brennan's" and served by a staff that "bends over backward to make you happy"; however, a number of grouchos grumble it's "overpriced."

GENOA   28 | 24 | 28 | $63
2832 SE Belmont St. (bet. 28th & 29th Aves.), 503-238-1464
■ Portland's No. 1 for Food as well as Most Popular, this 32-year-old "world-class" Belmont Italian offers "a sublime experience" – from the "gastronomic euphoria" of its seven-course prix fixe dinner to the service in which "no detail is overlooked" to the setting that's "opulent without being stuffy"; a "hugely expensive" tab puts off a few who also note that its three-hour meals are "easily the longest experience in town", but most concur "it's worth every penny" and minute.

Heathman S   26 | 24 | 24 | $41
Heathman Hotel, 1001 SW Broadway (Salmon St.), 503-790-7752
■ Normandy-born Philippe Boulot is the "outstanding" presiding force at this "dependably excellent" Downtown Northwest-French landmark where "elegance and class" define setting, service, food and wine; added attractions include "power breakfast and lunch", afternoon tea (holiday season only) or a rendezvous by the bar's fireplace for "heavenly crab cakes and Irish coffee."

HIGGINS [S] 26 24 25 $39

1239 SW Broadway (Jefferson St.), 503-222-9070

■ Local, organic "ingredients combined with imagination" are the hallmark of this Downtown "foodies' paradise", notable for "Mr. Natural's" (chef Greg Higgins) "flawless execution" of Northwest cuisine, which elicits repeat visits from carnivores and vegheads alike, not to mention fans of the 400-bottle wine list; the busy bar serves a "great hamburger", and the Broadway "location, location, location" makes it a magnet for theater- or concert-goers.

JOEL PALMER HOUSE 27 25 24 $42

600 Ferry St. (6th St.), Dayton, 503-864-2995

■ It's "worth the drive to Dayton", "in the heart of wine country", to dine at this "remodeled historic house" that's known for "classic gourmet" Northwest cuisine; "mushroom mavens" pop in for "fabulous" fungi appearing in everything from salad to cheesecake, but the "zingy grilled meats" and roast Oregon elk are also good picks; the "lovely setting", a "happy" staff and "caring" owners cap the experience, though it costs a little morel than some would like.

Mint [S] – – – M

816 N. Russell St. (bet. Albina & Mississippi Aves.), 503-284-5518

Fashionistas are flocking to this tropically hot scene in North Portland, where comfy banquettes and a cozy, chat-space-filled bar offer an inviting ambiance in which to sip fruity cocktails in giant glasses; the vibrant Latin cuisine stars such goodies as Cuban lamb burger, fried calamari salad with tomato and avocado, and the house's own coconut flan.

PALEY'S PLACE [S] 28 23 26 $43

1204 NW 21st Ave. (Northrup St.), 503-243-2403

■ For a "perfect experience", most places pale next to this "touch-of-class" Northwest-French bistro in a "charming" "converted house" in the Northwest District, where "gracious" owners preside over a "superior" kitchen and "knowledgeable staff" serving "exceptional entrees" mated with "well-chosen wines"; while treasure-hunters dig the "superb complimentary goodies" pre- and post-repast, wallet-watchers wail "you need to be William Paley to afford it."

Pazzo Ristorante [S] 23 23 22 $33

Hotel Vintage Plaza, 627 SW Washington St. (Broadway), 503-228-1515

■ "Classic" yet "imaginative" Italian fare keeps "everyone coming back" to this "perennial pleaser" in Downtown's Hotel Vintage Plaza thanks to chef Nathan Logan in the *cucina* cooking "yummy Piedmont beef", "orgasmic" filled pastas and "excellent desserts"; stylish touches like the "lively bar", open kitchen and "special-occasion wine room" make it "a good place to entertain" as well.

Pho Van Vietnamese Bistro – – – M

1012 NW Glisan St. (bet. 10th & 11th Aves.), 503-248-2172

The well-established Van family goes more upscale with its latest offering, this elegant, sophisticated bistro in the Pearl; its gorgeous space of earth tones and bamboo showcases Vietnamese culture through needlework wall hangings, traditional music and, of course, authentic dishes, such as shaking beef with watercress, lotus flower salad and ginger crème brûlée.

Saburo's Sushi House [S] 26 | 11 | 14 | $22

1667 SE Bybee Blvd. (bet. 16th & 17th Aves.), 503-236-4237

■ This Westmoreland "Tokyo-style phone booth of a restaurant" calls converts with "unbelievably fresh sushi" in "huge portions" as well as "good green-tea ice cream and plum wine"; though the decor is "humble" and seating limited, connoisseurs continue to redial, saying it's "worth it all."

Sungari [S] 25 | 21 | 22 | $25

735 SW First Ave. (Yamhill St.), 503-224-0800

■ "Everyone raves" about this "outstanding Chinese" Downtown three-year-old that champions cheer "does everything well"; its "subtly seasoned" Szechuan fare includes "the best moo shu pork", as well as other "high-style" dishes, all served with a touch of "formality" by "fabulous people" in an "upscale", "elegant" room; N.B. check out the adventurous choices on the wine list.

TINA'S [S] 28 | 22 | 25 | $40

760 Hwy. 99 W. (opp. fire station), Dundee, 503-538-8880

■ A "perennial wine country star", this "dependable" Dundee delight sparkles with a "sophisticated menu" of Northwest–French bistro fare fashioned from "interesting ingredients" that "shine through" in dishes such as "super sautéed oysters", braised rabbit and duck breast, all "well matched" with "superb" Oregon bottlings; though a few whine about the "city prices", others cite a "fireplace that warms the spirit" and "friendly" service that does the same as additional "excuses to make the trip."

WILDWOOD [S] 27 | 23 | 24 | $39

1221 NW 21st Ave. (Overton St.), 503-248-9663

■ Homegrown chef and best-selling author "Cory Schreiber gave Portland a gift when he opened" this "wildly popular" "Northwest cuisine icon" in the Northwest District that "does justice to local provender" and pays "attention to sustainable farming"; loyalists "love watching the open kitchen" turn out "consistently excellent" and "delicious" fare accompanied by "boutique wines" and served in an "intriguing milieu" (where "cheek-to-jowl" dining can result in "thunderous noise").

Winterborne 26 | 21 | 24 | $36

3520 NE 42nd Ave. (Fremont St.), 503-249-8486

■ Turning "meat-and-potatoes" sorts into fish fanatics for more than a quarter-century, this "small, cozy" Northeast old-timer brings "a nice touch of France" and the Northwest to its "excellent" seafood-only menu (though vegetarians be advised you "can ask for substitutes"); "whatever they suggest, order it", as "every entree is special" – from the "unique crab juniper" (available seasonally) to the "terrific sautéed oysters" – and "personal attention from the staff" will make you feel the same way.

Zinc Bistrot [S] – | – | – | M

500 NW 21st Ave. (Glisan St.), 503-223-9696

Long wood tables, a mirror and a bar topped with the namesake metal dominate the light-infused room of this Parisian-style bistro buzzing with the sound of politicos, trendy Northwest locals and Francophiles digging into traditional plates of steak frites, mussels marinière and seasonal fruit crêpes with homemade ice cream; N.B. *naturellement*, there's sidewalk seating in summer.

Salt Lake City & Mountain Resorts

TOP 10 FOOD RANKING

Restaurant	Cuisine Type
27 Seafood Buffet	Seafood
Fresco Italian Café	Northern Italian
Metropolitan	New American
Mariposa	New American
Tree Room	Western
26 Cafe Diablo	Southwestern
New Yorker Club	American
Center Cafe	International
Shallow Shaft	SW/Rocky Mountain
Mandarin	Asian

ADDITIONAL NOTEWORTHY PLACES

Bambara	New American
Chez Betty	Continental/American
Glitretind	New American
L'Avenue	French Bistro
Log Haven	International
Lugano	Northern Italian
Martine	Med./New American
Snake Creek Grill	American
Tuscany	Northern Italian
Wahso	Asian

F	D	S	C

Bambara S

24	25	22	$35

Hotel Monaco, 202 S. Main St., 801-363-5454

■ A "delectable experience" awaits at this "chic" New American bistro inside the Hotel Monaco, "a breath of fresh air" for jaded palates thanks to "beautifully prepared", "wonderfully presented" "unique" dishes that are some of the "most consistently interesting food in town", as well as service that makes folks feel "taken care of"; though a few find its "grand setting" (a former bank replete with "marble and ornamental iron") to be a "little froufrou", fans insist it's "top-notch."

Cafe Diablo S

26	20	23	$26

599 W. Main St. (N. Center St.), Torrey, 435-425-3070

■ Southwestern "favorites like trout, lamb, rattlesnake" and "pecan-crusted chicken – yee-haw!" are "great finds" at this "middle-of-nowhere" "oasis of excellence" in "tiny Torrey" near Capitol Reef National Park; you'll find "towers galore", as "the chef is big on vertical presentations", and what's more, the "fabulous food" is presented in a "must-see" high-desert atmosphere; N.B. open mid-April through mid-October.

Center Cafe S
26 | 19 | 23 | $33

60 N. 100 West (Center St.), Moab, 435-259-4295

■ It's a "not-to-be-missed Moab stop" say adventurous diners who seek out the "fantastic cuisine" at this International "desert jewel" "in the middle of red rock country", "the land of 4x4s and mountain bikers"; the "absolutely incredible" "variety of creative entrees" "delights the palate", and "great service" helps make it a "real gem" that "would be a hit anywhere"; P.S. the Decor rating does not reflect the post-*Survey* move to its much larger "new location."

Chez Betty S
26 | 20 | 24 | $42

Copperbottom Inn, 1637 Short Line Rd. (Deer Valley Dr.), Park City, 435-649-8181

■ After a day dodging "all those moguls" on the slopes, it's "nice to know" this "upbeat" spot in the "rustic" Copperbottom Inn "is there" to "soothe" the soul with "excellent service" and "inspiring" Continental-American fare that "outdoes that of some of its flashier Park City competitors" thanks to chef-owner Jerry Garcia (no relation to the Grateful Dead frontman), who makes "everyone feel comfortable"; insiders add that the "not-on-Main-Street" location "may be why the locals love it so much."

FRESCO ITALIAN CAFÉ S
27 | 24 | 25 | $33

1513 S. 1500 East (bet. Emerson & Kensington Aves.), 801-486-1300

■ "Bravo" applaud admirers who "can't say enough" about this "consistently delightful Northern Italian" Eastside "neighborhood bistro" where "fresh", "imaginative dishes" and "friendly service" "come together seamlessly"; while most dub the "romantic setting" "intimate" and "quaint", a handful say the interior "may be too cozy", "crowded" and "loud", opting instead for "the beautiful patio"; N.B. the Food rating does not reflect the post-*Survey* arrival of toque Todd Miller.

Glitretind S
26 | 26 | 24 | $48

Stein Eriksen Lodge, 7700 Stein Way (Royal St.), Deer Valley, 435-645-6455

■ "Never-disappointed" diners declare "it's worth the drive up the mountain" and into the stratosphere for a meal at this "top-notch" spot set in Deer Valley's "exquisite" Stein Eriksen Lodge because "you know you're going to eat well" thanks to "artistic chefs" who turn out "beautiful presentations" of "excellent" New American fare with Norwegian and European flourishes (including a "fantastic Sunday brunch"), served with an "outstanding wine list" and "without a stuffy attitude."

L'Avenue S
– | – | – | M

1355 E. 2100 South (1300 East), 801-485-4494

The quintessential model of a sassy French bistro – from its royal blue awnings to imported etched-glass mirrors – this chic new 'in' spot just north of Sugarhouse Park draws Francophiles like moths to a flame for its twice-fried *pommes frites*, fresh mussels, Gallic vino and chef Franck Peissel's hearty takes on everything from *canard* to gigot; its new garden- and tree-ringed patio has already become a sizzling scene on summer nights.

LOG HAVEN S
25 | 28 | 23 | $38

6451 E. 3800 South (Wasatch Blvd., 4 mi. up Millcreek Canyon), 801-272-8255

■ It's "the perfect place on a blustery winter evening" laud loyalists who love the "lavish" International fare (with Rocky Mountain,

Pacific Rim and New French influences) at this 82-year-old log cabin "mountain hideaway just outside of Salt Lake City" in the Wasatch National Forest; the atmosphere is "rustic and charming", but there's "nothing backwoodsy about" David Jones' "superlative" creations, so "take a date" and enjoy the "beautiful canyon setting" with a "gorgeous" waterfall view.

Lugano 🖸   24 | 20 | 22 | $29

3364 S. 2300 East, 801-412-9994

☑ "Finally, good food in Holladay" say diners who've discovered the "delicious" "homestyle" Northern Italian fare at chef-owner Greg Neville's Eastside two-year-old; the "consistently" "innovative cooking" and "reasonable prices" add up to an "unexpected treat" that's prepared in the "cool open kitchen" and "splendidly served"; "we feel like family here" say supporters who find it "warm, comfortable" and a "bit loud", but a few foes cry "oh, the noise! – you can't hear your dinner companions."

Mandarin   26 | 21 | 22 | $20

348 E. 900 North, Bountiful, 801-298-2406

■ "Greek hospitality" (the owners are Greco-American) mixed with "spectacular Chinese flavors" ("the chefs are from Hong Kong" and San Francisco) tote up to a "mouthwatering experience" that's definitely "not the same old" Asian at this "always crowded" Bountiful spot; sure, the no-reservations policy for parties of fewer than eight is a "hassle", but most say the "ridiculous wait" is "well worth" it "to savor every bite" of their "distinctly different dishes"; P.S. don't forget the "incredible dessert menu."

MARIPOSA 🖸   27 | 25 | 25 | $53

Silver Lake Lodge, Deer Valley Resort, 7600 Royal St., Deer Valley, 435-645-6715

☑ "Restaurant heaven" in an "alpine setting" enthuse enamored epicureans who head to Deer Valley Resort's "quaint" Silver Lake Lodge for "consistently innovative" New American fare; the "solid entrees" (including "always excellent" game dishes), "great wine list" and "polished service" are the big draws here, but it's the "unpretentious" cozy ski lodge ambiance (yes, there's a fireplace) that really wins romantics over; N.B. open December–April.

Martine   25 | 23 | 23 | $28

22 E. 100 South (bet. Main & State Sts.), 801-363-9328

■ "Simply divine" gush gastronomes who swear there's "nothing but fun" to be had at this "urbane", "cozy" and "romantic" Med–New American spot set in a historic "old Downtown brownstone"; "go with a large group and order" the "masterpiece plates" of "different tapas to sample" – it's some of the "best, most unique and innovative cooking in town", plus there's an "imaginative wine list" to boot.

METROPOLITAN   27 | 27 | 25 | $51

173 W. Broadway (300 South, bet. 200 West & W. Temple St.), 801-364-3472

☑ It's "the pinnacle of sophistication" sigh soigné surveyors who head Downtown to this New American for "artistic creations in an artfully recreated warehouse", a "contemporary", "New Yorkish experience"; the "exquisitely prepared meals" (including a "chef's tasting menu that's always a dream") are "a little extravagant" but "worth the money" and bolstered by "excellent service"; critics, however, say the "flavor combos are sometimes extreme" and claim the "humorless" staff is "high on attitude."

NEW YORKER CLUB   26 | 26 | 25 | $42

60 W. Market St. (Main St., bet. 300 & 400 South), 801-363-0166

■ "This is where we take clients" and "out-of-town guests" say acolytes "impressed" by this "kiss-kiss", "see-and-be-seen" Downtown "favorite" (voted Most Popular in Utah) where the "fantastic" Traditional American fare and "terrific service" "match the shimmering elegance" of the "clubby" surroundings; though a few nitpickers proclaim "pretension is served with every wonderful meal", most maintain it "succeeds on all fronts"; N.B. though it's a private club, visitor memberships are inexpensive.

SEAFOOD BUFFET   27 | 21 | 22 | $51

Snow Park Lodge, Deer Valley, 435-645-6632

■ "Come hungry, leave satiated" say insiders who rank this Deer Valley "favorite" seafood house No. 1 for Food in Utah; fans who flock to this "rustic mountain setting" each ski season for an "incredible spread" of sushi and shellfish advise "survey the extensive food stations before embarking on the wonderful culinary odyssey"; sure, it's a wintertime "treat", but that doesn't stop worshipers from wailing "if only they were open all year"; N.B. open during ski season, mid-December through early April.

Shallow Shaft S   26 | 22 | 24 | $41

Little Cottonwood Canyon (Little Cottonwood Rd.), Alta,
801-742-2177

■ "The view is to die for and the food is to live for" at this "Alta tradition", a "wonderful discovery" in Little Cottonwood Canyon for "excellent" Southwestern and Rocky Mountain fare; the "unique", "combinations of tastes make this a complex experience" say foodies, who confess they "dream about the lamb"; the "beautiful setting" with high-mountain ambiance is "more casual than the food would suggest", attracting skiers and non-skiers alike.

Snake Creek Grill S   25 | 20 | 22 | $32

650 W. 100 South, Heber City, 435-654-2133

■ American comfort food and a "charming" roadhouse ambiance, complete with "nostalgic photos" and retro "jazz sounds", attract admirers to this "friendly, welcoming" frontier-themed turn-of-the-century-style building in "beautiful" Heber; Barb Hill serves "unpretentious and delicious" "modern takes on the classics" and "terrific grill selections" that make this Snake "charmer" "well worth the drive"; loyal locals say "if it were closer to Salt Lake City, it would be standing room only."

TREE ROOM S   27 | 27 | 24 | $41

Sundance Resort, Rural Rte. 3 (North Fork Canyon Rd.),
801-223-4200

■ "Can a restaurant be sexy?" – oh yeah, say fans who fawn over Robert "Redford's best effort", this "classy", "romantic" Rocky Mountain "destination-dining" spot in the posh Sundance Resort, where the "consistently" "wonderful" "Western fare", including "scrumptious" "game and desserts, will make you weep" with joy while the "truly special" mountain views and "rustic decor", rich with "beautiful Native American art", will fill you with "immediate serenity and warmth"; P.S. a "real tree" grows "in the room" – hence the name.

TUSCANY S

23 | 27 | 23 | $35 |

2832 E. 6200 South (Holladay Blvd.), 801-277-9919

☑ Co-owned by former Utah Jazz basketball player Mark Eaton, this Northern Italian "delight" in Holladay is long on "old-world opulence", with "dynamite decor" and a "gorgeous garden"; enthusiastic diners say the "ambrosial" fare is a "gastronomic extravaganza" that "continues to wow" ("try the 7.4-inch chocolate cake" – it's a "slam dunk"), as do the "extensive wine list" and "impeccable service"; still, the "disappointed" declare that the "amazing atmosphere" outshines the "uneven food", imploring "get a chef who can rebound and score."

Wahso S

24 | 28 | 24 | $45 |

577 Main St., Park City, 435-615-0300

■ Famished fans frequently fly to this Park City "favorite", an "absolutely gorgeous" "rare bird" (whose name is the phonetic spelling of *oiseaux*, the Gallic word for our fine feathered friends) where "creative" "wonder-kid" chef-owner Bill White fashions "fabulous" "Asian-with-a-French-twist" fare – including "sea bass so good it's like sex on a plate" – that's "smoothly" served by a "slick" staff in a "Shanghai-feeling" space as "cool" as a "Hollywood set"; P.S. "don't miss the curtained booths!"

TOP 10 FOOD RANKING

	Restaurant	Cuisine Type
27	Sushi Ota	Japanese
	El Bizcocho	French/New French
	WineSellar & Brasserie	New French
	Pamplemousse Grille	New American/New French
26	George's at the Cove	Californian
	Mille Fleurs	New French
	Azzura Point	Californian/New French
	Tapenade	New French
	Vincent's Sirinos	French/Californian
	Rancho Valencia	Californian

ADDITIONAL NOTEWORTHY PLACES

Arterra	New American
A.R. Valentien	Californian
Bertrand at Mr. A's	New American
Cafe Japengo	Pacific Rim
Indigo Grill	Oaxacan/Alaskan
Laurel	Provençal
Marine Room	New French/Californian
Morton's of Chicago	Steakhouse
NINE-TEN	Californian
Roppongi	Asian Fusion

	F	D	S	C
Arterra [S]	–	–	–	E

San Diego Marriott Del Mar, 11966 El Camino Real (Carmel Valley Rd.), 858-369-6032

Eagerly anticipated, acclaimed chef-partner Bradley Ogden's chic new showcase (named after 'art of the earth') at the Marriott Del Mar in Carmel Valley pays homage to farm-fresh products from local specialty purveyors; his seasonal New American dishes, paired with a well-conceived domestic wine list, are delivered in a sophisticated space done up in an eye-opening palette of purple, ochre and crimson and appointed with comfortable furnishings.

	F	D	S	C
A. R. Valentien [S]	–	–	–	E

Lodge at Torrey Pines, 11480 N. Torrey Pines Rd. (Callan Rd.), La Jolla, 858-777-6635

An extensive collection of paintings by early 20th-century San Diego artist A. R. Valentien adds period authenticity to the Craftsman-style design of this handsome new hotel dining room in La Jolla; overlooking the famed Torrey Pines Golf Course and the Pacific, it's a swanky magnet for celebrities and moneyed locals who gather to sample chef Jeff Jackson's market-driven Californian menu, presented by young servers who try hard and usually succeed.

Azzura Point ⓈBold 26 | 26 | 24 | $53

Loews Coronado Bay Resort, 4000 Coronado Bay Rd. (Silver Strand Blvd.), Coronado, 619-424-4477

⬛ At this "special-occasion delight" in the Loews Coronado Bay Resort, an "indulgent" staff proffers "delectable" Californian-French dishes (to truly indulge, opt for one of the "outstanding tasting menus"); of course it's "expensive", but it's "worth it" for such a "romantic" dinner that's made even more "special" by the "elegant" waterside setting with "magnificent views."

Bertrand at Mr. A's Ⓢ 24 | 25 | 22 | $59

2550 Fifth Ave. (Laurel St.), 619-239-1377

☑ Created by Bertrand Hug of the renowned Mille Fleurs, this "special-occasion" spot near Balboa Park boasts "spectacular views" that "go on forever" and a "classy room" that provides a fitting backdrop for the kitchen's very "fine" New American fare tweaked with French and Mediterranean accents; even if some feel it's "outrageously expensive" and caution that service is the "weak link", devotees proclaim it an "instant classic."

Cafe Japengo Ⓢ 25 | 24 | 20 | $35

Hyatt Regency at The Aventine, 8960 University Center Ln. (bet. La Jolla Village & Lebon Drs.), 858-450-3355

⬛ Without a doubt the leading "beautiful-people hangout" in the Golden Triangle, this "chichi" Pacific Rim cafe is renowned for "fabulous" sushi "so fresh it practically moves", as well as "neat fusion" fare that "imaginatively" marries Japanese and Western flavors; a "too hip" staff serves an equally "trendy" clientele in a "busy, noisy" setting so buzzing with energy that groupies posit this "date magnet" could even "succeed in NYC or San Francisco."

EL BIZCOCHO Ⓢ 27 | 26 | 27 | $53

Rancho Bernardo Inn, 17550 Bernardo Oaks Dr. (Rancho Bernardo Rd.), Rancho Bernardo, 858-675-8550

⬛ This "romantic" stunner housed in the suburban Rancho Bernardo Inn is "elegance personified", dazzling "epicureans" with "exciting" French interpretations accompanied by an "extensive wine list" that's a "special treat"; "go to celebrate" any excuse and be "divinely" pampered by a "perfect" staff amid "spectacular" surroundings ("the pianist provides just the right background touch"); yes, it's "expensive", but a dinner here is "like being in heaven."

GEORGE'S AT THE COVE Ⓢ 26 | 26 | 25 | $44

1250 Prospect St. (bet. Cave & Ivanhoe Sts.), La Jolla, 858-454-4244

⬛ For a "must-do meal in La Jolla", head to this "romantic" "all-time winner" that's perennially voted the Most Popular restaurant in San Diego; no wonder, given the "absolutely superb" Californian dishes masterminded by "imaginative" chef Trey Foshee, decor that "oozes class" and the "top-notch" staff overseen by "great" owner George Hauer; sure it's "oh-so-expensive", but rest assured that "you get your money's worth" at this "special-occasion" "splurge" – and the "wow" of a view of the cove is free.

Indigo Grill Ⓢ — | — | — | M

1536 India St. (Cedar St.), 619-234-6802

Already known for its architectural presentations that make the dishes look ready to take flight, this newcomer courtesy of Deborah

Scott interestingly reworks Mexico's traditional Oaxacan cuisine to include Alaskan and Pacific Northwest influences; as a result, a table at her eatery in formerly sleepy Little Italy has become the hottest ticket in town, drawing a hip, youngish crowd; if you show up without a reservation, chill with a martini at the popular bar, where a waterfall cascades over a wall of pebbles.

LAUREL 🖫 | 26 | 25 | 23 | $45 |
505 Laurel St. (5th Ave.), 619-239-2222

■ "Always outstanding", this "class act" near Balboa Park is likely "as close as San Diego gets to Manhattan"; a "big-city" haunt that showcases a "cosmopolitan", "inventive" menu of "delicious" Southern French dishes, it features seasonal Provençal renditions paired with a "spectacular wine list" and served in a "chic" room populated by the local "elite"; factor in polished, "unobtrusive service" and the result is a "sublime experience"; N.B. new chef Jason Schaeffer is fully expected to maintain its high standards.

Marine Room 🖫 | 23 | 27 | 23 | $47 |
2000 Spindrift Dr. (Torrey Pines Rd.), La Jolla, 858-459-7222

■ "Catch a sunset here" right on the sands of La Jolla Shores, where the "breathtaking" experience of watching the ocean "waves splash against the windows" (brunch at "high tide is not to be missed") is nearly matched by chef Bernard Guillas' "dramatically presented" New French–Californian creations, delivered by a staff that "exceeds all expectations"; better bring a "large wallet", though.

MILLE FLEURS 🖫 | 26 | 25 | 25 | $58 |
Country Squire Courtyard, 6009 Paseo Delicias (Avenida de Acacias), Rancho Santa Fe, 858-756-3085

■ "A jewel nestled in the gilt village" of "lovely" Rancho Santa Fe, this "very special-occasion" New French is a "beautiful" place to indulge in equally "beautiful flavors", "artistically" choreographed by "dazzling" chef Martin Woesle (his menu changes daily); the service is just as "outstanding", so in spite of a "slightly stiff" ambiance, legions attest that this dining experience is "close to perfection – though even the wealthy might gasp at the prices."

Morton's of Chicago 🖫 | 26 | 23 | 23 | $53 |
285 J St. (bet. 2nd & 3rd Aves.), 619-696-3369

■ Be sure to "bring lots of dough" to this "superb" Downtown all-American steakery, "a carnivore's delight" where the "perfect" "beef doesn't get any better" and the portions are famously obscene; the "dark" setting ("looks like money") is "like a private men's club" and attracts lots of "beautiful people", which, of course, can make it "too crowded and noisy"; the major complaint: we certainly "could do without the showing of the raw meat" before placing our order.

NINE-TEN 🖫 | – | – | – | E |
Grande Colonial, 910 Prospect St. (Main St.), La Jolla, 858-454-2181

On the site where Gregory Peck once served sodas at the counter of his father's drugstore, chef Michael Stebner brings a healthy understanding of Californian cooking inspired by the wine country to this addition at La Jolla's historic, extravagantly appointed Grande Colonial hotel; his brief but pleasing daily menu focuses on thoughtfully prepared seafood and meat dishes, as well as ultra-high-quality local produce, proffered in a low-key setting by a young staff that strives mightily to please.

PAMPLEMOUSSE GRILLE [S] 27 24 25 $51

514 Via de la Valle (Jimmy Durante Blvd.), Solana Beach, 858-792-9090

■ "Amazingly good cooking" from "shining star" Jeffrey Strauss wows the "moneyed clientele" that flocks (especially during racing season) to this "first-class" New American–New French located across the road from the Del Mar Fairgrounds; devotees "love" the "casually sophisticated" ambiance, murals of rustic life and highly "attentive" service, and even if a less-enchanted few grouse "pretentious", the majority cheers "outstanding."

Rancho Valencia [S] 26 27 25 $52

Rancho Valencia Resort, 5921 Valencia Circle (Rancho Diegueno Rd.), Rancho Sante Fe, 858-759-6216

■ This "gorgeous" "retreat" is "a special place", an "intriguing hideout in the hills" of horsey Rancho Santa Fe that's situated in a "beautiful resort", which makes it a "paradise within paradise"; it attracts a "chic, sophisticated" crowd with its "old-money" ambiance, "extraordinary" contemporary Californian menu and "excellent" service, so wallet-stretching prices notwithstanding, it's "worth the drive" to experience this "refined" splurge.

Roppongi [S] 25 25 23 $37

875 Prospect St. (Fay Ave.), La Jolla, 858-551-5252

■ Anticipate "exciting", "exotic" Asian "fusion cuisine" at this "fabulously" "unique" "hip scene" for the "beautiful people" in La Jolla; "go with friends", "share" a "variety" of "original" tapas and other "wonderfully avant-garde" specialties and experience "perfect harmony in dining" (the interior design was determined by feng shui); P.S. "the caramelized bananas over vanilla ice cream with almond brittle is an orgasm on a plate."

SUSHI OTA [S] 27 12 18 $30

4529 Mission Bay Dr. (Balboa Ave.), 858-270-5670

■ "Absolutely awesome" is the unanimous verdict on the menu at this Pacific Beach Japanese retreat, rated No. 1 for Food in San Diego; despite a "spartan" setting in a "nondescript" strip mall and "brusque" service, it's "always crowded" because the eponymous Ota-san prepares the "best sushi in town, hands down" ("fish willingly sacrifice themselves to be turned into his incredible delicacies"), and he's a "wealth of fish information"; even "people visiting from Japan know to come here."

TAPENADE [S] 26 21 23 $47

7612 Fay Ave. (bet. Kline & Pearl Sts.), La Jolla, 858-551-7500

■ Francophiles gratefully tip their berets to the "inspired", "world-class" dining with a "sunny" Provençal accent at this La Jolla "gem" where "talented chef-owner" Jean-Michel Diot and his wife Sylvie know a thing or *deux* about creating an "elegant" environment with a "courtly" ambiance (even if a few deride the "somewhat arrogant service"); though it helps to be "financially flush", at least the "prix fixe meals are a relative bargain."

Vincent's Sirinos 26 18 21 $34

113 W. Grand Ave. (Broadway), Escondido, 760-745-3835

■ To savor a "great culinary experience in Escondido", head straight to this "classy" "sleeper" where "genius" chef-owner

Vincent Grumel "goes out of his way" to be "creative" and "cooks to order" "generous portions" of "consistently superb" French-Californian dishes; what's more, the room is nearly as "warm and inviting" as the "fine" staff, and its proximity to the California Center for the Arts makes it an ideal choice for pre-concert dining.

WINESELLAR & BRASSERIE   27 20 25 $48
9550 Waples St. (bet. Mira Mesa Blvd. & Steadman St.), 858-450-9557
■ Dionysians delight in this "classy", "special-occasion" New French in high-tech Sorrento Mesa, which has "stayed great since it opened in '89"; the kitchen masterfully uncorks "creative, fresh, focused flavors" that are only fortified by the "fantastic wine list" (2,500 selections), while the dining experience is further enhanced by the "lovely" decor and "attentive" staff; it may be saddled with a "difficult location" in a business park, but "it's worth every inch of the drive"; N.B. new chef Scott Diehl is expected to maintain its high standards.

San Francisco Bay Area

TOP 20 FOOD RANKING

Restaurant	Cuisine Type
29 Gary Danko	New American/New French
French Laundry	New American/French
28 Sierra Mar	Californian/New French
Masa's	New French
Ritz-Carlton Dining Rm.	New French
Chez Panisse	Californian/Med.
27 La Folie	New French
Sushi Ran	Japanese
Chez Panisse Café	Californian/Med.
Aqua	Seafood
Boulevard	American
Emile's	French
Acquerello	Northern Italian
Erna's Elderberry Hse.	Californian/New French
Terra	New French Fusion
La Toque	New French
Fleur de Lys	New French/Vegetarian
Le Poisson Japonais	Japanese
26 Le Papillon	New French
Charles Nob Hill	Californian/New French

ADDITIONAL NOTEWORTHY PLACES

Auberge du Soleil	French/Med.
Bistro Jeanty	French Bistro
Campton Place	French
Delfina	N&S Italian
Domaine Chandon	New French/Californian
Dry Creek Kitchen	New American
Elisabeth Daniel	New French
Farallon	Seafood
Fifth Floor	New French
Jardinière	Californian/French
Jeanty at Jack's	New French
Julia's Kitchen	Californian/New French
Lark Creek Inn	American
Merenda	N. Italian/French
Oliveto Cafe	Northern Italian
Redwood Park	New French
Rubicon	New French/Californian
Slanted Door	Vietnamese
Tra Vigne	Californian/N&S Italian
Zuni Cafe	N. Italian/Med.

Acquerello 27 | 23 | 27 | $60

1722 Sacramento St. (bet. Polk St. & Van Ness Ave.), 415-567-5432

■ It's no wonder this "fine dining" "gem" "hidden" off Polk Street is "still the *numero uno* [Northern] Italian" in the hearts and minds of surveyors, what with Suzette Gresham's "sublime combinations" ("foie gras truffle pasta to die for"), maitre d' Giancarlo Paterlini's "classic old-world service", an "impeccable" wine program and a "beautiful vaulted ceiling"; true, it's "very pricey" and "more formal" than its trendy brethren, but the refined regulars like it that way.

AQUA 27 | 25 | 24 | $64

252 California St. (bet. Battery & Front Sts.), 415-956-9662

◪ Chef/co-owner "Michael Mina's masterpiece" – a "glittering Downtown" destination that "drips with beautiful people" – "continues to perform swimmingly", with "floral arrangements as spectacular" as the "staggeringly good" seafood and "cutting-edge wine list"; while "professional" but "holier-than-thou" service and being "squeezed in" like sardines "dampen" some spirits, most "food sharks" willingly "mortgage the house" to power-dine here: when the "fish is this fantastic, you can put up with anything."

Auberge du Soleil [S] 26 | 27 | 25 | $66

Auberge du Soleil Inn, 180 Rutherford Hill Rd. (Silverado Trail), Rutherford, 707-967-3111

■ Dining at this "magnificent" Rutherford "romantic" is "like making it into heaven" – and not simply because it's got "one hell of a view" "overlooking the valley" and vineyards; chef Richard Reddington's "exquisite version" of French-Med fare "makes it nearly impossible to choose" and the international wine list (1,250 labels rich) "isn't bad either" – plus, there's "top-notch service" "to match"; P.S. those concerned about the "stiff prices" note that the vistas are "the same, and much cheaper, at lunch."

Bistro Jeanty ◐ [S] 26 | 21 | 23 | $43

6510 Washington St. (Mulberry St.), Yountville, 707-944-0103

■ "Food purists" who "make regular pilgrimages" to chef-owner Philippe Jeanty's "eponymous" French insist it "out-bistros Paris" because "it's friendlier" and you only have to drive to Yountville to savor its combination of "luscious" "hearty fare" ("no nouvelle or diets here"), "charming" "rustic decor" and "unpretentious" ambiance (including a "fantastic community table") that's "worth every decibel" and dollar – though actually the reasonable prices are pretty "*incroyable.*"

BOULEVARD [S] 27 | 25 | 24 | $54

1 Mission St. (Steuart St.), 415-543-6084

■ "Find the money, find the time" to "stroll down this Boulevard", again San Francisco's Most Popular restaurant, that "epitomizes all you'd ever want" – from Nancy Oakes' "sublime" American cuisine to Pat Kuleto's "splendid" "recreation of an art nouveau hangout" to a "staff intent on making your experience outstanding"; if you're not "lucky enough to get a window" table overlooking the Embarcadero, "sit at the counter and watch the chefs."

Campton Place [S] 25 | – | 26 | $60

Campton Place Hotel, 340 Stockton St. (bet. Post & Sutter Sts.), 415-955-5555

■ "Come well dressed" and be prepared to "get pampered" at this "elegant sophisticate" "tucked in an alley near busy Union

Square"; a post-*Survey* renovation of the "luxurious", intimate dining room has raised it to the level of chef Laurent Manrique's "refined" yet "soulful" Gascon- and Basque-influenced French fare, but you'll be tended to by the same "outstanding" staff, in charge of an "incredible cheese" tray and a new foie gras cart; true, "it's very pricey, but you get what you pay for."

Charles Nob Hill 🖺   26 | 24 | 26 | $75
1250 Jones St. (Clay St.), 415-771-5400

■ "Words like over-the-top, pampered and scrumptious come to mind" when describing this "polished diamond" that "didn't miss a step when" a new chef assumed the reins; go ahead, "play Nob Hill for a day" and "splurge" on the "Bacchanalian adventure" of "the two-hour tasting menu", during which the "highly professional staff seems to intuit your every need" as you sample bite after bite of "sumptuous" Californian–New French creations in "one of the most elegant – some say "stuffiest" – "rooms in town."

CHEZ PANISSE   28 | 24 | 26 | $71
1517 Shattuck Ave. (bet. Cedar & Vine Sts.), Berkeley, 510-548-5525

■ "Who knew that heaven was just a trip across the Bay" ask pilgrims who come to this Berkeley holy spot to "worship at the feet of Alice Waters" and report that eating the "flawless" "market-based" Cal-Med cuisine in a "Craftsman cathedral" with "well-orchestrated service" is an almost "religious experience"; though "the simplicity" of it all causes a few heretics to hiss about the "emperor's new clothes", most feel "it's worth every penny to be one step closer to nirvana."

Chez Panisse Café   27 | 23 | 24 | $41
1517 Shattuck Ave. (bet. Cedar & Vine Sts.), Berkeley, 510-548-5049

■ Luckily for "common people" "with gourmet tastes and student budgets", "Chez Panisse Jr." "is a lot like" the "acclaimed" "temple downstairs", only at about "half the price"; the Cal-Med menu "still has that incomparable Alice Waters touch", "paired with a welcoming staff", but the atmosphere is "more fun", the bookings are "a little easier to get" (though it's recommended to "call exactly one month in advance") and, free-choice advocates rejoice, "you can order what you like" "without being tied into that day's menu."

Delfina 🖺   26 | 19 | 22 | $38
3621 18th St. (bet. Dolores & Guerrero Sts.), 415-552-4055

◪ "If you're wondering where to have your last supper, look no further" than this "little treasure" of an Italian in the Mission that offers the "amazing blend of a phenomenal", "ever-evolving menu", served by "tattooed hotties" who are "slacker in appearance only", and a bill "half that of other restaurants of its caliber"; still, "it's hard to say which is more difficult – getting a reservation or finding parking" – and the room can be as loud as "an airport runway."

Domaine Chandon 🖺   26 | 26 | 25 | $58
1 California Dr. (Hwy. 29), Yountville, 707-944-2892

■ There isn't a better "spot to go broke" than this "magical" Yountville winery restaurant situated "only a few stumbles from an outstanding champagne cellar"; visitors can "tour" the facility "and then sit down" "in the lap of luxury" to "absolutely fantastic" New French–Cal cuisine, proffered by "attentive and discreet" servers; those without "excess cash to blow" can sit on the "patio looking over the well-manicured grounds" and opt for the "sparkling-wine sampler" and appetizers.

Dry Creek Kitchen Ⓢ   24 | 26 | 20 | $56

Hotel Healdsburg, 317 Healdsburg Ave. (Matheson St.), Healdsburg, 707-431-0330

◪ "Manhattan comes to Healdsburg in the best way" thanks to "the new star of Sonoma, Charlie Palmer", who "courts the upscale crowd" with "chic" decor, an all-local "wine list that could take you days to" read and "wonderfully prepared seasonal and regional food" from his New American kitchen; most welcome every aspect of the New York state of mind "except for the attitude" of the staff, which is "almost too sophisticated for laid-back wine country."

Elisabeth Daniel   26 | 22 | 25 | $84

550 Washington St. (bet. Montgomery & Sansome Sts.), 415-397-6129

◪ Disciples of this New French Downtown destination deem it "a temple of fine dining", offering a "glass-encased kitchen with the mystique of an altar", "austere" "decor that creates a reverential atmosphere" and "smooth-as-silk servers" "hovering" like angels; malcontents may moan that the "Internet-boom prices" "for micro-portions" "are going to kill" them, but before they go, even they "want [chef-owner] Daniel Patterson to cook their last meal."

Emile's   27 | 21 | 25 | $55

545 S. Second St. (bet. Reed & William Sts.), San Jose, 408-289-1960

■ This "hallowed institution" "put San Jose on the map 30 years ago" thanks to its "exquisite, old-fashioned French" food fashioned with "Swiss culinary artistry", owner Emile Mooser's "personal, attentive" "Continental service" and that "marvelous" wine list; if the "sedate atmosphere" and "prohibitive prices" seem "a little stifling" in the 21st century, the "adventurous specials" and "to-die-for soufflés" "more than make up for it."

Erna's Elderberry House Ⓢ   27 | 28 | 29 | $81

48688 Victoria Ln. (Hwy. 41), Oakhurst, 559-683-6800

■ Smitten surveyors who discover this "outstanding" Oakhurst wonder "on their way to Yosemite" "arrive exhausted and leave enchanted"; the "fairy-tale castle" makes an aptly "romantic" setting for the "exciting food-and-wine-pairing" experience offered by its six-course Cal–New French prix fixe, with owner Erna Kubin-Clanin herself overseeing service that "makes you feel both special and 'at home'"; N.B. travelers can stay at the château next door.

Farallon Ⓢ   24 | 27 | 23 | $54

450 Post St. (bet. Mason & Powell Sts.), 415-956-6969

■ "All that's lacking are the mermaids" at Pat Kuleto's Downtown seafood house, "awash in a sea of glitz" (think "Jules Verne on acid"); fanciers "would swim upstream" for chef/co-owner Mark Franz's "unbeatable way with fish" (the seasonal "Maine lobster with truffle oil is total food sex"), which is complemented by a "stellar wine list" and "accurate, attentive service"; yes, it's "a bit Disney-esque" and the prices may leave you gasping for air, but most feel dining in this "octopus' garden" is "divine."

Fifth Floor   25 | 25 | 24 | $71

Hotel Palomar, 12 Fourth St. (Market St.), 415-348-1555

■ The Hotel Palomar's "elegant", "abstract modern" "oasis" is on its second life with new chef Laurent Gras, whose "superb and innovative" menu of "thought-provoking" New French fare "keeps this place on the top shelf"; sommelier Rajat Parr's "encyclopedic" wine list remains, as does the "attentive" (if a tad "cold") service, but "bring the gold card" because at these "prodigious prices", "you're paying for the four floors beneath you"; P.S. the "full menu is available at the bar", "sans reservations."

Fleur de Lys 27 | 26 | 26 | $71 |
777 Sutter St. (bet. Jones & Taylor Sts.), 415-673-7779
■ Those who've been "missing" this "old-world, *très romantique*" "San Francisco institution" ("closed due to fire damage" in September 2001) must "anxiously await the reopening" no more – "consummate chef[-owner] Hubert Keller" is back in business, and diners can once again "splurge" on his "lavish", "pricey" New French and Vegetarian prix fixes (plus a new build-your-own tasting menu) under a "dreamy", "canopied ceiling" while being pampered by "impeccable", if slightly "snooty, service."

FRENCH LAUNDRY S 29 | 26 | 28 | $113 |
6640 Washington St. (Creek St.), Yountville, 707-944-2380
■ Getting "a table has become a badge of courage" at Yountville's New American–French "epicurean cathedral" – but "everything you've heard is true": "Thomas Keller should have his hands bronzed" for the "culinary pyrotechnics" that he achieves with his "ethereal", "humorous" tasting menus (both meat and veggie); even with "seamless service", you must "plan on three hours" in the "sublime setting", and expect "obscene prices", but it's an "experience" that every foodie "should indulge in" "before he dies."

GARY DANKO S 29 | 26 | 28 | $81 |
800 North Point St. (Hyde St.), 415-749-2060
■ "If God were a chef he would cook" at this Wharf "winner", but even in His absence, Gary Danko's eatery is "almost flawless in all respects", from his "drop-dead superb" New American–New French "build-your-own tasting menu" (rated No. 1 for Food among San Francisco restaurants) to the "perfectly orchestrated staff" and "Armani"-esque dining room; "you walk in a mere mortal but leave transformed" by "three hours of pure fantasy", so "sell the car, pawn the TV, do whatever you have to do to eat here."

Jardinière S 26 | 27 | 24 | $58 |
300 Grove St. (Franklin St.), 415-861-5555
■ This luminous Hayes Valley supper club "continues to burn bright" thanks to Traci Des Jardins' "amazing" Cal-French cuisine that "glides over the palate", Pat Kuleto's "glamorous" "upside-down champagne glass" decor and the "well-informed" staff's "amazing" service; "ask for a table on the balcony rail" for a "dramatic view overlooking" "one of SF's swankiest bars"; it's pretty "pricey", "but the memory will be with you long after the credit card bill is paid."

Jeanty at Jack's ●S ▽ 25 | 24 | 23 | $48 |
615 Sacramento St. (Montgomery St.), 415-693-0941
■ "Only Philippe Jeanty [of Bistro Jeanty] could slip into a classic San Francisco restaurant [the historic Jack's] and make it seem as if he'd always been there" swoon early-birds who come to roost at his new Downtown big-city brasserie with wine-country savoir faire; the New French menu includes a variety of seafood entrees, as well as the "unbelievable tomato soup" in puff pastry,

prompting city slickers to exclaim "now we don't have to drive to Napa for his wonderful food."

Julia's Kitchen [S] 25 | 15 | 21 | $44

COPIA, 500 First St. (Soscol Ave.), Napa, 707-265-5700

■ Living up to Julia Child's name is a tall order, but chef Mark Dommen rises to the challenge, creating "deftly balanced", "refined Cal–New French" dishes (utilizing organic produce) in the "open kitchen" at this newcomer in Napa's COPIA center; an all-American wine list, tendered by an "excellent staff", complements the cuisine, which is served in an "austere", "modern" room.

La Folie 27 | 22 | 26 | $73

2316 Polk St. (bet. Green & Union Sts.), 415-776-5577

■ "Take someone for a romantic date if you want another" one advise aficionados of Roland Passot's Polk Streeter showcasing his "flawless" New French dishes that are "works of art both in presentation and taste", with museum-quality "prices to match"; the "playful" decor of the main room festooned with marionettes creates "a decidedly un-Gallic atmosphere (i.e. warm, relaxed)" that encourages some amorous amis "to pursue a *folie à deux.*"

Lark Creek Inn [S] 25 | 24 | 23 | $47

234 Magnolia Ave. (Madrone Ave.), Larkspur, 415-924-7766

■ For frantic Friscans, Bradley Ogden's "classic" Larkspur "country getaway 20 minutes from the city" is "just what the doctor ordered": "extremely well-executed" "high-end" (and high-priced) American comfort fare, "a soothing", "serene setting" complete with a garden patio next to a creek (perfect for a dreamy "summer night") and "polite", "personal" service, all of which adds up to what many call the "best in dining in Marin", "for lunch", "anniversary dinners or any other event."

La Toque [S] 27 | 25 | 26 | VE

1140 Rutherford Rd. (Hwy. 29), Rutherford, 707-963-9770

■ Enthusiasts enraptured with Ken Frank's "romantic", refined Rutherford retreat exclaim "these people know what they're doing – in the kitchen" ("absolutely dazzling" "multiple-course prix fixe menus" of "fantastic" New French fare enhanced by "terrific sauces"), "in the cellar" ("inspired wine pairings" from an "extensive list") and "at the table" (an "exceptional staff"); so "why sit on hold for French Laundry" when it's "so much easier to get into" this "must-stop in the Napa Valley"?

Le Papillon [S] 26 | 24 | 25 | $60

410 Saratoga Ave. (Kiely Blvd.), San Jose, 408-296-3730

■ Though seemingly "cocooned in an uninspiring nest of streets" in San Jose, this "superlative" "butterfly" soars on the strength of "truly talented" chef Scott Cooper's "original" and "sublime" New French tasting menus, an "excellent wine cellar", a "charming", "subdued" interior and an "enthusiastic" staff that takes you "gently under its wings"; be prepared to "hold the pinkie high", for it's Sand Hill dining at "Beverly Hills prices."

Le Poisson Japonais [S] 27 | 16 | 20 | $51

642 Ramona St. (bet. Forest & Hamilton Aves.), Palo Alto, 650-330-1147

◪ In a town "ruled by computer nerds", you need to give this "nouvelle Japanese" credit for succeeding fairly well "at making Palo Alto hip", thanks to its co-owners, Wolfgang Puck protégés

Kenji Seki (with "his wild suits") and "artful, inventive" chef Naoki Uchiyama, whose exotic fish dishes (including "out-of-this-world miso-glazed sea bass") are "washed down with" selections from "an extensive sake list"; for "Internet-bubble prices", though, many expect more than "miniscule portions" and a "narrow, noisy layout."

MASA'S 28 | 26 | 27 | $83

Hotel Vintage Court, 648 Bush St. (bet. Powell & Stockton Sts.), 415-989-7154

■ With "Ron Siegal at the stoves", there's "never a wrong bite or a wrong move" at this Downtown special-occasion "classic" where "beyond-fabulous" New French tasting menus are accompanied by "a mind-blowing wine list"; the "first-class service" is almost as "impeccable", while the redone decor, "a mix of clean lines and warm tones", is possibly "the city's most elegant"; sure, the scary tabs are for those "without pocket problems", but you can't put a price on "consummate greatness."

Merenda [S] 25 | 19 | 24 | $42

1809 Union St. (bet. Laguna & Octavia Sts.), 415-346-7373

■ "Everyone feels like family" at this "fabulous addition to Cow Hollow"; despite "tight quarters", the "red-walled" room is quiet, and the "friendly staff is knowledgeable without being stuffy", but it's chef/co-owner Keith Luce's "terrific Northern Italian–Southern French" "dishes that are the star of the show"; unlike most prix fixe–only menus, you get to choose from "two-, three- and four-course" meals, so it can be "easy on your wallet"; P.S. the "great take-out" deli counter has now moved around the corner.

Oliveto Cafe [S] 24 | 21 | 21 | $45

5655 College Ave. (Shafter Ave.), Oakland, 510-547-5356

◪ If you ever "imagined what life would be like at a Tuscan villa", you can appreciate the allure of this Oakland "culinary institution" where "intensely flavored but small" portions of "homemade" fare have regulars recommending you do as "the Italians do" "and share" a full three courses; those put off by the "too-elegant" atmosphere and some staffer's "arrogance" opt for the "more informal" cafe downstairs.

Redwood Park 25 | 24 | 25 | $74

Transamerica Pyramid, 600 Montgomery St. (Battery St.), 415-283-1000

■ "It's another George Morrone miracle" – so say surveyors smitten with the former Fifth Floor chef's latest "over-the-top (in a good way)" venture Downtown; "from the moment you enter" its "architecturally exciting" art-filled dining room, "every gorgeous detail comes together effortlessly", from the "stellar" "modern French" cuisine to "service that matches it toe-to-toe"; it's no small wonder guests "want to go back immediately – as soon as the loan clears."

RITZ-CARLTON DINING ROOM 28 | 26 | 27 | $78

Ritz-Carlton Hotel, 600 Stockton St. (bet. California & Pine Sts.), 415-773-6198

■ When you really "want to impress him or her", this "old-world" "sumptuous" "sophisticate" "is the place to go"; chef "Sylvain Portay regales his audience with fantastic" contemporary "cuisine comparable to the best in France", while the nearly "flawless, without-any-snobbish-attitude" staff "treats you like royalty"; you may need to be among "the new rich of Silicon and the wine valleys" to afford it, but most feel "heaven cannot be as divine as dining at the Ritz"; P.S. "afternoon tea in the lobby lounge" "sets the standard."

Rubicon　　　　　　　　23 | 19 | 22 | $55
558 Sacramento St. (bet. Montgomery & Sansome Sts.), 415-434-4100
☒ "Who cares if DeNiro and Coppola own a partial share" in this Downtowner? – the "real star here" is "the unmatched wine list" of "Larry Stone, the master sommelier of master sommeliers", though chef Dennis Leary's "complex yet not precious" New French–Californian cuisine delivers a strong supporting performance; the "civilized" service ensures it's a top spot "for adults" doing "business lunch and dinner", but some "young people" complain of "corporate prices" and a "lack of trendiness."

SIERRA MAR S　　　　　28 | 28 | 27 | $76
Post Ranch Inn, Hwy. 1 (30 mi. south of Carmel), Big Sur, 831-667-2800
■ When visiting a place "where heaven appears to meet earth" (namely "breathtaking Big Sur"), why not "play it to the hilt at this" "superluxe" spot "perched atop a cliff 1,200 ft. above the Pacific"; "the food is something to marvel at" as well, since the "awesome setting" is "equaled" by the "exquisite", "passionate" Cal–New French menu, not to mention the "spectacular" service and a "wine list that's 4,000 bottles strong"; in short, "after a meal here you may melt away in utter bliss."

Slanted Door S　　　　26 | – | 20 | $37
100 Brannan St. (The Embarcadero), 415-861-8032
☒ Chef Charles Phan's "extraordinary" "upscale" "slant on" "Vietnamese street food" "takes [the cuisine] to a whole new level" of "vibrant", "pure, clean flavors" at this "casual, high-energy" "favorite" currently in temporary Embarcadero digs while its home undergoes a renovation (to be completed March 2003); "it's best to go with a group and order family-style", as the "beautifully plated portions" are "on the small side", but be warned: its "hyper-popularity" means "getting reservations can be difficult."

Sushi Ran S　　　　　27 | 20 | 21 | $41
107 Caledonia St. (bet. Pine & Turney Sts.), Sausalito, 415-332-3620
■ "Run", don't walk, to this jam-packed Sausalito Japanese that "doesn't need cartoons or house music" "to draw a crowd"; finatics feel its "inventive" and "amazing sushi" fashioned from "always-fresh" "fish that evaporates in your mouth" is "the best in Marin" and perhaps "the land"; the extensive "wine and sake bar next door" doesn't make the "looong waits" any shorter, though you can "have a snack there if you can't" tarry.

Terra S　　　　　　　27 | 24 | 25 | $56
1345 Railroad Ave. (bet. Adams & Hunt Sts.), St. Helena, 707-963-8931
■ "Unmatched creativity" is the hallmark of chef/co-owner Hiro Sone's "absolutely unbelievable", "imaginative" New French fusion fare with Northern Italian and "Asian influences" at this "quiet old stone building" "off the main drag of St. Helena" offering "refuge from the wine country's marauding masses" with its "gracious service" and an "out-of-this-world" vino list; so "let everyone duke it out to get reservations" at more high-profile places – this is a "true must-do" in the Valley.

Tra Vigne [S] 25 | 25 | 21 | $46

1050 Charter Oak Ave. (Hwy. 29), St. Helena, 707-963-4444

◪ Chef "Michael Chiarello is gone", but "this Napa Valley tradition" still "shines" with "absolutely glorious", "daring combinations" of Cal-Italian flavors ferried by "friendly, knowledgeable staffers" who "help you choose" from the "impeccable" wine list; the dining room "is reminiscent of an Italian cathedral", but "you may need to genuflect" to snare "a table in the summer" on the "idyllic outdoor patio among the vines" (if your prayers go unanswered, "eat at the bar and catch up on all the vineyard dirt").

Zuni Cafe ◐ [S] 23 | 20 | 18 | $40

1658 Market St. (bet. Franklin & Gough Sts.), 415-552-2522

◪ Judy Rodgers' Hayes Valley "legend" is the "embodiment of SF" dining; her now-"classic" roasted chicken and "best" whole-leaf Caesar salad are the apotheosis of "simple, impeccable" Northern Italian–Med fare, and the "long", "convivial" bar is the place to "rub elbows with the 'in' crowd"; while non-believers opine it's "as overrated as the New Economy was", "there's a reason" this "quietly cool" "treat" is "still a locals' favorite."

TOP 20 FOOD RANKING

Restaurant	Cuisine Type
29 Rover's	New French/Pacific NW
28 Herbfarm	Pacific Northwest
27 Georgian	Pacific Northwest
Mistral	Modern European
Campagne	French
Café Campagne	French Bistro
Harvest Vine	Spanish
Dahlia Lounge	Eclectic
26 Canlis	Pacific Northwest
Wild Ginger	Asian
Szmania's	Pacific NW/German
Le Gourmand	French
Nishino	Japanese
Shoalwater*	Pacific Northwest
Shiro's Sushi	Japanese
Il Terrazzo Carmine	Northern Italian
Metropolitan Grill	Steakhouse
Flying Fish	Seafood/Asian
JaK's Grill	Steakhouse
Nell's	New American

ADDITIONAL NOTEWORTHY PLACES

Brasa	Mediterranean
Cafe Juanita	Northern Italian
Cascadia	Pacific Northwest
Chez Shea	Pacific Northwest
El Gaucho	Steakhouse
Etta's	Seafood
Eva	Pacific NW/New American
Frontier Room	Barbecue
Hunt Club	Pacific Northwest
Kingfish Café	Southern
Lampreia	Pacific NW/New American
Le Pichet	French Bistro
Monsoon	Vietnamese
Oceanaire	Seafood
Palace Kitchen	Eclectic/New American
Restaurant Zoë	New American
Saito's	Japanese
727 Pine	Eclectic/Pacific NW
Union Bay Café	Pacific NW/New American
Vivanda Ristorante	Med./Seafood

* Tied with restaurant directly above it

Brasa S
24 | 25 | 22 | $42

2107 Third Ave. (bet. Blanchard & Lenora Sts.), 206-728-4220

■ Chef/co-owner "Tamara Murphy does it right" at this "gorgeous" Belltowner where the "inventive" "Mediterranean-with-a-twist" menu is almost as "impressive" as the "smashingly sharp, modern look" of the "spacious yet intimate" dining room; the "service can range from perfection to perfunctory, depending on who you get and who you know", but all in all, this is one "very civilized" and "classy" place; P.S. its "ultimate bar menu" is perfect for a post-midnight snack.

Café Campagne S
27 | 23 | 23 | $31

Pike Place Mkt., 1600 Post Alley (Pine St.), 206-728-2233

■ Smitten surveyors "want to move in" to this "ooh"- and "aah"-worthy "French bistro in the heart of Pike Place Market", which offers "wonderful" cassoulet and other "comfort food *à la française*"; it's also ideal for brunch, for "relaxing with a glass of Rhône wine" "on a blustery afternoon" or when you can't get into Campagne, its upstairs sibling; N.B. a recent expansion of the dining room and the addition of Post Alley sidewalk seating is not reflected in the Decor score.

Cafe Juanita S
25 | 20 | 24 | $39

9702 NE 120th Pl. (97th Ave. NE), Kirkland, 425-823-1505

■ "Hurrah" for Holly Smith, who has taken this hard-to-find "local institution to a new level" – one that's "worth searching for" if you're seeking "innovative" Northern Italian cooking, an "outstanding wine cellar" and "always-excellent service", all in a "quaint", "creekside" setting in Kirkland; no wonder cosmopolites croon it's one of the "most sophisticated" venues around.

CAMPAGNE ●S
27 | 24 | 25 | $49

Pike Place Mkt., 86 Pine St. (1st Ave.), 206-728-2800

■ Owner Peter Lewis' "classic Country French" "all-star" at Pike Place Market is "still one of the best in the city" by virtue of "exquisite food that's treated as respectfully as the customers", an "excellent wine list" and a "sexy yet refined" atmosphere; romance-seeking regulars "pop into the bar without a reservation", while penny-pinchers recommend the "bargain" prix fixe, but either way, "a great evening is assured."

CANLIS
26 | 27 | 27 | $55

2576 Aurora Ave. N. (Halladay St., south of Aurora Bridge), 206-283-3313

■ Passing its golden anniversary, this Seattle "landmark" in a "beautiful setting" overlooking Lake Union seems to get "more and more modern while staying completely timeless"; credit chef Greg Atkinson's seasonal menu of Pacific "Northwest treats" ("top-notch steaks", "out-of-this-world seafood"), complemented by a "superb" wine list of over 1,000 selections and "impeccable" service, especially the "impressive" valet parking; granted, this "classic" is "expensive", so "it should be perfect and usually is."

Cascadia
25 | 25 | 23 | $65

2328 First Ave. (bet. Battery & Bell Sts.), 206-448-8884

■ Pushing Pacific Northwest cuisine to ever greater heights, chef Kerry Sear uses only ingredients from the Cascade Mountain Range region in his "ambitious", "cutting-edge" cooking at this Belltown "original" that's further enhanced by "stunning decor" (including a "beautiful waterfall"); a few groan at the "temple-of-gastronomy attitude", but ultimately this "gift to Seattle" leaves most patrons feeling "incredibly pampered" from beginning to "pleasant adieu."

Chez Shea S   25 │ 25 │ 24 │ $42

Pike Place Mkt., 94 Pike St. (1st Ave.), 206-467-9990

■ When you're in the market (Pike Place Market, that is) for a "romantic, delightful oasis", make it a point to seek out this "quaint" Pacific Northwest eatery where "attentive" yet "discreet servers" deliver "inventive" offerings from a prix fixe menu; you "can't beat the view" of Puget Sound, nor the "candlelit" "elegance" of "one of the best, least-known restaurants in town"; N.B. adjacent Shea's Lounge offers a more casual à la carte menu until midnight.

DAHLIA LOUNGE S   27 │ 25 │ 25 │ $40

2001 Fourth Ave. (Virginia St.), 206-682-4142

■ The verdict is in: owner "Tom Douglas is a Seattle treasure" and his "sublime" lounge, a "perennial Downtown favorite", is "as good as ever" in "great digs" that are "roomy yet still intimate" and embellished with "fantastic red walls"; you can count on the "wonderful use of seasonal Northwest foods" and "just the right amount of creativity" in its "superbly presented" Eclectic dishes; P.S. "save room for the coconut cream pie."

El Gaucho ●S   24 │ 23 │ 24 │ $52

2505 First Ave. (bet. Vine & Wall Sts.), 206-728-1337

■ It's "class all the way" at this "sophisticated" Belltown shrine where the "martini, meat and Cuban-cigar crowd" worships the "superb service and superb steaks" (though, "surprisingly, the fish entrees are as good"); what with watching "Caesar salad and bananas Foster prepared tableside" and spotting the "local who's who", this is a real "dinner-as-theater" experience, set in a "dark and dramatic" space that "takes you back to a time long ago."

Etta's Seafood S   25 │ 20 │ 22 │ $36

2020 Western Ave. (bet. Lenora & Virginia Sts.), 206-443-6000

■ Fish fans say there's almost nothing b-etta than this "longtime favorite" (part of owner "Tom Douglas' dynasty") at the north edge of the Pike Place Market; it's "warm, friendly and informal", with an "eclectic menu" of "superbly fresh seafood" that "gets everything right" (even "the side dishes are a must"), and an "always-pleasant staff" rounds out the supremely "satisfying" experience; P.S. it's a "super weekend-breakfast place."

Eva S   – │ – │ – │ E

2227 N. 56th St. (Kirkwood Pl.), 206-633-3538

Both Green Lake locals and farther-flung folks flock to this charming bistro (in the former Brie & Bordeaux space) for its well-crafted Pacific Northwest–New American cuisine, interesting wine list and easygoing, friendly service; co-owners Amy McCray (chef, ex Chez Shea) and James Hondros (host and wine guy) each contribute to its distinctive and welcoming personality.

Flying Fish ●S   26 │ 22 │ 22 │ $38

2234 First Ave. (Bell St.), 206-728-8595

☑ "A lot of imagination goes into" the "superb seafood" with an Asian twist that's served at this "bustling, energetic" Belltowner;

fans' favorite include "out-of-this-world Thai crab cakes" and a platter of salt-and-pepper Dungeness crab that's "great for a crowd" (sharing's highly encouraged here); critics carp that it gets "way too noisy" and that "while the cash register flies, the service crawls", but satisfied regulars feel "this is a catch you should not miss."

Frontier Room ◐ — | — | — | M

2203 First Ave. (Blanchard St.), 206-956-7427

A dive no more, this infamous spot has been resurrected as an upmarket barbecue joint where chef Paul Michael offers up his signature dish, St. Louis ribs from the in-house smoker, as well as melt-in-your-mouth Tennessee-style pork, brisket and chicken (not to mention seafood and vegetarian chili); the mod urban-cowboy motif befits the hip neighborhood, though the down-home fare and moderate tabs make for a refreshing change from the Belltown standard.

GEORGIAN [S] 27 | 28 | 28 | $54

Four Seasons Hotel, 411 University St. (bet. 4th & 5th Aves.), 206-621-7889

■ There's just "no more elegant" place in town than this "posh" Downtowner, but this "class act" goes beyond opulent "carpets and chandeliers" to offer Pacific Northwest "meals fit for a king" and "luxuriant service"; "eventually all of Seattle shows up here", so "don't wait until a special occasion" – just "dress up" and "bring the credit card"; N.B. lofty though it is, the Decor score may not reflect a further refinement of the interior in late 2001.

Harvest Vine 27 | 20 | 22 | $33

2701 E. Madison St. (27th Ave.), 206-320-9771

■ "Good things come in small packages" at this "shoebox-size" Basque in Madison Valley that provides an "unparalleled ethnic experience"; since there are "no reservations", "get there early" for "exquisite tapas", accompanied by "great Spanish wine", and "sit at the copper-topped bar" so you can watch chef/co-owner Joseba Jimenez de Jimenez at work; wife and pastry chef Carolin "is a wonder", so save room for dessert.

HERBFARM [S] 28 | — | 27 | VE

Willows Lodge, 14590 NE 145th St. (Woodinville-Redmond Rd.), Woodinville, 206-784-2222

■ Supporters are full of superlatives for the "culinary adventure" that results when Jerry Traunfeld applies his art to the "creative uses of herbs": "sublime", "pure alchemy", "inventive [Pacific] Northwest cuisine at its best"; expect a multi-hour "gastronomic feast" (the nine-course prix fixe–only dinners range from $150–$180), supplemented by "exquisite service", that's "worth the long wait" for reservations; N.B. a post-*Survey* move to Woodinville means a larger, more luxurious space accented by warm colors.

Hunt Club [S] 25 | 25 | 24 | $45

Sorrento Hotel, 900 Madison St. (Terry Ave.), 206-343-6156

■ For some of Seattle's "most elegant, romantic dining", hedonists head to this "landmark" on First Hill where chef Brian Scheehser prepares "great, full-flavored" Pacific Northwest food (he "has a nice way with game" in particular) laced with Med influences that reflect the hotel's Italianate decor; the mahogany-"paneled room" is "quiet" and "comfortable", offering "old-world ambiance."

Il Terrazzo Carmine
| 26 | 24 | 24 | $40 |

411 First Ave. S. (bet. Jackson & King Sts.), 206-467-7797

■ Expect a "continuously superb" experience at this longtime favorite in Pioneer Square, an "elegant, old-school Italian" that relies on standards such as the "best carpaccio" and the signature osso buco Milanese, served in a setting that's simultaneously "sophisticated" and "comfortable"; the "ever-watchful eye of owner Carmine Smeraldo guarantees you" "seamless service", but the popular "classic" "can be loud."

JaK's Grill ⬛
| 26 | 18 | 22 | $32 |

4548 California Ave. SW (bet. Alaska & Oregon Sts.), 206-937-7809
14 Front St. N. (Sunset Way), Issaquah, 425-837-8834

■ "Great steak" at a "low price" might seem an oxymoron, but this "excellent" West Seattle and Issaquah beef duo does manage to be one of the "best buys in town" (the "no-frills" setting helps); "the fact that they don't take reservations is a pain" and because they're so often "crowded" they get "noisy", but "service that makes you feel like family" causes folks to be "weekly regulars."

Kingfish Café ⬛≠
| 25 | 22 | 21 | $26 |

602 19th Ave. E. (Mercer St.), 206-320-8757

■ "You go, girls!" cheer fans of the Coaston sisters, who run this "buzzing" "down-home" haunt, which offers "a taste of Southern tradition" at "very reasonable prices"; the "great cookin' with all the fixin's" includes "red beans, rice and cornbread to die for" and "buttermilk fried chicken worth every minute in line", so "put your name down and go for a drink" or a walk around the mellow Capitol Hill neighborhood.

Lampreia ⬛
| 25 | 21 | 23 | $58 |

2400 First Ave. (Battery St.), 206-443-3301

◪ No Seattle spot polarizes patrons as much as this Belltowner: the cult-like majority "would sit on an apple box in the alley to eat" chef-owner and "culinary genius" Scott Carsberg's "sublime" Italian-influenced Pacific Northwest–New American fare, though they prefer being pampered by the "indulgent staff" within its "stylish" interior; to heretics, however, it's a "stuck-up" spot that specializes in "confrontational dining" in the form of "skimpy portions", "robotic waiters" and "austere decor."

Le Gourmand
| 26 | 21 | 26 | $54 |

425 NW Market St. (6th Ave. NW), 206-784-3463

■ "A little off the beaten path", this Ballard "oasis of comfortable elegance" offers an "escape from the trendy set" as you enjoy "top-of-the-line French fare"; chef-owner Bruce Naftaly "delights" with his "impeccable use of Northwest ingredients" (some of which may be "grown 20 yards from where you sit", in the garden); with "exquisite fine food, romantic atmosphere and prompt service, what more can you ask for?"

Le Pichet ⬛◖
| 23 | 22 | 20 | $30 |

Pike Place Mkt., 1933 First Ave. (Virginia St.), 206-256-1499

■ There's now a "little piece of Paris" at the Pike Place Market, offering the "hearty flavors" of "artful" French bistro fare on a selective (some say "limited") menu; "authentic details" include a tiled floor, hefty zinc bar, earthenware *pichets* of wine and a bill with phrases *en français*.

METROPOLITAN GRILL [S] 26 | 23 | 24 | $45

820 Second Ave. (Marion St.), 206-624-3287

■ "If you need meat, it can't be beat" say supporters of this Downtowner, an oldie that's still "the best place for steak in Seattle"; expect "always-done-to-a-turn" "portions the size of Texas" served by a "bright, funny, attentive staff" and an "expense-account" ambiance that, when fueled by the "good happy hour", is "busy, energetic, vibrant" – and a tad "too noisy" at times; all in all, though, this is one prime beef baron.

MISTRAL 27 | 20 | 24 | $67

113 Blanchard St. (bet. 1st & 2nd Aves.), 206-770-7799

■ This "intriguing" place blew into Belltown, establishing itself for "serious, *very* serious, foodies": you pick your prix fixe price point, choose "fresh ingredients" from the daily printed menu, then "relax and enjoy" chef-owner William Belickis' "wonderful, daring" Modern European preparations, "impeccably served"; though reviewers register "sticker shock" over the bill, they admit that "every course is exquisite" – "maybe too good for Seattle."

Monsoon [S] 25 | 19 | 20 | $30

615 19th Ave. E. (bet. Mercer & Roy Sts.), 206-325-2111

■ Tucked into a section of Capitol Hill, this "delicious Vietnamese" run by the Banh clan delights with meals that start with "incredibly fragrant soups" then move on to signature dishes that "combine subtle and spicy flavors", such as crispy crabmeat-and-shrimp spring rolls or grilled baby squid stuffed with duck meat, all complemented by "well-chosen wines"; just be prepared – only a monsoon could drown out the "terrible din" when the "spare, bright" room gets packed.

Nell's [S] 26 | 21 | 24 | $45

6804 E. Green Lake Way N. (bet. 2nd & 4th Aves.), 206-524-4044

■ Chef-owner "Philip Mihalski is clearly a rising star", and his New American with regional influences serves as a "great successor" to the beloved Saleh al Lago, late of this Green Lake locale; the setting and "excellent service" make for a "friendly atmosphere" in which to enjoy "faultless food"; whether it's an "old favorite" (beef tenderloin) or an occasional special (black cod), "each dish is a masterpiece", so some say this spot "will become one of the city's best."

Nishino [S] 26 | 22 | 23 | $39

3130 E. Madison St. (Lake Washington Blvd.), 206-322-5800

■ A careful balance of "inventive Japanese fare and the great classics" is maintained at this "elegant, serene" Madison Park hot spot; "there is no better sushi in Seattle", and the rest of the menu is pretty "divine" too, but regulars recommend "splurge on the omakase meal" (which you must reserve in advance) and "let chef-owner Tatsu Nishino feed you whatever he wants", knowing full well that it will be something "exceptional."

Oceanaire Seafood Room [S] – | – | – | E

1700 Seventh Ave. (Olive Way), 206-267-2277

With its luxurious cherry wood detail and red leather booths, the grand room of this Downtown seafood house (part of a small, upscale chain) evokes a bygone era, and its menu, which you'll be perusing over a complimentary relish tray, does the same with classics like oysters Rockefeller, stuffed sole and baked Alaska, though the focus is on the wide world of super-fresh fish cooked with great care; the eye-catching oyster bar is an additional lure.

Palace Kitchen ◐ [S] 24 | 22 | 21 | $36

2030 Fifth Ave. (Lenora St.), 206-448-2001

■ Need we say it again?; owner "Tom Douglas is the best", and folks have "nothing but kudos" for his "very hip" "hot spot" Downtown; the "imaginative", made-for-grazing menu serves up Eclectic–New American "food with real flavor", from the "fabulous house-baked bread" to the applewood-grilled meats, fish and poultry to the cheese plate; add in the "great bar scene" and you've got a "festive atmosphere" that makes for hordes of "happy people"; P.S. it's also "the perfect place for late at night."

Restaurant Zoë 25 | 23 | 25 | $37

2137 Second Ave. (Blanchard St.), 206-256-2060

■ This favorite has jogged even the most jaded diners with "flavorful food", "fab cocktails", "exceptional service" and a "totally tony" interior, all "in the middle of the action" of Belltown; chef-owner Scott Staples hits the right notes with a New American menu that's concise and consistently well executed; no wonder Zoë-goers say they "want more places like this."

ROVER'S 29 | 25 | 28 | $82

2808 E. Madison St. (28th Ave.), 206-325-7442

■ Once again Seattle's No. 1 for Food, this longtime "champion" in Madison Valley is truly "the tops" for its Pacific Northwest–accented New French "edible art" prepared by chef-owner Thierry Rautureau and presented in "fantastic tasting menus" (including a veggie version) that are "well worth the splurge"; a staff that's "knowledgeable without being stuffy" and a "lovely", "elegant" setting add up to an "always exceptional" experience, leaving one surveyor to sigh "I'd be a regular if I were Bill Gates."

Saito's Japanese Café & Bar ▽ 25 | 23 | 20 | $22

2122 Second Ave. (bet. Blanchard & Lenora Sts.), 206-728-1333

■ Chef-owner Yutaka Saito's Belltown Japanese "shows some real class" with "most excellent sushi" and creative sake-it-to-me cocktails; the "graceful" setting, accented with splashes of color, also offers diners their choice of seats at the "entertaining" bar.

727 Pine [S] – | – | – | VE

Elliott Grand Hyatt, 727 Pine St. (8th Ave.), 206-774-6400

Set in the sleek Elliott Grand Hyatt, this stylish multilevel venue cascades downward from the casual lounge at street level (perfect for cocktailing) through the bustling bar to the elegant dining room, a restful refuge from the Downtown din; chef Kyle H. Nelson's Eclectic menu features Northwest-inspired seasonal fare done up with some interesting twists, such as vichyssoise with sorrel panna cotta and sumac-crusted Colorado lamb rack, followed by decadent desserts worth saving room for.

Shiro's Sushi [S] 26 | 17 | 20 | $35

2401 Second Ave. (Battery St.), 206-443-9844

■ If you're lucky enough to snag a spot at the sushi bar at this Belltowner (hint: be there when it opens), "ignore the menu and have Shiro order for you", because this "master chef" uses only the "highest-grade ingredients" in his "incredible" dishes and he often has "wonderful seasonal surprises" to share; it's "extremely traditional" in decor (some say "stark") and some detractors find it "disappointing", but most maintain it's "worth every yen."

Shoalwater [S] 26 | 24 | 23 | $41

Shelburne Inn, 4415 Pacific Hwy. (45th St.), Seaview, 360-642-4142

■ For more than 20 years, this Long Beach Peninsula destination has provided the region with a "tradition of excellent [Pacific] Northwest fare", including Willapa Bay oysters and Alaskan halibut, though meat dishes shine as well; the "wine selection is great" and the "service is friendly", making this a solid choice for some of the "best dining on the Washington coast."

Szmania's [S] 26 | 22 | 24 | $40

3321 W. McGraw St. (34th Ave.), 206-284-7305

148 Lake St. S. (Kirkland Ave.), Kirkland, 425-803-3310

■ "A great dining experience even if no one can pronounce the name" (hint: the 'z' is silent), this Magnolia "jewel" sparkles, offering "creative Northwest cuisine with German flair"; chef-owner Ludger Szmania "does everything right", from "imaginative" dishes like the "awesome Jäger schnitzel" to the "warm and welcoming atmosphere" and "pampering" service; N.B. the Downtown Kirkland branch opened post-*Survey.*

Union Bay Café [S] 25 | 21 | 23 | $36

3515 NE 45th St. (bet. Mary Gates Dr. & 36th Ave.), 206-527-8364

■ "Just plain wonderful, from starters through dessert" – so say supporters of this "snazzy" Laurelhurst "find" that provides diners with "creative" Pacific Northwest–New American fare, "unobtrusive service" and a "great wine list" in a "simple but elegant" setting; some unionists even name it one of the "top underrated restaurants in town."

Vivanda Ristorante [S] – | – | – | E

Pike Place Mkt., 95 Pine St. (1st Ave.), 206-442-1121

A new addition to the popular Pike Place Market, this Med seafood house supplies an attractive urban setting with warm tones and a view (from some tables) of beautiful Elliott Bay; the menu draws its inspirations from, and liberally interprets, the cuisines of coastal regions in Italy (panzanella salad), Greece (deep-fried calamari with skordalia), Spain (a marinated seafood and gazpacho 'martini') and France (stuffed escargot with sherry-chive hollandaise).

WILD GINGER [S] 26 | 24 | 22 | $36

1401 Third Ave. (Union St.), 206-623-4450

■ Folks are just wild about this Downtown Southeast Asian, voting it the Most Popular restaurant in Seattle thanks to the "incredible 'fragrant duck'" and other "fabulous flavors" that make it a "culinary adventure in smells and spices"; though its move two years ago to a "gorgeous" bigger space did create "more room for the throngs", it's still "always packed", making it "hard to get a table" ("even with reservations, expect a wait") at the "hottest place in town."

TOP 20 FOOD RANKING

Restaurant	Cuisine Type
29 Xaviar's at Piermont	New American
Xaviar's at Garrison	New American
28 Freelance Café	New American
La Panetière	New French
27 Escoffier	New French
La Crémaillère	French
Harralds	International
American Bounty	New American
Azuma Sushi	Japanese
Buffet de la Gare	French
Terrapin	New American
Arch	Eclectic/French
26 Le Château	French
Zephs'	Eclectic
Rest. X & Bully Boy Bar	New American
Auberge Maxime	French
Equus	New French
Iron Horse Grill	New American
Crabtree's Kittle House	New American
L'Europe	French/Continental

ADDITIONAL NOTEWORTHY PLACES

American Bistro	New American
Aubergine	French/New American
Cafe Mezé	Mediterranean
Citrus Grille	New American
Conte's Fishmarket	Seafood
Cripple Creek	Eclectic/New American
DePuy Canal House	American/Eclectic
Hajime	Japanese
Halstead Avenue Bistro	New American
Harry's of Hartsdale	Steakhouse
Il Cenácolo	Northern Italian
Inn at Pound Ridge	American
Le Canard Enchainé	French Bistro
Lusardi's	Northern Italian
Mulino's	Northern Italian
Old Drovers Inn	American/International
Peter Pratt's Inn	New American
Purdys Homestead	New American
Sonora	Nuevo Latino
Would	New American

AMERICAN BISTRO, AN 🖪　　25　–　22　$37
296 Columbus Ave. (bet. Fisher & Lincoln Aves.), Tuckahoe,
914-793-0807

■ "Tucked away in Tuckahoe", this "reasonably priced" "little gem" is home to "creative chef"-owner Robert Horton, "an artist" whose "inventive" New American preparations "never miss", and "his wife", Denise, "the friendly hostess", who oversees a staff that "couldn't be nicer"; a post-*Survey* "move" to "a bigger space" across from the Crestwood train station and the recent reversal of its old "no-reservations policy" may stifle criticism about "no-frills" decor and "impossible waits."

American Bounty　　27　25　25　$44
Culinary Institute of America, 1946 Campus Dr. (Rte. 9), Hyde Park,
845-471-6608

■ Proclaimed "a wonderful showcase for hardworking students", who operate "every facet" of it, this CIA-based Hyde Park New American features "out-of-this-world" cuisine, a "handsome room with beautiful tableware" and "sweet", "gracious" service; in sum, a true "class act" and an "ideal way to finish off a day of touring wineries"; N.B. the Decor score may not reflect a recent renovation.

Arch 🖪　　27　27　26　$60
Rte. 22N (end of I-684), Brewster, 845-279-5011

■ Patrons predict "you'll feel like royalty" at this vaunted Brewster Eclectic-French, revered for its "glamorous" yet "intimate" interior (ask for the "great garden room"), pleasing patio, "personal, attentive" service and "excellent wine list"; chef-owner George Seitz's "terrific", prix fixe dinner (à la carte at lunch) "changes with the times" but is "a treat for the palate", if not the pocketbook.

Auberge Maxime 🖪　　26　25　25　$56
721 Titicus Rd. (Rtes. 116 & 121), North Salem, 914-669-5450

■ "Strictly for grown-ups", this Gallic entry in North Salem's "horse country" is lauded for "great soufflés" and "original ways of serving duck", as well as a "wonderful French country" feel, highlighted by two "heavenly" patios; a few feel that it's getting "a bit stale on ideas" but wouldn't think of declining an invite for a "special-occasion" dinner here.

Aubergine 🖪　　25　25　25　$53
Aubergine Fine Food and Lodging, Rtes. 22 & 23, Hillsdale,
518-325-3412

■ Set in a "gorgeous", circa-1783 auberge, chef-owner David Lawson's "country mecca" is "as good as it gets in Columbia [County]" thanks to "beautiful rooms" furnished with antiques, a "calm", "comforting" aura, "wonderful" French-American cuisine and a "great cellar"; while "expensive", it makes "a perfect coda to a Sunday afternoon at Tanglewood (a half hour away)."

Azuma Sushi 🖪　　27　15　18　$38
219 E. Hartsdale Ave. (Central Ave.), Hartsdale, 914-725-0660

■ Raw "fish doesn't get much fresher" than the "top-quality" "traditional" sushi that's crafted inside this "tiny" Hartsdale Japanese storefront whose "very high standards" attract "hordes of people from Manhattan" (it's "convenient to Metro-North"); just "don't expect any atmosphere", many cooked dishes or coddling by the "intimidating" staff.

Buffet de la Gare
27 | 22 | 24 | $54

155 Southside Ave. (Spring St.), Hastings-on-Hudson, 914-478-1671

■ "Excellent in all ways" exclaim enthusiasts of this "family-run" French near the Hastings train station, a "special-occasion favorite" that "can compete with the best of Manhattan" thanks to "first-rate" (albeit "expensive") cuisine served in "elegant", "cozy rooms"; though a few interpret the "Gallic reserve" as "pretentious", most say the "considerate staff" provides "warm and attentive service"; N.B. jacket preferred.

Cafe Mezé 🖫
23 | 19 | 21 | $42

20 N. Central Ave. (Hartsdale Ave.), Hartsdale, 914-428-2400

■ "Hail to the Livanos!" boom boosters of this family that "knows how to run a restaurant" – namely, this Hartsdale Med; "excellent chef" Mark Filippo scores "points for inventiveness" with his "soul-satisfying" cuisine; though the "rushed waiters" are sometimes "overwhelmed" by large "weekend crowds", it continues to be a "sophisticated dining experience."

Citrus Grille 🖫
25 | 19 | 22 | $45

430 E. Saddle River Rd. (bet. Lake St. & Rte. 59), Airmont, 845-352-5533

■ Chef-owner Steven Christianson's "creative, superior cuisine" and "interesting vertical presentations" elevate his Rockland County New American to the status of an area favorite; "welcoming service", a "cozy atmosphere" and "friendly patrons" make it "feel like a country restaurant", and though a few find the "intimate" seating a bit too close for private conversation, most conclude the experience is "charming."

Conte's Fishmarket ⊅
25 | 12 | 19 | $35

448 Main St. (St. Mark's Pl.), Mount Kisco, 914-666-6929

■ Despite a tiny "no-frills" setting in a Mount Kisco fish market ("on a nice night, sit outside"), this BYO seafood house is a "high-priced", must-reserve spot for "simply prepared" but "wonderful" *mer* fare; N.B. lunch Tuesday–Friday, dinner Thursday–Saturday.

CRABTREE'S KITTLE HOUSE 🖫
26 | 25 | 25 | $49

Crabtree's Kittle House Inn, 11 Kittle Rd. (Rte. 117), Chappaqua, 914-666-8044

■ An "old inn [circa 1790] provides the perfect backdrop" for this Chappaqua New American, one of "the yardsticks for fine dining" in Westchester, with "heavenly" cuisine, a "world-class wine cellar", "garden views" and service that "truly caters to you"; not surprising, it's also "a favorite" choice "for special occasions."

Cripple Creek 🖫
26 | 21 | 22 | $44

22 Garden St. (Market St.), Rhinebeck, 845-876-4355

■ "A delight from the minute you walk in" say admirers of this Eclectic–New American in Rhinebeck where the "charming touches" include "red rose petals" strewn on the linens; chef Benjamin Mauk's regularly changing menu features local produce, and you can expect "excellent service" from staffers "under the stewardship of co-owner Patrick Hays, a Juilliard-trained musician" who provides classical piano accompaniment; N.B. dinner only.

DePuy Canal House 🖫
25 | 27 | 24 | $55

1315 Rte. 213 (Rte. 209), High Falls, 845-687-7700

■ "A must-stop" "for the adventurous palate" say fans of chef-owner and "food artist" John Novi's "spectacular" American-

Eclectic that's now in its fourth decade of offering "creative combinations"; the "beautiful", antique-filled "1797 stone" house and "excellent service" make this "*the* place to take first-time Hudson Valley visitors"; while wallet-watchers find it "expensive", most feel "it's worth it."

Equus [S] 26 | 29 | 25 | $59

Castle at Tarrytown, 400 Benedict Ave. (bet. Maple St. & Martling Ave.), Tarrytown, 914-631-3646

■ "Stunning!" enthuse aesthetes over the "beautiful" dining rooms, "breathtaking" "views of the Hudson" and "scenic gardens" surrounding this "fairy-tale castle" in Tarrytown; similarly "elegant in every detail" are its "exquisite" New French creations and "top-notch" service; N.B. the Food rating does not reflect the post-Survey arrival of chef Michael Coldrick.

ESCOFFIER [S] 27 | 26 | 26 | $50

Culinary Institute of America, 1946 Campus Dr. (Rte. 9), Hyde Park, 845-471-6608

■ If legendary chef Auguste Escoffier "ate here he'd be proud of his namesake" insist epicures about this New French "treat" that offers a "superb dining experience at the Culinary Institute" in Hyde Park; the "outstanding" food makes it "a place to pamper the palate", and there's also that "wonderful setting" and "friendly service by students" whose "instructors keep standards high"; P.S. better "make reservations in advance."

FREELANCE CAFÉ & WINE BAR [S] ≠ 28 | 20 | 25 | $41

506 Piermont Ave. (Ash St.), Piermont, 845-365-3250

■ "Always reinventing itself", this "less-expensive" "little sister to Xaviar's" at Piermont fashions "superb ingredients" into "artful", "sublime" New American fare offered with "fabulous wines by the glass" and "bend-over-backward service" amid an "informal-yet-sophisticated ambiance" that has some wishing they "could eat here every night"; if not for the "no-reservations policy", supporters say, this "tiny" spot would be "perfect."

Hajime [S] 25 | 16 | 19 | $32

267 Halstead Ave. (Harrison Ave.), Harrison, 914-777-1543

■ With a Food score that puts it near the top of its category, it should be no surprise that reservations are recommended for weekend dinners at this Downtown Harrison Japanese where owner Sam Takahashi (who's been practicing his craft for over 35 years) creates "wonderful" sushi, including "terrific" *omakase* (chef's choice) dinners.

Halstead Avenue Bistro [S] – | – | – | M

123 Halstead Ave. (West St.), Harrison, 914-777-1181

This mahogany-adorned two-year-old is causing a stir in Harrison with its attention to detail, from the amuse-bouches that kick dinner off to the complimentary biscotti presented with the check; thanks to reasonable prices, New American dishes like slow-roasted duck and Belgian chocolate beggar's purse shouldn't make a pauper out of anyone; N.B. reservations requested for parties of five or more.

Harralds ≠ 27 | 26 | 27 | $66

3760 Rte. 52 (bet. Durrschmidt & Mountain Rds.), Stormville, 845-878-6595

■ The "old-world charm" makes for "a delightful, delicious experience" at this Dutchess County International; host Harrald

Boerger "treats you like a favored guest" in a "lovely country setting" where you'll dine on "nonpareil" fare from the kitchen of his wife, Eva Durrschmidt; though many find the prix fixe tariff "*très cher*", most would agree "it's worth it"; N.B. reservations required.

Harry's of Hartsdale [S] – | – | – | E

230 E. Hartsdale Ave. (Bronx River Pkwy. & Central Park Ave.), Hartsdale, 914-472-8777

This bi-level Hartsdale haven with a steakhouse and raw-bar focus offers innovative entrees (including farfalle served with cured salmon, capers, fava beans and tomato concasse finished with a dill lemon crème) plus housemade desserts and a nice selection of beers and wines, along with live jazz Thursday nights.

Il Cenácolo [S] 25 | 19 | 24 | $51

228 S. Plank Rd. (Union Ave.), Newburgh, 845-564-4494

◪ Partisans agree it's "worth the drive" to this perennially top-rated Northern Italian "treasure in Orange County" that's "like a one-night trip to Tuscany" thanks to "brilliant" cooking and attention to service and presentation"; a few declare it's "pricey and not worth it", but for the majority it "never disappoints"; N.B. a post-*Survey* refurbishment is not reflected in the Decor score.

Inn at Pound Ridge [S] 25 | 25 | 23 | $51

258 Westchester Ave./Rte. 137 (Rte. 172), Pound Ridge, 914-764-5779

■ A visit to this "absolutely beautiful" American set on "lovely grounds" in Pound Ridge is "like stepping back in time", with "superior" "country inn fare" "carefully served" in a "romantic" "New England atmosphere" that offers the "best of both worlds" – "classy" and "tasteful", yet "not too stuffy"; indeed, guests may face only one "hard decision: dine upstairs (more elegant) or downstairs (cozier)?"; either way, "this one is not to be missed."

Iron Horse Grill 26 | 21 | 23 | $47

20 Wheeler Ave. (Manville Rd.), Pleasantville, 914-741-0717

■ This "consummately professional" New American set in a "charming" "converted railway station" "remains on track" after its "brilliant start" in 1998, with chef-owner Philip McGrath creating "inspired", "scrumptious" cuisine that's "nicely presented" by a "caring" staff; some call the prices "too steep" for Pleasantville, but given that it's almost "impossible to get reservations", cost concerns "don't seem to be holding people back."

LA CRÉMAILLÈRE [S] 27 | 27 | 25 | $61

46 Bedford-Banksville Rd. (bet. Noah St. & Roundhouse Rd.), Banksville, 914-234-9647

■ For a "charming" "slice of France" "transported" to Banksville, "chichi" types "dress up" and head to this Classic Gallic destination where chef William Savarese prepares "superb" cuisine, bolstered by an "impressive" 14,000-bottle cellar and "attentive, unobtrusive" staff; "an extravagance, but well worth it" for a "classy evening", it can also be experienced more affordably through its prix fixe lunch (available Thursday–Saturday).

LA PANETIÈRE [S] 28 | 27 | 26 | $63

530 Milton Rd. (Oakland Beach Ave.), Rye, 914-967-8140

■ Once again voted No. 1 for Popularity in the So. NY area, this Provençal-themed Rye New French destination is lauded for "outstanding food" that's "a joy to behold and eat", a "great" (if "pricey") wine list and superb service led by "dignified" owner Jacques Loupiac; quibblers find it a tad "pretentious" ("women's menus don't have prices") but are outvoted by those who gladly don a jacket and "take out a home-equity loan to pay for" a visit.

Le Canard Enchainé [S] 25 | 22 | 23 | $40

276 Fair St. (bet. Maiden Ln. & Pearl St.), Kingston, 845-339-2003

■ Like a "Left Bank bistro off the banks of the Hudson", this Uptown Kingston classic is "warm and friendly"; better still, the "lunch is a bargain and the dinner worth the price", as "extraordinary" chef-owner Jean-Jacques Carquillat is "one of the most amazing sauciers on planet earth" and his "tarte Tatin is the best"; devotees dub it the greatest "restaurant north of Manhattan."

Le Château [S] 26 | 28 | 26 | $57

Rte. 35 (Rte. 123), South Salem, 914-533-6631

■ Situated in a mansion on "beautiful grounds" that afford "sweeping views of uninterrupted forest", this "elegant" South Salem classic French "makes you feel as if you've come home to your private château" to enjoy "sunset cocktails" and "superb" cuisine ("try all the soufflés") proffered by an "excellent" staff; P.S. you may "want to hold your daughter's wedding" here.

L'Europe [S] 26 | 21 | 24 | $54

407 Smith Ridge Rd./Rte. 123 (Tommys Ln.), South Salem, 914-533-2570

■ The "meticulous" but "friendly service" scores almost as well as the "first-class menu" of "superb", "finely tuned food" (such as "great rack of lamb") at this "old-world" French-Continental hidden away in the Vista neighborhood of South Salem, "in rural Westchester"; voters also praise the "lovely atmosphere", prix fixe dinner (on Saturday) and "wonderful" Sunday brunch, summing up by saying "it may be a little hard to find, but it's well worth it."

Lusardi's [S] 24 | 21 | 22 | $46

1885 Palmer Ave. (bet. Chatsworth Ave. & Weaver St.), Larchmont, 914-834-5555

■ "Arguably" one of "the best Italians north of NYC", this "enjoyable" eatery "brings a bit of polish to Larchmont" with "consistently excellent" "food fit for the fussiest palate", "gracious service" from a "warm", "doting staff" and an "elegant" setting ("in the winter, sit by the fireplace for a romantic meal"); since this "winner" is such a crowd-pleaser, you'll need to "call far in advance to get reservations" on weekends.

Mulino's of Westchester ◐ 25 | 23 | 24 | $48

99 Court St. (bet. Martine Ave. & Quarropas St.), White Plains, 914-761-1818

■ "What a pleasant surprise to find this" "excellent upscale Northern Italian" "in Downtown White Plains" say savorers of its "blend of comfort and sophistication" and its "generous portions" of "wonderful food" presented by a "staff that will bend over backward" for you; like "its no-relation namesake in NYC", it can be "pricey", but its popularity with "power-scene" "politicos" and "romantics" alike means it "tends to book up", so "reserve early."

Old Drovers Inn [S] 25 | 26 | 25 | $56

Old Rte. 22 (E. Duncan Hill Rd.), Dover Plains, 845-832-9311

■ "You almost expect to see George" Washington sinking his wooden teeth into an "exceptional" colonial American meal at this "historic, romantic" Dover Plains inn that fully "deserves its stellar reputation"; dining here is like "stepping back in time", but since folks were shorter in 1750, better "watch your head"; N.B. executive chef Peter Wallace, whose post-*Survey* arrival is not reflected in the Food score, has supplemented its 'classics' menu with International dishes.

Peter Pratt's Inn 🖪   23 | 20 | 20 | $42
673 Croton Heights Rd. (Rte. 118), Yorktown, 914-962-4090
■ One of "Yorktown's restaurant jewels", this "charming and innovative" New American is "romantically" nestled within a "wood-beamed" "colonial farmhouse" that's seen "a good slice of" history; it's "hard to find" but "well worth" it if you're game for "talented" chef-owner Jonathan Pratt's "creative cuisine" featuring "rare-in-the-suburbs" wild meats; P.S. those who found the "musty" decor in "need of a tune-up" may appreciate the recent post-*Survey* refurbishment.

Purdys Homestead 🖪   24 | 25 | 23 | $52
100 Titicus Rd. (bet. Rtes. 22 & 116), North Salem, 914-277-2301
■ Customers coo that the "modern flair" of the "delicious and imaginative" New American menu is as bright as the "fireplaces in every room" of this "beautifully restored" 1775 North Salem homestead; though it's "especially welcoming on a snowy night", the "old colonial house's" "cozy and romantic" charm is ever-present, thanks to chef-owners Charles and Maureen Steppe, who provide a "quiet, dressy dining" "experience that's seamless from beginning to end."

Restaurant X & Bully Boy Bar 🖪   26 | 25 | 25 | $51
117 Rte. 303 (bet. Lake Rd. & Rte. 9W), Congers, 845-268-6555
■ "Wow, what a hit" the "x-uberant" x-claim about this "go-to" New American "masterpiece", x-plaining that owner Peter Kelly (of the always top-rated Xaviar's duo) may be the "Alain Ducasse" of the Congers "boondocks" because he "does everything right" at this "divine" venture: the "cutting-edge" cuisine is "x–quisitely prepared", the "ambiance is terrific" (particularly in the "garden room overlooking the pond") and the "solicitous and efficient" staff has a "magical touch" that "leaves you happy."

Sonora 🖪   – | – | – | M
179 Rectory St. (Willett Ave.), Port Chester, 914-933-0200
Native Colombian chef, cookbook author and whiz kid Rafael Palomino brings his lively Nuevo Latino touch to this Port Chester outpost; the surroundings, appointed with high-backed wooden chairs and Nazca Indian symbols on sandstone-colored walls, create a Peruvian backdrop for meals that might begin with assorted seviches and end with one of several *dulce de leche* desserts; N.B. now offering Latin jazz on Thursdays.

Terrapin 🖪   27 | 19 | 26 | $42
250 Spillway Rd. (Rte. 28A), West Hurley, 845-331-3663
■ "Inventive combinations of flavors" characterize chef-owner Josh Kroner's "shockingly brilliant" New American cooking at this West Hurley "find" where patrons are served by a "friendly staff" within a "cozy, woody dining room"; its "backwoods location" near the Ashokan Reservoir allows ample room for the organic garden that supplies the kitchen; N.B. a $19.95 prix fixe three-course menu on Wednesdays wows wallet-watchers.

Would S   26 | 17 | 21 | $42

Inn at Applewood, 120 North Rd. (Rte. 9W), Highland, 845-691-9883
■ "Wonderful on all counts" say cognoscenti who know the way "through winding apple orchards" to this New American "favorite" atop a hill in Highland, where the "fresh, distinctive" dishes are made of local and organic ingredients and enhanced by an "amazing wine list"; there's also "great service", but "the decor definitely needs work", despite some remodeling.

XAVIAR'S AT GARRISON S⌁   29 | 26 | 28 | VE

Highlands Country Club, Rte. 9D (Rte. 403), Garrison, 845-424-4228
■ "Always memorable", Peter Kelly's "jewel" in Garrison offers "sublime" New American tasting menus that inspire "fine-dining gluttony", with each course "paired with perfect wines"; N.B. the prix fixe dinner on Friday and Saturday ($85) includes wine, and the Sunday brunch ($40) is a little slice of "sheer heaven."

XAVIAR'S AT PIERMONT S⌁   29 | 25 | 27 | VE

506 Piermont Ave. (Ash St.), Piermont, 845-359-7007
■ A little sibling rivalry has paid off for Peter Kelly's "smaller, more intimate" and younger Piermont offspring, which has edged out its Garrison big brother in a photo finish for top-rated Food in So. NY; the "glorious" New American prix fixe menu ($60, not including wine) "makes you glad you have something to celebrate", as do the "impeccable" staff and "elegant", "beautiful setting"; in fact, only those who don't have a reservation are unhappy, so be sure to book early.

Zephs' S   26 | 17 | 24 | $45

638 Central Ave. (bet. Union Ave. & Water St.), Peekskill, 914-736-2159
■ "Don't tell anyone about this" "jewel" supplicate selfish supporters of this "out-of-the-way" Peekskill Eclectic where dining feels "like being a pampered guest in a great cook's home"; though the "spartan-at-best" interior of this refurbished brick grist mill could be "more inviting" ("bring on the decorator!"), the staff's "friendliness" and the "reasonable prices" on the "original" menu "whet one's appetite" for the "glorious" creations to come.

TOP 10 FOOD RANKING

	Restaurant	Cuisine Type
26	Sidney Street Cafe	New American
	Trattoria Marcella	N&S Italian
25	Crossing	New American
	Tony's	N&S Italian/Seafood
	Zinnia	New American
24	Dominic's	Northern Italian
	Pho Grand	Vietnamese
23	Kemoll's	Continental/N&S Italian
	Cardwell's at the Plaza	International
	Harvest	New American

ADDITIONAL NOTEWORTHY PLACES

Annie Gunn's	New American
Bar Italia	Northern Italian
Eau Cafe & Bistro	New American/Asian
Frazer's	New American/Seafood
Giovanni's	N&S Italian
India Palace	Indian
Portabella	Mediterranean
Pueblo Solis	Mexican
Remy's Kitchen & Wine Bar	Mediterranean
Shiitake	Pan-Asian

F | D | S | C

Annie Gunn's [S] — | — | — | M

16806 Chesterfield Airport Rd. (Boone's Crossing), Chesterfield, 636-532-7684
Destroyed by the Flood of '93, this New American was rebuilt, bigger and better, and has been packin' them in ever since; chef Lou Rook III, assisted by his dad, works magic with meats and fish from the adjacent Smoke House Market, but sure shots should note (with apologies to Irving Berlin) that you can't get a table with a gun – you'll just have to wait like everyone else.

BAR ITALIA RISTORANTE [S] 21 | 19 | 17 | $32

13 Maryland Ave. (Euclid Ave.), 314-361-7010
◪ Patrons praise this "trendy alternative" Central West Ender for its "fresh and imaginative" Italian cuisine (mostly Northern, with a few Southern specialties) and its "fantastic patio" that's "perfect for watching" the "beautiful people" ("good luck getting an outside table after 5:30 on a Friday"); though "inconsistent service" troubles some, more say this "fun experience" "is all about the charm" of the "pleasant" "Ethiopian owners."

Cardwell's at the Plaza [S] 23 | 20 | 19 | $33

94 Plaza Frontenac (Lindbergh Blvd.), 314-997-8885
◪ "Chef David Owens is on the money" with his "consistently delicious and imaginative" fare at this "trendy" International in

Plaza Frontenac that "always has something interesting" on the menu ("vegetarians love this joint", as do "the tony ladies who lunch"); while dissenters think "facing onto a mall (albeit an upscale one) does detract from the atmosphere" and say it can get "noisy" and "hectic", the acquisitive insist this "popular" "favorite" is "a treat" "during [or after] a full day of shopping."

CROSSING 25 | 19 | 21 | $47

7823 Forsyth Blvd. (Central Ave.), Clayton, 314-721-7375

■ Two "ambitious and accomplished chef-owners", James Fiala and Cary McDowell, design "superb dishes" (especially with "fresh fish") at this "chic Clayton" spot where a "formal but relaxed" dining room and a "warm, welcoming" attitude have gourmands gushing; while the New American fare and international wines are "certainly pricey", most feel the place is "getting better all the time."

Dominic's on the Hill 24 | 23 | 24 | $52

5101 Wilson Ave. (Hereford St.), 314-771-1632

Dominic's Trattoria

200 S. Brentwood Blvd. (Bonhomme Ave.), Clayton, 314-863-4567

■ "A longtime favorite", this "elegant" Northern Italian "icon for special occasions" on the Hill still attracts with its "fabulous" fare ("love their veal dishes") and "excellent service" – even if the "calm and civil" atmosphere is "a bit stiff" for those who tire of "hovering waiters"; "bring a fat wallet" because "prices are steep", but "food that speaks for itself" makes all worthwhile; P.S. the "trattoria in Clayton is also very good."

Eau Cafe & Bistro [S] 21 | 23 | 17 | $41

Chase Park Plaza Hotel, 212 N. Kingshighway Blvd. (Lindell Blvd.), 314-454-9000

■ "Nestled in" the Central West End's "elegantly" "renovated Chase Park Plaza" Hotel, these "popular" "hot spots" are actually two separate restaurants, but "both" the "bustling" bistro and the smaller yet "pleasantly hip" cafe across the hall offer a "shining dining experience" thanks to "imaginative" executive chef Rob Uyemura, who blends New American and "Asian influences" in his overlapping and "ambitious menus", each complemented by a "superb wine list"; P.S. the larger venue's "fantastic [Sunday] brunch" "is to die for."

Frazer's 22 | 14 | 19 | $28

(fka Frazer's Traveling Brown Bag)

1811 Pestalozzi St. (Lemp Ave.), 314-773-8646

■ Head to this "quirky", "fun" "happening place" (a "stone's throw" from the Anheuser-Busch brewery) for "fresh seafood" dishes, including eponymous chef Frazer Cameron's "famous salmon", and a blackboard of "wildly eclectic" New American specials; though fans "wish others hadn't talked" about this once-"undiscovered wonder" – "it's tougher to get a table" now – the "friendly staff" and "groovy digs" keep them traveling here.

Giovanni's ▽ 22 | 20 | 20 | $48

5201 Shaw Ave. (Marconi Ave.), 314-772-5958

◪ A "well-known landmark on the Hill", this Italian still offers an "old-fashioned, very formal" experience; enthusiasts insist the "traditionally rich entrees" and tuxedo-clad staff ensure "you never go away unhappy", but critics, while conceding it's "still a fine special-occasion choice", cite "decor of faded elegance" and "jaded, stuffy service" as signs this vet "could use a bit of an overhaul all around."

HARVEST [S] 23 | 22 | 20 | $42

1059 S. Big Bend Blvd. (Clayton Rd.), 314-645-3522

◪ Happy harvesters hail this "intriguing" Richmond Heights New American for chef-owner Steve Gontram's "fantastic use of seasonal ingredients" in his "constantly changing" menu of "wonderful cuisine", as well as the "best bread pudding ever", "an out-of-this-world wine list" and a "friendly, polished staff"; despite this, detractors decry what they call "overdone" dishes with "food piled on the plate like a sculpture", saying "save me from their unrelenting creativity"; P.S. "don't try to get in at dinnertime without a reservation."

India Palace [S] 23 | 17 | 19 | $22

Howard Johnson Hotel, 4534 N. Lindbergh Blvd. (I-70), Bridgeton, 314-731-3333

■ Devotees delight in devouring the "moist and flavorful tandoori" at this Indian "on top of a Howard Johnson's" in North County, "particularly" during the "great lunch buffet" when they're "in extreme danger of overeating" (as one reviewer reveals, "I could eat here seven days a week, but I'd never be size 6 again"); while some say the Polynesian decor "makes you feel like a *Gilligan's Island* stowaway", the "spectacular views of the airport" and "courteous" service more than compensate.

Kemoll's [S] 23 | 21 | 21 | $44

Metropolitan Square Bldg., 1 Metropolitan Sq. (bet. Olive & Pine Sts.), 314-421-0555

■ Owned by the same family since 1927, this "special-occasion institution" offers "upscale Continental-Italian dining Downtown", with "*molto*-size portions" of "rich food that's not for the diet-conscious" (e.g. "incredible cheese bread", "fantastic fried artichokes"); a "cozy and enveloping atmosphere" as well as an "experienced staff" round out the "absolutely decadent" dinners and lunches; P.S. "the early-bird menu is a steal."

Pho Grand [S] 24 | 17 | 21 | $14

3195 S. Grand Blvd. (Connecticut St.), 314-664-7435

■ From the "great spring rolls" to the *bo luc lac* (shaking beef) to the wide variety of "wonderful veggie dishes" to the "must-have iced coffee", the "food is grand" at this "unbelievably popular" South City Vietnamese with a "well-deserved reputation", "low prices" and a "super staff" that provides "warm and efficient service"; in fact, those who don't like "waiting on weekends" want to "keep it a secret from out-of-towners", suggesting "don't tell anyone about this" "totally wonderful experience."

Portabella 22 | 18 | 19 | $38

15 N. Central Ave. (bet. Forsyth Blvd. & Maryland Ave.), Clayton, 314-725-6588

◪ Though no longer new, this "trendy place" remains "action central" "for Clayton movers and shakers" ("get a window table and watch Downtown go by"); but while the "well-dressed" insist the Mediterranean "fare still works" (especially at lunch), the "unimpressed" proletariat pouts "it's a little too chichi", adding that "the noise level and racing waiters are distracting"; P.S. check out the "savvy bar scene", which "attracts a smart set."

Pueblo Solis [S] 22 | 12 | 18 | $23

5127 Hampton Ave. (Delor St.), 314-351-9000

■ "Watch the Solis family smoothly run the show" (mama Oralia's in the kitchen, son Alfredo's out front) at this "cramped South City" cantina that serves the "hands-down best Mexican [fare] in St. Louis", including "shrimp diablo that's just about the best thing you could do to a shrimp"; the "*auténtico*" food, plus "a wide variety of tequilas", ensures "you don't notice" that the "dark" "decor looks like somebody's basement rec room."

Remy's Kitchen & Wine Bar 23 | 20 | 20 | $32

222 S. Bemiston Ave. (Bonhomme Ave.), Clayton, 314-726-5757

■ "What a delightful place" report reviewers about owner Tim Mallett's "hoppin'" hangout in Clayton, "always a favorite" since "there's always something new to try" on the "wide-ranging menu that leans toward Mediterranean flavors" and the "tapas-like" "large and small plates to share" and "wine flights add to the fun atmosphere"; though it gets "sorta crowded", the decor (a "nice mix of casual and elegant") and "eager-to-please" staff help ease the squeeze.

Shiitake 22 | 23 | 22 | $36

7927 Forsyth Blvd. (Central Ave.), Clayton, 314-725-4334

■ A "chichi" crowd comes to this Clayton creation, an avatar of "imaginative Pan-Asian fare" that ranges from "wonderful lettuce-cup appetizers" to sushi to lobster pad Thai, served amid "striking black-and-white decor"; a few fuss that the "fusion seems confused" and insist that "earplugs are needed on weekends", but the majority rules that "eating here is as fun as it is delicious."

SIDNEY STREET CAFE 26 | 21 | 24 | $42

2000 Sidney St. (Salena St.), 314-771-5777

■ The "storefront style and chalkboard menu belie the fine food" (rated No. 1 in St. Louis) served at this New American, "the place to go on the South Side"; surveyors "always leave stuffed", thanks to the "phenomenal lobster-filled fillet", "great beignets" and other "delicious" "food for people with a cholesterol deficiency", served by "well-seasoned staffers"; the "only downside: you can't go on impulse", since "reservations are hard to get."

TONY'S 25 | 24 | 24 | $63

410 Market St. (bet. Broadway & 4th Ave.), 314-231-7007

■ Established in 1946, this "fancy" Italian seafood house remains "a landmark in Downtown St. Louis" and is "still the best on all counts" maintain many who marvel at the "excellent" eats ("you can get anything you want, any way you want it"), "attentive staff" and "classically classy" digs; the irreverent insist its "reputation has exceeded reality", citing a "tired menu" and "overbearing service"; but pro or con, all agree that owner Vince Bommarito puts on "a big production, ending with a big check."

TRATTORIA MARCELLA 26 | 17 | 23 | $36

3600 Watson Rd. (Pernod Ave.), 314-352-7706

■ "Those Komorek brothers sure know how to run a restaurant" sing surveyors about Steve and Jamie's South City establishment, voted St. Louis' Most Popular; yes, the "stark surroundings" (there's "basically a lot of wall") get "crowded and noisy, but it's worth it" for "imaginative and exquisitely executed" "rustic Italian" dishes such as "sublime [lobster] risotto" and "miraculous fried spinach and calamari" dished up by a "superb staff"; best of all, it's "still a bargain", so "plan far in advance" to get a table.

ZINNIA [S] 25 | 20 | 23 | $38

7491 Big Bend Blvd. (Shrewsbury Ave.), Webster Groves, 314-962-0572

■ "The lilac-colored exterior lets you know you've found" this "Webster Groves gem", which some St. Louisans can't forget "used to be a gas station"; clearly, it's been the "best conversion ever", since surveyors salivate over the "creative, nuanced New American cooking" ("especially the outstanding seafood") of "genius David Guempel"; the "hosts and servers are always welcoming" too, making this flower a "perennial favorite."

Tampa/Sarasota

TOP 10 FOOD RANKING

	Restaurant	Cuisine Type
29	Ritz-Carlton Dining Rm.	French
28	Caffe Paradiso	Northern Italian
	Lafite	Continental/New American
	Blue Heron	Eclectic
27	Beach Bistro	New American/Med.
	Bijou Café	Continental/New American
	Bern's	Steakhouse
	Mise en Place	Eclectic
	Bistro 41	New American
	Grill at Feather Sound	New American

ADDITIONAL NOTEWORTHY PLACES

Café L'Europe	Continental/European
Euphemia Haye	International
Jasmine	Thai
Jonathan's	Continental/Eclectic
Maison Blanche	French
Maritana Grille	Floribbean
Michael's on East	New American
Ophelia's	Eclectic
SideBern's	Asian Fusion
Zoria	Eclectic/New American

F | D | S | C

BEACH BISTRO [S] 27 | 24 | 26 | $48

Resort 66, 6600 Gulf Dr. (66th St.), Holmes Beach, 941-778-6444

■ "In a word, fabulous!" gush gastronomes about this "little" New American–Med "jewel" tucked away in unassuming quarters on the "water's edge" in Holmes Beach; yes, it's "cramped", but "what it lacks in elbow room" it more than "makes up" for in its "subtle, complex" and "excellent" fare, award-winning wine list and "knowledgeable" service, not to mention its "spectacular sunset" views; it's so "marvelous all around" that the charmed sigh "when I die, I hope this is heaven."

BERN'S STEAK HOUSE [S] 27 | 22 | 27 | $49

1208 S. Howard Ave. (bet. Marjorie & Watrous Sts.), Tampa, 813-251-2421

■ Just about "the best place in Florida for steaks", this "institution" has been drawing carnivores to Tampa's Hyde Park since 1957 with its "outstanding" aged cuts served by a "knowledgeable staff" in multi-roomed, "bordello"-like quarters; "it's as much a show as a meal" if you go on "the must tour" of the kitchen and the award-winning wine cellar; P.S. "don't miss the dessert room" upstairs, which boasts an exhaustive menu of decadent finales.

BIJOU CAFÉ [S] 27 | – | 25 | $40

1287 First St. (Pineapple St.), Sarasota, 941-366-8111

■ After a fire and nine-month renovation, this "Downtown delight" in Sarasota's Theater District is back, "never disappointing" its tony devotees thanks to chef-owner Jean-Pierre Knaggs's "outstanding" menu of "divine" Continental–New American "classics" and the pampering attention of his "caring staff"; the newly expanded interior brings breathing room to what was once a "cramped" "old gas station" from the '30s.

Bistro 41 [S] 27 | 21 | 25 | $33

Bell Tower Shops, 13499 S. Cleveland Ave. (Daniels Pkwy.), Ft. Myers, 941-466-4141

■ "Located in an upscale shopping center", this "surprise treat" with "really good decor" and a "nice bar area" is "convenient for shoppers as well as residents" of Ft. Myers, many of whom report they're "never disappointed" by its "good variety" of "innovative" New American dishes, "finely presented" by a "top-notch" staff whose "attentive service" befits the "fashionable surroundings"; P.S. regulars "like to eat outside" on the thatch-covered patio.

BLUE HERON [S] 28 | 24 | 27 | $37

Shoppes at Clover Pl., 3285 Tampa Rd. (bet. Lake St. George & US 19), Palm Harbor, 727-789-5176

■ Perhaps the "best stop in North Pinellas County" for "fine upscale dining" is this "romantic" Palm Harbor "gem" renowned for chef and co-owner Robert Stea's "unique" Eclectic menu of "exciting" "fusion" "creations" that are "unsurpassed in quality" ("particularly the seafood"), accompanied by a "well-appointed wine list" and served by a "quick and sharp" staff; the Decor score does not reflect a recent remodeling.

Café L'Europe [S] 23 | 25 | 24 | $42

431 St. Armands Circle (Hwy. 41), Sarasota, 941-388-4415

◪ "Traditional"-ists who've been "missing the old standards" since this "longtime Sarasota" institution on "lively St. Armands Circle" "switched cooking styles" will be "pleased" to know that owner Titus Letschert has "changed direction in the kitchen" yet again, hiring chef Keith Daum and abandoning the "cutting-edge" approach in favor of a classic "old-world" Continental-European menu; with its "superb wine list", "elegant" setting and "exceptional service", this "class" act is hard to beat as a "dress-up" place for "special occasions."

CAFFE PARADISO 28 | 24 | 26 | $35

St. Croix Plaza, 4205 S. MacDill Ave. (bet. Knight & Wallcraft Aves.), Tampa, 813-835-6622

■ *"Perfecto!"* cheer admirers of this "family-run" hideaway in South Tampa that feels just "like being in Italy" thanks to its "authentic", "delicious" Northern-style dishes and "relaxing yet elegant" surroundings; the "friendly" service is indulgently "personalized", and with such "moderate prices" patrons can often return to "feel pampered."

Euphemia Haye [S] 26 | 23 | 24 | $45

5540 Gulf of Mexico Dr. (Gulfbay Rd.), Longboat Key, 941-383-3633

■ "Absolutely the best restaurant for roast duckling" (the house specialty), this "consistently excellent" Longboat Key treasure offers seating options in the "quirkily" decorated yet "romantic" downstairs space and upstairs in the "casual" Haye Loft piano bar; either way, expect a "superb" International dinner delivered by a staff that pays "attention to every detail"; just be sure to check out the "awesome dessert room", "the place to go" for sweets.

Grill at Feather Sound | 27 | 22 | 22 | $39 |

2325 Ulmerton Rd. (Egret Blvd.), Clearwater, 727-571-3400

■ "Trendy in the best sense of the word", this Clearwater American grill manages to be *très* "chic" despite its location in a "strip mall" (with "no view of Feather Sound" to boot); its hip clientele is drawn to its "outstanding" menu (house-smoked pork tenderloin with peach chutney is a signature dish), "sophisticated" ambiance and "excellent, knowledgeable" service; the only downside: the "terrible noise" when the house is full.

Jasmine Thai 🖪 | 26 | 22 | 24 | $24 |

13248 N. Dale Mabry Hwy. (Fletcher Ave.), Tampa, 813-968-1501

■ Management's assertion that the princess of Thailand ate at this "smallish strip-mall eatery" on a visit to the Tampa area is wholly plausible considering the high ratings for its "great food", such as "excellent pad Thai" or "good" whole red snapper followed by "yummy coconut ice cream"; the decor sports a purple-hued garden look, and a "pleasant" staff that provides "polite service" rounds out its appeal.

Jonathan's | – | – | – | M |

6777 Manatee Ave. W. (67th St.), Bradenton, 941-761-1177

With this fine-dining destination, creative chef-owner Jonathan Shute has raised the bar in a Bradenton strip mall previously unaccustomed to white tablecloths and fresh flowers; true to his New Orleans heritage, he offers his own take on haute Creole classics such as crawfish étouffée, but his ambitious Continental-Eclectic cuisine reaches further afield than across the Gulf for its inspiration; similarly, the cozy bar boasts an international array of wines, single-malt scotches and rare cognacs; N.B. now open for lunch from October through May.

LAFITE AT THE REGISTRY RESORT | 28 | 28 | 27 | $53 |

Registry Resort, 475 Seagate Dr. (south of Vanderbilt Beach Rd.), Naples, 941-597-3232

■ Housed in one of the tonier properties in tony Naples, this Continental–New American resplendent with crystal chandeliers and beveled mirrors is the embodiment of opulence; its sumptuous dishes are simply "excellent" and presented with "elegance", but with such "break-the-bank" prices, it may be best reserved for "special occasions"; N.B. be sure to call for the latest information on off-season closures.

Maison Blanche 🖪 | – | – | – | E |

Four Winds Beach Resort, 2605 Gulf of Mexico Dr. (Bay Isles Pkwy.), Longboat Key, 941-383-8088

After a decade in Paris, chef-owners Jose Martinez and Pascal Feraud transplanted their restaurant to the Four Winds Resort at Longboat Key's Gulf beach; resplendent with a chic, starkly modern design, it features fine French food fashioned from the freshest local ingredients – from seafood and meats to homemade breads and ice creams – accented by attentive service and a wine list that's half Gallic and half American; N.B. the sea bass and warm chocolate cake are standouts, as is the degustation menu.

Maritana Grille [S] 27 | 26 | 25 | $53

Don CeSar Beach Resort, 3400 Gulf Blvd. (Pinellas Bayway), St. Petersburg Beach, 727-360-1882

■ The signature dining room at St. Pete's historic Don CeSar Beach Resort, this "wonderful" "jewel of a restaurant" earns enthusiastic accolades for its "innovative", "delicious" Floribbean menu, "classy" environment decorated with an aquatic motif and "top"-notch service; though it may be a "little overpriced", it's "fabulous in all regards" and even boasts a chef's table, set up right in the kitchen.

MICHAEL'S ON EAST 26 | 26 | 24 | $43

Midtown Plaza, 1212 East Ave. S. (bet. Bahia Vista & Prospect Sts.), Sarasota, 941-366-0007

■ You'll think you've "died and gone to NYC" at this Sarasota "institution" (the Gulf Coast's Most Popular restaurant) that "seduces" with "outstanding" New American fare "served with elegance" in a "sweeping neo-art deco" setting, a "sophisticated" surprise given its strip-mall location; "dependably terrific in all departments", it's a "lively" "'in' spot for power lunches", "fine wine tasting events" and dinners that are near-"perfect every time"; N.B. the Food score does not reflect the post-*Survey* arrival of chef John Zottoli.

Mise en Place 27 | 23 | 24 | $41

442 W. Kennedy Blvd. (Grand Central St.), Tampa, 813-254-5373

■ Expect a "big-city buzz" upon entering this "comfortable", pastel-colored Eclectic in Downtown Tampa, where chef-owner Marty Blitz proffers an "innovative" weekly menu of "outstanding" dishes employing "exotic ingredients" (ostrich, wild boar, purple potatoes); a "great wine program" featuring California bottlings (including selections "from smaller wineries") and "good-value" prices further explain why admirers "do not miss" a chance to dine here.

OPHELIA'S [S] 26 | 25 | 24 | $41

9105 Midnight Pass Rd. (south of Turtle Beach), Siesta Key, 941-349-2212

■ "Siesta Key's most romantic waterfront" eatery may well be this Eclectic "date place" where "superior chef" Mitch Rosenbaum creates "imaginative", "superb" fare enhanced by an "beautiful" interior and outdoor seating with a "can't-be-beat view" of the bay; factor in an "excellent" wine selection and "outstanding" service from a "high-class" staff and ("pricey" though it may be) the whole package is simply "tops" for a "formal special evening."

RITZ-CARLTON DINING ROOM [S] 29 | 29 | 28 | $56

The Ritz-Carlton Naples, 280 Vanderbilt Beach Rd. (US 41), Naples, 941-598-6644

■ "What all fine restaurants should be", this "really special", beautifully appointed dining room in the Ritz-Carlton Naples (voted No. 1 for Food on the Gulf Coast) provides "luxury at its best", showcasing "excellent" classic French cuisine accompanied by a wine selection of nearly 700 labels and proffered by an impeccable pro staff ("if you want to feel pampered, this is the place"); P.S. the eight-course blind "tasting menu is expensive but a real challenge."

SideBern's S   27 | 23 | 23 | $36

2208 Morrison Ave. (S. Howard Ave.), Tampa, 813-258-2233

■ Fans of the "excellent Bern's Steak House" say "hats off" to this SoHo "spin-off" that gives chef-partner Jeannie Pierola a "chance to show off" with her "innovative" Asian-accented "fusion" dishes (don't miss the "unique" dim sum or exquisite desserts); factor in an "incredible wine list", "chic" atmosphere and "smooth" service, and it's easy to see why so many admirers "love this place."

Zoria S   26 | 18 | 24 | $36

1934 Hillview St. (Tamiami Trail S.), Sarasota, 941-955-4457

■ Lovers of "superb cuisine" insist "it doesn't get much better than this" Eclectic–New American in Sarasota's trendy Southside Village, where the "inventive menu" features "excellent" dishes marked by "lovely presentations" (including deliciously "deadly" desserts); the only drawback is the somewhat "modest" (some say "blah") decor.

TOP 10 FOOD RANKING

	Restaurant	Cuisine Type
28	Dish, The	New American
27	Grill at Hacienda del Sol	New American
26	Vivace	Northern Italian
	Ventana Room	New American
	Janos	Southwestern
	Le Rendez-Vous	French
25	Cafe Poca Cosa	Mexican
	Wildflower	New American
	Stone Ashley	New French
	Gold Room	SW/Continental

ADDITIONAL NOTEWORTHY PLACES

Anthony's/Catalinas	Continental
Arizona Inn	Continental
Bistro Zin	New American
Café Terra Cotta	Southwestern
Fuego!	Southwestern
J Bar	Latin American
Jonathan's Tucson Cork	Steakhouse/SW
Kingfisher	New American/Seafood
McMahon's	Steakhouse
Tack Room	Southwestern

F | D | S | C

Anthony's in the Catalinas [S] 22 | 24 | 22 | $50

6440 N. Campbell Ave. (E. Skyline Dr.), 520-299-1771

◪ Though you may "need two credit cards to pay for dinner", this "beautiful" Continental showcase's "legendary wine list" and "dynamite city views" are "first-class"; disappointed diners, however, who cite the "old-fashioned menu" and "pretentious" service as proof that it's "overrated", lament that it's now a mere "shadow of what used to be a great Tucson experience."

Arizona Inn [S] 21 | 25 | 23 | $42

Arizona Inn, 2200 E. Elm St. (bet. N. Campbell Ave. & N. Tucson Blvd.), 520-325-1541

■ Graced with a timeless "serenity", this "lovely" Continental "throwback" in a "secluded" old hotel is revered for its "exquisite" gardens and "solicitous", "old-style" service, capturing the "understated elegance" of the "'30s West"; it may "not be a place for the young crowd", but it does provide a "charming" glimpse of "old Arizona at its best", especially at "afternoon tea in the parlor."

Bistro Zin ◐[S] 23 | 22 | 23 | $38

1865 E. River Rd. (Campbell Rd.), 520-299-7799

■ "Wear black and bring a megaphone" if you visit this "big-city" bistro (owned by Sam Fox of Wildflower) because it's as "chic" as it is "noisy"; the main draw is the "impressive" selection of wines by the glass (also offered in nearly two dozen "interesting flights"), which teams well with the "excellent", "eclectic" French-accented New American dishes, all "attractively presented" (the servers are "knowledgeable", so listen to their pairing suggestions); P.S. "don't miss the chocolate desserts."

Cafe Poca Cosa 🖺 | 25 | 21 | 21 | $26 |
Clarion Santa Rita Hotel, 88 E. Broadway Blvd. (Scott Ave.), 520-622-6400

■ "Rollicking yet somehow intimate", this Downtown "treasure" may well be the "number one spot to take out-of-town guests" thanks to Suzana Davila's "amazing" Mexican cooking (her chalkboard menu changes twice daily, but you "can't go wrong with the chef's tasting plate") and the "unique" vibe; adding to the "festive" atmosphere are the colorful Oaxacan folk art masks mounted on bright walls and the south-of-the-border music, making this an "absolutely essential dining experience in Tucson."

CAFÉ TERRA COTTA 🖺 | 21 | 21 | 19 | $33 |
3500 E. Sunrise Dr. (E. River Rd.), 520-577-8100

☑ Voted the Most Popular restaurant in Tucson, this "happening" Southwestern "scene" is "as culturally important as the San Xavier Mission" to its many acolytes; boasting a "beautiful view of the valley", it's an "upbeat" place with an "imaginative menu", "excellent wine list" and "great diablo margaritas (infused with chiles)", along with a "lovely" patio; nevertheless, former friends contend that it's "not what it used to be" (having "lost some of its charm in its new location").

DISH, THE | 28 | 19 | 25 | $38 |
3200 E. Speedway Blvd. (Country Club Blvd.), 520-326-1714

■ "Wow!" exclaim enthusiasts about this "tiny" New American "diamond" "hidden behind" the Rum Runner Wine & Cheese shop, the "finest gourmet spot in town"; ranked No. 1 for Food in Tucson, it's a "perfect place for a quiet dinner" over "original" "dishes of delectable delights", accompanied by a "fantastic wine selection" and presented by a "knowledgeable" staff; it may be "a bit cramped" (there are "very few tables", so "reservations are a must"), "but who cares given the quality and service?"

Fuego! 🖺 | 23 | 17 | 21 | $38 |
6958 E. Tanque Verde Rd. (Sabino Canyon Rd.), 520-886-1745

☑ "Local personality" Alan Zeman "keeps his eye on the details" at his "festive" Southwestern bistro whose name "means fire" in Spanish and whose "innovative" menu highlights "flaming platters" of "devilishly good" appetizers and wild game; though he exhibits a particularly "deft hand" with exotica like ostrich, all his creations offer a "successful combination of flavors and textures", so despite "inconsistent" service, fans swear it's "well worth it."

Gold Room 🖺 | 25 | 26 | 23 | $48 |
Westward Look Resort, 245 E. Ina Rd. (bet. N. 1st Ave. & Oracle Rd.), 520-297-1151

☑ "Sublime views" of Downtown enhance the experience at this "magical" dining room, "a major treat for the eyes and palate"; the "lovely surroundings", "superb" Southwestern-Continental menu and "exhaustive wine list" bolster its reputation as an "elegant" "celebration place", but be forewarned that some say the "snotty" staff ("pretentious to the nth degree") "can leave you wondering if you're invisible."

GRILL AT HACIENDA DEL SOL 🖸   27 | 27 | 24 | $51
Hacienda del Sol, 5601 N. Hacienda del Sol (bet. E. River Rd. & E. Sunrise Dr.), 520-529-3500

☑ Once a "favorite rendezvous spot for Tracy and Hepburn", this "romantic jewel on a hill" with an "interesting history" epitomizes "Tucson's casual elegance"; surveyors suggest you "get a window table" in the "gorgeous" dining room to best enjoy the "city lights" (a "memorable view") while splurging on "fabulous" New American fare; the smitten insist that it's "a must-try for a special occasion", but cynics feel it "doesn't live up to expectations."

JANOS   26 | 25 | 24 | $57
Westin La Paloma, 3770 E. Sunrise Dr. (bet. N. Campbell Ave. & N. Swan Rd.), 520-615-6100

☑ "Still one of Arizona's best" for "special-occasion" dining, this "formal" "oasis" in the foothills is the brainchild of Janos Wilder, whose "sublime" French-inspired Southwestern cooking is "inventively presented" and beautifully paired with an award-winning wine list; turned out in an "exquisite" setting with a "spectacular view of Tucson", dinner here is "always an exciting surprise", even if dissenters feel that it's "too pricey for the portions" and "too pretentious for this town."

J Bar   23 | 22 | 22 | $31
Westin La Paloma, 3770 E. Sunrise Dr. (bet. N. Campbell Ave. & N. Swan Rd.), 520-615-6100

■ Cost-conscious diners crow about getting "Janos Wilder's food at half the price" at his "spirited" and far more "casual" offshoot (adjacent to Janos); from the open kitchen emerge "blissful" grilled Latin American specialties infused with "wonderfully original flavors" (the "jerked pork is fantastic"), while the handsome bar, custom-made of tin and mirrors, hosts a convivial social scene; "big food without big attitude" plus "a mean margarita" – "you can't ask for much more."

Jonathan's Tucson Cork 🖸   24 | 19 | 21 | $34
6320 E. Tanque Verde Rd. (bet. E. Pima St. & N. Wilmot Rd.), 520-296-1631

■ Loyalists continue to beat a path to this "dependable" '60s-era steakhouse for its "great" Southwestern spin on certified angus beef, as well as its "well-prepared" game dishes ("outstanding ostrich"); regulars say it's "always a pleasure" to dine here because they know they'll get a "friendly greeting" and an "excellent meal for the price" (it's "been on the Tucson scene for a long time, and it knows its business").

Kingfisher ●🖸   22 | 17 | 21 | $32
2564 E. Grant Rd. (N. Tucson Blvd.), 520-323-7739

■ Though the decor at this New American seafood house draws divided opinions – "weird" vs. "cool" – not so the "eclectic" menu (starring some of the "freshest fish without a sea nearby"), which is praised as one of the most "original" in Tucson; backed by a "great" wine list and "exceptionally accommodating" service, it's "excellent across the board", and "thank goodness there's a fine restaurant that's still open after a play or concert."

Le Rendez-Vous 🅂   26 | 17 | 22 | $44
3844 E. Ft. Lowell Rd. (N. Alvernon Way), 520-323-7373
■ Tucson Francophiles finagle a "trip to France without leaving town" by visiting this time-honored "quality act" where the "honest, authentic" cooking is "rich" and "wonderfully decadent"; the "traditional" menu may hold "no surprises", but when "classics" such as duck à l'orange, sweetbreads and crêpes suzette are "prepared so artfully with top-notch ingredients", who cares?

McMahon's   21 | 24 | 20 | $50
Prime Steakhouse 🅂
2959 N. Swan Rd. (bet. E. Ft. Lowell Rd. & E. Glenn St.), 520-327-2333
◪ "Contemporary Western art" provides a "stylish" backdrop for the "local power brokers" who patronize this "elegant" "expense-account enclave", long a "favorite" for "fine cuts of meat", an "outstanding wine cellar" and its "excellent" piano lounge, live nightly music and "great cigar bar"; the less impressed, however, conclude "everything is good but overpriced."

Stone Ashley ●🅂   25 | 29 | 26 | $62
6400 E. El Dorado Circle (bet. Speedway & Wilmont Blvds.), 520-886-9700
■ Make your "big night out" a "memorable", "over-the-top experience" by taking a splurge at this "ornate" villa where the ambiance is "formal yet relaxing" and the appointments most "comfortable"; nearly rivaling the "gorgeous" surroundings are the "superb" New French menu and "impeccable" service (perhaps the "most attentive in the city"); of course it's "very pricey", but it's "truly worth a visit" for a "special occasion", so "just go and be enchanted."

Tack Room   23 | 25 | 25 | $62
7300 E. Vactor Ranch Trail (Tanque Verde Rd.), 520-722-2800
◪ Since 1965, this adobe hacienda has been an "excellent choice for out-of-town guests" hungry for a taste of the Old West; still a "sentimental favorite" among "cattle-ranching types" because it has had the "good sense not to change" much, it continues to serve "excellent" Southwestern fare and a "distinctive wine list" by an "exemplary" staff; skeptics, though, sniff "not as sharp as it used to be."

VENTANA ROOM   26 | 27 | 26 | $63
Loews Ventana Canyon Resort, 7000 N. Resort Dr. (N. Kolb Rd.), 520-299-2020
■ Nestled in the foothills and affording a "beautiful view of the city", this "fancy" New American "gem" is "a hotel restaurant of the best kind"; in an "elegant" setting made "romantic" by "lovely" live music, look forward to "outstanding" dishes made "with only the finest ingredients", an "excellent wine list" and "crisp" service; for an even more "superlative dining experience", book the private chef's table in the kitchen; sure "it costs, but they do it right."

VIVACE   26 | 22 | 25 | $37
St. Philip's Plaza, 4310 N. Campbell Ave. (River Rd.), 520-795-7221
■ Loquacious locals can't say enough about chef-owner Daniel Scordato's Northern Italian "class act" (he "deserves more credit than he gets"); better "forget about your diet" here because his

"inspired" cooking is so "yummy" that it's hard to stop eating the "amazing pesto olive oil dip", "divine fish" and "desserts that give new meaning to fruit"; consider too the "wonderful" atmosphere ("never stuffy") and "attentive yet unobtrusive" service and it's easy to see why regulars come "back for more again and again."

Wildflower 🖫

25 | 21 | 21 | $32

Casas Adobes, 7037 N. Oracle Rd. (Ina Rd.), 520-219-4230
☑ A trompe l'oeil ceiling depicting clouds and giant paintings of wildflowers give this "eclectic" "hot spot" a "stylish" look despite its "strip-mall" setting; it's an "excellent choice" for "exceptional" New American fare (including "can't-miss" desserts) and a "solid wine list" presented by a staff that treats each guest "with care"; though the "impossibly noisy" interior "detracts" from the experience, the "pretty" covered patio, a "quieter but still lively venue" with a view of the mountains, comes "recommended."

Washington, DC

TOP 20 FOOD RANKING

Restaurant	Cuisine Type
29 Inn at Little Washington	New American
28 L'Auberge Chez François	Country French
27 Makoto	Japanese
Kinkead's	New American/Seafood
Maestro	N&S Italian
Gerard's Place	New French
Citronelle	New French
Prime Rib	Steakhouse
Obelisk	Northern Italian
26 Marcel's	New French/Belgian
Galileo	N&S Italian
Melrose	New American
Vidalia	New American/Southern
Four & Twenty Blackbirds	New American
1789	New American
Tosca	Northern Italian
25 Taberna del Alabardero	Spanish
Nora	New American
L'Auberge Provençale	French
Bistrot Lepic	French Bistro

ADDITIONAL NOTEWORTHY PLACES

Bistro Bis	French Bistro
Bombay Club	Indian
Bread Line	International/Bakery
Cafe Atlantico	Nuevo Latino
Cafe 15	New French
Caucus Room	New American/Steakhouse
Colvin Run Tavern	New American
DC Coast	New American/Seafood
Equinox	New American
Jaleo	Spanish
Johnny's Half Shell	Seafood
Majestic Cafe	New American
Old Ebbitt Grill	American
Palena	New American
Pizzeria Paradiso	Pizza
Seasons	New American
701	New American
TenPenh	Pan-Asian
2 Amys	Pizza
Zola	New American

Bistro Bis ⬛　　　24 | 24 | 22 | $45

*Hotel George, 15 E St., NW (bet. Capitol St. & New Jersey Ave.),
202-661-2700*

⬛ Just "steps from the Capitol", this "sophisticated" French bistro
housed in the Hotel George cossets with a "film noir elegance"
and "polished" but "not intimidating" manners; the kitchen's
"clever" takes on Gallic classics and the cellar's *très* "fine"
collection of regional wines make it a "great place for celebrating
an event", while the "who's who" scene around the "fabulous"
zinc-topped bar earns it the sobriquet "Manhattan in DC."

Bistrot Lepic ⬛　　　25 | 20 | 22 | $42

1736 Wisconsin Ave., NW (S St.), 202-333-0111

◪ Chef-owner Bruno Fortin's "adorable little French place" in
Upper Georgetown turns out "top-notch" bistro dishes with
"panache" (his signature veal cheeks are the "best" in the city,
and he does "wonders with fish"); the cooking is such a "wonderful
treat" that his many admirers readily forgive the flaws, namely
the "tight" spacing, the "noise" and the "Franco-efficient (read:
chilly)" service.

Bombay Club ⬛　　　25 | 26 | 25 | $40

815 Connecticut Ave., NW (bet. H & I Sts.), 202-659-3727

⬛ Only steps from the White House, this "lovely" Indian "oasis"
distinguished by "refined elegance" transports visitors "back to
the days of the Raj" with "gracious", "unobtrusive" pampering
that makes even bureaucrats "feel like viceroys"; as "first-class"
as the service is the "superb" fare, "subtly spiced" yet "bursting
with flavor", making this "special-occasion" destination one of
the "best dining experiences in DC."

Bread Line　　　23 | 11 | 14 | $12

1751 Pennsylvania Ave., NW (bet. 17th & 18th Sts.), 202-822-8900

◪ "Elevating fast food" to high art, Mark Furstenberg's International
bakery/cafe on Pennsylvania Avenue has made many an addict out
of the employees at the White House and World Bank, who can't
get enough of his "fantastic" artisanal breads, "clever" sandwiches
or "divine" desserts; "first-timers shouldn't be thrown off by the
noise", the "spartan" decor or the "confusing lines", because
this place is really an "amazingly" "well-oiled machine" and it
may be the "best cheap lunch ever."

Cafe Atlantico ⬛　　　23 | 22 | 21 | $37

405 Eighth St., NW (bet. D & E Sts.), 202-393-0812

⬛ This "sexy", "multilevel" Penn Quarter Nuevo Latino will "spice
up your evening" with "innovative" dishes such as "outstanding"
guacamole ("made at the table"), "not-to-be-missed" quesadilla
de huitlacoche, "fantastic desserts" and "dangerous" cocktails;
not only is it "chaotic fun" and a "unique" "adventure", but it
offers a "fabulous" Saturday dim sum–style brunch; N.B. given
its smooth management, chef Christy Velie's departure shouldn't
diminish its wide appeal.

Cafe 15 ⬛　　　‒ | ‒ | ‒ | VE

Sofitel Lafayette Sq., 806 15th St., NW (bet. H & I Sts.), 202-737-8800
New French luxe is the lure at the White House precinct's latest
lobbying lair, a petite boîte with a seasonal menu overseen by
three-star Michelin chef Antoine Westermann that's well suited

to the dignified, deco-feeling hotel dining room; Le Bar, its jewel-toned lounge with plush armchairs and couches arranged for informal meetings, offers more casual dining options; be warned, though, that the lofty prices are as Parisian as the fare.

Caucus Room 22 | 24 | 23 | $49

401 Ninth St., NW (D St.), 202-393-1300

[◪] Just a stone's throw from Capitol Hill, this "state-of-the-art lobbyist's hangout" with an "imposing gentlemen's club" ambiance is a "very Washingtonian" political hub; whether you opt for a "leather booth" or a "private" room, you can expect "very good" steaks ("so big it should be called the Carcass Room") and New American fare served by, "seemingly, one waiter per chair", though the powerful tabs lead pundits to quip "with these prices, [co-investors] Tom Boggs and Haley Barbour can leave their day jobs."

CITRONELLE [S] 27 | 26 | 25 | $66

(aka Michel Richard's Citronelle)

Latham Hotel, 3000 M St., NW (30th St.), 202-625-2150

■ Revel in a "gastronomic tour de force" at this "attractive" "destination" in Georgetown, the "unforgettable" brainchild of "jovial" chef-owner Michel Richard; from the show kitchen emerge "intricate", "inventive" New French dishes, accompanied by "superb" wines and "expertly served" in an California-"chic" interior with a color-shifting mood wall; "from start to finish", "it doesn't get much better than this", but for an even more "extraordinary" evening, book the private chef's table.

Colvin Run Tavern [S] 25 | 25 | 24 | $56

Fairfax Sq., 8045 Leesburg Pike (Gallows Rd.), Tysons Corner, VA, 703-356-9500

[◪] An "upbeat" haven of "city sophistication among the glut of Tysons Corner steakhouses", this "exciting" "addition" courtesy of Bob Kinkead looks nothing at all like a tavern; it's a "warm", "comfortable" "class act" with an "outstanding" New American menu that specializes in "exceptional" roasted meats "carved at the table" by "polished" servers; though a few faultfinders quibble that it "needs to smooth out some edges", plenty of groupies already consider it "easily one of the best in Northern Virginia."

DC Coast 25 | 24 | 23 | $45

Tower Bldg., 1401 K St., NW (14th St.), 202-216-5988

[◪] "Electricity is in the air" at this "young power brokers'" haunt Downtown that boasts a "gorgeous" deco-style, two-tiered space and a "fabulous" New American seafood-slanted menu "inspired by three coasts"; despite "unacceptable" noise (sit upstairs if you can), a "velvet-rope" vibe and tabs in the "luxury" stratosphere, followers promise that you'll have a "memorable" meal, because, after all, "food is the real star here."

Equinox [S] 25 | 21 | 23 | $49

818 Connecticut Ave., NW (I St.), 202-331-8118

[◪] Owners Todd and Ellen Gray and their "warmhearted" staff obviously "really like what they're doing" at this "superb" New American "centrally located" near the White House, and they lend it "genuine" appeal; a recent James Beard award nominee, "talented" chef Todd showcases his "original", "sumptuous" seasonal dishes in "tasteful", "comfortable" surroundings, eliciting "huzzahs" from admirers, even if a minority "expects more from such hype."

Four & Twenty Blackbirds [S] 26 | 21 | 23 | $44

650 Zachary Taylor Hwy. (Rte. 647), Flint Hill, VA, 540-675-1111

■ Nestled in the "scenic" Virginia foothills, this "delightful" New American "destination" is a "welcoming" "country gem" "in the middle of nowhere", making it a "perfect getaway from DC"; though the "imaginative" gourmet menu changes every three weeks, you "can't go wrong" with any selection because everything is homemade, "very fresh" and "exceptional"; it's "well worth the drive", so "if you haven't taken the time to dine here, you need to reevaluate your priorities."

GALILEO [S] 26 | 23 | 24 | $58

1110 21st St., NW (bet. L & M Sts.), 202-293-7191

LABORATORIO DEL GALILEO ◐

1110 21st St., NW (bet. L & M Sts.), 202-331-0880

■ Esteemed as the "Prada of Italian cuisine", this "epicurean must" in the Golden Triangle is where DC players take their "best clients" for an "unmatched" "experience" orchestrated by Roberto Donna; for the "ultimate insider's dinner", book a table in the Laboratorio adjacent to the main room at Galileo, a private dining space with a showcase kitchen, from which emerges a "spectacular", custom-designed series of 10–12 "complex" tasting courses "perfectly matched" with wines from the "divine" cellar.

Gerard's Place 27 | 22 | 24 | $63

915 15th St., NW (bet. I & K Sts.), 202-737-4445

■ "Tasteful and restrained", Downtown's most "Parisian" of places "wows" devotees with "fabulous", "imaginative" New French interpretations prepared with "finesse" (don't miss the "outstanding lobster" or "indescribable" chocolate soup); it's "always among the best" destinations in DC thanks to chef-owner Gerard Pangaud's "exquisite" touch, "elegant" surroundings and "precise" (if "arrogant") service; it's "in a class by itself – too bad the prices are as well", but "on Mondays, you can BYO."

INN AT LITTLE WASHINGTON [S] 29 | 28 | 29 | VE

Main & Middle Sts., Washington, VA, 540-675-3800

◪ "Two perfectionists" – Patrick O'Connell and Reinhardt Lynch – treat "dining as an art form" at their "exquisite" Virginia country inn, and it shows, as this "unequalled star" has again been voted No. 1 for Food in the Washington area; the owners have long made it their mission to ensure that "each guest enjoys the whole evening", from the moment they step into the "over-the-top" "fantasy" setting through every bite of the "magical" New American courses served by an "exceptional" staff; "could any meal be worth this much money?" – this one is.

Jaleo [S] 23 | 21 | 19 | $29

480 Seventh St., NW (E St.), 202-628-7949

7271 Woodmont Ave. (Elm St.), Bethesda, MD, 301-913-0003

◪ What gives these "cool" "crowd-pleasers" in the Penn Quarter and Bethesda their "amazing staying power"? – more than 1,500 surveyors say it's their "upbeat" energy, "delectable" Spanish tapas that are "fun to share" ("every pick is better than the last", so have a "little of everything") and "superb" Iberian wines; of

course, the "downside" of their raging success is the "frustrating"
mob scene ("wish they took reservations"), though the "best"
sangria going makes "waiting" in the "jam-packed bar" bearable.

Johnny's Half Shell | 23 | 17 | 20 | $34 |

2002 P St., NW (bet. 20th & 21st Sts.), 202-296-2021

◪ "Beautifully simple decor and simply great food" is the story
at this "fresh and sassy" Dupont Circle seafood bistro whose
"dreamy" "crispy oysters", inviting "little touches" (like the
homemade malt vinegar for the "great" fries) and "refreshingly
casual" vibe have many admirers clamoring for a seat; nitpickers,
on the other hand, find the portions "too small" and gripe that the
"lovely lighting" doesn't do enough to dress up the "spare" setting.

KINKEAD'S Ⓢ | 27 | 24 | 25 | $51 |

*2000 Pennsylvania Ctr., 2000 Pennsylvania Ave., NW (I St.),
202-296-7700*

■ Voted yet again Washington's Most Popular restaurant, chef-
owner Bob Kinkead's "winning" New American brasserie is lauded
for maintaining its "high standards"; as Foggy Bottom's "power
food" HQ, it's a "professionally run" "special-occasion" destination
that delivers "astounding" seafood dishes and a "superior" wine
list in a "supercharged atmosphere"; "a class act in all aspects",
it's "hands down" one of the "best" establishments in the capital,
even if "the elite" get "preferential" treatment.

L'AUBERGE CHEZ FRANÇOIS Ⓢ | 28 | 27 | 28 | $59 |

*332 Springvale Rd. (Beach Mill Rd.), Great Falls, VA,
703-759-3800*

■ A "magical" "pleasure from apéritif to soufflé", this "truly
special" Country French "treat" set on "lovely" bucolic grounds
in Great Falls has "epitomized" "romantic" dining for generations;
in "cozily" rustic quarters whose "charm can't be beat" and out
in the "glorious" garden, an "informed" but "not snotty" staff
brings to table "hearty", "outstanding" Alsatian dishes; despite
the "reservations hassle", the "experience as a whole" is so
"superb" that you're sure to "leave feeling tingly" all over.

L'Auberge Provençale Ⓢ | 25 | 26 | 25 | $66 |

13630 Lord Fairfax Hwy. (Rte. 50), Boyce, VA, 540-837-1375

◪ "French country dining with a Virginia hunt country address" is
the appeal of this "delightful escape" set in a "lovely", antique-
filled manor house, circa 1753, that "oozes charm" and "easy
elegance"; devotees laud the "rich" dishes and "polished"
service and recommend an "overnight stay" in the inn (if only
to "get the fantastic breakfast"), but a "disappointed" minority
feels it "doesn't live up to its reputation."

MAESTRO Ⓢ | 27 | 28 | 28 | $69 |

*Ritz-Carlton Tysons Corner, 1700 Tysons Blvd. (International Dr.),
Tysons Corner, VA, 703-917-5498*

■ Open only since last year, this "exquisite" "gourmet heaven" at
Tysons Corner's Ritz-Carlton is already a "top contender" in the
"fine-dining" stakes; "genius chef" Fabio Trabocchi, who dares to
"take risks", orchestrates a "world-class" "symphony of Italian
flavors" from a "gorgeous open kitchen" that only "adds to the
evening entertainment"; enhanced by a "luxuriously" appointed
space and an "impeccable" staff, it adds up to an "ultimate dining
performance" that's "worth every penny" of admission.

Majestic Cafe S   23 | 21 | 21 | $36

911 King St. (Patrick St.), Alexandria, VA, 703-837-9117

◪ "Chef Susan Lindeborg does it again", this time in Old Town, where she has "re-created an atmospheric" art deco–style cafe from the "WWII" era; it's a "chic" spot to "be seen in" while partaking of "some of the classiest" Southern-accented New American cooking "you'll ever have" (save room for the "fabulous" layer cake); it may need to "work out a few kinks", but groupies already want to "sell our kitchen and eat every meal here."

MAKOTO S   27 | 24 | 25 | $53

4822 MacArthur Blvd., NW (Reservoir Rd.), 202-298-6866

■ Anticipate a "genuine Japanese experience" at this "peaceful little enclave" in the NW Palisades, designed for those "willing to be adventurous" (after removing their shoes); while the prix fixe menu offers a "great introduction for the novice", presenting a series of "tiny jewels", sushi connoisseurs swoon over the "sweet" morsels of fish that are "fresh beyond description"; legions attest that this is "as good as any place in Tokyo, at one third the price."

Marcel's S   26 | 25 | 25 | $58

2401 Pennsylvania Ave., NW (24th St.), 202-296-1166

■ Robert Wiedmaier's "brilliant", "inventive" French dishes tweaked with a Flemish flair and "lavishly presented" have earned him a devoted following at this "plush", "sophisticated" West End "star" that may "look stuffy but isn't" (though it is "accoustically challenged"); he and his "courtly" crew woo guests with "tip-top wine selections", "great" live music nightly in the bar and even complimentary "limousine service to and from the Kennedy Center", while still keeping the focus "on the food."

Melrose S   26 | 24 | 25 | $53

Park Hyatt Washington, 1201 24th St., NW (M St.), 202-955-3899

■ "Efficient for lunch, delightful for dinner", this "light and airy" "special-occasion" destination in the West End is an "oasis of calm", soothing with an "impressive" fountain-bedecked patio and "thoughtful" service; "talented" chef Brian McBride "does equally well cooking for a table of two or for a banquet", turning out "fabulous" New American fare; to the many fans who can't wait to "dine and dance the night away" on weekends, this "class act" "belies the hotel restaurant curse."

Nora   25 | 23 | 24 | $53

2132 Florida Ave., NW (bet. Connecticut & Massachusetts Aves.), 202-462-5143

◪ "Eat luxuriously and don't feel guilty" at this "outstanding" New American quartered in a "charming" carriage house above Dupont Circle; Nora Pouillon's "feel-good" ethic – create "beautiful" dishes based on "first-rate" "organic" products – is not only beneficial "for both your health and the environment", it also results in a "memorable" "feast"; though a "senator may well be at the next table", the staff will "make you feel like the center of attention", though foes don't buy the "arrogantly" PC philosophy.

Obelisk   27 | 22 | 26 | $60

2029 P St., NW (bet. 20th & 21st Sts.), 202-872-1180

◪ For gourmands who love food and wine, this "exquisite" Dupont Circle Northern Italian "treasure" is home to "36 of the best seats in town"; the "superb" five-course prix fixe menu changes daily, but it's always "thoughtfully" conceived and combines an "element of surprise along with authentic" touches; though the quarters are a bit "tight" and a few beaus feel that the decor is akin to an "old flame who could use some new makeup", the "first-rate" service team really "cares about doing it right."

Old Ebbitt Grill ●S   20 | 22 | 20 | $33 |
675 15th St., NW (bet. F & G Sts.), 202-347-4801
☑ "Who knows which Cabinet secretary will stop by for lunch" at this handsome "must-see" "legend" Downtown; a "powerhouse" at breakfast too and a "tradition" late at night at its four bars, this is a "classic" saloon with "brass and wood everywhere" and "well-prepared" all-American food on the plate; though spoilsports hiss "tired and touristy", with way "too many Republicans" in the house, you "can't get more DC" than here.

Palena   25 | 23 | 22 | $60 |
3529 Connecticut Ave., NW (Porter St.), 202-537-9250
☑ At their "refined" Cleveland Park venue, Frank Ruta's seasonal New American dishes (inspired by the cuisines of France and Italy) "awaken taste buds you didn't even know existed", while Ann Amernick's "fabulous" desserts are legendary; everything is "painstakingly prepared" (read: "slowly") and served in a "serene" room by a staff that's either "attentive" or "forgetful" (depending on the night); though most can't wait to "return", a few skeptics conclude "for all the lineage, not enough impact for the money."

Pizzeria Paradiso S   25 | 15 | 18 | $21 |
2029 P St., NW (bet. 20th & 21st Sts.), 202-223-1245
■ Paradise found rhapsodize acolytes of this "civilized" Dupont Circle pizzeria's "heavenly" wood-fired pies – the "best in DC" – made with a "crisp, light" crust and topped with all sorts of "scrumptious" "goodies" (its "great sandwiches and salads are only a bonus"); aside from the "long" prime-time "wait", most surveyors "come with high expectations – and they're fully "met."

Prime Rib   27 | 26 | 26 | $57 |
2020 K St., NW (bet. 20th & 21st Sts.), 202-466-8811
■ Surprisingly "snazzy" for a lobbyists' lair, this "high-class" K Street powerhouse is nearly as famed for its "wonderful" crab imperial as for its "melt-in-your-mouth" prime rib and "reasonably" priced fine wines; amid "gleaming" lacquered walls and "fresh flowers" all about, "gentlemen and ladies" are cosseted with "royal treatment"; though some find the ambiance a bit "stuffy", most appreciate its ageless appeal and advise when you want to "feel like a character in a '50s movie", dress up (jacket and tie required) and come here.

Seasons S   25 | 26 | 26 | $57 |
Four Seasons Hotel, 2800 Pennsylvania Ave., NW (28th St.), 202-944-2000
■ "Elegant in every respect", this "especially attractive" hotel dining room in Georgetown "maintains the high standards of the Four Seasons"; appointed with every "luxurious" detail, it promises "a wonderful experience" – from the "relaxing" ambiance to the "comfortably spaced tables" to the "impeccable" service; the "toque sits well" on new chef Doug Anderson, whose New American menu is "imaginative" and "superb" and who has made the Sunday brunch more "incredible" than ever.

701 S   23 | 23 | 23 | $45

701 Pennsylvania Ave., NW (7th St.), 202-393-0701
■ For a "great swanky night out" in the Penn Quarter, replete with "caviar and champagne" and "quiet jazz", it's hard to beat this "perpetual" New American favorite where "elegant is done right"; patrons come to be treated like "grown-ups" in a "sophisticated" setting that actually allows for conversation while dining on "tasteful" dishes brought to table by a "knowledgeable" team; delivering "true value for the quality", it "rarely disappoints."

1789 S   26 | 25 | 25 | $53

1226 36th St., NW (Prospect St.), 202-965-1789
■ Much, much more than just a "place to take your visiting parents", this "inviting" Federal period piece in Georgetown provides "formality" "without intimidation"; "genius" chef Ris Lacoste deftly "blends" old and new seasonal American recipes into "top-notch" renditions (her "superb" rack of lamb makes sure that "food is the star of the show" here), while the "outstanding" staff "goes out of its way for guests"; it's a "splurge", but the prix fixe menus are a "steal."

Taberna del Alabardero   25 | 26 | 25 | $52

1776 I St., NW (18th St.), 202-429-2200
■ "Old-world Spain comes alive" at this "gorgeous" "standout" near the World Bank, where "you can be romantic or all business" and still have a "memorable" meal; at the bar, the "international elite sips wine and eats tapas", while earthy regional dishes (including the "best paella this side of Valencia" and "perfect" stews) are served "with flair" in the "sumptuous" dining rooms by a "pampering" staff.

TenPenh   25 | 25 | 23 | $45

1001 Pennsylvania Ave., NW (10th St.), 202-393-4500
☑ "Atmosphere and attitude" reign at one of Downtown's most glamorous "destinations", a "dramatic" pastiche of Pan-Asian visuals and victuals where the "beautiful people" are part of the show; don't think for a second, though, that the food is secondary, because Jeff Tunks will "astonish" your taste buds with his "clever, creative" plays on the cuisines of Thailand, Vietnam, China, the Philippines and beyond, presenting his dishes as works of "art" on a plate; still, holdouts hoot "too bad you can't eat hipness."

Tosca S   26 | 24 | 23 | $53

1112 F St., NW (bet. 11th & 12th Sts.), 202-367-1990
☑ Downtown's "rising star" is this "svelte" showroom where chef Cesare Lanfranconi (ex Galileo) masterminds "fabulous" Northern Italian fare that pulls off a "refined" "balance of traditional and contemporary" styles, with many dishes inspired by his native Lombardy; his tasting menu is particularly "heavenly" and the "sophisticated" dining room is "a place to dress up for" and feel oh-so-"Cary Grant", but it's "still finding its way", and a few discordant notes can be detected in the "arrogant" service.

2 Amys S   22 | 14 | 17 | $22

3715 Macomb St., NW (Wisconsin Ave.), 202-885-5700
☑ Peter Pastan's (of Obelisk renown) "very special" new Italian gift brings wood-fired artisanal pies (crafted according to exacting standards set by the Verrace Pizza Napoletana trade association)

to this sunny, tiled venue in Northwest DC; his "dedication" to the "authenticity" of the art is obvious, even if those weaned on Domino's find these refined pizzas a bit "bland" and "not crunchy enough"; the consensus: "on its way to greatness, but it needs to work out a few kinks."

Vidalia S　　　26　23　24　$51
1990 M St., NW (bet. 19th & 20th Sts.), 202-659-1990

☑ Look forward to "a little love on every plate" and an "explosion of tastes" in your mouth at this "stylish" Dixie-influenced New American in the Golden Triangle; despite its basement setting, it delivers a "top-notch" "culinary adventure when you want something both delicious and a little different" (think pork short ribs with new turnips and baby carrots), but be forewarned that the service can be "slow"; P.S. turn "luxury dining" into a "deal" with the prix fixe lunch.

Zola　　　–　–　–　E
800 F St., NW (8th St.), 202-654-0999

Shadows, peepholes and sleek lines define this intriguing New American set in the Penn Quarter's new International Spy Museum, where windows in the rear of the booths let diners keep tabs on the kitchen as it turns out market-driven comfort foods that are equally appealing to your Kansas cousins, their congressmen and *their* young clerks; check it all out from a bar-stool perch or cater to your inner James Bond by booking a private room stocked with state-of-the-art audiovisual gadgets.

Indexes

CUISINES BY AREA

Atlanta

American (New)
Aria
Asher
Bacchanalia
BluePointe
Buckhead Diner
Canoe
dick & harry's
Food Studio
Mumbo Jumbo
Oscar's
Park 75
Van Gogh's
Asian
BluePointe
Sia's
Bakery
Alon's
Brazilian
Fogo de Chão
Chinese
Chopstix
Continental
Nikolai's Roof
Pano's & Paul's
Seeger's
European
Babette's Cafe
French
Nikolai's Roof
French (Bistro)
Floataway Cafe
French (New)
Brasserie Le Coze
Joël
Ritz-Carlton Buck. Café
Ritz-Carlton Buck. Din. Rm.
Greek
Kyma
Hawaiian Fusion
Roy's
Italian (N=Northern; S=Southern; N&S=includes both)
Abruzzi (N&S)
di Paolo (N)
La Grotta (N)
Sotto Sotto (N)

Japanese
Soto
Sushi Huku
Pan-Latin
Tierra
Russian
Nikolai's Roof
Sandwich Shops
Alon's
Seafood
Atlanta Fish Market
Chops/Lobster Bar
Kyma
Southern
Watershed
Southwestern
Nava
Sia's
Steakhouse
Bone's
Chops/Lobster Bar
Fogo de Chão
Thai
Tamarind

Atlantic City

American
Knife & Fork Inn
Italian (N=Northern; S=Southern; N&S=includes both)
Angelo's Fairmount (N&S)
Capriccio (N&S)
Chef Vola's (N&S)
Girasole (N&S)
Medici (N&S)
Mexican
Los Amigos
Sandwich Shop
White House
Seafood
Dock's Oyster Hse.
Southwestern
Los Amigos
Steakhouse
Brighton

Baltimore/Annapolis

Afghan
Helmand

Cuisines by Area Index

American
Milton Inn
American (New)
Charleston
Hampton's
Linwood's
Stone Manor
Chesapeake Bay
Harry Browne's
Continental
Harry Browne's
Eclectic
Bicycle
French (Bistro)
Petit Louis
Greek
Samos
Italian (N=Northern; S=Southern; N&S=includes both)
Boccaccio (N)
Trattoria Alberto (N)
Japanese
Joss Cafe
Mediterranean
Black Olive
Pacific Rim
Soigné
Seafood
Black Olive
Cantler's
Spanish
Tio Pepe
Steakhouse
Lewnes'
Prime Rib
Ruth's Chris

Boston

American
Grill 23 & Bar
Harvest
Yanks
American (New)
Aujourd'hui
blu
Hamersly's Bistro
Harvest
Icarus
Perdix
Salts

Asian
Ambrosia on Huntington
Blue Ginger
Barbecue
East Coast Grill
Californian
Yanks
Continental
Locke-Ober
Eclectic
Blue Room
Evoo
European
No. 9 Park
Salts
French
Caffe Umbra
Maison Robert
Mantra
Mistral
Pigalle
French (Bistro)
Hamersley's Bistro
French (New)
Ambrosia on Huntington
Clio
Federalist
Julien
Le Soir
L'Espalier
Lumière
Mistral
Radius
Indian
Mantra
Italian (N=Northern; S=Southern; N&S=includes both)
Bistro 5 (N)
Caffe Umbra (N&S)
Il Capriccio (N)
La Campania (N&S)
Prezza (N&S)
Saporito's (N)
Japanese
Ginza
Mediterranean
Blue Room
Caffe Bella
Oleana
Olives
Rialto

Middle Eastern
  Oleana
New England
  Rowes Wharf
Steakhouse
  Grill 23 & Bar
  Morton's of Chicago

Charlotte

American (New)
  Barrington's
  Bonterra
  Carpe Diem
  Guytano's
Californian
  Sonoma
Eclectic/International
  Dearstyne's Bistro
  McNinch House
  Pewter Rose
French (New)
  Noble's
  Zebra
Indian
  Woodlands
Italian (N=Northern; S=Southern; N&S=includes both)
  Guytano's (N)
  Toscana (N)
  Volare (N&S)
Mediterranean
  Noble's
Seafood
  LaVecchia's
  McIntosh's
  Upstream
Soul Food
  Coffee Cup
Spanish
  Miró
Steakhouse
  McIntosh's
  Mickey & Mooch
  Sullivan's
Vegetarian
  Woodlands

Chicago

American (New)
  Blackbird
  Charlie Trotter's

  Kevin
  mk
  Naha
  North Pond
  Oceanique
  one sixtyblue
  Seasons
  Spring
  302 West
  Twelve 12
Asian
  NoMI
Californian
  Caliterra B&G
French
  Les Deux Gros
  Le Titi de Paris
  Oceanique
  Pasteur
French (Bistro)
  Le Bouchon
  Retro Bistro
French (New)
  Ambria
  Avenues
  Carlos'
  Everest
  Gabriel's
  Kevin
  Le Français
  Les Nomades
  NoMI
  Ritz-Carlton Din. Rm.
  Tallgrass
  Trio
  Tru
Italian (N=Northern; S=Southern; N&S=includes both)
  Caliterra B&G (N&S)
  Gabriel's (N&S)
  Spiaggia (N&S)
Japanese
  Mirai Sushi
Mediterranean
  Naha
Mexican
  Frontera Grill
  Salbute
  Topolobampo
Seafood
  Atlantique
  Joe's Seafood

Steakhouse
  Gibsons
  Joe's
  Morton's of Chicago
Thai
  Arun's
Vietnamese
  Pasteur

Cincinnati

American
  Daveed's at 934
  Phoenix
American (New)
  Brown Dog Cafe
  JUMP Café
  Palace
  Palomino
Barbecue
  Montgomery Inn
Chinese
  China Gourmet
Continental
  Phoenix
Eclectic
  Aioli
  Boca
  Daveed's at 934
  Vineyard Café
Eurasian
  Beluga
French
  Maisonette
Indian
  Ambar India
Italian (N=Northern; S=Southern;
N&S=includes both)
  Boca (N&S)
  Nicola's (N&S)
  Primavista (N)
Mediterranean
  Palomino
Pan-Asian
  Pacific Moon Cafe
Pizza
  Dewey's
Seafood
  Precinct
Steakhouse
  Jeff Ruby's
  Precinct

Cleveland

American
  fire
American (New)
  Lola Bistro
  Moxie
  One Walnut
  Parker's
Asian
  Phnom Penh
  Weia Teia
Brazilian
  Sergio's
Continental
  Baricelli Inn
  Johnny's Bar
  Johnny's Downtown
Eclectic
  Mise
French
  Chez François
French (Bistro)
  Johnny's Bistro
Italian (N=Northern; S=Southern;
N&S=includes both)
  Circo Zibibbo (N&S)
  Giovanni's (N)
  Johnny's Bar (N)
  Johnny's Downtown (N)
Mediterranean
  Sans Souci
Seafood
  Blue Point Grille
  Century
South American
  Sergio's
Spanish
  Viva Barcelona

Columbus, OH

American
  Lindey's
  Yard Club
American (New)
  Cameron's
  M
Cuban
  Starliner Diner
Eclectic/International
  Alana's
  Handke's Cuisine
  M

Eurasian
SuLan Eurasian Bistro
French
L'Antibes
Refectory
French (New)
Refectory
French (Provençal)
Rigsby's
Irish
Yard Club
Italian (N=Northern; S=Southern; N&S=includes both)
La Tavola (N&S)
Rigsby's (N)
Trattoria Roma (N)
Japanese
Restaurant Japan
Shoku
Low Country
Braddock's Grandview
Mexican
Starliner Diner
Vaqueros
Seafood
Columbus Fish Mkt.
Steakhouse
Mitchell's
Morton's of Chicago

Connecticut

American
Golden Lamb Buttery
Mayflower
American (New)
Carole Peck's
Jeffrey's
Max Downtown
Metro Bis
Rebeccas
Steve's Centerbrook
Terra Mar Grille
West Street Grill
Asian
Baang Café
Chinese
Great Taste
Continental
Jeffrey's
Mayflower
Roger Sherman Inn
Stonehenge

French
Baang Café
Bernard's Inn
Da Pietro's
Restaurant du Village
Thomas Henkelmann
French (Bistro)
Cafe Routier
Union League Cafe
French (New)
Cavey's
Jean-Louis
La Colline Verte
Ondine
Italian (N=Northern; S=Southern; N&S=includes both)
Cavey's (N)
Da Pietro's (N)
Gennaro's (N&S)
Max Amore (N)
Peppercorn's Grill (N&S)
Piccolo Arancio (N&S)
Quattro's (N&S)
Restaurant Bricco (N)
Valbella (N)
Mediterranean
Restaurant Bricco
Nuevo Latino
Roomba
Pizza
Frank Pepe
Frank Pepe's The Spot
Harry's
Sally's Apizza
Seafood
Max's Oyster Bar
Spanish
Meigas
Steakhouse
Max Downtown
Morton's of Chicago
Ruth's Chris

Dallas

American (New)
City Cafe
French Room
Grape
Green Room
Lola
Mercury Grill

Nana
Pyramid Grill
Sevy's Grill
Tramontana
Voltaire
Barbecue
Sonny Bryan's
Brazilian
Fogo de Chão
Continental
Hôtel St. Germain
Old Warsaw
Eclectic/International
Abacus
Grape
York Street
French
Old Warsaw
Riviera
French (Bistro)
Jeroboam
French (New)
French Room
Hôtel St. Germain
Voltaire
Italian (N=Northern; S=Southern;
N&S=includes both)
Arcodoro/Pomodoro (N&S)
Ferré (N)
Il Sole (N&S)
Mi Piaci (N)
Modo Mio (N)
Japanese
Tei Tei Robata Bar
Mediterranean
Riviera
Mexican
Ciudad
Pan-Asian
Citizen
Sea Grill
Steel
Seafood
Al Biernat's
Cafe Pacific
Chamberlain's
Sea Grill
South American
La Duni Latin
Southwestern
Mansion/Turtle Creek
Star Canyon

Steakhouse
Al Biernat's
Bob's
Capital Grille
Chamberlain's
Del Frisco's
Fogo de Chão
Nick & Sam's
Pappas Bros.

Denver Area & Mountain Resorts
American
Bang!
Briarwood Inn
American (New)
Adega
Aix
Beano's Cabin
Charles Court
Conundrum
Flagstaff House
Fourth Story
Highlands Garden Cafe
Hilltop Café
Kevin Taylor
La Petite Maison
Mel's
Mizuna
Palace Arms
Q's
Renaissance
Solera
Splendido
Strings
Sweet Basil
Vesta Dipping Grill
Wildflower
Continental
Briarwood Inn
Charles Court
Palace Arms
Penrose Room
Eclectic
Flagstaff House
Solera
French
Aix
Clair de Lune
La Petite Maison
Left Bank
Tante Louise

French (New)
Penrose Room
Indian
India's
*Italian (N=Northern; S=Southern;
N&S=includes both)*
Barolo Grill (N)
Full Moon Grill (N)
Panzano (N)
Japanese
Sushi Den
Mediterranean
Mel's
Renaissance
Mexican
Tamayo
Rocky Mountain
Alpenglow Stube
Grouse Mountain Grill
Keystone Ranch
Piñons
South American
Cafe Brazil
Steakhouse
Del Frisco's

Detroit

American
Morels
Opus One
Ritz-Carlton Grill
American (New)
Daniel's on Liberty
Five Lakes Grill
Whitney
Asian
Mon Jin Lau
Tribute
Continental
Golden Mushroom
Opus One
Ritz-Carlton Grill
Deli
Zingerman's
Eclectic
Common Grill
French
Earle
French (New)
Cafe Bon Homme
Emily's

Lark
Tribute
*Italian (N=Northern; S=Southern;
N&S=includes both)*
Earle (N&S)
Il Posto Ristorante (N&S)
Rist. Café Cortina (N&S)
Mediterranean
Emily's
Middle Eastern
Steve's Backroom
Steakhouse
Capital Grille
Vietnamese
Annam

Ft. Lauderdale

American (New)
By Word of Mouth
Caribbean
Blue Moon Fish
Chinese
Silver Pond
Continental
Black Orchid Cafe
Floridian
Mark's Las Olas
*Italian (N=Northern; S=Southern;
N&S=includes both)*
Cafe Martorano (N&S)
Cafe Vico (N)
Casa D'Angelo (N&S)
La Tavernetta (N)
Primavera (N&S)
Mexican
Eduardo de San Angel
New World
Darrel & Oliver's Cafe
Seafood
Blue Moon Fish
Charley's Crab
Hobo's Fish Joint
Sunfish Grill
Southwestern
Armadillo Cafe
Canyon
Spanish
Cafe Seville
Steakhouse
Outback
Ruth's Chris

Ft. Worth

American (New)
Bistro Louise
Café Ashton
Classic Cafe
Rough Creek Lodge
Barbecue
Angelo's
Railhead Smokehouse
Burgers
Kincaid's
Eclectic/International
Angeluna
Grape Escape
Pegasus
Randall's Cafe
French
Cacharel
Escargot
Saint-Emilion
Italian (N=Northern; S=Southern; N&S=includes both)
La Piazza (N&S)
Mediterranean
Bistro Louise
Pegasus
Southwestern
Cool River Cafe
Reata
Steakhouse
Del Frisco's
Texan
Chisholm Club
Western
Lonesome Dove

Honolulu

American
Orchids
Asian
Hoku's
Indigo
OnJin's Cafe
Chinese
Golden Dragon
Eurasian
Bali by the Sea
French
OnJin's Cafe
Padovani's
French (New)
Chef Mavro's
La Mer

Hawaiian
Sansei
Side Street Inn
Hawaiian Fusion
Roy's
Hawaiian Regional
Alan Wong's
Chef Mavro's
Diamond Head Grill
Pineapple Room
International
Hoku's
Indigo
Japanese
L'Uraku
Sansei
Mediterranean
Padovani's
Pacific Rim
3660 on the Rise
Seafood
Orchids
Steakhouse
Hy's
Ruth's Chris
Thai
Mekong

Houston

American
Rotisserie/Beef & Bird
American (New)
Anthony's
Aries
benjy's
Daily Review Café
Mark's
Mockingbird Bistro
Quattro
Ruggles Grill
Ruggles Grille 5115
Zula
Asian
benjy's
Saba Blue Water Cafe
Scott's Cellar
Barbecue
Good Co.
Cajun
Tony Mandola's

Caribbean
Saba Blue Water Cafe
Continental
Anthony's
Scott's Cellar
Tony's
Creole
Brennan's
Eclectic
Mosquito Cafe
Ouisie's Table
French
Chez Nous
La Réserve
Ruggles Grille 5115
French (Bistro)
Café/Pâtisserie Descours
Gulf Coast
Rainbow Lodge
Indian
Indika
Italian (N=Northern; S=Southern; N&S=includes both)
Aldo's (N)
Amerigo's Grille (N)
Da Marco (N&S)
Damian's (N)
La Griglia (N&S)
La Mora (N)
Quattro (N&S)
Tony Mandola's (N&S)
Latin American
Américas
Cafe Red Onion
Mexican
Irma's
Seafood
Good Co. Texas
Rainbow Lodge
South American
Churrascos
Southern
Ouisie's Table
Southwestern
Brennan's
Cafe Annie
Ruggles Grill
Steakhouse
Capital Grille
Churrascos
Morton's of Chicago
Pappas Bros.
Ruth's Chris

Kansas City

American
Stroud's
American (New)
American
Café Sebastienne
City Tavern
40 Sardines
Grille on Broadway
MelBee's
Starker's Reserve
zin
Barbecue
Fiorella's Jack Stack
Eclectic
Grand St. Cafe
French
Tatsu's
French (Bistro)
Le Fou Frog
Italian (N=Northern; S=Southern; N&S=includes both)
Garozzo's (N&S)
Lidia's (N)
Pizza
d'Bronx
Sandwich Shop
d'Bronx
Seafood
Bristol B&G
City Tavern
McCormick & Schmick's
Steakhouse
Plaza III
Ruth's Chris

Las Vegas

American
Michael's
NOBHILL
Verandah
American (New)
Aureole
Charlie Palmer
Postrio
Rosemary's
Trumpets
Wild Sage Café

Brazilian
  Samba
Cajun/Creole
  Commander's Palace
  Emeril's New Orleans
Californian
  Spago
Chinese
  Mayflower Cuisinier
  Pearl
Continental
  Hugo's Cellar
  Michael's
  Top of the World
Eclectic
  Verandah
French
  Andre's
  Eiffel Tower
  Le Cirque
French (Bistro)
  Mon Ami Gabi
French (New)
  Lutèce
  Picasso
  Renoir
Fusion
  808
*Italian (N=Northern; S=Southern;
N&S=includes both)*
  Osteria del Circo (N)
  Piero's (N)
  Piero Selvaggio (N)
  Spiedini (N&S)
  Terrazza (N)
Japanese
  Nobu
Pacific Rim
  808
Peruvian
  Nobu
Seafood
  Aqua
  Emeril's New Orleans
  Palm
Steakhouse
  Charlie Palmer
  Craftsteak
  Del Frisco's
  Delmonico
  Hugo's Cellar

  Morton's of Chicago
  Palm
  Prime
  Ruth's Chris
  Samba
  Steak House

Long Island

American
  Maidstone Arms
American (New)
  Barney's
  Coolfish
  Della Femina
  Focaccia Grill
  Mill River Inn
  Palm Court/Carltun
  Panama Hatties
  Piccolo
  Plaza Cafe
  Polo
  Tupelo Honey
Continental
  Mazzi
  Mirko's
  Palm Court/Carltun
Eclectic/International
  La Plage
  Mirepoix
  Mirko's
  Tupelo Honey
French
  American Hotel
  La Marmite
  L'Endroit
  Stone Creek Inn
French (Bistro)
  Le Soir
French (New)
  Barney's
  Louis XVI
  Mirabelle
*Italian (N=Northern; S=Southern;
N&S=includes both)*
  Casa Rustica (N&S)
  Da Ugo (N&S)
  Focaccia Grill (N&S)
  Harvest on Fort Pond (N)
  La Marmite (N&S)
  La Pace (N)
  La Piccola Liguria (N)

Cuisines by Area Index

Argentinean
Gaucho Room
Graziano's Parrilla
Asian
Azul
Brazilian
Porcao
Versailles
Wish
Caribbean
Azul
Ortanique on the Mile
Chinese
Tropical
Continental
Crystal Cafe
Forge
Cuban
Versailles
Floridian
Mark's South Beach
French
La Palme d'Or
French (New)
Azul
Blue Door
La Palme d'Or
Pascal's on Ponce
Tantra
Wish
Italian (N=Northern; S=Southern; N&S=includes both)
Cafe Prima Pasta (N)
Caffe Abbracci (N)
Carpaccio (N)
Escopazzo (N&S)
Grazie Cafe (N)
Osteria del Teatro (N)
Romeo's Cafe (N)
Japanese
Nobu Miami Beach
Shoji
Toni's Sushi Bar
Mediterranean
Tantra
New World
Baleen
Chef Allen's
Norman's
Pan-Asian
Pacific Time

Peruvian
Nobu Miami Beach
Seafood
Baleen
Garcia's
Joe's Stone Crab
Pacific Time
Palm
Spanish
Casa Juancho
Steakhouse
Forge
Morton's of Chicago
Palm
Vietnamese
Hy-Vong
Miss Saigon Bistro

Minneapolis/St. Paul

American
St. Paul Grill
American (New)
Dish
Goodfellow's
Lucia's
128 Cafe
Restaurant Alma
Vincent
Zander Cafe
Eclectic/International
Bayport Cookery
3 Muses
French (Bistro)
Vincent
French (New)
La Belle Vie
Greek
Gardens of Salonica
Italian (N=Northern; S=Southern; N&S=includes both)
D'Amico Cucina (N&S)
Ristorante Luci (N&S)
Japanese
Origami
Mediterranean
La Belle Vie
Pizza
Punch Neapolitan
Seafood
Kincaid's
Oceanaire

Steakhouse
    Kincaid's
    Manny's
Swedish
    Aquavit

New Jersey

American
    Manor
    Moonstruck
    Washington Inn
American (New)
    Acacia
    Bernards Inn
    Daniel's on Broadway
    Dining Room
    Ebbitt Room
    Esty Street
    Frog & the Peach
    Harvest Moon Inn
    Highlawn Pavilion
    Jeffrey's
    Karen & Rei's
    Saddle River Inn
    Union Park
    Waters Edge
    Zarolé
Continental
    Highlawn Pavilion
    Manor
Eclectic/International
    Cafe Matisse
    Little Cafe
    Park & Orchard
French
    410 Bank Street
    Fromagerie
    Madeleine's Petit Paris
    Saddle River Inn
    Siri's
French (Bistro)
    Le Rendez-Vous
French (New)
    Cafe Panache
    Jocelyne's
    Rat's
    Ryland Inn
    Serenäde
    Stage House

Italian (N=Northern; S=Southern; N&S=includes both)
    Scalini Fedeli (N)
Japanese
    Sagami
    Shumi
Mediterranean
    Le Rendez-Vous
    Mazi
    Moonstruck
New Orleans
    410 Bank Street
Pizza
    DeLorenzo's Tomato Pies
Seafood
    Bobby Chez
    Doris & Ed's
Steakhouse
    River Palm Terrace
Thai
    Siri's
Vegetarian
    Park & Orchard

New Orleans

American (New)
    Bayona
    Dakota
    Emeril's
    Grill Room
    Herbsaint
    Pelican Club
Asian
    Kim Son
Cajun/Creole
    Antoine's
    Arnaud's
    Brennan's
    Clancy's
    Commander's Palace
    Dick & Jenny's
    Emeril's
    Gabrielle
    Galatoire's
    Gautreau's
    Jacques-Imo's Cafe
    Lafitte's Landing
    Mr. B's Bistro
    Muriel's
    Sal & Judy's
    Upperline

Continental
Rib Room
French
Antoine's
Brennan's
Dick & Jenny's
Irene's Cuisine
La Provence
Peristyle
French (Bistro)
Bistro at Maison de Ville
Martinique Bistro
Rene Bistrot
French (New)
Artesia
August
Gautreau's
Herbsaint
Italian (N=Northern; S=Southern; N&S=includes both)
Eleven 79 (N&S)
Irene's Cuisine (N&S)
Mosca's (N&S)
Sal & Judy's (S)
Japanese
Sake Cafe
Latin American
RioMar
Louisiana
Brigtsen's
Cuvée
Dakota
New Orleans
NOLA
Peristyle
Seafood
Martinique Bistro
Soul Food
Jacques-Imo's Cafe
Spanish
RioMar
Steakhouse
Rib Room
Ruth's Chris
Vietnamese
Nine Roses

New York City

American
Bayard's
'21' Club

American (New)
Aureole
Blue Hill
Craft
Eleven Madison Park
Gotham Bar & Grill
Gramercy Tavern
Harrison
Ilo
Park Avenue Cafe
River Cafe
Tavern on the Green
Town
Union Pacific
Veritas
Washington Park
Austrian
Danube
Chinese
Shun Lee Palace
Deli
Carnegie Deli
Eclectic
Blue Ribbon
French
Alain Ducasse
Bayard's
Café des Artistes
Chanterelle
Daniel
La Caravelle
La Côte Basque
Le Bernardin
Lespinasse
Montrachet
French (Bistro)
Artisanal
Balthazar
db Bistro Moderne
French (New)
Atelier
Bouley
Jean Georges
Le Cirque 2000
Greek
Milos, Estiatorio
Italian (N=Northern; S=Southern; N&S=includes both)
Babbo (N&S)
Fiamma Osteria (N&S)
Il Mulino (N)
Scalini Fedeli (N)

Japanese
Nobu
Nobu, Next Door
Sushi of Gari
Sushi Yasuda
Mediterranean
Harrison
Picholine
Peruvian
Nobu
Nobu, Next Door
Scandinavian
Aquavit
Seafood
Le Bernardin
Milos, Estiatorio
Oceana
Steakhouse
Peter Luger
Smith & Wollensky

Orange County, CA

American
Cheesecake Factory
Ramos House Cafe
American (New)
Mr. Stox
Sage
Californian
Aubergine
Napa Rose
Pavilion
Chinese
P.F. Chang's
Continental
Hobbit
Ritz
French
Aubergine
Cellar
Hobbit
Pascal
Pinot Provence
Ritz-Carlton Lag. Niguel
French (New)
Troquet
Italian (N=Northern; S=Southern; N&S=includes both)
Antonello (N&S)
Il Fornaio (N&S)

Mediterranean
Pavilion
Ritz-Carlton Lag. Niguel
Pizza
California Pizza Kitchen
Southern
Ramos House Cafe
Steakhouse
Ruth's Chris
Swedish
Gustaf Anders

Orlando

American
Cinderella's Royal Table
Houston's
Stonewood Tavern & Grill
Victoria & Albert's
American (New)
Dux
Flying Fish Cafe
Harvey's Bistro
Californian
California Grill
Continental
Arthur's 27
Boheme
Café de France
Chatham's Place
Maison et Jardin
Peter Scott's
Creole
Emeril's
Cuban
Rolando's
Eastern European
Chef Henry's Cafe
Eclectic/International
Jiko
La Coquina
Manuel's on the 28th
French
Citricos
French (Bistro)
Chefs de France
Le Coq au Vin
German
Chef Henry's Cafe
Italian (N=Northern; S=Southern; N&S=includes both)
Antonio's La Fiamma (N&S)
Christini's (N)

Delfino Riviera (N)
Enzo's on the Lake (N)
Mediterranean
Spoodles
Pacific Northwest
Artist Point
Seafood
Flying Fish Cafe
Narcoossee's
Steakhouse
Charley's
Del Frisco's
Le Cellier
Outback
Ruth's Chris
Vito's Chop House
Yachtsman
Thai
Thai House
Thai Passion
Thai Place

Palm Beach

American
Cheesecake Factory
John G's
American (New)
Cafe Chardonnay
11 Maple Street
L'Escalier
32 East
Caribbean
Captain Charlie's
Continental
Cafe L'Europe
Kathy's Gazebo
Le Mont
Eclectic
Zemi
Floridian
Four Seasons
Le Mont
French (Bistro)
Chez Jean-Pierre
French (New)
La Belle Epoque
Le Mistral
L'Escalier
French (Provincial)
La Vieille Maison

Italian (N=Northern; S=Southern; N&S=includes both)
Marcello's (N&S)
Renato's (N&S)
Seafood
Captain Charlie's
Fathom
Steakhouse
New York Prime

Philadelphia

American (New)
Dilworthtown Inn
Fork
Founders
Fountain
Jake's
Mainland Inn
Opus 251
Swann Lounge
20 Manning
Asian
20 Manning
Asian Fusion
Buddakan
Chinese
Susanna Foo
Yangming
Continental
Yangming
Cuban
Alma de Cuba
European
Django
French
Birchrunville Store Cafe
Deux Cheminées
La Bonne Auberge
Le Bec-Fin
Overtures
French (Bistro)
Bistro St. Tropez
Inn at Phillips Mill
Le Bar Lyonnais
Pif
Pigalle
French (New)
Brasserie Perrier
Fountain
Nan
Susanna Foo
Swann Lounge

Domaine Chandon
Erna's Elderberry Hse.
Jardinière
Julia's Kitchen
Rubicon
Sierra Mar
Tra Vigne
French
Auberge du Soleil
Campton Place
Emile's
French Laundry
Jardinière
Merenda
French (Bistro)
Bistro Jeanty
French (New)
Charles Nob Hill
Domaine Chandon
Elisabeth Daniel
Erna's Elderberry Hse.
Fifth Floor
Fleur de Lys
Gary Danko
Jeanty at Jack's
Julia's Kitchen
La Folie
La Toque
Le Papillon
Masa's
Redwood Park
Ritz-Carlton Dining Rm.
Rubicon
Sierra Mar
Terra
Fusion
Terra
Italian (N=Northern; S=Southern;
N&S=includes both)
Acquerello (N)
Delfina (N&S)
Merenda (N)
Oliveto Cafe (N)
Tra Vigne (N&S)
Zuni Cafe (N)
Japanese
Le Poisson Japonais
Sushi Ran
Mediterranean
Auberge du Soleil
Chez Panisse

Chez Panisse Café
Zuni Cafe
Seafood
Aqua
Farallon
Vegetarian
Fleur de Lys
Vietnamese
Slanted Door

Seattle

American (New)
Eva
Lampreia
Nell's
Palace Kitchen
Restaurant Zoë
Union Bay Cafe
Asian
Flying Fish
Wild Ginger
Barbecue
Frontier Room
Eclectic
Dahlia Lounge
Palace Kitchen
727 Pine
European
Mistral
French
Campagne
Le Gourmand
French (Bistro)
Café Campagne
Le Pichet
French (New)
Rover's
German
Szmania's
Italian (N=Northern; S=Southern;
N&S=includes both)
Cafe Juanita (N)
Il Terrazzo Carmine (N)
Japanese
Nishino
Saito's
Shiro's Sushi
Mediterranean
Brasa
Vivanda

Pacific Northwest
Canlis
Cascadia
Chez Shea
Eva
Georgian
Herbfarm
Hunt Club
Lampreia
Rover's
727 Pine
Shoalwater
Szmania's
Union Bay Cafe
Seafood
Etta's
Flying Fish
Oceanaire
Vivanda
Southern
Kingfish Café
Spanish
Harvest Vine
Steakhouse
El Gaucho
JaK's Grill
Metropolitan Grill
Vietnamese
Monsoon

Southern NY State

American
DePuy Canal House
Inn at Pound Ridge
Old Drovers Inn
American (New)
American Bistro
American Bounty
Aubergine
Citrus Grille
Crabtree's Kittle House
Cripple Creek
Freelance Café
Halstead Avenue Bistro
Iron Horse Grill
Peter Pratt's Inn
Purdys Homestead
Rest. X & Bully Boy Bar
Terrapin
Would
Xaviar's at Garrison
Xaviar's at Piermont

Continental
L'Europe
Eclectic/International
Arch
Cripple Creek
DePuy Canal House
Harralds
Old Drovers Inn
Zephs'
French
Arch
Auberge Maxime
Aubergine
Buffet de la Gare
La Crémaillère
Le Château
L'Europe
French (Bistro)
Le Canard Enchaîné
French (New)
Equus
Escoffier
La Panetière
*Italian (N=Northern; S=Southern;
N&S=includes both)*
Il Cenácolo (N)
Lusardi's (N)
Mulino's (N)
Japanese
Azuma Sushi
Hajime
Mediterranean
Cafe Mezé
Nuevo Latino
Sonora
Seafood
Conte's Fishmarket
Steakhouse
Harry's of Hartsdale

St. Louis

American (New)
Annie Gunn's
Crossing
Eau Cafe & Bistro
Frazer's
Harvest
Sidney Street Cafe
Zinnia
Asian
Eau Cafe & Bistro

Continental
Kemoll's
Eclectic/International
Cardwell's at the Plaza
Indian
India Palace
Italian (N=Northern; S=Southern; N&S=includes both)
Bar Italia (N)
Dominic's (N)
Giovanni's (N&S)
Kemoll's (N&S)
Tony's (N&S)
Trattoria Marcella (N&S)
Mediterranean
Portabella
Remy's Kitchen
Mexican
Pueblo Solis
Pan-Asian
Shiitake
Seafood
Frazer's
Tony's
Vietnamese
Pho Grand

Tampa/Sarasota

American (New)
Beach Bistro
Bijou Café
Bistro 41
Grill at Feather Sound
Lafite
Michael's on East
Zoria
Asian Fusion
SideBern's
Continental
Bijou Café
Café L'Europe
Jonathan's
Lafite
Eclectic/International
Blue Heron
Euphemia Haye
Jonathan's
Mise en Place
Ophelia's
Zoria

European
Cafe L'Europe
Floribbean
Maritana Grille
French
Maison Blanche
Ritz-Carlton Din. Rm.
Italian (N=Northern; S=Southern; N&S=includes both)
Caffe Paradiso (N)
Mediterranean
Beach Bistro
Steakhouse
Bern's
Thai
Jasmine

Tucson

American (New)
Bistro Zin
Dish
Grill at Hacienda del Sol
Kingfisher
Ventana Room
Wildflower
Continental
Anthony's/Catalinas
Arizona Inn
Gold Room
French
Le Rendez-Vous
French (New)
Stone Ashley
Italian (N=Northern; S=Southern; N&S=includes both)
Vivace (N)
Latin American
J Bar
Mexican
Cafe Poca Cosa
Seafood
Kingfisher
Southwestern
Café Terra Cotta
Fuego!
Gold Room
Janos
Jonathan's Tucson Cork
Tack Room
Steakhouse
Jonathan's Tucson Cork
McMahon's

Washington, DC

American
  Old Ebbitt Grill
American (New)
  Caucus Room
  Colvin Run Tavern
  DC Coast
  Equinox
  Four & Twenty Blackbirds
  Inn at Little Washington
  Kinkead's
  Majestic Cafe
  Melrose
  Nora
  Palena
  Seasons
  701
  1789
  Vidalia
  Zola
Bakery
  Bread Line
Belgian
  Marcel's
Eclectic/International
  Bread Line
French
  L'Auberge Chez François
  L'Auberge Provençale
French (Bistro)
  Bistro Bis
  Bistrot Lepic
French (New)
  Cafe 15
  Citronelle

  Gerard's Place
  Marcel's
Indian
  Bombay Club
Italian (N=Northern; S=Southern; N&S=includes both)
  Galileo (N&S)
  Maestro (N&S)
  Obelisk (N)
  Tosca (N)
Japanese
  Makoto
Nuevo Latino
  Cafe Atlantico
Pan-Asian
  TenPenh
Pizza
  Pizzeria Paradiso
  2 Amys
Seafood
  DC Coast
  Johnny's Half Shell
  Kinkead's
Southern
  Vidalia
Spanish
  Jaleo
  Taberna del Alabardero
Steakhouse
  Caucus Room
  Prime Rib
Tapas
  Jaleo

AREA ABBREVIATIONS

ALPHABETICAL PAGE INDEX

Alphabetical Page Index

Alphabetical Page Index

subscribe to zagat.com

Alphabetical Page Index

Alphabetical Page Index

Alphabetical Page Index

Alphabetical Page Index

Alphabetical Page Index

Alphabetical Page Index

Alphabetical Page Index

Alphabetical Page Index

Alphabetical Page Index

Wine Vintage Chart

This chart is designed to help you select wine to go with your meal. It is based on the same 0 to 30 scale used throughout this *Survey*. The ratings (prepared by our friend **Howard Stravitz**, a professor at the University of South Carolina) reflect both the quality of the vintage and the wine's readiness for present consumption. Thus, if a wine is not fully mature or is over the hill, its rating has been reduced. We do not include 1987, 1991–1993 vintages because they are not especially recommended for most areas.

	'85	'86	'88	'89	'90	'94	'95	'96	'97	'98	'99	'00	'01
WHITES													
French:													
Alsace	24	18	22	28	28	26	25	23	23	25	23	25	26
Burgundy	26	25	17	25	24	15	29	28	25	24	25	22	20
Loire Valley	–	–	–	–	25	23	24	26	24	23	24	25	23
Champagne	28	25	24	26	29	–	26	27	24	24	25	25	–
Sauternes	21	28	29	25	27	–	20	23	27	22	22	22	28
California (Napa, Sonoma, Mendocino):													
Chardonnay	–	–	–	–	–	22	27	23	27	25	25	23	26
Sauvignon Blanc/Semillon	–	–	–	–	–	–	–	–	24	24	25	22	26
REDS													
French:													
Bordeaux	25	26	24	27	29	22	26	25	23	24	23	25	23
Burgundy	23	–	21	25	28	–	26	27	25	22	27	22	20
Rhône	25	19	27	29	29	24	25	23	25	28	26	27	24
Beaujolais	–	–	–	–	–	–	–	–	23	22	25	25	18
California (Napa, Sonoma, Mendocino):													
Cab./Merlot	26	26	–	21	28	29	27	25	28	23	26	23	26
Pinot Noir	–	–	–	–	–	27	24	24	26	25	26	25	27
Zinfandel	–	–	–	–	–	25	22	23	21	22	24	19	24
Italian:													
Tuscany	26	–	24	–	26	22	25	20	28	24	27	26	25
Piedmont	26	–	26	28	29	–	23	26	28	26	25	24	22

Ready for your
next course?

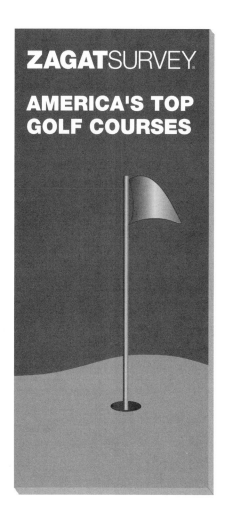

ZAGATSURVEY.

AMERICA'S TOP GOLF COURSES

Introducing America's Top Golf Courses, rated and reviewed by avid golfers. Besides telling you what the courses and facilities are like, we'll tell you how much you'll pay and even how well you'll eat.

Available wherever books are sold, at zagat.com or by calling **888-371-5440.**

Is that a Zagat in your pocket?

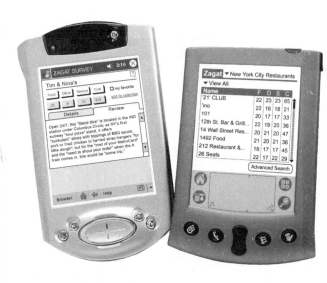

INTRODUCING

ZAGAT TO GO℠
2003 Restaurant and Nightlife Guide
FOR POCKET PC & PALM OS® DEVICES

- **Extensive Coverage:** Includes over 18,000 establishments in 30+ cities

- **Custom Search:** Pinpoint the perfect spot by locale, price, cuisine and more

- **Free Updates:** Stay current with new content downloads throughout the year

- **One-Touch Scheduling:** Add your plans directly to your Date Book or Calendar

Available wherever books and software are sold

or for download at www.zagat.com/software